A Celebration of Sex

Dr. Douglas E. Rosenau

OLIVER
NELSON

THOMAS NELSON PUBLISHERS
Nashville • Atlanta • London • Vancouver

Published in Nashville, Tennessee, by Thomas Nelson, Inc.

Scripture quotations marked NKJV are taken from THE NEW KING JAMES VERSION. Copyright © 1979, 1980, 1982, Thomas Nelson, Inc., Publishers.

Scripture quotations marked NIV are taken from the HOLY BIBLE: NEW INTERNATIONAL VERSION®, copyright © 1973, 1978, 1984 by the International Bible Society, used by permission of Zondervan Publishing House. All rights reserved.

Illustrations by Alan Tiegreen

Printed in the United States of America

Library of Congress Cataloging-in Publication Data

Rosenau, Douglas.
    A celebration of sex / Douglas E. Rosenau.
      p. cm.
    Includes bibliographical references and index.
    ISBN 0-8407-9180-1 (hardcover)
    ISBN 0-7852-7366-2 (paperback)
    1. Sex in marriage. 2. Sex—Religious aspects. I. Title.
HQ31.R8425   1994
306.7—dc20   93-32904
                                                        CIP

12 11 10 9 8 – 99 98

To

a wise and loving Creator, who graciously gave us
the joy of marriage and making love.
Thank You, Lord, for the intimate playfulness
and bonding warmth of a sexual companionship.

And to

each of my fellow pilgrims, who is courageously
reading this book and embarking on the journey toward
true intimacy according to our Creator's formula.

Contents

Foreword

I remember my first conversation with Doug Rosenau after receiving his letter asking me to write a foreword for his book. I told him I could not do this as a Christian expert. This was an area of marriage in which God was still helping me make some important changes. I needed this manual, too. I could only write as someone who was in the beginning stages of learning and growing.

Doug assured me that there are no experts on sex. All Christians are struggling to appropriate God's answers. He actually preferred observations and comments from this novice viewpoint, as we humbly help each other practically apply truth.

As I have grown in the Lord, I've discovered how selfish I've been in many areas of my life. I shouldn't have been surprised when I learned I had been extremely selfish in sex. I want to change that pattern. Tacitus, a Latin Father, wrote profoundly, "Self-interest is the enemy of all true affection."

God has such wonderful guidelines for intimate relationships. The book of Ruth gives us a powerful picture of self-sacrifice and commitment that needs to capture our hearts. We are also told to clothe ourselves with "compassion, kindness, humility, gentleness" (Col. 3:12 NIV). I want to be affectionate and giving in sex with my wife, Lyndi. I want to wisely get beyond self-interest and other enemies of fulfilling intimacy.

I know I need more education. I am eager for godly discourse on this subject. I hope the church can provide formats for this to occur. I hope couples can be encouraged to work on this area of their marriage. Men can often be reluctant to talk about sexual concerns, but we must encourage dialogue about sex and mutual learning.

Doug Rosenau has provided a wonderful resource to help heal this problem for me and others. This book should be helpful to most Christians and especially men. Men, read this book together with your wives and mutually learn about each other's needs. Accept and enjoy Christ's yoke of servanthood as you nurture each other and find true fulfillment.

Take specific chapters and use them as discussion starters in your accountability groups. Help each other embrace mature biblical principles and act on them. Accept God's invitation to a truly affectionate sex life.

We don't have to agree on every point to engage in godly discourse. I hope you can use this book as a starting point in finding solutions and overcoming ignorance and self-interest. Sexual enrichment and reconciliation will come as you are gripped and transformed by God's answers and the love of Christ.

Bill McCartney
Founder and CEO, Promise Keepers

Acknowledgments

Catherine, wonderful partner, you have my heartfelt gratitude for your support and encouragement. Without you, *A Celebration of Sex* would never have been created. Thank you for sacrificing so much to make this book possible.

I deeply appreciate two important relationships in my life and the part they have played in my sex education: my parents who modeled an intimate companionship as they hugged and kissed each other and were great partners; my wife, Catherine, who over the years has helped me learn the rich and deep concept of making love.

I want to thank two wise teachers who have greatly increased my ability as a sex therapist: Domeena Renshaw, M.D., who started me on my journey and gave me the beginning skills; William Talmadge, Ph.D., who continues to be a thoughtful teacher and supervisor.

A special thanks is extended to each of you who read over parts of my manuscript and added immensely to the quality and helpfulness of the book: Kathy Butler, Mike and Karen Sytsma, Bill and Linda Talmadge, Carole Smith, Debra King, Jerry Lancaster, Fred and Vivien Folsom, Walt Handford, Susan Wagner, Jim Mallory, Mike Lyles, and Vern Rosenau.

I appreciate my two editors who made such crucial contributions to guiding, shaping, and polishing *A Celebration of Sex*: Victor Oliver who took a chance on an unknown author and made many important changes in the manuscript; Lila Empson who wisely shaped and pushed through the final product.

I could never have written this book without my new computer. Thank you, David Novak and Christy Weaver, for bringing me from computer illiteracy to accomplishing this mammoth task.

Thanks, Al, for patiently making changes in illustrations and helping me create the needed drawings for this book.

I am grateful for the loving and prayerful support of my men's Bible study and fellowship group who have helped me struggle through the past two years.

A hearty thank-you to the Atlanta Counseling Center and my colleagues who were always open for a quick consult or the need to unload frustration around the accomplishment of this manual. I can be reached at that address:

Dr. Douglas Rosenau
Atlanta Counseling Center
6111-C Peachtree-Dunwoody Road
Atlanta, Georgia 30328

A
Celebration
of Sex

Introduction

God has a fantastic formula for your sex life.

An Intimate Marriage + Mature Lovers = A Fulfilling Sex Life

If you want powerful techniques and easy answers, you may be disappointed in this book. God's plan often involves time, effort, and difficult changes. It can be a wonderful journey if you are willing to take on this fun challenge. You will discover that sex is more of an exciting process and way of life than it is a simple acquisition of techniques.

In God's design, sex and an intimate marriage can never be separated. He wove sexual fulfillment intricately into the fabric of marital companionship and created the concept of two becoming one flesh.

Instant sex cannot create instant intimacy. Fulfilling sex flows out of fulfilling intimacy. Developing a fun, trusting companionship takes time and an intimate knowledge of one's partner. In God's design, this companionship precedes fulfilling sexual interaction. Sex is not the most important part of a marriage. A loving companionship and a right relationship with God are the essentials. Even though a great sex life does not ensure a great marriage, a great marital companionship can provide the foundation for fantastic lovemaking.

Sex can't resolve your fights or replace intimate communication. Making love is more than an exciting rush or buzz that serves as antidote to boredom or stimulant for quick closeness. Sexual intimacy enhances the one-flesh partnership. And this book will encourage you as a couple to more fully enjoy God's wonderful gift of sexual pleasure as you pursue God's dynamic concept.

If you are approaching marriage, this book is written for you. With knowledge and understanding, you can head off many potential sexual problems and never fall into sabotaging habits. If you are already married and have a good sex life, this book can increase your communication and give you some tips on building a close companionship and enjoying greater sexual variety. It can also help you alter some attitudes or behaviors that could ultimately hinder a deeper intimacy in your marriage and damage your lovemaking.

The last two sections of the book are written for you who are struggling with specific concerns. If you are concerned about aging, infertility, impotence, or diminished sexual desire, be assured there is help. Read the appropriate chapter(s) and know you are not alone. There is hope.

Principles for an Intimate Marriage and a Great Sex Life

If a good sex life is built on an intimate marital companionship, what are the components of this companionship and how do you build one? Here are some vital principles for an intimate relationship, marriage, and a fulfilling sexual union.

Three Kinds of Love Must Be Present

In the Greek language of New Testament times, there were different words for love. These suggest three different kinds of love. Each type helps achieve an intimate marital and sexual relationship. *Agape* depicts the unconditional love and commitment God has for His children. It is an act of will and a specific choice. *Eros* contains the idea of fusion and passion with a strong attraction and some crazy excitement. Newness and variety are significant and stimulating. Eros abandons defensive walls and enjoys the rush of erotic and romantic feelings. *Philia* can be described as brotherly love and a comfortable companionship. It is enhanced with time spent together, mutual interests, and self-disclosing, bonding experiences.

Each way of loving adds a richness and a different dimension to marriage. All three loves must be present for your intimate companionship and lovemaking to thrive. A bonded, safe relationship needs agape love to foster commitment, trust, and honesty—vital ingredients for lasting over the long haul. Agape love chooses to be committed to the spiritual and sexual well-being of your mate. It protects the exclusivity of your companionship and is unconditional: "A friend loves at all times, and a brother is born for adversity" (Prov. 17:17 NKJV).

Eros provides sparks and feelings that are crucial to feeling in love. Passionate eros love energizes your togetherness with feelings of fun and fusion. It is more than just sexual; it is a magnetic field that creates a special attraction with warmth and excitement and mystery. A wife and husband should not simply be in a brother-sister relationship. Attraction and chemistry are vital ingredients.

Above all else, you and your mate must be intimate companions. You need a deep and profound sense of philia to abound. Philia love connects companionably. It flourishes with shared experiences and greater time together. This may be the most mature and bonding type of love.

Philia allows you to enjoy your mate sexually over the years as you develop sexual comfortableness and warm acceptance. You intimately know and love your mate's body with its beauty and flaws. You build an exciting desire and need for the loving completion your mate brings to you. As companions, you look forward to sharing every aspect of your lives; you revel in truly knowing and being known by your partner. This is intimate companionship at its best.

Time Out . . .

How do you need to incorporate agape, eros, and philia into your marriage?

Which symbolic word or words would you use to define the concept of loving companions? Interdependency? Playmates? One-flesh? Fusion? Best friends? Unconditional commitment?

A Dynamic, Bonded Partnership Must Be Formed

The Bible describes the beauty and complexity of the marital companionship that creates the context for lovemaking. The loving, intimate relationship of you and your spouse is modeled after the relationship of God and His chosen people. A mature companionship fashions itself after *redemption* in that you die to yourself and let go of any defensiveness. You create a bonded partnership in which you submit your will for the good of your mate. Your union is based on love and trust.

Your trust is well founded because each of you reaches out and lovingly nurtures the other as carefully as you would watch out for your own body. In this union, you look honestly at your own rough edges and shortcomings and humbly try to change them. You choose to give as precious gifts the things that your mate desires and needs. It is a marvelous atmosphere for fun sexual relating and intimate connecting when this kind of tenderness, trust, genuine empathy, and cooperation abound.

I love the words *nurture* and *connected*, and I will use them many times in this book. Great examples of nurturing are parents lovingly caring for their children or gardeners carefully watering and tending their plants. Mates lovingly nurture each other. You are connected with your mate in a way more profound than the splicing of two electric wires or the tying of two ropes. You are connected in a partnership that grows ever richer and deeper but takes constant attention and renewal. This is the concept of soul mates and of lives cleaving together. Like steel, a unique synthesis is created, and a profound connection is formed.

A wonderful synergistic dynamic can occur in marriage. The whole is much greater than the sum of its parts. Individuality, personal pleasure, and separate responsibility are not lost. In dying to self and becoming a one-flesh companion, each partner becomes stronger and achieves things that could not be accomplished alone. The two have the best of both worlds: they are a nurturing couple, and each flourishes as an individual. A totally unique and powerful partnership is created. From this unique relationship of marriage can come sexual enjoyment as individuals and as a couple. It will seem like one plus one equals four.

Reasonable Biblical Expectations Must Be Incorporated

Most couples enter marriage with a variety of expectations about how it should be. Which of the following expectations did you bring into your marriage?

- You would never fight.
- The husband would automatically take the garbage out and vacuum.
- Your partner would never be attracted to anyone else.
- You would eat dinner together at the table most nights.
- Christmas Eve would be spent with your family—or with neither family.
- Sex would fall into place easily.
- Money would be handled wisely, and there would be a joint checking account.

In my book *Slaying the Marriage Dragons,* I help couples define a great marriage by sorting through their expectations. One couple told me that if they could only let go of all their expectations, they would have a happy marriage. I asked them, "Why get married if you don't expect anything from the relationship and your mate?" The task you face is not getting rid of all your expectations but basing them realistically on biblical principles.

Here are ten reasonable desires based on God's economy for intimate companionship. May He give you wisdom and courage to make the changes you need within your partnership. Great sex flows out of a great marriage. It may seem like strange advice, but the quality of your sex life may depend on turning off the television, picking a good fight, becoming independent of your parents, setting up a budget, or taking regular vacations.

1. Each of us will have a partner and soul mate offering unconditional love, understanding, and support. We will be best friends.

The Lord God said, "It is not good that man should be alone" (Gen. 2:18 NKJV).
Husbands, . . . dwell with them with understanding, giving honor to the wife. . . .
All of you be of one mind (1 Peter 3:7–8 NKJV).

Husbands ought to love their wives as their own bodies. . . . No one ever hated his own body, but he feeds and cares for it. . . . And the two will become one flesh (Eph. 5:28–29, 31 NIV).

A friend loves at all times,
and a brother [mate] is born for adversity. . .
but there is a friend who sticks closer than a brother (Prov. 17:17; 18:24 NIV).
Love is patient. . . . It is not rude, it is not self-seeking. . . . It always protects, always trusts, always hopes, always perseveres (1 Cor. 13:4–5, 7 NIV).

In a boxing match, the boxer has in his corner a manager who is unconditionally committed to helping the fighter use his best shots, encouraging him, correcting mistakes, taking care of any wounds, and preparing him for maximum efficiency. Mates are each other's managers. Marriage is a safe retreat from the fight of daily living. You have an ally in your corner who will persevere in loving support and who knows you better than anyone else in the world.

An important part of cleaving together and becoming one flesh is being intimate companions. You become soul mates and best friends in marriage as you share your souls—your needs, your innermost feelings and desires, your future goals. It is important to have a same-sex best friend, but your partner should also be a best friend. Both mates, and often especially husbands, struggle with this—at times being too private and not disclosing needs and feelings. (Later on in the book, you'll learn the art of connecting conversation.)

2. Neither of us will expect the other to meet all needs or take sole responsibility for personal happiness. We will give each other space to breathe.

Work out your own salvation with fear and trembling; for it is God who works in you both to will and to do for His good pleasure (Phil. 2:12–13 NKJV).
Each one should test his own actions. Then he can take pride in himself, without comparing himself to somebody else, for each one should carry his own load (Gal. 6:4–5 NIV).

Each of you must build support networks consisting of helpful friends and the Lord. Ultimately, you must rely on God because He is the only unfailing source of peace, purpose, and happiness. Your mate can meet your sexual needs, but you have many other needs that are impossible for one person to meet. You need a best friend of the same sex, supporting couple friendships, and fellowship groups. You will perhaps need tennis buddies, kindred political souls, good baby-sitters, efficient accountants, or surrogate grandparents.

You must also learn to nurture yourself and work out your own salvation as you become self-sufficient and confident. God indeed blesses those who help themselves. If you are insecure and possessive, you can smother your mate. Real love is free of fear and gives breathing room for you and your mate to grow and experience life. You must work on your own happiness as you take responsibility to grow and experience contentment.

3. We will leave our fathers and mothers and create a new, independent, special family unit.

> For this reason a man will leave his father and mother and be united to his wife, and the two will become one flesh (Eph. 5:31 NIV).

Disentangling yourself financially and emotionally from your parents and family is important. Together, you are creating a new partnership and family. You cannot hold on to the need to run back to your parents for constant nurturing. You need to make a definite, symbolic statement that your spouse is your first priority. It is the husband who is specifically commanded to leave father and mother. It's difficult to learn the wisdom and maturity of gently separating from parents and making your marriage special.

Sometimes this process of becoming independent and separate is called *individuating*. This needs to happen individually before it can happen as a couple. Sometimes with age and maturity comes the ability to do this better. It does not mean either disrespecting your parents or never leaning on them for support. The act of leaving your parents makes your mate feel special and protected—a priority as you meet your mate's needs. It creates that new and unique partnership. If you are having trouble individuating from your parents, you will probably need to move away from them geographically. You may also need to stay in a motel when you visit parents to give your partner a chance to regroup, to tell your parents you don't want to hear your mate put down, or to expand your group of wise counselors and sounding boards beyond your parents.

4. We will have one healthy fight a week. Confrontation around our unmet personal needs will be believed and not dismissed.

> Correct, rebuke and encourage—with great patience and careful instruction (2 Tim. 4:2 NIV).
>
> Speaking the truth in love.... Therefore, putting away lying, "Let each one of you speak truth with his neighbor."... Do not let the sun go down on your wrath (Eph. 4:15, 25–26 NKJV).
>
> For even if I made you sorry with my letter, I do not regret it (2 Cor. 7:8 NKJV).
>
> Now no chastening seems to be joyful for the present, but painful; nevertheless, afterward it yields the peaceable fruit of righteousness to those who have been trained by it (Heb. 12:11 NKJV).
>
> Brothers, if someone is caught in a sin, you who are spiritual should restore him gently (Gal. 6:1 NIV).
>
> Exhort one another daily... lest any of you be hardened through the deceitfulness of sin (Heb. 3:13 NKJV).
>
> Make straight paths for your feet, so that what is lame may not be dislocated, but rather be healed.... [Look] carefully lest anyone fall short of the grace of God; lest

any root of bitterness springing up cause trouble, and by this many become defiled (Heb. 12:13, 15 NKJV).

Disappointed expectations, frustrated needs, stored hurt, and retained anger create bitterness and distance and destroy intimacy. You as a couple will have to have the courage for healthy conflict and confrontation. Learn conflict-resolution skills (see chapter 8), practice forgiveness, and let go of hurt as you resolve differences.

Mates are unique individuals who will be incompatible. The differences can actually enhance a marriage. With good communication skills and the resolution to not let the sun go down on your anger, you will be able to work through these differences. Frequent confrontation and conflict resolve issues. Drawn-out disagreements are more likely to create resentment and bitterness.

Courage and honesty are needed to deal immediately with disagreements. Healthy conflict that resolves issues and clears the air is an important discipline within intimate companionship. Confronting issues and learning to fight effectively are reasonable expectations in a good marriage. You should be humble and loving enough to hear your partner and believe what is being said, and your mate should be willing to do the same for you.

Don't attempt to use submission as an agent of change in your spouse's life. Loving rebuke and exhortation are God's method for correcting harmful behaviors—not submission. Work out a patient, logical, and kind plan of correction, and (perhaps to your surprise) your spouse may humbly listen, agree, and make needed changes. Have at least one good fight or confrontation a week.

5. We will take regular vacations and honeymoons throughout our marriage as we mend and enhance our intimacy.

There is a time for everything,
and a season for every activity under heaven . . .
a time to tear down and a time to build, . . .
a time to mourn and a time to dance, . . .
a time to search and a time to give up, . . .
a time to tear and a time to mend (Eccles. 3:1, 3, 4, 6, 7 NIV).
When a man has taken a new wife, he shall not go out to war or be charged with any business; he shall be free at home one year, and bring happiness to his wife (Deut. 24:5 NKJV).

There should be some special time set aside for a honeymoon and more concentrated, focused time in that first year together. It is a time of adjusting and getting to know each other. Getting away is a great principle for all married couples, no matter how long they have been married. In chapter 6, I explain the importance of couples' taking vacations and rejuvenating their companionship and sex life. They need time away from home and free of duties as they concentrate on bringing happiness to each other and renewing their friendship.

The marital plague of the twenty-first century will be over-involvement and busyness. We seldom plan to spend enough time and money to revive our companionship. You may need to plan for a baby-sitter and a date night every week or two, an overnight away, or a complete second honeymoon. Give yourself permission to budget time and money for your partnership. A reasonable expectation of your marriage is a fun friendship and quality playtime together.

6. We will use credit carefully as we become wise stewards of our finances.

> Owe no one anything except to love one another (Rom. 13:8 NKJV).
>
> Then he who had received the five talents went and traded with them, and made another five talents. . . . His lord said to him, "Well done, good and faithful servant; you were faithful over a few things, I will make you ruler over many things. Enter into the joy of your lord" (Matt. 25:16, 21 NKJV).

A great sex life is closely dependent on staying out of debt and learning to handle finances wisely. It makes sense that any stressors in a marriage will weaken intimacy and the desire to make love.

Christian financial counselor Ron Blue has this marvelously simple principle for couples who want to avoid financial stress: Spend less than you make. Financial counselors especially advise against spending excessive money on depreciating items like a car, clothes, or furniture. Not borrowing money certainly means not using credit cards as you create sound spending and budget habits. Learn to be self-disciplined in this area of your life. Effective stewardship of your finances will indeed help your sex life.

God requires sound thinking and self-discipline of Christians in all important areas of life that can tend to the destructiveness of excess: "For God has not given us a spirit of fear, but of power and of love and of a sound mind"(2 Tim. 1:7 NKJV). Do a quick reality check in your marriage. Are you being undisciplined and blocking a deeper intimacy in some area other than finances? Television? Children? Work? Parents? Friends? Hobbies? Sports? Get your act together, or like financial trouble, the stress will begin to have an impact on your marriage and love life. It is amazing how couples improve their marriages simply by turning off the television.

7. My mate will be faithful and committed to me.

> You shall not commit adultery (Exod. 20:14 NKJV).

A great marital partnership has room for only two people in it. Commitment is vital to intimate companionship, and the creation of good boundaries is irreplaceable for a fantastic marriage and sex life.

Adulterate means "to contaminate by adding a foreign substance or watering down a product." You can adulterate your marital companionship in many ways other than by having a sexual affair. You can adulterate your marriage by overcommitting to work, children, or church. It is a valid desire and decision that mates avoid adulterating their marriage.

God's injunction of "thou shalt not commit adultery" is often portrayed in terms of a protective fence that guards the beautiful marital and sexual garden. So often we look at fences as something to jump so we can get to greener grass. Actually, the no-adultery fence is there so you can have the intimacy to create an unbelievable relationship within that enclosure—a deeper level of emotional and sexual connecting that can occur and flourish only in an intimate marriage. It protects you from contaminating elements that can threaten the quality of your companionship.

Faithfulness and commitment are interesting concepts. They are processes that create an exclusive partnership with your mate. Some of the choices in mating are highly visible and are special and easily remembered symbols of commitment. The wedding vows are one of these symbols, similar to the pillar Jacob erected in Bethel to serve as a reminder of God's promise and blessing (Gen. 28:18). Other obvious choices are children, a home mortgage, and retirement planning.

Probably more important but less obvious are commitments to your mate that come in a series of daily choices. Every day when you say, "I have my mate," and refuse to entertain thoughts about someone else, you are reaffirming your commitment. You are allowing sex to be relational and setting good boundaries as you choose to control your sexual impulses and preserve sexual integrity.

These little commitment choices to preserve and deepen intimacy pop up in all areas of marriage. It could mean calling off a lunch with a colleague, deciding whether to have that third child, going to a bed and breakfast for a weekend renewal, leaving work early, or buying that funny card and leaving it in the car for your spouse. It can be going to that marriage seminar, reading a book on sexual technique, apologizing for that unkind remark, or working harder to correct a personal character defect.

These choices are not always huge and obvious, but they create the glue that keeps a marriage and sexual relationship together. Daily you have to choose not to adulterate and water down your companionship. Daily you take those little steps that create the fences protecting your garden of fantastic intimacy and sexual pleasure. This is a reasonable expectation.

8. Either of us will be able to initiate marriage counseling, and the other will be willing to go.

> A scoffer does not love one who corrects him,
> Nor will he go to the wise (Prov. 15:12 NKJV).

> The heart of him who has understanding seeks knowledge,
> But the mouth of fools feeds on foolishness (Prov. 15:14 NKJV).

> He who heeds the word wisely will find good (Prov. 16:20 NKJV).

> The sweetness of a man's friend gives delight by hearty counsel (Prov. 27:9 NKJV).

In a humble, loving marital partnership, you want your mate to be happy and fulfilled. You also value wise counsel. If an impasse occurs, either mate will be able and encouraged to initiate counseling with the appropriate wise person.

The partner should willingly participate in protecting and nurturing the companionship. Wise counsel is a constant source of marital enrichment. It may be a marriage counselor to learn better communication skills or a financial advisor to help set up an effective budget; it may be your pastor to work on confession and forgiveness or a sex therapist to work on sexual problems.

9. We will have regular, satisfying sexual interaction.

The husband should fulfill his marital duty to his wife, and likewise the wife to her husband. The wife's body does not belong to her alone but also to her husband. In the same way, the husband's body does not belong to him alone but also to his wife. Do not deprive each other (1 Cor. 7:3–5 NIV).

A reasonable expectation in a good marriage is frequent and mutually fulfilling sexual activity. Each partner can expect help from the other to experience personal sexual satisfaction. It is realistic to desire and work toward intimacy-enhancing sexual companionship that grows over the years—sexual communication that is much more than just intercourse or orgasm.

It will require an investment by both mates to ensure time, provide variety, and avoid routine. It may also require some counseling to break through any difficulty: an inability of the wife to experience an orgasm, an inability of the husband to achieve erection, a wife's or husband's lack of desire, or other problems. Don't put it off; these problems usually won't go away but get worse. Get help if you are not enjoying regular, satisfying sexual interaction.

10. We will enjoy a growing spiritual life together with prayer and Bible study.

If any of you lacks wisdom, let him ask of God, who gives to all liberally and without reproach (James 1:5 NKJV).

Husbands, love your wives, just as Christ loved the church . . . cleansing her by the washing with water through the word (Eph. 5:25–26 NIV).

Let the word of Christ dwell in you richly. . . . Continue earnestly in prayer (Col. 3:16; 4:2 NKJV).

Bible study and prayer enhance intimacy and allow you to become more Christlike. God is the author of intimacy, and keeping centered in Him is the beginning of wisdom and an intimate marriage. If you are humble and open, He will shine His truth and love into your life and relationships.

One husband was excited about a discovery he had made: Christians have the ability to be the best lovers in the world. He had read Galatians 5:22–23: "But the fruit of the Spirit is love, joy, peace, longsuffering, kindness, goodness, faithfulness, gentleness, self-control" (NKJV). What a list of traits as a foundation for a great marriage and sex life! If you are filled with God's Spirit and living out these virtues, you will never be excelled as a marital partner or sexual lover. God bless your lovemaking as you apply His principles for a great marriage and meet each other's realistic expectations within your partnership.

Using This Book

I appreciate your letting me be your mentor as you deepen your intimate companionship and learn more about making love. You, with God's help, must implement these changes in your marriage. For my part, I promise to help you go through this experience in a thoughtful, yet playful and fun, way. We will let honesty, God's love, and guidelines for great relationships be the foundation of this book.

In working with couples over the past fifteen years as a Christian sex therapist, I have come to some definite convictions. I am determined that Christians reclaim God's wonderful gift of sexuality. There are many myths we will seek to destroy with love and truth. As Christians, we know, in a way others cannot, the importance of marriage and the joy of commitment and becoming one flesh. We can bring intimate bonding to new heights with love, trust, and excitement.

Some of the sexual ideas we explore will seem commonplace, and some will challenge you. They may somehow seem inconsistent with our common Christian faith. We usually don't talk about sex and making love as explicitly as we will in this book. You may occasionally feel uncomfortable because the values of the world have distorted God's intentions for married couples.

This book is written to adult couples who are married or contemplating marriage. Slang has been deliberately omitted; sex has been treated with respect. I will challenge you to make your lovemaking congruent with God's economy. Christlike values and character traits are the bedrock of a great sex life and are a strong part of this book. Being a Christian should never be separated from being playful, passionate, and romantic.

We have an obligation to be "wise as serpents and harmless as doves" (Matt. 10:16 NKJV). My desire is that this manual be truly educational and help you enjoy God's great gift of making love.

Don't skip over what you feel may be the boring parts. Take the time to work on your intimate companionship. Meaningful lovemaking takes energy, but most of the needed changes will be in your attitude, not your technique.

As you learn how to celebrate more completely your intimate companionship, the sexual part of your marriage will never be the same. Playfulness, fun, and deep love will permeate your relationship. You will embark on the awesome journey into God's wonderful, exciting world of making love with a richness you never thought possible.

Section One

Setting the Scene

Chapter One

A Biblical Celebration

Making love reached its peak expression in the Garden of Eden with Adam and Eve before the Fall. That is the model Christians should aspire to. And in this chapter we'll develop a theology of sexuality from Genesis on. Since the Fall, sex has been in a downhill spiral of immaturity and distortion. As Christians, we have a responsibility to redeem and reclaim God's wonderful gift of sexual union as we experience making love in its Garden-of-Eden fullness.

God's Image

Genesis 1:27 states, "So God created man in His own image; in the image of God He created him; male and female He created them" (NKJV). Wow! God's image is reflected in both maleness and femaleness and the way they interface. As we better understand the Creator of man and woman and the interaction of the Trinity, we gain an intimate glance into the nature of gender and sexuality: differences and similarities within a complementary partnership, the needs for intimate relationship, excitement and nurturing, procreation and recreation.

In exploring these concepts, we must be careful not to anthropomorphize God. (*Anthropomorphize* is a five-syllable word that means "to make human.") We as human beings are limited to our experiences, and they do not give us enough vocabulary and concepts to truly understand God. We as Christians should also be careful not to keep

God so far away from sexuality and marriage that we lose our Creator's insights into the nature of gender and becoming one flesh.

We can gain helpful understanding of gender differences by observing God's relationship with others. God the Father is an excellent model for the male role. God wanted to be respected by and to be a loving Father to the Israelites as He led and provided. God the Son is an excellent model for the female role. Jesus said He wanted to protect and nurture "as a hen gathers her chicks under her wings" (Matt. 23:37 NIV). At Lazarus's death, Jesus wept and showed His emotions (John 11:35). Jesus gave us insights into femininity with His enjoyment of nurturing, intimate relating, and maternal protectiveness of people important to Him. He appreciated the nourishing wholeness of valuing emotions and disclosing Himself within intimate friendships, embodying the concept of femaleness He created.

Another fascinating aspect in God's creation is that there is as much similarity in two-gender humanness as there is in the three-person Godhead. Males and females have more common emotions, needs, and attributes than they have differences. Each human being contains aspects of both genders. Carl Jung called these two principles *anima* and *animus*. I, Doug, am male but also have a female side to me that I can acknowledge and maximize. I can be a mother hen as I hover protectively; I will sometimes gently hold someone's hand as we cry together. Each of us, whether male or female, has both gender traits interacting in us in a way that brings a richness to personality and meaning to relationships, along with an awareness and appreciation of difference.

This idea of course leads into perplexing speculation about what exactly are the differences between maleness and femaleness, between husband and wife. The physical differences are readily apparent. There are other God-created differences, but it is easy to confuse them with prejudice, stereotypes, and power struggles. This is not God's design, for in Christ men and women are different but equal (Gal. 3:28; Col. 3:5–13).

We need to understand that some of these differences are not God-given distinctions but learned behaviors. For example, you have probably heard the saying that "men give affection to get sex and women give sex to get affection." This is not part of God's gender and sexual design. As a society, we have squelched female sexuality while allowing males to diminish the importance of emotions and intimate relating. These attitudes and actions should be disputed and changed by Christians.

We cannot deny that there are definite differences, and we can learn from each other as we incorporate the best of both gender worlds. What if men are more sexually immediate and women do value romance more? What if men do want challenge and women do desire security? Then our goal should be to combine the best of both genders, with men becoming more sensually romantic and women more aggressively sexual.

Some gender differences will always be a mystery, much as is the image of our wonderfully complex God. However, recognizing basic differences is important because these differences directly affect your understanding and ability to please your mate, create an intimate marriage, and be a great lover. Here are some common generalizations. They may or may not apply to your situation, so be careful not to presume your spouse conforms to less than universal concepts of masculinity and femininity. Most people blend characteristics from both lists.

Characteristics of men:
- Need to feel respected, and to have their egos stroked as they are told what great providers they are
- Take risks (e.g., no disability insurance) more easily
- Are one track (e.g., can't watch television and listen at the same time)
- Often see life as a contest that needs to be challenged
- Can come across as defensive
- Enjoy leading and providing but often insist on doing both in their own way—not necessarily in the manner the mate desires
- Sit on feelings or lack the skills to express them
- Tune in more visually to erotic sexual cues and like to touch what they see and enjoy in the wife's body
- Are more prone to be superficial and obsessive in their sexual behaviors—but can be childlike in a fun way in their enjoyment
- Are more predictable in what arouses them

Characteristics of women:
- Need to feel secure and to have a comfortable nest as their safety and emotional needs are met
- Do not take risks as readily
- Want to feel connected and included
- See life as more of a cooperative community
- Want to nurture and protect
- Are better at asking connecting questions and engaging in conversation
- Are freer in expressing emotions
- Enjoy sensuality and tune in visually to the whole person as well as erogenous zones
- Desire romance and emotional affiliation
- Are unpredictable in sexual arousal, both mentally and physically

One Flesh

God stated in the beginning of creation, "It is not good that man should be alone; I will make him a helper comparable to him" (Gen. 2:18 NKJV). Not only did God create the genders, but He designed a special, unique mating relationship. The scriptural account details, "A man shall leave his father and mother and be joined to his wife, and they shall become one flesh. And they were both naked, the man and his wife, and were not ashamed" (Gen. 2:24–25 NKJV).

It is tremendously moving to think of God's original one-flesh companionship. Adam and Eve, before the fall of Eden, had the marvelous capacity of being totally naked, physically and emotionally, with no shame or fear. They reveled in a childlike trust and curiosity—laughing, exploring, giving and receiving love. Sex was a glorious, innocent celebration lived out with instinctual honesty, respect, and zest for life. It was naked and unashamed with no performance anxiety, inhibitions, pain, or skill deficits. What a relationship and sex life they were able to have as they truly "knew" each other, inside and out!

Being God's special creation gives us the power to control nature and make choices in a way different from animal sexuality. We can decide when we want to have children and how many we can lovingly provide for. We can love and enjoy our children and families for a lifetime of purpose and intimacy. We can choose to have loveplay and lovemaking for intimate bonding and fun. We can enjoy the whole sexual process for recreation and the enhancement of intimacy. Unfortunately, sex has not always been regarded so positively.

Within Christianity, sex has often been portrayed as sinful or dangerous. Not too long ago, sex was justified only as a means of procreation. God was considered distant and mildly opposed to marital sexual pleasure. Some of this type of thinking dates back to St. Augustine and his conversion from a completely undisciplined and salacious sexuality. He and other church fathers created a restrictive, legalistic sexual economy because of their own struggles, and in so doing they incorporated a theology that strayed from Scripture. Church prohibitions robbed couples, and especially women, of the ability to enjoy God's intended pleasure.

One-flesh unity is an exciting concept, replete with sexual uniting and recreating. This is indeed God's plan, and we as Christians need to claim, sanctify, and celebrate the wonder and enjoyment of our sexuality. God intended for men and women to appreciate sexual fun and recreation. We need to claim our birthright of sexual pleasure and intimacy.

However, with greater freedom and grace in our sexuality comes the ability to make both constructive and destructive choices, and that is scary. The legalism of the early church fathers required less thought and energy on the part of Christians. Sexuality is indeed a powerful force in our lives with tremendous potential for intimate bonding or harmful behaviors. We must constantly make the choices that will enhance our one-flesh partnership.

First Corinthians 7:3, 5 tells about the importance of keeping sexually united in marriage: "Let the husband render to his wife the affection due her, and likewise also the wife to her husband. . . . Do not deprive one another except with consent for a time . . . and come together again so that Satan does not tempt you because of your lack of self-control" (NKJV). In a loving partnership, enjoying sexuality and connecting with a mate are gifts each brings to the other willingly—not by demands or coercion.

Please don't use God's loving guidelines as weapons on each other. Some husbands and wives club their mates with this passage and say things like, "If you don't have sex with me tonight, you are sinning." The real sin is theirs because they usually have never taken the time, lovingkindness, and energy to make changes needed to appeal to their mates romantically. Becoming one flesh has ceased to be the loving gift of meeting each other's needs and uniting.

Are you too fatigued or busy or inhibited to have sexual relations regularly? You are missing God's plan for marriage and the enjoyment of one of His avenues for increasing intimacy. Failing to structure frequent sexual activity into your companionship may open you up for Satan's temptations.

Satan tempts and destroys marriages by extramarital affairs, extreme inhibitions, and many more ways. Often it is a subtle drifting apart and a lack of warm, connecting companionship. God has given spouses something precious in the ability as husband and wife to share a physical intimacy that cannot be matched in any other relationship. There is no replacement for what God intended sex to do for intimate marriages. It is the framework for expressing many powerful and exciting emotions, like joy, love, trust, and playfulness. Making love also helps dissipate and defuse negative emotions and behaviors, like hostility, nit-picking, and defensive distancing. Spouses who frequently play sexually together stay together in warm, bonded ways and keep at bay many of the dragons that can haunt intimate companionship.

Godly Submission and Selfishness

Christians need to be able to practice righteous selfishness. But being selfish appears to be in direct conflict with the traditional Christian teaching of putting others first and ourselves last. We as Christians are indeed encouraged to be submissive. That is, we are encouraged to place our partners' needs and feelings ahead of our own. And submission is a significant part of a great sex life. Through submission, we honor our mates and nurture them unselfishly in ways they truly enjoy. But fulfilling sex also requires being selfish. If we are always other-focused and if we always repress our needs, we forfeit complete sexual fulfillment. Intimate lovemaking is a partnership with both selfishness and unselfishness.

The Bible often develops two principles that seem conflicting but actually are two balancing parts of a paradoxical concept. Some examples are law/grace, masculinity/femininity, bear your own burdens/bear one another's burdens, and unselfishness/selfishness. When we emphasize only *one* half of these balanced concepts, their effectiveness is diminished. We must add to submissiveness and unselfishness the complementary principles of self-esteem and selfishness.

Selfishness doesn't seem to get equal time in practical Christian training. Self-awareness and the assumption of personal responsibility are crucial to building a fun sexuality. The Bible commands us to "love your neighbor as yourself" (Mark 12:31 NKJV), and it states that "husbands ought to love their own wives as their own bodies" (Eph. 5:28 NKJV). These teachings are based on the idea of a healthy self-concept.

As Christians, we are accountable to God for creating a good sexual self-image and accepting ourselves without comparing ourselves to others. We are answerable individually to build a vibrant self-awareness and to learn to love and appreciate our bodies' potential for sensuality. As individuals, we are responsible for developing our own sexuality and celebrating love. We need to understand our own sexual needs and assertively fulfill them. God encourages autonomy and personal responsibility for our lives, our bodies, and our sexuality.

Orgasms are an excellent example of healthy sexual selfishness. Your mate does not experience your orgasm. You focus on your sexual feelings and allow them to build to a climax. This is an intensely personal pleasure within your mind and body. You selfishly let your mind enjoy the intensity of your excitement.

As so often happens in God's complementary principles, selfishness and unselfishness balance each other and create a more complete wholeness. You selfishly enjoy your orgasm but unselfishly allow your mate to observe how much pleasure your mate brings to you. Your partner is aroused by your personal excitement and intense experiencing of erotic release. This selfishness creates a mutual intimacy that is fun and bonding. Selfishness is indeed a great turn-on to you and your mate.

The question may be hovering in your mind: Isn't there a destructive, sinful way of misusing submission and selfishness? Anytime you have a principle, it usually can be distorted and become destructive. Godly submission does not imply that you allow your mate to take advantage of you sexually as you build resentment. Putting the other's needs ahead of your own does not mean discounting your needs or ignoring them. Submission does not prevent a mate from being assertive and confronting behaviors that are personally or relationally damaging.

The downside of selfishness is being self-centered and thinking the world revolves around your needs. This creates an unwillingness to empathize with another person's needs and lovingly satisfy them. Greed, insecurity, false pride, and laziness create a negative self-centeredness and play havoc with sexual intimacy. This destructive selfishness may be quite subtle and come under the guise of caretaking so you don't have to face dealing with your needs or you may allow your mate to nurture you ("no, let me stroke you; don't worry about me"). Or you may be a martyr and manipulate with guilt ("I've got a headache—but if you need to"). Or you may be fragile or supersensitive ("I don't think I can ever be as sexy as you need," or "I know it's been ten days, but you really hurt my feelings").

Here are three suggestions for minimizing destructive selfishness and submission:

1. Keep a balance of healthy selfishness and unselfishness. Opposites need to be balanced out, and you can make a mental note when the ledger is starting to get uneven.

2. Be truly selfish and submissive. You must ask for your needs to be met and relish your sexual pleasure. You must submit your needs and give as loving gifts the things that your spouse needs.

3. Work on your personal spiritual growth as you humbly become Christlike. God's Spirit can help you become mature with playfulness, love, honesty, gentleness, and positive assertiveness.

A Spiritual and Emotional Union

Commenting on the beauty and depth of marital companionship, Paul writes, "For this reason a man will leave his father and mother and be united to his wife, and the two will become one flesh. This is a profound mystery—but I am talking about Christ and the church" (Eph. 5:31–32 NIV). Making love and creating a one-flesh partnership are a profound, mysterious, and dynamic process.

As we launch into our exploration of sexuality, we must remember that we lose something if we treat making love as simply physical excitement, intercourse, and techniques. Making love offers insight into Christ's relationship and modus operandi with His beloved followers, the church. It includes joy, excitement, trust, commitment, unselfish nurturing, self-esteem, and a mutually fulfilling, playful companionship. It is truly intimate, and we will never completely understand this mystery.

The apostle Paul deals more with the fuller meaning of sexual interaction and intercourse as he talks about the temple prostitutes in the pagan worship of Aphrodite (1 Cor. 6:9–20). Some of the Corinthian Christians were getting sexual excitement and release by visiting the temple prostitutes. He writes, "Foods for the stomach and the stomach for foods. . . . The body is not for sexual immorality but for the Lord. . . . Do you not know that he who is joined to a harlot is one body with her? For 'the two,' He says, 'shall become one flesh.' . . . Do you not know that your body is the temple of the Holy Spirit?" (NKJV). Paul emphasizes that sexual union has an emotional and a spiritual dimension to it; it is not like eating a meal or casually satisfying a bodily desire.

Making love needs to be based on an intimate marital partnership. Without the playful, loving companionship, sex becomes another buzz that loses its perspective and has increasingly diminishing returns. Going on a roller coaster or eating a big steak is fun, but we wouldn't want to do that two or three times a week the rest of our lives. A one-flesh marriage—that is, the *spiritual* merger of wife and husband—allows sex to be ever new and exciting. Sex is a means to an end and never an end in itself. Making love unites and excites, but the relationship gives the context and meaning. Without the intimate relationship, we find that sex becomes an activity (like eating steak or shooting white-water rapids) that rapidly loses its dynamic appeal.

Making love in a special and meaningful way is modeled after Christ's relationship with the church. We as Christians must learn to bring God's love and values into our marriages, especially into making love. We need to understand Christ's deep commitment, gentleness and humility, the ability to lead and serve, to speak the truth with love. He demonstrated the basis for true spiritual and emotional union.

Marriage and making love are complex and mysterious concepts. Sexual union is an exciting emotional and spiritual experience. Bringing its Creator into the equation adds immensely to our understanding and appreciation of the process.

A Well of Water

My favorite scriptural passage as a sex therapist is Proverbs 5:15–19:

> Drink water from your own cistern,
>   running water from your own well.
> Should your springs overflow in the streets,
>   your streams of water in the public squares?
> Let them be yours alone,
>   never to be shared with strangers.
> May your fountain be blessed,
>   and may you rejoice in the wife of your youth.
> A loving doe, a graceful deer—
>   may her breasts satisfy you always,
>   may you ever be captivated by her love (NIV).

We could paraphrase this for wives:

> Rejoice in the husband of your youth.
> A gentle stag, a strong deer—
>   may his hands and mouth satisfy you always,
>   may you ever be captivated by his love.

The Bible often uses water as a very powerful and fitting metaphor for cleansing, healing, and rejuvenating. There are beautiful images like "streams in the desert," "water of life," and "beside the still waters." What a tremendous portrayal of the dynamic nature of lovemaking to compare it to a cistern, a well, a stream, and a fountain of water. It is like a cool, refreshing drink from your own safe supply.

In one way, your sex life is like a cistern in which you have stored many amorous memories and a sexy repertoire of arousing activities. You can dip into it again and again in your fantasy life and lovemaking for excitement and fun. In another way, making love is like a stream or spring of water. Sex in marriage has an ever-changing, renewing quality to it. As the ancient Greek philosopher Heraclitus gazed into the river and realized life was a dynamic process that never stayed the same, so you can anticipate infinite variety and newness in making love.

A routine sex life is not God's design. Read this book, renew your minds and attitudes, and get sexy and playful. You can make love four times a week for the next fifty years and still never plumb the surprising depths of this mysterious sexual "stream" of becoming one flesh.

I appreciate the words *rejoice, satisfy,* and *captivated* in the Proverbs passage. Pleasure and fun are an intended part of making love. It is important for mates to enjoy playing together. We can rejoice with the mate of our youth. Our creativity, imagination, and love allow us to remain ever enthralled sexually with the lover of our youth. We can be ever satisfied and captivated.

I really appreciate this saying from the Talmud, the Jewish teachings on the first five books of the Bible: "God will hold us accountable for every permitted pleasure that we forfeit." We as Christian couples and individuals may need to adjust our attitudes on rejoicing, being satisfied and enthralled, and enjoying sexual pleasure. You can experience tremendous joy, excitement, and fulfillment if you allow God to bless your lovemaking and you follow His design of being a fresh spring of water to your partner.

An Erotic Celebration

In my earlier years, before I had listened to so much sexual tragedy, I used to think the Christian emphasis on sex as a spiritual and emotional union was a cop-out. I was tired of hearing about the importance of having a committed relationship and building good fences. I wanted more solid information and explicit discussion about sex. I often thought that we spiritualized sex because we were afraid to talk about bodies, positions of intercourse, erotic fantasies, and the excitement of making love. We were afraid to face the concepts of pleasure and sexual techniques and erotic arousal.

As a sex therapist, I now realize how many problems are created by spiritual and soul deficits (e.g., lack of honesty, a poor body image, or an inability to play or experience pleasure). I now understand better the need for relational skills, deeper commitment, and emotional bonding. Yet I still think the church has been reluctant to talk openly and honestly about sex, especially the erotic pleasure of it.

Sex is an erotic celebration! *Eros,* the Greek word for sexual love, includes the ideas of fusion, passion, attraction, and bonding. Erotic love is getting lost in someone's eyes. Erotic love is mental imagery, anticipation, playfulness, ambiance, and lovers physically enjoying each other.

The Song of Solomon contains many beautiful images of erotic love:

> Let him kiss me with the kisses of his mouth—
> For your love is better than wine (1:2 NKJV).
> My lover is mine and I am his;
>   he browses among the lilies (2:16 NIV).
> Your two breasts are like two fawns. . . .
> Your plants are an orchard of pomegranates
>   with choice fruits. . . .
> You are a garden fountain,
>   a well of flowing water. . . .
> Let my lover come into his garden
>   and taste its choice fruits (4:5, 13, 15–16 NIV).
> But my own vineyard is mine to give. . . .
> Thus I have become . . . like one bringing contentment (8:12, 10 NIV).

These passages so beautifully and poetically describe erotic passion with body, emotion, fantasy, and soul. Sex is the curious and excited exploration of each other's erogenous zones to create pleasure. It is creating stimulating atmospheres and frolicking in each other's garden, sharing choice fruit, and drinking till contented from the flowing water of your sexual relationship.

There have been many different interpretations about what is permissible for a Christian in genital pleasuring as you browse among the lilies and taste the choice fruits of your marital sexual garden. An example of this would be the different views about oral sex and pleasuring your mate's genitals with your mouth. The Bible is silent about this topic. The Christian community has often been skeptical of oral sex, sometimes for unworthy reasons like thinking that the genital area is "dirty" or "too private" or thinking that Christians should be cautious about overindulging in playful sexual pleasure. Christians also may wonder if oral sex encourages emphasis on orgasm to the point where other methods of making love become less preferred. Viewed in this way, some may feel that oral sex may take away from the importance of intercourse as a God-given part of becoming one flesh. When the Bible does not directly deal with a topic, however, we turn to other scriptural values to help govern our sexual behaviors. In light of other injunctions, oral sex can be enjoyed as one of many ways to enjoy making love, though some couples may choose not to engage in this expression of love.

In Scripture we are called to be considerate and gentle. Never should we do anything that violates our mate's sensibilities or offends our mate sexually. Our bodies are God's temple, and the tissue should be treated respectfully and not damaged. (For a small percentage of women, oral sex may increase the risk of yeast infections. These women should abstain.) We are told to be self-disciplined and balanced, with oral sex, or any erotic stimulation, never becoming the focus of our whole lovemaking and intimate connecting. Making love is a celebration of our one-flesh companionship and should never be associated simply with orgasm, intercourse, or genital pleasuring. We as lovers are to entrust our private parts only to our mates, but indeed "my own vineyard is mine to give," and we should learn to have no shame or inhibitions with the genital area.

With biblically-neutral behaviors, such as oral sex, Christians will disagree about whether they are productive or counterproductive to married lovemaking. That is okay. God promises in Philippians 3:15, 16 that if we act on the truth we do understand, He will help each of us mature and come to an understanding of His will and way. A purpose of this book is to encourage each of us to think carefully and bring our sexuality and lovemaking into accord with God's truth and economy. This book is humbly based on God's truth. Together we as Christians need to carefully reclaim from distorted worldly values God's precious gift of sexuality. Let's create a practical and accurate sexual theology and practice.

Making love is intimate connecting and a breaking down of walls so that "my lover is mine and I am his [hers]." You are willingly naked and vulnerable. Lovers are able to experience freedom and abandonment together based on love, trust, and commitment. It is a totally unique companionship and so exciting to be naked and not ashamed as you celebrate marriage. Making love is a cycle you can repeat with intensity throughout the years of your marriage because it is founded on your intimate companionship. The next chapter will develop further the importance of this loving partnership and the need to be a mature lover.

Chapter Two

The World's Greatest Lover

Fantastic lovemaking is based on being a fantastic person. Attitudes are what count. True sexiness and a fantastic sex life depend first upon being a mature, sexy person.

So you want to be the world's greatest lover? Build into your mind and heart the following character traits possessed by all great lovers: playfulness, love, knowledge, honesty, creative romance, and discipline. These guidelines, gleaned from the Bible, will lead to great sex. Their effective use will show you how to truly arouse your mate's desire. Success is practically guaranteed, but it will take some real effort to incorporate them into your life.

Playfulness

We as adults so easily forget the art of playfulness. It is the ability to let go of control and to frolic and be silly. It is feeling you deserve to have fun and being able to anticipate it, then enjoying the fun you create.

You can learn from children's playfulness. They can be self-directed and demand pleasure. In their childlike mentality, life is a big playground, and they expect to have fun. Children can get excited a whole day about an anticipated ice-cream cone. Adults, however, sometimes have to be on vacation for two days before getting relaxed and starting to have fun. Playfulness is perhaps best described by the terms *excitement, curiosity, eagerness,* and *spontaneity.* Playfulness is the ability to be unpretentious and candid as you demand things with enthusiasm and laughter—expecting your needs to be met.

You cannot *work* at creating better lovemaking—you and your mate have to *play* at it. This character trait can be practiced in other areas of your life and the lessons brought back into your sex life. Get silly; anticipate an event for a week or more; risk a new behavior; laugh until you have tears in your eyes or roll on the floor; tickle and chase each other around the whole house; get wide-eyed with awe and wonder about something. You are becoming a great lover.

Playing has a way of connecting people. Gentle teasing, shared games, and mutual laughter can be bonding. Even sexual mistakes can create a playful memory. So often in making love, partners do things that are silly or embarrassing. As playful partners, you can laugh rather than be awkward.

Making love is certainly built on the foundation of play. I am reminded of Christ's teaching that to truly experience the kingdom of God, we need to become like little children. An important part of being childlike is valuing play and reveling in the awe of the moment. Children are great teachers of amusement, as you learn every time you take them to a park. I've taken the liberty of paraphrasing Christ's advice: "Unless you become childlike and learn to be playful, you will never experience God's gift of great sexual intimacy." You each have this childlike playfulness that is longing to be unleashed.

Time Out . . .

Take time when you are out this week to stop and buy yourself a toy or two that would encourage you to play. You may want some that you and your mate can enjoy together, such as water pistols, jump ropes, rub-on tattoos, or Tinkertoy building blocks.

Love

The Bible says you are to love your neighbor or your mate just as you love yourself. Fun sex depends on a husband and wife who have learned to love themselves. This means you take care of your health and exercise your body to keep it in shape. You should also enjoy and accept the body God gave you. Self-acceptance, self-esteem, and a good body image are healthy parts of sexiness and Christian self-love. Think of how difficult it is to sexually focus on your mate when you are embarrassed, inhibited, or self-conscious.

Psychological research has shown us that the people and things we are more familiar with, we tend to like more. People who live in the same apartment complex or go to church together seem to grow to like one another just by being in proximity with one another and sharing common things. As you get more comfortable with seeing your body and allowing it to be in your thoughts without negative criticism, you will start to like it more.

Time Out . . .

Stand nude in front of a full-length mirror. Now observe yourself and resist making any judgments. After observing a few minutes, start with your hair and proceed down to your feet and accept and describe every one of your body parts with no negative judgments: "This is my hair, and it is brown with a cowlick."

Sometimes when you're in front of the mirror, you may want to dispute some of the negative messages going around in your head. Start by looking at a part of your body that you appreciate and truly affirm that: "My eyes are big and brown and quite striking." Now observe more closely parts you don't like and verbally make yourself accept them and say something affirming about them: "God gave me these thighs, and they are strong and support me in many things I enjoy doing." "My shoulders have changed at age forty-eight, but I still hit the softball well."

An important part of love is respecting and unconditionally accepting your mate. If you want to find and focus on flaws, you will put a damper on your partner's sexiness and the whole lovemaking process. First Corinthians tells us that true love protects, forgets, and doesn't keep a record of wrong (13:4–7). Allowing your mind to become preoccupied with the size of body parts or sags is very destructive.

You reap the benefit (or the destructiveness if you stay obsessive) of nurturing and helping your lover revel in sexual appeal. Every time you affirm some particular aspect of masculinity or femininity that you admire and enjoy, you lovingly increase your mate's sex appeal. It is such a growth-producing process when you are unconditionally committed to accepting your own sexiness and affirming the sexiness of your partner. It creates the environment for a comfortable, safe, sexual greenhouse in which playfulness and risk taking blossom. Unconditional love and acceptance and affirmation set the temperature for some fantastic sex.

I like the word *lover* to describe your sexual partner. This is an important part of God's boundary and provision for great sex—one who loves within the commitment of an intimate marriage. Love creates trust so you can try new behaviors and risk appearing silly. Love produces warm excitement and fun companionship. Love helps you remember and desire to meet your mate's needs. Learn to be a lover! The best sex is long-term, and love is the oil that keeps this type of lovemaking running smoothly.

Love is also gentle, kind, and forgiving as mates nurture each other. Mature love doesn't pout or harbor grudges and is able to reach out beyond your own needs—all vital for great sex. A great love life depends on allowing your mate to apologize and change. We will all do dumb things that can damage our lovemaking, and we need to be able to forgive and move on. Mature love incorporates loving gestures that are nonsexual as well as sexual. Wives especially value hugs and caresses outside the bedroom that build a loving ambiance and lay the groundwork for fun romance.

Practicing loving behaviors (unconditional acceptance, gentleness, forgiveness, meeting your mate's needs) produces strong, warm feelings of being in love. As you learn to love, your sexiness will increase.

Knowledge

There are two parts of being a wise and knowledgeable lover. First, become a student of your mate and yourself. The apostle Peter tells husbands: "Be considerate as you live with your wives" (1 Pet. 3:7 NIV). An integral aspect of true consideration is constantly trying to know and understand your partner better.

In the language of the King James Version of the Bible, the word *know* is used to describe intercourse. For example, Isaac knew his wife, Rebekah, and they conceived a son. I used to think this wording was due to the reluctance of those times to deal with sex openly. Now, I like this word *know* in our era of casual sexual encounters. Lovemaking should be knowing what your mate enjoys and needs. This knowledge takes time, curiosity, a good memory, and the willingness to be a student.

Time Out . . .

Take a minute and do a quick personal inventory. Which areas of your sex life can benefit from greater knowledge? Which do you hope to improve by reading this book? How are you going to implement change?

Study your mate's responses to know what is most enjoyable. No book can give you that information. Women even more than men vary about what feels good—the strokes and rhythms that are most pleasurable. Be an eternal student of your partner's body and reactions. Acquire a reservoir of knowledge of what excites your partner physically and mentally. Set the romantic ambiance, practice the right moves, and reap the exciting benefits of being a wise lover.

Another aspect of being an informed and sexy lover is knowing your own body and sexual responses. You are the teacher of your mate. Do you know what turns you on and increases your desire? It will be difficult teaching your erotic needs to your partner if you are not aware of them. Tune in to your sexuality, and keep expanding your repertoire of sensual delights. A healthy, selfish focusing on your sexual feelings not only allows you to get excited but also turns your mate on. Knowledge of yourself and your mate is crucial to great sex.

The second part of being a knowledgeable lover is your technical knowledge of sexuality. Sexual technique is not the be-all and end-all of a great sexual relationship, but its importance can't be denied.

Many chapters of this book are about technique. The couple with their act together sexually know how to create ambiance and be uninhibitedly sensual and playful. They understand various positions of intercourse, and they have built a comfortable, exciting repertoire of sexual moves. The wife understands how to ring her husband's chimes. The husband knows how to orchestrate his wife's responses to produce exciting, sexual music together. Each is wise and skillful sexually.

Sexiness = a knowledgeable, together person + a great relationship!

Honesty

In making love, dishonesty destroys trust, allows boredom, and creates confusion and hostility. It may take the form of the dishonest husband who lacks skills but can't admit to himself he is a nonromantic sexual illiterate. He may think, "She says sex isn't very fun, but she reaches a climax most of the time." A wife may play manipulative sexual games. Instead of confronting issues, she angrily vows to herself, "If he forgets our anniversary again, he won't get any sex for a month." Both may be unaware of their sexual needs and feelings—a more subtle form of dishonesty.

Time Out . . .

Do you have any dishonest sexual games you need to eliminate from your sex life? Do you sulk or pout rather than talk through your needs? Have you asked your mate what he or she needs? Do you avoid becoming passionate because you are afraid to let go of control, but you rationalize it by saying your partner is so pushy? Do you fear confrontation and settle for mediocrity? Do you fake orgasms? Do you neglect to share your feelings? When your needs are satisfied, do you stop?

Many couples find it uncomfortable to initiate sexual conversations and openly discuss individual needs and desires. The wife may be upset because her husband gets defensive or pouts if she openly refuses sex or makes a small suggestion. The husband may be angry because his wife turns him down after he plays the romantic rituals like taking a quick shower or rubbing her back. These are times for great air-clearing, honest discussion and confrontation to openly express feelings and needs.

God's guidelines are very explicit for relationships: He tells us to speak "the truth in love" and put away lying (Eph. 4:15, 25). Even in love, the truth is sometimes tough to take. Even in little sexual communications during making love, it is sometimes difficult to say, "That doesn't feel good tonight," or "Please rub harder." Great sex is based on mature lovers who can be honest with themselves and their mates. They are self-aware and can assertively communicate.

Before leaving the character trait of honesty, let's acknowledge the ultimate dishonest kiss of death to a great sex life: the extramarital affair. Nothing can sabotage trust and the specialness of a love life more thoroughly than adultery. Sneaking, broken promises, and divided loyalties rob a couple of sexual celebration in their marriage. An affair is a powerful negative illustration of the importance of honesty for sexual love to flourish.

Creative Romance

Sexy lovers take the time to develop the sensual, romantic part of their minds and personalities. Every person has an exciting romantic side, but few take the time and energy to unleash their passionate capacities. Mates can be surprised how talented and creative they are in planning sexy surprises for each other. They easily come up with exciting unique ideas as they focus on the importance of sensuality and mood setting—anticipation builds, and fresh attitudes pervade the whole sexual scene.

Time Out . . .

How would you define *romantic?* Creating moods, sexy, mysterious, spontaneous, passionate, sentimental? Many wives and husbands wish their spouses would be more romantic. Make a brief list of behaviors that you consider romantic and do one or two this week.

Couples always enjoy letting their romantic part out. This may include surprise gifts, foot and leg massages, verbal demonstrativeness, mutual showers, or dinners with candlelight and soft glances. Of course, romantic lovemaking doesn't always involve completely new techniques and experiences. There are certain positions, ways of caressing, places, rhythms, restaurants, moods, and vocabulary that remain enjoyable favorites.

Being creatively romantic is such an important quality to incorporate. Why then do you think it is so easy to fall into ruts and forget to employ this character trait for a great sex life?

1. *Problem*: too busy; a modern plague demonstrated by an inability to say no and scale down as priorities are constantly violated. *Solution*: create date nights and time together.

2. *Problem*: no plan. *Solution*: mobilize willpower and create goals while structuring a varied, exciting sex life into life-style.

3. *Problem*: inhibitions and ignorance; a lack of time and energy invested in changing attitudes and increasing sexual knowledge. *Solution*: read, go to workshops, talk, and attempt new behaviors.

4. *Problem*: tension; conflict in the relationship with unresolved traumas, hurt, and anger. *Solution*: learn to communicate and resolve conflict.

5. *Problem*: demands of child rearing on time and energy. *Solution*: structure and set careful boundaries.

6. *Problem*: procrastination. *Solution*: start making love at 9:30 P.M.; enjoy quickies once in a while; turn off the television; ignore fatigue, and just do it.

Time Out . . .

They are making a movie of your sex life. What would its title be? The theme song? Type of movie? Length? Do this exercise twice: (1) the way your love life is presently, and (2) the way you would like it to be.

You as an individual and couple breathe life and excitement into the material of this book with your imagination and relationship and character traits. Sexiness comes from your imaginative creativity and romantic inspirations—and the discipline (time and energy) to carry them out. You want to be a great, sexy lover? Become a creative romantic.

Discipline

Discipline may seem an odd character trait to include for a lover, and the opposite of spontaneity, playfulness, and creativity. The truth of the matter is that an undisciplined life-style will end up with very infrequent sex. Perhaps you think that discipline would completely destroy the fun and spontaneity of sex and put pressure on you. But if you don't plan sex into your schedules, you will never make love! The ambiance, activities, place, timing, and technique are up to your romantic creativity. Just keep a time sacredly reserved for sex.

Time Out . . .

Put your heads together and plan when and how often you are going to make love each week as you allow time for spontaneous sex into your intimate companionship.

One of my supervisors in my sex therapy training, Dr. Domeena Renshaw, said she was always amazed by couples. Both would heartily agree the activity was fun, relaxing, and important to them. Then they placed it around number twenty-five on their list of priorities and wrote it in pencil so they could move it lower if something else came up.

There are few couples whose sex life has not been seriously sabotaged by lack of discipline and priority. They may start making love at 11:00 P.M. when one or both have already turned into pumpkins—physically and emotionally spent. They may try to get all the chores done first or not plan carefully enough around the children's needs. They may make love only when the mood and circumstances are perfect—averaging about once every two months. A few disciplined adjustments create more sexiness: go to bed at the same time, teach the children to respect a locked door, and agree to schedule lovemaking so many times a week regardless of distractions or fatigue.

A fundamental aspect of discipline in relation to a quality sex life is developing in a healthy, godly way the emotions of shame and guilt. These emotions play a crucial part in keeping your sex life pleasurable. Paul, when he wrote to the Corinthians, did not try to distinguish between guilt and shame but called those emotions *godly sorrow*. He explained the importance of godly sorrow in the Christian's life as a motivational feeling to protect and mold a productive life. "Godly sorrow brings repentance that leads to salvation and leaves no regret. . . . See what this godly sorrow has produced in you: what earnestness, what eagerness to clear yourselves, what indignation, what alarm, what longing, what concern, what readiness to see justice done" (2 Cor. 7:10–11 NIV). God does not want you to feel shame for having sexual feelings. But there should be healthy shame in your sex life throughout your marriage. Shame and guilt might come because you neglect lovemaking as a wonderful avenue for bonding or are complacent in not incorporating variety and new skills. You may feel guilty for choices that hurt your intimacy. As long as shame and guilt drive you to seek out God's best, your love life will thrive, and you will maintain healthy discipline.

You have the promise of being a great lover. Incorporate the character traits of being loving, honest, playful, knowledgeable, and disciplined. Build real commitment. Tune in to God's emotional signals of shame and guilt and make necessary changes. As you become more disciplined, you actually will become more spontaneous and will have a more intimate, comfortable, sexual fulfillment.

In a world of new techniques, bigger-is-better beliefs, and instant answers, it is difficult but truly rewarding to take the time and energy to improve yourself and your relationship.

May you have wisdom and courage as you appreciate and conform to God's economy for great lovemaking:

An Intimate Marriage + Mature Lovers = A Fulfilling Sex Life

Chapter Three

Your Erogenous Zones

Let's consider a husband and wife who enjoy making love and have discovered various spots on each other's body that are sensitive to touch and produce great sexual feelings. Sometimes both are a little lazy in searching out new areas of arousal or in letting the other know what feels particularly good. Neither is completely comfortable letting the other explore the genital area intimately.

The husband wishes his wife would be more active in pleasuring all of his erogenous zones. He appreciates her enjoyment of his penis and its key role in arousing him, but he wishes she would caress other parts of his body, too, sometimes. He enjoys giving her pleasure and it is very stimulating to him, but recently, he has felt a little neglected. He isn't sure exactly what he needs, but his worry and dissatisfaction are starting to get in the way. He doesn't want to lose the tremendous enjoyment they experience in making love.

The wife gets upset because she wishes her husband would stimulate her clitoris differently. She wants more friction with a firmer touch on the shaft rather than lower toward her vagina—which misses her spot of most arousal. She would also like greater variety in caressing and loveplay. He seldom focuses on her stomach or face, and they are very sensitive areas for her. She has told him a couple of times, but he seems to forget. If anyone were making a list of the attributes for a great lover, she would want to include an excellent memory. It isn't enough for her to tell him; he has to remember what she likes when they make love.

If you asked this couple, they would say they have a good sex life overall. They do.

They are great companions and have fun playing together as friends and lovers. Their bed is a fun sexual playground, and they try to take the time to create a romantic atmosphere. Overall, both like their bodies and trust that the other will enjoy what is seen and touched. They may never need sex therapy for a specific problem, but they could profit tremendously from education about erogenous zones. These zones are parts of the body that have a concentration of sensory nerve endings, which can be stimulated to cause sexual arousal.

Sexual Reflexes

Your body's mechanism for sexual arousal demonstrates a beautifully complex relationship among hormones, nerves, blood vessels, and muscles. Yet all you have to do is simply relax and tune in to your God-given erogenous zones and responses. The sexual part of your mind and body may be repressed or lying dormant, but it is there. Making love and stimulating erogenous zones are the essence of simplicity, but it is important to first understand your sexual reflexes and how arousal occurs. This is the foundation for enjoying the erogenous zones. Many couples short-circuit their love-making by sometimes worrying too much about sexual arousal and not enjoying their reflexive sexual reactions enough.

Hormones and the Autonomic Nervous System

Why do we experience a sexual touch and begin to get an erection or vaginal lubrication? God has designed our bodies so that our hormones, nerve endings, and minds can create sexual arousal. It is a cooperative process of hormones and the nervous system. The hormones activate the process in our bodies and bloodstream, and then our nerves relay sexual information from our senses to our brains, and back to our genitals to create physical arousal. Without getting too technical, the autonomic, or involuntary, nervous system is involved in the sexual arousal cycle. I was referring to it when I said that both the husband and the wife in the opening example were worrying too much and getting upset and, in the process, sabotaging the natural, reflexive sexual responses. They needed to get out of the way of God's natural automatic arousal patterns and enjoy their bodies and erogenous zones more.

The autonomic, or involuntary, nervous system has two branches called the sympathetic (SNS) and the parasympathetic (PNS). The PNS and the SNS operate in opposite manners. The parasympathetic is operative when we are relaxed, and it has a creative, building effect on the body. The sympathetic springs into action when we are intensely aroused to trigger orgasm or when we are threatened to shut down the PNS. Both arousal and orgasm are involuntary, reflexive actions. You simply have to relax and enjoy erogenous zones.

Sabotaging Arousal and Erogenous Zones

So the husband in our example, and in some ways the wife, too, was short-circuiting God's design of relaxing with erogenous zones and allowing pleasurable sensations (PNS) to build. He was anxious about not getting enough attention from his wife. Anxiety, anger, boredom, and resentment trigger SNS reactions and are great saboteurs of having stimulating times making love. The husband was not going with his automatic parasympathetic system as he allowed arousal to mount. He was too worried about having his body caressed, while wondering whether they were having fun yet. His wife was not that much different because she built some resentment about the way he stimulated her clitoris. Both could experience some sabotaging results from blocking their PNS unless they begin to relax and enjoy.

This couple were blocking their enjoyment of erogenous zones with resentment and worry and lack of variety. Other people have never allowed their erogenous zones to be sensitized and create sexual arousal. They are inexperienced at tuning in to sexual feelings and identifying sexual arousal. All of us have nerve endings that can produce sexual feelings, but they do have to be activated by allowing our hormones to create sexual arousal and our minds to interpret these sensations as sexual.

Because of a conservative Christian background, natural shyness, or discomfort with their bodies, some mates have never explored their physical sexual responses. The hormones and nervous system are obviously in place, and they enjoy some types of arousal. The parasympathetic system needs to be turned loose with less effort and more turning into sexual feelings without intense effort.

Too many couples are guilty of sabotaging their erogenous zones and sexual enjoyment with ignorance, anxiety, and intense efforts. Intimate marital companions have usually never developed their sexual awareness to include even half of the erogenous zones in their bodies, and they often short-circuit their sexual reflexes. Mates have many fun sexual discoveries to make in their erogenous zones.

Erogenous Zones

Sensuality and sensitivity to touch have to be developed and connected to your sexual lovemaking. Overall, our erogenous zones are more alike than different, whether we are male or female, experienced or inexperienced, overweight or underweight, active or inactive. But some individuals will experience more sensitivity and arousal from certain erogenous points than from others. These may also change over time. In the last section of this chapter we will explore how some of this can be a product of sensual erotic conditioning. There can be individual differences, though. That is why you must continually be a student of your mate and learn every inch of the body—remembering what is arousing but not locking into boring patterns of stimulation.

The erogenous areas can be divided into three levels according to their sensitivity in producing sexual arousal. Level three areas are less sexual in nature but capable of producing sensual arousal and sexual excitement. Level two areas contain a greater concentration of nerve endings and can be more sexual. Mucous membranes (e.g., the mouth and surrounding tissue) and tissue in the areas around the genitals are very sensitive and arousing sexually. Level one areas are the nipples and the genitals. These are the most sensitive areas and capable of building greater sexual tension—with the most crucial organs for triggering the orgasmic response being the penis and the clitoris.

Level Three

This level includes the entire body with its skin and nerve endings. You may be exclaiming, "Why is the whole skin area considered erogenous? When I rub my arm, I don't get turned on." The skin is the most extensive area of sensuality. A whole chapter on sensual massage is included in this book for this very reason. If you want to become a sensual lover, learn to revel in and appreciate your whole body's being caressed. Lie back, close your eyes, and discover the erogenous zone God has created with your skin.

You don't have to have special training or expensive equipment to enjoy massage. The object is to pleasure your mate's skin by touching and caressing. The experience can be enhanced by warming some oil and letting him or her rest comfortably on a pallet you have created on the floor. Sensuously stroke in smooth, continuous motions as you move from one area of the body to another. You can give so much enjoyment as you use your hands and fingers to create pleasure and intimate bonding.

Massage and caress your lover's arms, shoulders, outer ears and earlobes, scalp, upper chest, buttocks, and calves. They may not have the concentration of sensory nerve endings as other parts of the body, but they are still very sensual. They can contribute to a delightfully sensual experience.

Level Two

This level includes the parts of the body that are normally stimulated during foreplay. If you desire to be a great lover, become familiar with these areas of your partner's body. Have your mate take fingertips or mouth and tongue and explore the level two erogenous zones. Communicate with each other and determine if you do or do not feel greater sensitivity in these areas than level three parts of the body. If you focus your mind on enjoying the sensual feelings, you will find your ticklishness is less. You can also ask your partner to apply firmer pressure.

Take time and do some prospecting in these sensual areas. Stimulate the sensory nerve endings as you experience the pleasurable feelings of (1) the back of the knees, (2) the inner thighs, (3) the armpits and breast area, (4) the abdomen area and the navel, (5) the small of the back, (6) the neck from back to front, (7) the palms of the hands and bottoms of the feet, (8) the face, especially the (9) eyelids, (10) the edges of the nose over the sinus cavities, (11) the temples, and (12) the mouth and tongue. These areas are rich in sensory nerve endings. Allow these gentle touches and nuzzling to be a sensual treat and to become arousing sexually, too.

Sensate focus is an exercise developed by Masters and Johnson and other sex therapists as they helped couples overcome performance anxiety and become sensual lovers. As you play with your mate and focus on sensual feelings, you relax and a sense of companionship emerges. You experience a connection and stimulate your sensory nerve endings for more fulfilling sexual arousal.

Time Out . . .

Set aside at least a half hour. One partner will be the passive receiver and the other will be the active giver for fifteen minutes—then exchange roles. Both partners should be nude for this experience. If you are the active giver, touch and caress your mate in ways that bring pleasure to you. There is no right way to do this because you are touching for your own pleasure. If your mate does not like to be touched in certain areas, refrain out of love and respect. The passive partner will enjoy receiving pleasurable massage and pleasing you. The passive receiver is learning what touch feels best personally and what kind of active touch you like to give. This exercise focuses on level three and level two erogenous zones. There should be no touching of the genital area and nipples. Do not go on to making love during this session.

It is fun to incorporate sensate focus into your companionship as a relaxing, educational, and bonding exercise. You may want to incorporate aspects of this sensual massage into your lovemaking, but it is important to be able to touch and not always have the activity progress to intercourse and orgasm. This is a great way to learn about level two erogenous zones.

Level One

The most sensitive and sexually stimulating erogenous zones are the nipples and the genitals. The genitals most directly stimulate sexual arousal, and the third section of this chapter carefully explores this aspect of lovemaking. The nipples are a favorite spot of both men and women for stimulating sexual excitement. The nerve endings are especially sensitive and connected to sexual arousal. The nipples show sexual arousal by becoming erect, and the center portion (papilla) hardens.

Remember! Level one erogenous zones should not be the immediate focus of loveplay. Tease and caress the areas around the nipples and genitals before turning attention to the nipples, penis, or clitoris. Both men and women will enjoy a quickie occasionally. They will want their mates to stimulate the genitals with the goal of achieving a rapid orgasm. This is fun and exciting but often fails to achieve the same level of arousal as taking time to tease and play.

Men especially need to learn to go from general arousal to specific locations. Be mysterious, surprising, and tantalizing. Great lovers practice the sexual process of amplifying tension by gradually increasing stimulation in a teasing and slow manner.

There seem to be some gender differences but they are not universal. A man doesn't seem to mind immediate and direct, firm stimulation of the penis and even the nipples. This quick approach is often not to his wife's advantage if she wishes to prolong the lovemaking process. A woman seems to prefer a slower and more teasing approach with more firm and rapid stimulation when approaching climax. A woman also seems to need more varied stroking and techniques. She appreciates her husband's being an expert lover and having many alternatives to caressing and arousing her body and stimulating her erogenous zones.

The Genitals

Male and female genitals conform to the same general pattern but vary uniquely in shape, color, angles, and size. Variations have nothing to do with the ability to be a great lover and experience or give sexual pleasure. The following figures will develop an understanding of genital erogenous zones so you can better pleasure your mate.

The Male Genitals

The male genitals are more visible to the eye and familiar to the man because he handles his penis every time he urinates. Yet many men have never taken the time to truly examine the penis.

At birth the penis is uncircumcised with the foreskin covering the glans. The foreskin can be removed surgically for hygienic reasons. There is no truth to the myth that the uncircumcised penis is much more sensitive to touch.

The penis. The penis is composed of three columns of spongy tissue with the urethra running through the bottom column (corpus spongiosum). These spongy tissues fill with blood in a type of hydraulic system that creates the erection. The whole penis is an intricate network of blood vessels and nerves, with the head or glans of the penis being especially sensitive. The skin of the penis is loosely attached to allow for more easy stimulation. Penises can vary in the angle of erection, shape of the head of the penis, length, and color. This has nothing to do with the ability to give and receive pleasure. The myth of the importance of penis size in making love must forever be put to rest. When flaccid, the size of the penis will vary greatly; when erect, the size for most men falls into the five- to seven-inch category. The outer third of the vagina is most sensitive, and it would take a penis only three inches or less in length to create great pleasure. Men, quit being obsessed with penis size—it is not on the list of needed qualities for being a great lover.

The scrotum and testes. The scrotum is a sac of skin enclosing the testes. Under the skin is a muscle that can contract in response to cold or during sexual arousal, causing

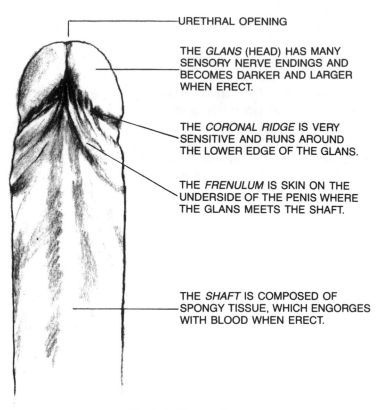

URETHRAL OPENING

THE *GLANS* (HEAD) HAS MANY
SENSORY NERVE ENDINGS AND
BECOMES DARKER AND LARGER
WHEN ERECT.

THE *CORONAL RIDGE* IS VERY
SENSITIVE AND RUNS AROUND
THE LOWER EDGE OF THE GLANS.

THE *FRENULUM* IS SKIN ON THE
UNDERSIDE OF THE PENIS WHERE
THE GLANS MEETS THE SHAFT.

THE *SHAFT* IS COMPOSED OF
SPONGY TISSUE, WHICH ENGORGES
WITH BLOOD WHEN ERECT.

FIG. 3.1. The penis.

the scrotum to hang lower or get tighter to the body. The scrotum and the base of the penis contain hair and sebaceous glands that can become ingrown and infected, much like a pimple. Sometimes a varicocele occurs in the scrotum. It is a bundle of dilated veins of the spermatic cord, much like varicose veins. This condition can be painful and may require minor surgery to repair.

The testicles will hang with one lower than the other. The testes are outside the body and contract toward the body with cold because the sperm need to develop in a

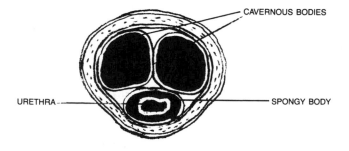

CAVERNOUS BODIES

URETHRA

SPONGY BODY

FIG. 3.2. Cross-section of penis showing urethra with corpora cavernosa and spongiosum.

40 *Setting the Scene*

constant temperature that is several degrees lower than body temperature. The testes produce sperm and hormones.

The epididymis is a coil of small tubes attached to a testis. The coil can sometimes get infected (epididymitis) and need to be medically treated. The epididymis ends in the vas deferens, which is the tube conducting sperm to the seminal vesicles and the ejaculatory duct. During a vasectomy, the vas is cut and tied off to prevent sperm from reaching the semen.

The seminal vesicles, bladder, prostate, and urethra. As you trace the vas deferens, it becomes a complex valve system with the seminal vesicles, the bladder, and the urethra, which passes through the prostate. The vas deferens brings sperm to the seminal vesicles that form the ejaculatory duct. This duct runs through and joins the urethra in the prostate. The prostate is about the size of a chestnut and produces fluid that forms part of the semen. The prostate can become infected (prostatitis) or cancerous, which necessitates medical treatment. Cancer may require a prostatectomy, which can create retrograde ejaculation: the ejaculate goes back into the bladder rather than out through the urethra and penis. This condition does not have to affect sexual pleasure. In an orgasm the muscles around the prostate and ejaculatory duct and the base of the penis contract, propelling the semen out through the urethra.

The Male Genital Erogenous Zones

Nipples. The male's nipples are sensitive to touch and create pleasurable feelings when stimulated orally or manually, often becoming hard just like the female's.

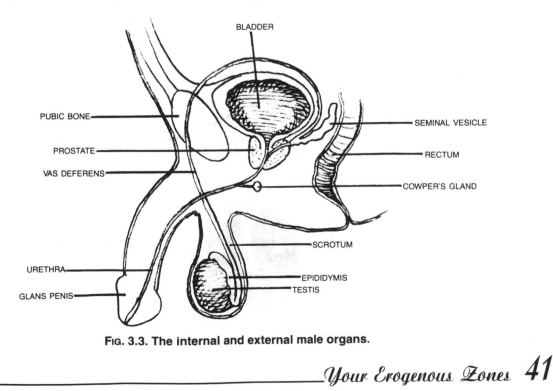

FIG. 3.3. The internal and external male organs.

Penis. The wife will often need her husband to demonstrate the strokes he appreciates most on his penis. It usually is firmer with the whole hand encircling the organ and often more rapid, especially when approaching orgasm, than she might expect. The underside of the penis is often very sensitive and responds well to fingertip stroking. The greatest concentration of nerve endings is in the head of the penis. Oral stimulation, the hand well-lubricated, or the vagina create arousal. Again, it will need to be firm stimulation, or it will not be felt or appreciated as much. A wife can place her hand over her husband's hand and learn the strokes and rhythms he enjoys the most.

Scrotum and testicles. The testicles are sensitive to being hit but can be touched quite firmly if done gently. These very erotic parts of a man's body create pleasant sensations with caressing or lightly tugging on the scrotal sac.

Perineum. This is the area between the scrotum and the anus. It is over the prostate gland as well as being at the base of the penis. It can be quite exciting to rub this area with moderate firmness—especially if done in conjunction with manually stroking the penis with the other hand. You, as partners, will have to explore and experiment, as you have done with level three and level two erogenous zones, while discovering what feels most exciting and pleasurable.

The Female Genitals

The vulva comprises the external genitals of the female. The vulva varies greatly in shape and size of outer and inner lips and density of pubic hair.

The vulva begins in front with the mons pubis covered with pubic hair and extends down to the perineum above the anus. On either side are the outer labia and inner labia with the clitoris, followed by the urethral opening and the vagina.

The mons pubis and labia majora. The pubic mound (mons pubis) is soft tissue over the pelvic bones. It is covered with hair and acts as a cushion during the thrusting of intercourse. The outer lips (labia majora) start down at the anus and extend up to meet at the mons. They are soft folds of tissue that, with the hair on them, protect the inner organs and are often all that are visible as they come together over the inner lips. During sexual arousal, the outer lips become engorged with blood and become flatter.

The clitoral hood and labia minora. The inner lips (labia minora) are hairless and start at the vaginal opening and extend upward to meet at the clitoral hood. If the hood is pulled back, the external part of the clitoris can be seen, like a small pea in size. The inner lips vary greatly in size and shape among females. With some women they are larger and extend outside the outer lips. There is no perfect size, but each unique shape will become intensely erotic to the woman's husband. The inner labia become engorged during sexual arousal and change color and increase in thickness. They create a chute that the penis travels down to the vagina for penetration.

The clitoris and shaft. The clitoris is homologous to the penis and contains the most sensitivity. It is given to the female solely for sexual pleasure, and stimulating it is the key to tension buildup and climax. The clitoris doubles in size and becomes hard like the penis. The clitoral shaft is primarily beneath the surface of the skin under the clitoral hood. (See fig. 3.4.)

The urethral opening. The urethral opening is between the clitoris and vaginal opening but is small and sometimes difficult to detect. The urethra has nothing to do with sexual arousal but is located near the wall of the vagina and can become irritated with the thrusting of intercourse.

The hymen. At birth the opening to the vagina is covered by a thin perforated piece of skin called the hymen. It is often broken with the insertion of tampons or physical activities. In rare cases it is so strong that a physician must perform a hymenectomy and surgically cut the hymen to allow intercourse. Usually, it is broken without intense pain and can be stretched by inserting the thumb or two fingers and gently pushing or pulling before first intercourse.

The vagina. The vagina is a shaft or tube of tissue with the sides touching. It is around three inches in length; it is muscular and expands so that it can accommodate any size of penis, especially with arousal. With arousal, the outer third of the vagina swells and creates the orgasmic platform, and the inner part balloons. After arousal, the greater penile stimulation will occur at the mouth, or outer third, of the vagina.

The cervix is at the upper end of the vagina and opens into the uterus. It can be sensitive to the hard thrusting of intercourse, but there are front and rear fornices on either side of the cervix. The rear fornix takes most of the hard thrusts of vigorous intercourse and is designed to collect the semen and hold it near the cervix to increase the likelihood of insemination. The vagina has folds of skin and sweats out lubrication

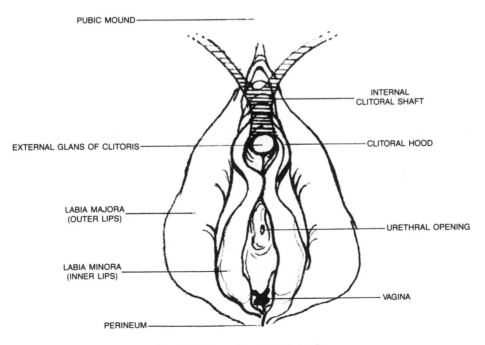

PUBIC MOUND

INTERNAL CLITORAL SHAFT

EXTERNAL GLANS OF CLITORIS

CLITORAL HOOD

LABIA MAJORA (OUTER LIPS)

URETHRAL OPENING

LABIA MINORA (INNER LIPS)

VAGINA

PERINEUM

FIG. 3.4. The clitoris with labia.

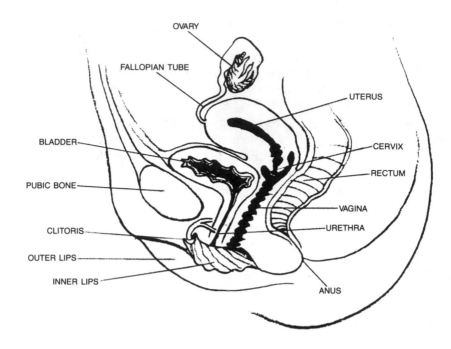

FIG. 3.5. The internal female organs.

when sexually aroused to allow intercourse. The vagina is delicately balanced with bacteria and acidic fluids to slow down bacterial growth. Be cautious with douches or placing a finger that has been near the bacteria of the anus within the vagina and upsetting the balance.

The Female Genital Erogenous Zones

The breasts and nipples. The breasts and nipples are very exciting to both husband and wife. The husband enjoys the unique femininity of his wife's breasts and sees the nipples becoming erect as an obvious sign of sexual arousal. He needs to remember that his wife will not usually appreciate a direct attack on the nipples or genital area. A woman more often appreciates an indirect, teasing approach. It is also wise to understand that a woman more than a man will vary in what feels stimulating or irritating from one lovemaking session to another. Nipples, for instance, can be affected by hormonal fluctuations. Always be creative as you caress, nibble, lightly touch, or stroke more firmly. Vary the direction and types of stroking as you invite and remember suggestions.

The labia. The outer and inner lips have many nerve endings and create sexual excitement. Again, vary the touch as you start with the outer lips and mons. Place the

whole hand over the genital area; run a finger from bottom to top of outer labia; lightly rub the labia together over the clitoral area. Allow sexual tension to build. The penis is a marvelous wand for creating pleasure, especially the soft head. Use it to gently stimulate the inner labia and the clitoris. Let the tension begin to build before active stimulation of the clitoris.

The clitoris. The wife will have to discover the strokes and places that she prefers for clitoral stimulation and teach her partner. She may have to slowly sensitize herself to experiencing the fun sensations her clitoris can provide. She can suggest techniques for her husband to use that are helpful for arousing her. One wife had trouble showing her husband the place she preferred to be stimulated. She liked a firm sideways stroke with his finger over the erect clitoral shaft right above the hood as she thrust up to meet the pressure. Eventually, she and her husband coordinated their movements, and it was tremendously arousing for her. The husband came to realize that the stimulation of his wife's clitoris was very similar to that of his penis. She desired rapid stroking as she approached her climax, with firmer and vigorous caressing. Your partner is unique; learn to nurture and excite her.

The vagina. The outer third of the vagina is the most sensitive. This sensitivity should be kept in mind with either manual or penile stimulation. Quick, shallow thrusts, as well as slow, sensual, longer motions, can be very arousing. Often there is greater sensation at twelve o'clock (toward the clitoris) and six o'clock (toward the anus) within the vagina. Positions that stimulate these areas create exciting sensations. (The G spot, which is located about an inch within the vagina at twelve o'clock and can be most easily located when the woman is aroused, will be discussed in a later chapter. With some women, the G spot creates particular pleasure and arousal.)

The perineum and areas adjacent to vulva. The perineum, or tissue between the anus and vagina, is sensitive to touch. Any skin or tissues immediately surrounding the vulva categorized as level two erogenous zones would include areas such as the inner thighs and stomach. Though not the direct genital area, they are very sensitive to caresses, licking, and teasing strokes—almost becoming an extension of the vulva. Remain creative and varied as you enjoy level one erogenous zones. Stimulating the genital area does not always have to lead to orgasm but can be done with nondemanding pleasuring. (See chapter 11.)

Sensual Erotic Pairing

Hormones stimulate sexual feelings and the nervous system communicates this to the brain. The brain then signals the muscles and blood system of the genitals and creates arousal. Your task is to be sensual and learn the erogenous zones so that you can caress your mate's body and both can experience the automatic sexual arousal that will occur as the hormones are released and the brain automatically sends signals through the nervous system. Your body and mind will cooperate, but you may need to be sensitized to enjoy a fuller range of sexual feelings as you stimulate erogenous zones and experience greater sexual arousal.

Time Out . . .

Let the husband get into a comfortable position lying on his back. The wife is going to gently and carefully explore and touch the genital area from perineum to the tip of the penis. Observe the penis both flaccid and erect. Let him tell her what feels especially sensitive and arousing. Now let the wife lie on her back and the husband do the same, taking time to explore what feels best in the vagina as well as the labia and clitoris. Pull back the clitoral hood and notice the clitoris—massage to greater arousal and feel the clitoris become erect. Become a student of your mate's body.

Another concept that can help you understand and enjoy the erogenous zones is a psychological principle that Russian psychologist Ivan Pavlov discovered. He taught dogs to salivate at a ringing bell by associating the bell with food. We call this classical conditioning. Perhaps it is easier to understand this conditioning process by calling it *pairing*. Figure 3.6 shows you how sexual pairing occurs. An unconditioned stimulus is paired with a conditioned stimulus, and you get aroused in time simply with the conditioned stimulus.

Unconditioned Stimulus (hormones) → *Unconditioned Response (excitement)*
Conditioned Stimulus (kiss) → *Conditioned Response (excitement)*

FIG. 3.6. Pairing of sexual stimulus and sexual response.

Pairing takes place in your mind as you stimulate the erogenous zones or sensually (touch, sight, smell) notice them and associate (pair) these experiences with hormones and sexual arousal. As you become more aroused, more hormones are released, and you can continue to pair various touches and visual experiences so that they become sexually arousing to you—like kissing or observing your mate's genitals. This is the beauty of a long-term intimate companionship. The pairing/conditioning never ceases, and stored in your mind are many sexually arousing symbols that you can draw on to create or enhance sexual arousal. Stimulating the erogenous zones can continually become charged with sensual and erotic pleasure over a lifetime of lovemaking.

Relax, explore, caress, pair, discover, stroke, expand, touch, and sensuously feel as you fully enjoy God's wonderful gift of sexual pleasure.

Chapter Four

The Lovemaking Cycle

God has designed a marvelously complex process to be set in motion when a couple makes love. A *process* can be defined as "a continuing series of changes that develop over a span of time to accomplish a purpose." This is true of making love. Lovemaking is commonly sabotaged by neglecting to allow the sexual cycle to be a fulfilling and exciting process that takes time and unfolds slowly with sensuous, pleasurable, and arousing changes. Lovemaking is also sabotaged by incorrectly defining the purpose of the sexual process or cycle. The purpose is *not* having intercourse or achieving an orgasm. The purpose of the lovemaking process is to unite with your one-flesh companion as God designed—with anticipation, warmth, excitement, mutual pleasure, and intimate bonding.

Because males and females have different emotional needs, men should be aware that it's dissatisfying to most women if lovemaking is not allowed to be a process. Here is a common example. The wife feels that her lovemaking with her husband is very unfulfilling. He doesn't seem to understand that she needs him to take more time to stimulate her sexually before intercourse. She enjoys the loveplay and feels very romantic and special when he pays attention to her even before they get into bed. She doesn't know if he suffers from premature ejaculation, but he climaxes more quickly than either of them want, and she feels she is often left dangling. Not only is there never enough foreplay, but afterward she wants him to hold her and be close, not jump out of bed or go to sleep.

Women likewise need to be aware that husbands often prefer for their wives to be more involved in the arousal part of sex and to initiate seductive activity. The husband sometimes wishes that his wife did not have rigid expectations—a preset plan of making love, with a certain amount of foreplay, with him climaxing first and then bringing her to an orgasm. He also wants to intersperse intercourse throughout the lovemaking process. He may know he needs to slow down his ejaculation, but he isn't sure how. He admits to falling asleep after the lovemaking, but he often is so relaxed and doesn't seem to need the pleasure of the afterglow.

Lovemaking is a cycle of physical and emotional arousal that helps us understand the importance of letting it be an unfolding series of changes. Sex researchers Masters and Johnson developed this lovemaking cycle to help couples understand four separate phases of physical sexual buildup and changes. These four phases are (1) excitement, (2) plateau, (3) orgasm, and (4) resolution. Every wise lover should understand this basic knowledge in order to focus energy on any neglected phase. Every phase needs a balanced amount of attention.

The Four-Phase Cycle

A four-phase cycle sounds like part of a course in electrical engineering. Actually, it is the exciting way our bodies function in the lovemaking process. (See fig. 4.1.)

During the excitement phase, with physical and mental stimulation our bodies become aroused. We then enter the plateau phase with loveplay increasing the sexual tension and fewer physical changes happening. This is a fun time of playing and enjoying arousal. The orgasm phase occurs with muscle spasms in both male and female. Then the organs, following their increased blood supply and muscle contractions, return to their normal prearoused state during resolution. We will explore each phase. Figure 4.2 summarizes each phase.

1. The Excitement Phase

Male arousal is seen by the penis becoming erect. God has designed a marvelous hydraulic system in the penis with spongy tissue that engorges with blood to create the hardness. The autonomic nervous system triggers arousal as the veins and muscles contract to maintain the erection. The aging process may mean that erections are less

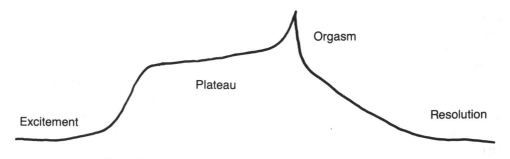

FIG. 4.1. The four phases of arousal and satisfaction.

48 *Setting the Scene*_____

Phases	Women	Men
Excitement	Nipples erect Breast enlargement Sex flush (75%) Clitoral tumescence Vaginal lubrication Outer lips flatten and enlarge Inner lips enlarge Heart rate and blood pressure increase	Nipples erect (60%) Sex flush (25%) Penis erect/tumescent Scrotum thickens and sac elevates Heart rate and blood pressure increase
Plateau	Orgasmic platform with ballooning Increased sex flush and cardiorespiratory Involuntary muscle contractions Increased blood flow in breasts and vulva; color changes	Seepage from penis; prostate and seminal vesicles contract Increased cardiorespiratory Involuntary muscle contractions Head of penis enlarges and color deepens; testes rise and rotate
Orgasm	Muscle contractions at 0.8 second in orgasmic platform, rectal sphincter, uterus Involuntary muscle spasm in pelvis and entire body Heart and breathing rate elevated	Muscle contractions at 0.8 second in prostate, seminal duct system, base of penis/rectal area Produce ejaculation Involuntary muscle spasm in pelvis and entire body Heart and breathing rate elevated
Resolution	Relief of vasocongestion and enlargement of breasts and genitals Muscles relax Skin flush disappears Heart rate, blood pressure, and breathing return to normal	Relief of vasocongestion and enlargement of penis, scrotum and testes Muscles relax Skin flush disappears Heart rate, blood pressure, and breathing return to normal

FIG. 4.2. Characteristics of the four phases of arousal and satisfaction.

firm and that it will take more direct stimulation of the penis to produce an erection. The size and angle of the erect penis can vary from man to man. As stated earlier, erections normally vary from around five inches to seven inches, and sexual excitement does not depend on a large penis or rock-hard erection.

Erections are interesting phenomena and are almost taken for granted until there are erectile difficulties. All men will struggle with getting or maintaining an erection at some point. Fatigue, alcohol, medication, and performance anxiety are common causes. The key is not to panic because that will just compound the problem. Don't worry about the temporary impotence and it will usually go away.

With continued stimulation and arousal, an erection can last from ten minutes to over an hour. Often during the excitement and plateau phases, the erection becomes partial/softer or completely subsides because the husband focuses on pleasuring his mate and has less direct penile stimulation. He also may get distracted and less focused and lose the erection. That is normal. As he enjoys the loveplay and erotic stimulation, the erection will return.

The husband's sexual excitement is a blend of physical friction in the erogenous zones and mental arousal through sensual stimulation. Men often enjoy looking at their wives' genitals and touching what is appealing to them. With husbands and wives, what has happened during the day may already have begun the excitement phase even before focused sexual activity. Husbands could enhance their wives' romantic mood by unloading the dishwasher, taking ten minutes to talk when they walk in the door, or helping with the children during supper preparation. During the excitement and plateau phases, men are more predictable than women; most appreciate direct and firm stimulation of the penis.

Female arousal in the excitement phase is demonstrated by vaginal lubrication, which is like beads of saliva that sweat through the outer walls of the vagina. This occurs within the first minute or two of arousal but can vary, especially with aging or distraction and an inability to focus on pleasure. The vaginal secretions have an odor much like saliva. Some foods (e.g. asparagus) will affect the odor of the secretions. The mind is a wonderful tool as it can pair the odors of making love (semen, vaginal secretions, perspiration) with sexual excitement and pleasure as they become exciting stimuli.

The nipples of the female become erect in the central papillae area during sexual excitement. There is also some enlargement of the breasts, which is visually exciting to the husband. The nipples are a fun part of sexual loveplay. Within the vagina, the outer third becomes more engorged with blood (tumescent) during the excitement phase. It is called the orgasmic platform and increases during the plateau phase. The outer third of the vagina is more sensitive anyway, and stimulating the orgasmic platform feels great for both partners. (See fig. 4.3.)

During arousal, the outer lips flatten and the inner lips of the vulva enlarge, creating a chute for the penis to travel down to the vagina. The clitoris enlarges to two or three times its relaxed size. This occurs under the skin at the clitoral hood and is not readily observable. It can be felt by rolling a finger over this area right above the clitoral hood, feeling much like a firm cord under the skin. Women vary immensely as

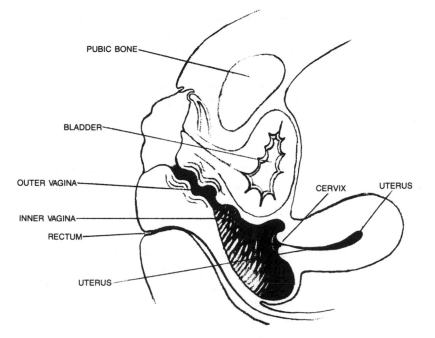

PUBIC BONE

BLADDER

OUTER VAGINA

INNER VAGINA

RECTUM

UTERUS

CERVIX UTERUS

Fig. 4.3. Orgasmic platform with ballooning.

to how they enjoy clitoral stimulation and can change over the various phases. It is crucial for every couple to build effective communication skills and learn about each other. The wife may need to demonstrate how she prefers the clitoris to be stimulated.

2. The Plateau Phase

This phase should be the longest and perhaps the most enjoyable one of the sexual cycle. The initial arousal is there, and the loveplay can build on this tension as it progresses from general stimulation to specific locations. The penis becomes fuller and the head a deeper color as it is further engorged. The orgasmic platform in the outer third of the vagina also becomes larger, giving firmer friction on the penis during intercourse. The inner two-thirds of the vagina expands, creating a receptacle for the semen, and the uterus elevates, giving greater comfort with thrusting because the cervix is pulled away.

In the male, preparation for ejaculation is taking place as the prostate and seminal vesicles contract. Some seepage from the penis occurs; it does contain sperm, so be cautious to have birth control in place. In an ejaculation there are 250 to 500 million sperm, and it takes only one to create a baby. The seminal fluid is building in the urethra and area around the prostate preparatory for orgasm.

Both males and females experience increased heart rates, the blood pressure rises, and the breathing intensifies. With some, there is a sex flush on the upper torso, neck, and face. Muscles involuntarily contract, and sexual excitement continues to build gradually during this plateau phase. The loveplay will increase in intensity with active intercourse and more vigorous direct stimulation of the erogenous zones. Mental and emotional arousal are focused with sensual touch, sight, taste, smell, and sound intensified.

The plateau phase is a sensual celebration and the focus of the majority of the loveplay. Research has found that a man, if actively thrusting, will often climax in less than two minutes while a woman may take longer to reach an orgasm. The wise couple intersperse intercourse throughout the plateau phase as the husband starts and stops and keeps his arousal on a plateau without peaking too soon. Both husband and wife can learn to approach an orgasm and then back off as they maintain the plateau phase for extended periods of pleasurable and sensuous lovemaking.

3. The Orgasm Phase

This phase focuses on producing an orgasm in one or both partners. The plateau phase has increased excitement, and now both partners are ready to climb that last peak with focused stimulation. In a great marriage, mates need to build an assertive, responsible selfishness. Orgasm is a great example of Christian selfishness. Great sex, like a good marriage, allows an individual to strategically focus on personal pleasure as well as the mate's.

In allowing the reflexive action of an orgasm to occur, you must focus on your body and the tension that is building. Allow your mind to give in to the increasing arousal and revel in the approaching climax. At orgasm, you become self-focused and trust your partner with grimaces and squeals and muscle contractions. You are oblivious to how you look as your mind is selfishly centered on your growing excitement.

A fascinating paradox occurs here! Your selfish inward journey to orgasm and intense personal excitement becomes a mutual experience and a marvelous turn-on for your mate—feeling and indeed being an integral part of the whole process. There is a lot of joyful connecting in the one-flesh process of making love—sharing an orgasm is something special.

Orgasms retain their long-term and repeated satisfaction, as well as their immediate capacity to strongly jolt your system, by remaining a part of a committed and intimate companionship and a part, not the whole, of the lovemaking cycle. Although the orgasm phase is the shortest in the sexual cycle, it can take over as the primary focus because of its intensity and feelings of release.

As a great lover, you remember to keep orgasm in perspective within your lovemaking as you relate, play, nurture, build and extend excitement, and create intimate companionship. Fortunately, God's design for satisfying sex keeps you honest. Whenever you become too preoccupied with achieving a bigger sexual buzz or casually using your mate, your sex life quickly has diminishing returns. The pleasure lags and the excitement wanes—you are forced back to the wisdom of basing orgasms on a nurturing relationship and the complete sexual cycle.

Physically, both male and female experience muscle contractions, eight-tenths of a second in duration, as the central part of the orgasmic response. For the female, the contractions center in the vaginal area in the orgasmic platform with the PC (pubococcygeal) muscle and the rectal sphincter (circular muscle at the opening of the rectum). The uterus also contracts, much as in labor pains. The female experiences a series of spasms, four to twelve in duration depending on the intensity of the orgasm. The male experiences spasms during his ejaculation, which also vary in intensity depending on level of arousal and abandonment to the experience. His contractions occur around the prostate gland and then along the seminal duct system and penis as the semen is propelled outward through the urethra.

Ejaculation occurs in two phases. In the first stage, the prostate gland has contractions, and the sphincter muscle to the bladder closes off so semen does not back up into the bladder. The left testicle (with most men, the left hangs lower) elevates and rotates, and semen gathers in the urethra at the base of the penis. In the second phase, which is unable to be interrupted, ejaculation inevitably takes place with muscle contractions. The semen that has collected in the upper urethra is propelled outward.

With orgasm also come involuntary contractions of the muscles of the arms, legs, pelvis, and back. Breathing, blood pressure, and heart rate will increase. Sometimes deliberately simulating these physiological aspects of an orgasm with tensing muscles and breathing heavily can trigger the climax.

Men experience orgasm with an intense genital focus. Their descriptions are more of explosions, fireworks of release, and intense feelings that build and then come with a rush. These feelings are often centered on the penis and, at the moment of release, include the muscle spasms in the genital area and ejaculation. Women, too, can have intense orgasms with exciting explosions of feelings in the clitoral and vaginal area. They often describe their release as waves of pleasure and a flooding of feelings. These intense feelings, which are more than the vaginal and uterine contractions, may begin in the genital area but seem to diffuse throughout the body—through the abdomen, breasts, legs, and head. For both sexes, the mind is a fantastic tool for focusing and increasing the intensity of the climax.

One wife in the course of therapy was surprised to hear her husband say that sometimes it felt like a volcano and at other times it was a mild, pleasurable pulsing of feelings. She thought that because males ejaculated, their orgasms were all strong and identical in nature. She found her husband similar to herself, with orgasms varying from lovemaking incident to incident.

There are interesting distinctions between male and female orgasmic capabilities. Males have a refractory period, or recuperative time, between orgasms. At age nineteen, this rest period may be a few minutes; with aging, it increases to a few hours or days. The second orgasm following close on the first may take more stimulation and may be less intense.

Females, on the other hand, do not have a refractory period. They are capable of having repeated orgasms, and rather than diminish—succeeding orgasms may be more intense. Females also have the capability for multiple orgasms. They may experience separate orgasms minutes apart, or during an intense lovemaking session with increasing arousal, they may experience them in rapid succession. This rapid succession may also be explained as a more intense orgasm, which can have ten to twelve spasms. Some women also experience a gushing of vaginal secretions and a greater wetness.

Before leaving the orgasm phase, we need to discuss two common concerns: clitoral versus vaginal orgasms, and the attempt to climax simultaneously. One wife was worried because she could never climax during lovemaking by penile thrusting alone. She had to have manual or oral stimulation of her clitoris. She is not unusual because the majority of women can't achieve an orgasm without direct stimulation of the clitoris. It would be like helping the husband have an orgasm by stroking his testicles but not his penis.

Originally, Freud stated that there were two types of orgasms: vaginal and clitoral, with the vaginal supposedly superior. Research has shown that the clitoris is the focal point of sexual stimulation in the female. Orgasms in both male and female are muscle contractions, no matter what type of stimulation created the arousal. More accurate sexual knowledge has done away with misunderstandings regarding vaginal and clitoral orgasms, but what lingers is the notion that a wife should be able to climax with thrusting alone.

Remember that an orgasm is a reflexive response; it is not an intentional act of the will. You cannot consciously will yourself to have an orgasm. Orgasms are a product of sufficient buildup of physical, mental, and emotional stimulation as the mind focuses on that increasing sexual tension. For most women, the stimulation needs to be in the clitoral area where there is a concentration of nerve endings.

Having orgasms simultaneously was, during part of the seventies, thought to be the epitome of making love and coordinating sexual rhythms. Fortunately, few couples now chase the need to climax simultaneously. Some women enjoy their orgasms with the penis in the vagina and experience greater intensity, while some prefer not to have the penis in the vagina as they focus on their own sensations. Some couples like orgasms close together, and others prefer allowing the woman to climax several times before the man. Create the patterns and rhythms that fit you as an individual and as a couple.

4. The Resolution Phase

After an orgasm, both men and women experience a release of tension as the body returns to its original state before sexual arousal. This is physically the final enjoyment of an orgasm as the muscles relax, blood vessels and tissue release the engorging blood, and the congestion abruptly eases. Sometimes with men and women, the genitals become very sensitive after an orgasm. As in all aspects of lovemaking, communication is vital as you talk to your partner about what you need during this resolution phase.

For the male, this process takes place quite quickly. The penis becomes flaccid (soft), and the testicles descend from their position of being tighter to the body during arousal.

For the female, the vagina, cervix, and uterus return to their prestimulated state. There is a feeling of tension release with an orgasm as the blood congestion leaves the

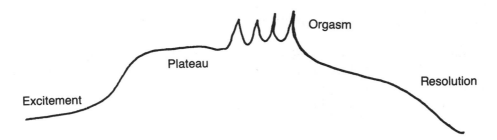

FIG. 4.4. The four phases of arousal and satisfaction in the multiorgasmic female.

genital, pelvic area with a pleasant, perhaps tingling, sensation. In the woman, unlike the man, there is the potential to return quite quickly to an aroused state and experience multiple orgasms. The wife may learn to experience several orgasms as she then returns to the plateau phase with her husband. It can be fulfilling for both of them. The sexual cycle could be portrayed as above if the wife had four orgasms. (See fig. 4.4.)

The husband and wife may need to make adjustments to accommodate each other in the various phases of the lovemaking cycle. The husband may save up things to tell his wife and share during the resolution phase. He may hold her for a few minutes and find she really appreciates the expression of his love at that time. It seems a more important time of affirmation for her than for him, but he loves her and wants to meet her needs. In the same way mates learn to prolong the plateau phase, they may enjoy the pleasures of an extended resolution phase. With intimate conversations, warm cuddling, smiles, and communicating with their eyes the enjoyment they feel, they affirm their love for each other and create wonderful companionship.

If we graph the sexual cycles of the husband and wife before they understand the phases of the lovemaking cycle (frustrated) and after (currently fulfilled), figure **4.5** shows how they would look.

They are able to begin more gradually and lengthen the excitement phase as they thoroughly arouse each other with ambiance, romance, sensuous massage, sexual talk, and a variety of techniques. The plateau is tantalizing, building right to orgasm, then backing off and prolonging the pleasure, or the wife going on to climax several times. Because of greater arousal and pleasuring, both have more intense and fulfilling

FIG. 4.5. The four phases of arousal and satisfaction: frustrated (left) and fulfilled.

orgasms. The afterglow keeps lengthening as they find the time very intimate and affirming.

Ecclesiastes 8:6 admonishes, "For there is a proper time and procedure for every matter" (NIV). Making love is a marvelous process—a cyclical series of exciting changes. Understand and enjoy each phase as you cycle through excitement, plateau, orgasm, and resolution while becoming an expert lover and an intimate companion.

Chapter Five

Minimizing the Muss

The word *muss* is defined as "anything messy and untidy." It certainly fits many aspects of sex. It is unfortunate, but many couples let the muss seriously dampen their lovemaking. Here is a sample of the complaints from marriage partners:

- "He never wants to make love during the menstrual cycle even if the flow is very light."
- "She always jumps up and runs to the bathroom to clean up right after we make love."
- "We were using some lubrication and he squeezed the tube too hard and I became one gooey mess."
- "Life can get in the way of a good sex life—at first it was my pregnancy, then his bladder infection, and now the demands of the children."
- "He wants to make love at the most inopportune times when I am dressed, have my hair done and my lipstick on, and am ready to leave the house."
- "He enjoys having sex on Saturdays after working in the yard when he is all sweaty and smelly—he also hasn't shaved and gives me beard burn."
- She: "We're in the mood and fooling around, then we have to mess with inserting birth control and lose our spontaneity." He: "I hate condoms. They don't feel natural and are such a nuisance."
- He: "She and I both enjoy oral sex. But sometimes it's awkward for me if she

didn't have time to bathe first." She: "I love it when he climaxes. But I can't seem to get used to how sticky semen feels."

- "Sex is so embarrassing with all its noises and funny faces and awkward positions. The personal intensity of sex with its passion and perspiration intimidates me."
- She: "I hate sex in the morning—I'm not a morning person, and then I seep semen all day." He: "She turns into a pumpkin at nine at night, and that is when I am just getting going."

Your environment does not always cooperate to encourage and support lovemaking. Time is difficult to come by, and children's many demands interfere. The physicalness of sex is not always stately and smooth. Birth control can be a nuisance, and bodies are more real than romantic at times. Minimizing the muss and controlling the environment are integral parts of making love. You can learn to relax and handle the muss in style, or you can let God's wonderful gift of sex be sabotaged. You may discover that what you thought was an untidy aspect of sex can actually be a fun part of mutual lovemaking.

The above complaints are organized into four separate categories that we will work through together. This is not an exciting or erotically arousing chapter, but it is very practical and important. Often the little things mess up a great sex life. Many couples permanently hamper their lovemaking by not minimizing its messiness. We will start off by looking at sex as getting physical with noises, secretions, and funny positions, as well as the physical facts of periods, pregnancy, and physical problems. The second section will consider how to deal with birth control and artificial lubrication. Then we will explore the importance of timing in a great sex life, minimizing the demands of children, being a day person, or having to get undressed. Finally, we will talk about hygiene and cleaning up before and after making love.

Getting Physical

One woman felt that sex was animalistic. She was a romantic who much preferred her dating days. At that time, she and her husband-to-be were usually at their best (clean, rested, and dressed up), on their way out on a date. She enjoyed kissing and flirting and being feminine without the physicalness of their present sexuality. She detested his demands and the coarse thrusting of intercourse, and all the secretions seemed so uncouth. She was disappointed that sex involved the reality of bodies and could not remain more romantic and civilized.

Though this reaction is more uncommon than not, all of us are sometimes put off by the reality of semen, vaginal secretions, the noises of the penis in the vagina or the vagina releasing trapped air, and the funny contortions of sexual ecstasy or intercourse. But these are all part of making love. They can actually create erotic arousal and playfulness or at least be minimized as they are dealt with matter-of-factly in a trusting, spirited relationship.

Physical Sexuality

A fundamental part of making love is that it is passionate, with physical arousal, active loveplay, and noise. If you are an emotional person who can go down a waterslide with your mouth wide open screaming, the passionate part of sex won't seem that messy. If you enjoy sports and perspiring and don't worry about making a face and grunting when you hit a tennis ball, you probably won't be put off by the sheer physicalness of making love on a summer afternoon.

But you may not like to sweat or get too involved in feelings. You may have to give yourself permission to be erotically physical as you allow this activity to grow into being more romantic. As adults, we often forget how to be truly excited and let go of control. Being wildly abandoned as you revel in your body and the body of your mate can seem very untidy and uncontrolled. To be a great lover, you will have to be open to becoming passionate and be adaptable to change as you learn to enjoy new and exciting experiences.

You will make funny noises and unsettling mistakes as you enjoy making love. At some point the husband may miscalculate his ejaculatory aim. Or his vocal excitement may render his wife nearly deaf if his mouth is too close to her head. Or the wife may dribble evidence of her husband's recently spent passion when she sits astride his body. If you don't have a sense of humor or can't forgive yourself and your mate, sex won't be very much fun. Being sensual, passionate, and playful is never neat. Bodies and their functions are never totally romantic, but they can create some marvelous sexual connecting.

It won't happen overnight, but active thrusting, sweat, semen, and vaginal secretions will become arousing stimulants of pleasure and sexual excitement as you associate them with your mate and fun times together. You and your mate can be open to each other's feelings. And you both can make an effort to anticipate when the other may consider seepage of the body's natural fluids to be unpleasant. The love you have for each other encourages you to control various activities so that enjoyment is equal. A box of tissues is a smart thing to keep around your bed to help you minimize the muss anyway. Making love will slowly cease to seem as messy or out of control as you take steps to minimize the interferences and slowly change some attitudes.

Menstrual Cycle

What is a good rule of thumb for lovemaking when the wife is in her menstrual cycle? Like other types of sexual interaction, it depends on the sensibilities of the individual and the couple. Please sort through this situation carefully. Many couples lose some opportune times for making love by completely avoiding intercourse or other loveplay during this time. Here are some commonsense ideas that you will need to discuss together as sexual lovers and partners:

1. There is nothing dirty about the menstrual flow, and there is nothing wrong with having sex during this time if a couple wishes. Both mates may have negative attitudes they need to talk through and resolve.

2. The vagina and genitals can be tender during the menstrual cycle, and during the heavy flow, many men and women prefer not to have intercourse. That does not negate making love—which you never want to associate solely with intercourse. There can still be mutual pleasuring through to orgasm and fun sex play. Because of aesthetics or tenderness, you may wish to avoid the days of heavy flow, however.

3. Though not foolproof, during and immediately after the cycle are safe times to have sex with a very low risk of pregnancy. Many couples enjoy sex during the lighter flow at the end of the period. They may put a towel under them during intercourse and keep tissues or a washcloth handy for cleanup afterward. Some couples find it enjoyable to have intercourse regardless of flow and take a quick shower after or even make love in the shower. It depends on your and your mate's sensitivities.

If you have not taken the time to talk through this aspect of minimizing the muss, do it now. You may assume you know what your mate thinks and feels, and you leave implicit (implied but never verbally expressed) too much of sex and mutual guidelines for making love. Implicit will get you in trouble and rob you of many permitted pleasures. Let the wife tell of her growing-up experiences and how she has felt about her period over her developmental years. Let the husband talk about the ideas about menstruation he had as a youth. How does each of you feel aesthetically, and what would you feel comfortable trying sexually, during the menstrual cycle? Talk it through and come to some mutual understandings.

Pregnancy

The exciting time of conceiving or expecting a child is a hurdle that many couples face, along with the demands of children, in keeping their sex life active and enjoyable. The issues of conceiving and infertility, with their impact on making love, will be covered in chapter 21. Couples have some real fears about having sex during pregnancy. Let me list some commonsense advice:

Sex During Pregnancy

- Consult your physician and follow her or his suggestions. Your body and pregnancy are unique and may need special guidelines (e.g., if you are prone to miscarriages).
- If there is any bleeding or change in condition, immediately seek medical help.
- Unless there is nausea or complications, most couples can enjoy making love throughout the nine months.
- Sexual intercourse is permissible right up to the last week unless your physician advises otherwise. Refrain from intercourse when labor begins or when your water breaks.

A couple's sex life during pregnancy will often reflect the frequency and level of enjoyment prior to pregnancy. If a couple have a low frequency of making love before pregnancy, they may stop completely during these months. Many women report a normal desire for sex or even an increased arousal with the hormonal fluctuations of pregnancy. During the first trimester, some women experience problems with morning sickness, which dampens desire. In the third trimester, especially near the birth of the baby, the mother-to-be will feel big and tired and awkward. These feelings will slow sexual ardor and activity.

Two concerns that can squelch lovemaking during pregnancy need to be actively addressed. The first is that the baby may be hurt. Consult your physician for reassurance. Both the mucous plug in the cervix and the amniotic sac protect the baby from semen or infections in the vagina. The baby is suspended in its own protective environment (amniotic sac and fluid), which is a shock absorber. It doesn't hurt to be active, but you as a couple can become more gentle as time goes on. Another way to overcome the factor of pregnancy in your love life is to employ more comfortable positions of intercourse. The rear entry as spoons, the crosswise position with legs scissored, the edge-of-the-bed position—all are effective during pregnancy (see chapter 12).

Time Out . . .

Stop a minute and talk about the physical aspects of sex with your mate. What part of physical sex is tough for you or causes some misgivings? Don't simply hint around. Be specific in your comments and communicate your feelings in love.

A second common concern in pregnancy is body image. A woman can feel very unsexy as she gains weight and her stomach distends. A man may actually find himself more excited by his wife's body and the fact she is carrying his child. Though his wife's breasts can be tender and sensitive, the changes in them are also exciting and arousing. As the pregnancy progresses, both of you may be eager for the wife's body to return to normalcy. This is a great opportunity the Lord has given you to allow making love and sexiness to extend beyond body shape and size. As you age, you also have to practice this skill more.

If you struggle with body image anyway, you may want to go to chapter 17 and experience some healing. Everyone has flaws, and if you make them the focus, you will destroy your ability to truly enjoy and be aroused by your mate.

Wife, let your pregnant body symbolize femininity in a beautiful, sexy manner. Do some self-talk. Husband, affirm her in ways you haven't in the past. She needs it now.

A final word about sex and pregnancy: Some couples have difficulty getting their sex life started again after the baby comes. This is especially so if the pregnancy was difficult or surgery was necessary. You may wish to incorporate some of the techniques for making love discussed in chapter 19 and get beyond the awkwardness. If it has been more than two months since you have made love, make a choice to do so this weekend or seek counseling.

Birth Control and Lubrication

The Genesis passage on being fruitful and multiplying is in the context of God's giving humankind control of the natural world. We are to be wise stewards of the children God places in our care. To choose to have one or two or five has to be a thoughtful and prayerful decision.

Here are nine common methods of birth control. You as a couple will have to sort through which one best fits you as you consider personal sensitivities, health, and who takes responsibility. Withdrawal of the penis before ejaculation is not included as a method of birth control because of its ineffectiveness. There are 250 to 500 million sperm in one ejaculation, and it takes only one to cause fertilization. Sperm are present in the seepage before ejaculation as well, and it is difficult to time the withdrawal exactly. Recognize that *some of the failures of birth control are due to improper usage.* Putting on a condom after thrusting has begun is like practicing the withdrawal method with sperm already present in the vagina.

Types of Birth Control

1. Rhythm Method

This method is based on the fact that pregnancy occurs during ovulation when the sperm meets the egg. If you are trying to keep from getting pregnant, you will not want to have intercourse during the time of ovulation. Sperm live approximately two days and the female egg one day unless fertilized. That means there is a three-day period (two days before and the day after) around ovulation during which a pregnancy could result. Some research gives the rhythm method a 30 percent failure rate, which attests to the difficulty of predicting ovulation.

Three methods are used to predict ovulation and gauge a "safe" period of time for intercourse. Each of these methods requires charting to determine length of menstrual cycle and to establish a pattern. The first uses the calendar and considers that ovulation occurs around fourteen days before the onset of the menstrual flow. To provide an adequate cushion of time, it discourages intercourse four days on each side. If the cycle is twenty-eight days, ovulation would occur around the fourteenth day, and days ten through eighteen would be considered unsafe. A thirty-five-day cycle would be days seventeen through twenty-five.

The second way of determining ovulation is through the woman's charting her temperature upon awakening. In most women at the time of ovulation, there is a rise of one-half to seven-tenths of a degree in temperature. This elevation continues about three days and is the fertile time. The temperature is taken with a basal body thermometer which measures smaller increments than an ordinary thermometer. Intercourse should be avoided during this period of elevation and two days before it. The ovulation is then charted over months to determine the optimal time for intercourse. A physician may need to help interpret your temperature chart and the safest time for you. You may need to chart for several months to a year to better predict ovulation.

The third method involves observing the cervical mucous and learning the natural changes in its consistency around ovulation. The mucous, which can be felt by inserting a finger into the vagina to the cervical area, changes from more tacky to more fluid at ovulation. At ovulation the fluid will stretch between the fingers like an egg white. Many women can feel the change in the vagina without actually checking. This method can help predict the times that are unsafe for intercourse. The difficulty in predicting ovulation is that the monthly cycles can vary as much as ten days, and both ovaries can ovulate rather than alternate each month.

The rhythm method poses no health risk and does not include apparatus to dampen spontaneity. It does put a damper on intercourse during a significant part of the month, and it is not very effective unless the monthly cycle is very consistent.

2. Contraceptive Pill

Birth control pills contain the synthetic hormone estrogen or progestin or a combination of the two. The pills alter the body's hormone balance and (a) prevent the ovaries from ovulating, (b) change the consistency of the cervical mucous, and (c) change the consistency of the fallopian tubes and the uterus. A physician's care is needed to monitor their use because there can be side effects of hormonal imbalance (mood swings, headaches, irregular bleeding) if improperly regulated. It is also important to schedule regular gynecological exams with breast exams and Pap smears. Depending on the type of pill, it is taken for twenty-one to twenty-eight days, and the menstrual period starts after this cycle of pills is finished.

There are now lower dosage pills of the estrogen and progestin combination, as well as a minipill that just uses progestin. These pills minimize the health risks and side effects but do not completely inhibit ovulation. Some women will therefore

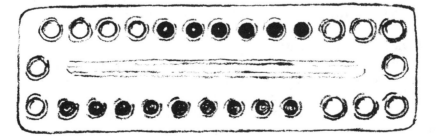

FIG. 5.1. Birth control pills.

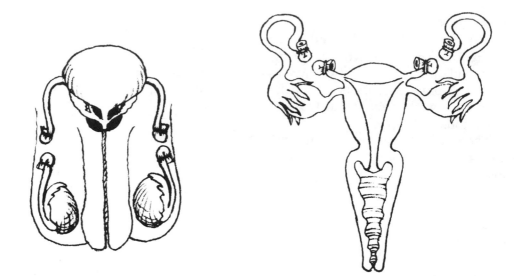

Fɪɢ. 5.2. Vasectomy (left) and tubal ligation.

experience an irregular menstrual cycle with their use. They are effective and work by changing the consistency of cervical mucous and the lining of the uterus and fallopian tubes. A doctor can help you decide when a type of pill is contraindicated because of health issues (heart problems, obesity, smoking, etc.). The pill is sometimes prescribed not for birth control but for regulation of the menstrual cycle and helps with cramping and an unusually heavy flow.

An advantage of the pill is that it does not interfere with spontaneity. A couple can make love as the mood strikes. It does not involve an artificial device, like a condom or a diaphragm, which can sometimes interfere with sensations and spontaneity. The pill, if properly used, has a high success rate of preventing pregnancy, although nothing is foolproof.

3. Vasectomy or Tubal Ligation

A vasectomy is a fairly simple office procedure in which the physician makes a small incision in the scrotal sac and a portion of each vas deferens is cut off and the ends are tied. The ends are then replaced in the scrotum. Sperm are prevented from swimming from the testicles to the seminal fluid, which is primarily created by the prostate. A vasectomy does not alter ejaculation or the presence of semen and does not interfere with hormones and sexual desire.

The procedure is nearly 100 percent effective—but only if done properly. Occasionally, a tube will come untied and heal back, but that is very rare. Vasectomy should be considered irreversible and be done only as a permanent form of birth control. Surgical procedures may reverse a vasectomy, but they are not always effective. After a vasectomy, at least two sperm counts in the following months are taken to be certain that all sperm is out of the system and intercourse is safe without risk of pregnancy.

A tubal ligation is a hospital procedure and more complex than a vasectomy. Like a vasectomy, this method should be seen as irreversible and done only when no more children are desired. In this procedure, the female tubes are tied or cut and sutured to prevent the egg from meeting with the sperm. This is accomplished through a small incision in the abdomen.

The advantage of a vasectomy or tubal ligation is its permanence. It is perhaps as foolproof as any method in preventing pregnancy. There are occasional complications from the surgery, but they are rare.

4. Condoms

Condom use and a vasectomy are the two methods of birth control that the husband can take responsibility for. Condoms are made of thin latex or a natural membrane and come in various textures, colors, shapes, and sizes. As you read the advertising on the boxes, you may be led to think they are marvelous aphrodisiacs, with the extra ribbing or exotic colors. Actually, you may want to sample several for size and sensitivity, but there is not that much difference. Most women don't feel or appreciate the extra bumps in the latex that supposedly stimulate the vagina. Condoms are placed over the erect penis and can be used for only one act of intercourse. They come with or without lubrication or spermicide already on them. Here are some important instructions:

- Blow condoms erect (like a balloon) as you check for any holes that could destroy their effectiveness.
- Put the condom on before approaching the vagina, and be careful not to get seepage on the outside of the condom.
- Use a new condom for every ejaculation or act of intercourse—this prevents seepage or breakage with sperm in the condom.
- Withdraw the penis before the erection is fully lost, and above all, hold the condom as you withdraw the penis to prevent its slipping off.

Fig. 5.3. Condoms.

An advantage of condoms is that they are easily available and effective if properly used, perhaps in conjunction with a spermicidal jelly. A disadvantage is that some men and women dislike the reduced sensation in the penis or the vagina. A disadvantage of the natural membrane condom is its inability to protect from HIV. They can be a nuisance and on occasion cause an allergic reaction—as can any spermicide. Condoms and other methods of birth control like a diaphragm can be incorporated into your lovemaking. The wife can help create a romantic mood by unrolling the condom on her husband's penis as part of the loveplay.

5. Female Condom

Female condoms are not a new concept but have recently been brought back on the market. Like the male condom, they are made of a thin, strong latex and are a sheath. The female variety has a flexible ring at each end and is inserted into the vagina before intercourse. The rings keep it in place and it creates a protective lining in the vagina that contains the penis and sperm.

The instructions for the male condom apply also to the female condom: Insert it before any intercourse and remove from vagina with care to prevent tearing the latex or spilling any semen. Like the male condom, the female condom can limit sensitivity, but used properly it can be an effective barrier method.

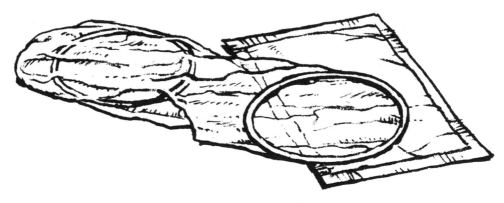

Fig. 5.4. Female condom.

6. Diaphragm and Cervical Cap

A diaphragm and a cervical cap are round rubber devices with a covered metal rim. Each is inserted into the vagina with spermicidal jelly, foam, or suppository as a barrier against the sperm swimming into the cervix and uterus. The diaphragm is inserted behind the pubic bone and holds the spermicide over the cervix. The cervical cap is a smaller version of the diaphragm and covers only the cervix. The cervical cap can be left in place longer, but neither should be left in the vagina for days. When removed, each is washed with warm water and stored to prevent tears.

A diaphragm or a cap needs to be fitted and prescribed by a gynecologist. Neither is

Fig. 5.5. Diaphragm (left) and cervical cap.

available over the counter. After pregnancy or weight gain, the device needs to be refitted. The vagina can change its shape and size.

It is recommended that the spermicide not be in the vagina for more than three to six hours without renewal. This time lag gives some flexibility in inserting the diaphragm or cap before lovemaking to prevent interruption and encourage spontaneity. The diaphragm or cap should be left in the vagina for six to eight hours after intercourse and ejaculation.

7. Spermicidal Sponge

Available over the counter, the spermicidal sponge is dampened with water before inserting it into the vagina. This action releases the spermicidal foam. The sponge acts as a barrier, and it has spermicide to counteract impregnation. Like the diaphragm and cap, it should be left in the vagina after intercourse for six hours. Instructions come with the product. Don't read quickly or ignore the instructions with any form of birth control. Too much is at stake.

The sponge's advantages are that it is easy to use and can be inserted prior to making love. Like any barrier method, it is still intrusive and has to be prepared for ahead of time. Toxic shock syndrome is a possibility in rare cases.

Fig. 5.6. Spermicidal sponge.

8. Intrauterine Devices

Some IUDs have caused infections in the uterus and must be used with caution. For some women, they are still effective when used under a physician's care. The intrauterine device is a small coil or loop inserted into the uterus with a short plastic string attached. This string can be felt in the vagina projecting from the uterus through the cervix. Once inserted, it can be left in place for a year or more. It works

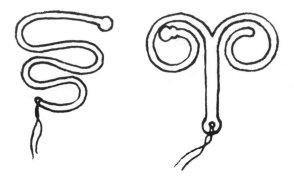

Fig. 5.7. IUD.

by causing the uterus to reject the fertilized egg. For some couples, this might violate personal ethics.

The IUD is long-term and effective and does not have the mess of the barrier methods. Once removed, it does not delay a woman's ability to become pregnant. It does not affect hormones and fertility. Again, because of the possibility of infections and negative side effects, these devices are used with caution under the care of a physician.

9. Spermicidal Foam, Jelly, and Suppository

These chemicals are inserted into the vagina and kill the sperm. Some women have to experiment to find ones that don't cause an allergic reaction. The spermicides can be used alone as a method of birth control, but this is not recommended. They are much more effective if used with a condom or a diaphragm. The suppositories are recommended for only an hour of protection, though the spermicidal action continues after this time span, and they should be inserted at least ten minutes in advance.

Foams and jellies come with a syringe that allows them to be inserted deeper into the vagina. The jelly is often placed in the diaphragm or cervical cap before insertion. Within the vagina foams and jellies have a certain lifespan of effectiveness. They

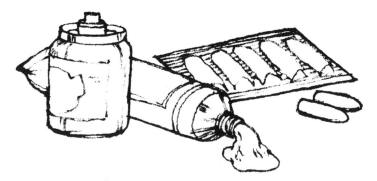

Fig. 5.8. Spermicidal foam, jelly, and suppository.

should be replaced after six hours at the most. Consult the instructions for correct usage. *Many failures of any method of birth control are due to the improper and careless application of that method.* This is not something you can afford to get sloppy or take chances with. Pray that God will help you keep wise, careful, and disciplined in this area of your life.

Types of Lubrication

In response to thrusting and other stimulation, our bodies produce lubrication to prepare for intercourse. The fact of the matter is that this will not always be adequate. With hormonal changes there may be less vaginal secretion. You may wish to stimulate sensitive tissues as a part of arousal or during prolonged lovemaking. Every couple should have some artificial lubrication handy to use as needed as an aid to great lovemaking.

Many drugstores sell a variety of artificial lubricants in the same section as the condoms and spermicides. Vaseline is an old standby, but because it is not water soluble, it can be more difficult for the vagina to be self-cleansing and for cleanup in general. Physicians prefer a water-soluble product, but petroleum jelly is safe to use when other products aren't available. It still may be your lubrication of choice because of its density and consistency. K-Y Jelly is another standby that works well. Other similar jelly lubricants are on the market now. Some couples complain that K-Y dries out, and they prefer a different type like Astroglide. It is more liquid and comes in a small plastic dispenser. Actually, both K-Y and Astroglide contain glycerin as part of the base.

Many couples find natural oils from coconut to olive oil appealing for smell and consistency. They are edible and don't interfere with oral stimulation of the genitals. Vegetable oils (corn or safflower) work fine if you have forgotten to get something you like better. Another type of lubrication that some women appreciate is a vaginal suppository. It is not a spermicidal suppository but a lubricant that slowly dissolves. One of these vaginal suppositories, called Lubrin, assists and mixes with the vaginal secretions. It can be inserted fifteen to thirty minutes before intercourse to allow it to dissolve. Take some time to experiment and find out what works best for you.

Minimizing Birth Control and Lubrication

A theme of this chapter is minimizing the messy or needed but nuisance parts of sex. However, even better than minimizing the muss is taking these untidy aspects of sex and incorporating them in such a way that they enhance your lovemaking. You as lovers can make birth control and lubrication easier and more erotic.

Keep supplies readily available and easy to put into action. Getting up from bed and going to get them, not having them handy, or forgetting to purchase them puts a damper on spontaneity.

Incorporate them into your loveplay and erotic arousal. Putting on the condom or inserting the diaphragm can be very stimulating. Lubrication can be slowly and sensuously applied.

Both of you take responsibility for birth control and lubrication. Don't make it the sole job of either mate. Share in the purchase and use of whatever method you choose.

Stay creative and keep a fun variety. Try different kinds of lubrication. Sometimes don't include intercourse so you don't have to deal with birth control if you are using a barrier method. Keep as spontaneous, playful, and sensual as you can.

Personal and Environmental Timing

As much as a couple might like it, spontaneous and exciting sex doesn't happen that often. Let's take a couple with two children. The husband works out of the home and has to do some traveling, and the wife works part-time at a dentist's office. She doesn't start functioning until three cups of coffee and a time to slowly wake herself in the mornings. Her family has learned through painful experiences not to talk to her until she is fully awake. The husband turns into a pumpkin at ten o'clock every night. Every once in a while he surprises his wife on a Saturday night and makes it to midnight. The two boys are very active and demand their share of attention.

It does not take a marriage and sex therapist to see some problems plaguing this couple's sex life. You also have to throw into this equation that the wife is a perfectionist who needs structure and routines in her life. The husband flies by the seat of his pants, is always late, and has a penchant for procrastinating. She is not known for her flexibility nor he for his sensitivity. With some work, they actually ended up with a very active and fulfilling sex life as they learned to minimize environmental distractions.

Children

The effort to control the children's sabotaging effect on their lovemaking involved five practical steps: (1) enforcing bedtimes, (2) getting the boys to respect a locked door and the privacy of the parents' bedroom, (3) risking interruption, which was tough on the wife, (4) taking regular mini-vacations alone as the parents employed their baby-sitting system and getting separate rooms while on vacation with the boys, and (5) training the boys to get their own breakfast on Saturday morning. These steps work better now that the boys are four and six years old, but even at age three children can begin to respect a locked door.

Enforcing bedtimes was tough until the parents told the boys that every time they interrupted the parents after 8:30, they would have to be in their rooms that much earlier the next night. One boy asked for a drink of water at 9:30 on a Thursday night and was in his room at 7:30 that Friday night. It did not take long for them to get the idea that Mom and Dad would deduct from their stay-up time for every minute they stole from their parents' private time after 8:30 P.M. They did not have to go to sleep, but they had to be in their rooms and not bother the folks.

Locking the bedroom door and refusing the children entry until the couple was ready were not too hard. One morning when the husband got up, he found the younger son asleep outside their door, but that soon stopped, too. Even with the locked door, the wife struggled with focusing and letting go without worrying about interruptions. It slowly became easier after they had trained the boys better and she trusted the locked door. Oftentimes she was able to get back into the lovemaking even after an interruption. Sometimes the mood was completely broken, and they simply got up and agreed to resume later. Saturday mornings became special because she could sleep in, and then they luxuriously made love while the boys ate and watched television.

The overnight getaways became their favorite. Their lovemaking needed the extra boost of being out of town and completely away from responsibility and interruptions in order to keep thriving. They reconnected emotionally and physically on short one- or two-day junkets. Both planned some special surprises and appreciated being away from the boys and the demands of home on the mini-honeymoons.

Personality Differences

The husband had a good friend to whom he could talk about anything. He had great discussions with his friend, who had the same personality differences in his sex life. The friend was a morning person, too. They both loved vacations for the same reason. The friend said he had made an agreement with his wife that once a month she would surprise him with a quickie in the morning before work. He in turn agreed that they would, at least once a month, have a long, leisurely late night session after a romantic date.

The friend was fussy and could get in sexual routines without much spontaneity and variety. He and his wife tried once a week to make love using variety as their theme. They would try different places, techniques, lengths of time, and loveplay. This challenged him and thrilled his wife, who grew weary of his need for controlled routine. With the first couple, it was interesting that though the wife was more controlled and structured, she could actually be more playful and adventurous in expressing feelings than her husband. He was the one who had to allow himself to truly enjoy the roller-coaster ride of feelings.

It helped the husband to talk to his friend. He got rid of some of his self-pity and helplessness. He decided to become more proactive in minimizing personality differences with his wife. They were just a part of the sex life of any normal couple. He could become more passionate, and she could become more flexible. They could continue to seek compromises on issues, like being a night person versus a day person. He also fretted over basic gender differences and his need for more visual variety and her desire for erotic romanticism with extended loveplay. With creativity, they often came up with solutions that met the needs of both partners.

Timing

Any way she sliced it, however, the wife did not appreciate her husband's timing, and there were occasions she saw it as a big nuisance to take all of her clothes off. Having sex without messing up her makeup and hair was very difficult. It wasn't that she minded getting sweaty and making love actively. But the mornings before work just weren't very convenient, and on weekends the boys interfered or the family was supposed to participate in some activity. As much as she enjoyed sex, she was surprised she thought that it was an inconvenience and that it was tough to increase the frequency.

The more you make love, the more you will make love. Greater frequency has a way of overcoming inertia and picking up steam. As sex starts to be an expected activity, making love becomes more enjoyable and easier to make time for. Busy couples don't have a choice but to structure times that they make sacred and reserve for lovemaking. This couple found a real solution with their Saturday mornings, and they tried to seek out one weeknight that would work. They ended up having to plan a different night each week, but they decided which one on Sunday evening when they knew their schedule for the week.

The husband found he could help his wife minimize the muss with more sensitive initiating, and he felt she became more adaptable. They sometimes made love without taking all their clothes off, or she would pleasure him to an orgasm and then take off on her errands. He learned to catch her earlier before she had taken her bath or was completely dressed. He helped her with chores and got her to come to bed earlier so they could make love before he conked out. It was a constant effort to work on timing and prioritizing sex in their busy schedules. Vacations really helped, and they did better in making quality time to connect and play sexually during the week.

Hygiene and Cleanup

The husband, in his hang-loose attitude toward life, did not always pay attention to whether he was shaved and showered. He slowly discovered that a freshly shaved face with cologne and a body smelling of soap made his wife feel romantic and special. He had to admit he associated many erotic memories with the smell of lilacs. Her favorite bubble bath was lilac scented, and she was much more open to sex after a leisurely soak. He never thought of her genital area as dirty in any way, but he appreciated its soft lilac fragrance after her bath.

Fortunately, they learned to talk and share openly with each other and express their needs around hygiene and personal sensitivities. She actually found active sex very stimulating, and perspiring with her man was exciting. She explained that in her mind, freshly brushed teeth and a quick shower showed respect and forethought to their lovemaking process. She also agreed that a spontaneous romp once in a while was fun.

The husband remembers the vacation they ended up alone together during the wife's period. The circumstances forced them to discuss their relational guidelines on when to make love during her monthly cycle. It turned out that neither minded as much as each thought the other did. They had just never talked it out before. Both agreed on the importance of cleanup, and she removed her tampon right before intercourse. With a little lubrication and a quick shower immediately after, it was a close and mutually enjoyable experience.

The wife was on the pill and appreciated the freedom it gave her in making love. That was one time, though, she envied her friend who used a diaphragm and inserted it right before making love during her period. She thought about getting fitted for one just to make sex easier during that time of the month.

When they were first married, the wife had thought she would need to douche after sex or during her period to keep odors at a minimum. Her gynecologist told her that would not be good for her vagina. It could upset the bacterial balance and make her prone to yeast infections. And it is actually unnecessary because the vagina is self-cleansing and some odors are just a part of sex and periods.

The biggest fight the couple had was over his irritating habit of jumping up immediately after ejaculation to run to the bathroom and wipe himself off. After he climaxed, she wanted him to lie there with her and feel close. Even after his erection went down, she did not want the afterglow interrupted. He said that he not only worried about dripping on the sheets but also assumed she felt very uncomfortable. Usually, that would be true of the wife, but in reality very little semen leaked out. Basking in her warm, close connectedness overrode her need for tidiness, and she wanted her husband to lie still and hold her.

The compromise was really quite simple, and they felt a little silly later when thinking what a major issue it had become. They kept some tissues beside the bed. He could wipe off, and she could quickly place a couple between her legs without ruining the mood. She also bought some panty shields. After a quickie in the morning, she wore them as protection against any seepage during the day.

Often couples learn that minimizing the muss has many creative compromises and solutions. Keeping tissues or a washcloth by the bed, planning ahead on birth control and lubrication, and relaxing with the normalness of the human body and its functioning greatly help.

Consider these key qualities you need in dealing with the messiness of a great sex life:

- *Sense of humor.* Laughing together and not taking yourself so seriously are invaluable. Sex will be funny and full of mishaps and playfulness.
- *Flexibility.* Keep out of routines and let go of a strong need to always be in control. You will enjoy yourself more in making love if you can go with the flow and are able to adapt.
- *Forgiveness.* Let each other make mistakes, and let go of resentment and hurt. Allow each other to change as both work through tough areas, and cut each other some slack as both focus on positive solutions.
- *Effective communication.* A couple must be able to assertively express needs and feelings and truly hear each other. No topic is off bounds, and with dialogue and compromise, solutions can be reached.
- *Love and trust.* If you like each other and believe your mate wants you to be happy and sexually fulfilled, it is easier to discuss and negotiate. An intimate relationship is vital in responsibly using birth control, creatively experimenting, and flexibly communicating.
- *Being uninhibited.* Let yourself go as you enjoy your mate and God's gift of sex. Being uninhibited and sensual has a way of overcoming and transforming the muss of sex into an aphrodisiac.

You and your partner can ensure that the untidiness of sex never gets in the way of a thriving love life.

Section Two

Enhancing Pleasure

Chapter Six

Natural Aphrodisiacs and Creating a Mood

The question is often asked and has been pursued down through the centuries: Are there sexual aphrodisiacs? No chemical has been found and documented that truly increases sexual desire. Ginseng root, vitamin E, special herbs or teas—nothing has been proven to work, though some couples would say differently. If it seems to help, you may not want to discontinue it. Some chemicals that can be harmful to physical or relational health should be avoided. However, one chemical—Spanish fly—actually irritates the urethral tract and can cause physical damage. Drugs like alcohol or marijuana may relax you or lower inhibitions, but they do nothing for sexual performance. If taken in excess, they dampen sexual arousal and the ability to enjoy making love.

Our gracious Creator has provided us as couples many natural and revitalizing aphrodisiacs that we constantly neglect—to the detriment of our lovemaking. These aphrodisiacs help set the mood for a more fulfilling sex life. The first section of this chapter identifies these natural aphrodisiacs. The second section discusses setting sexual goals for your relationship. An overcommitted couple won't have much quantity or quality in lovemaking unless goals are set and a bonding sex life is given a priority. The third section explores further ideas for creating an ambiance for making love—focusing on the bedroom environment.

Natural Aphrodisiacs

God has freely given you many natural ways to enhance your lovemaking. Discover them with your mate.

Time

Take more time to enjoy each other sexually. Taking more time increases loveplay and, in a fun way, forces you into being more creative. One of the building blocks of a great sex life is taking sufficient time to enjoy each other, and both enjoy the extra attention and playfulness.

Taking time is a marvelous aphrodisiac because it allows a couple to create an ambiance and be more imaginatively sensual. If ten minutes of mood setting and loveplay enhance sensuality, forty minutes may do four times as much. Time gives you the luxury of thinking about and enjoying sexuality in old and new ways. You don't have to feel sad for neglecting things you want to do in your sex life. Take the time and initiative and make up for it now.

Frequency and Inertia

On vacation couples expect to make love. They often make a mental note of things they have been avoiding in enhancing their sex life and want to be sure and include while on vacation. They take props, like sexy outfits and books like this. The mind and attitude are more sexually specific and expectant than at home.

So many things in life have a way of snowballing. The more you do them, the easier they become and the more you want to do them—like a snowball rolling downhill

Time Out . . .

You don't have to wait for vacation to enhance your sex life. Make love every day for five days in a row! Start on Thursday and have sexual activity every day through to the following Monday. The weekend times should be easier than weekdays. Sex will become an expected part of each day's activity rather than a neglected part.

and picking up snow as it goes. It is like the law of inertia that states that a body in motion tends to stay in motion and a body at rest tends to stay at rest. If sex has become awkward or if it has been placed on the back burner, mates will consciously have to get the lovemaking started again.

Spouses who structure into their schedules the time for frequent sexual activity seem to enjoy it more and want to make love more often. The more they enjoy it, the more frequently they make love, and the cycle goes on.

Physically Fit, Rested, and Focused

Good health and physical fitness are marvelous aphrodisiacs. Being rested vitalizes attitudes and gives added capacity for sex. Getting the body in shape with long walks or other forms of exercise enhances sex. Making vigorous love affirms your sense of physical well-being.

Rest and a lack of distractions have a marvelous effect on the mind. Tuning out the world and focusing only on each other and the relationship may be tough in the busyness of life. Maybe somehow you can create your own insulated island where you can retreat for passionate lovemaking. You may need to deal with your environment better so it can encourage being rested and focused.

Adventure and Variety

God has created us with a desire for variety and adventure. Uninhibited and varied sex is arousing. The wife's wearing see-through lingerie may sexually excite both partners. You may want to try some new positions. Or the wife may allow the husband to orally bring her to an orgasm for the first time.

Make sure you stay within God's economy in enjoying variety. Keep adventures within the love and respect each has for the other's feelings, and don't pressure each other. Let your creative minds and loving companionship produce the ultimate electricity and adventure. Determine to be more experimental, curious, and adventuresome in lovemaking.

Intimate Companionship

A fun companionship stimulates a great sex life. If you feel *in* love, you will be more likely to *make* love. Here are some ways to maintain sexual closeness:

Plan more regular vacations. Be creative. A vacation doesn't have to be a week in the Bahamas. But busy couples should plan at least two one-week vacations and six other overnights or long weekends in a year. It isn't an option if you are a busy couple wanting to revitalize your companionship and lovemaking.

Create a safe harbor. Create a safe, romantic place (e.g., your bedroom) where you tune out the world when you make love. Practice the skill of centering your minds on each other and the pleasure of the moment. Strategically choose times for lovemaking when you are as rested as possible.

Set goals and prioritize. Commit to certain days to make love. Negotiate and structure in time for sex. Make it a priority that you won't bump from your schedule.

Plan date nights for romantic companionship. Make a date night at least twice a month, and go out to enjoy each other. Find a window of time to talk each night, and concentrate more on simple nurturing gestures like kissing each other when one or both get home from work. Keeping in better touch with each other really helps both partners feel like making love more often.

Plan surprises for variety. Try new sexual techniques. Make sure you've taken privacy precautions and then make love in every room of the house, in the shower, or in both cars. Plan surprises for each other from a romantic video to some fabulous-smelling body lotion. Be playful with each other.

Sexual Goal Setting

A Rose Parade float is an excellent analogy for a couple's sex life. The beauty, creativity, delightful movements, and sensuous appeal are awe-inspiring. All of this is made possible because of the inner framework, motors, and a driver. The beautiful flowers and fun motions of the float that are visible to the eye are anchored to and driven by an inner structure of steel, wood, and ingeniously programmed motors, all consciously guided by a human driver.

Does your float lack beauty, creativity, motion, and sensuality because its inner structure is defective? Begin working from the inside out. Consciously decide together that sex is going to be a priority.

Every busy couple needs a structured framework on which to create a beautiful love life. There are two separate tasks that comprise this framework: negotiating realistic goals, and prioritizing them.

Remember that sex is *not* the most important part of your marriage. You may need to take these goal-setting and prioritizing ideas and apply them to many other areas of your partnership in addition to your lovemaking. Do you pray together, have regular companionship time, enjoy family devotions, and budget your money? These are vital areas to set effective goals and may need to be implemented before your sex life can flourish.

Setting Effective Sexual Goals

Beginning goals may be to choose when during the week and when during the weekend you are going to make love, and set that time aside as sacred to each of you. As busy as your schedules are, if you don't structure in making love, you will have sex about once a month. And you do not have to destroy your spontaneity. Goal setting is simply the inner structure and doesn't have to dampen excitement and creativity.

Sexual goals involve more than frequency. They should also deal with the quality of your lovemaking and the quality of your intimate companionship. Goals may include reading at least a chapter a month in a book on sex, each mate initiating one new technique or idea as a contribution to creativity and variety, scheduling regular vacation time. Goals need to be:

1. Specific. "We will make love more often" is not an effective goal. It must be more specific and include behavioral steps so you can tell if you have accomplished it. "We will have the kids in bed by 9:00 P.M. on Tuesday and make love immediately before doing any chores" is specific and measurable. Having a quickie once in a while is not specific enough for the busy couple. You can allow for spontaneity and yet still be more specific: "Wednesday and Friday mornings I don't have to go to work as early. I would enjoy making love a couple times a month on these days. If it's okay with you, since I am a morning person, I will initiate and get the birth control ready."

2. Realistic and attainable. Goals should take small steps as mates start to make changes so they won't be overwhelming. Goals that are not reasonable and do not consider time, energy, and money demands will quickly be sabotaged. "We will make love four times a week" or "Let's redecorate the bedroom" may be too optimistic.

3. Scheduled. If you don't give your goals specific time guidelines, you may not accomplish them. Scheduling includes not only when you will do something but also when you will begin doing it and how long you will try to keep doing it. "Let's try to be more creative in our lovemaking" is neither specific enough nor is it scheduled. This goal will probably never be accomplished, or it may be done sporadically. Effective scheduling would redefine this goal: "Each of us will read about and incorporate one new idea into our lovemaking each month, starting in September."

Goal setting takes negotiating and much thoughtful introspection and prayer. Each of you may want to think through individually what is important sexually and then discuss it. You may need to do this on a weekend away with time for discussion and companionable mutuality. You are wisely committing to nurturing your marital companionship.

Time Out . . .

Negotiate together how many times a week you would like to make love. Be specific and realistic. Schedule definite days and hours. This internal structure will help you be spontaneous, creative, and playful. How might you both sabotage this scheduled time and not keep it sacred?

---

4. Prioritized. It is not enough to have goals that are specific, realistic, and scheduled. You as a couple will have to consciously choose to make them a priority and follow through on them. Here are some ways to make your sexual goals a priority that will help you accomplish them over the long haul:

- Choose a limited number of goals and make them baby steps. (Example: "We will have sexual closeness twice a week on Tuesday and Sunday.")
- Mutually explore and acknowledge the vital importance of your selected goals and covenant together to follow through on them. (Example: "We will pray and ask God to help us see how vital these goals are to our companionship as we choose to follow through.")
- Create individual and marital attitudes that will support your goals. (Example: "I will hug my mate three times every day.")
- Establish a life-style conducive to accomplishing the goals. (Example: "We will create a great baby-sitting network.")
- Set up specific behaviors that you flag as warning signals when your goals are being sabotaged. (Example: "Neither of us can cancel a vacation without a long discussion and another time agreed upon.")

Creating a Mood

Setting the mood is the backbone of being romantic and creating exciting variety in your love life, and it involves at least three different aspects of your lovemaking.

1. Mental mood setting. Mental mood setting includes using your mind and will to fantasize about sex and choose to tune in to sexual cues as you structure making love into your marriage. Tuning in to sexual cues mentally, you can relax in your masculinity or femininity, fantasize about your mate, and set goals.

2. Emotional atmosphere. Emotional mood setting means creating an atmosphere in which you can be rested, excited, and warmly intimate. Good sex is predicated on an emotional mood or atmosphere. It involves enjoying adventure and being stress-free enough to focus on your sexual feelings.

3. Environmental ambiance. Environmental mood setting encourages romantic ambiance by altering your surroundings. It involves creating an environment that enhances and stimulates sexual arousal and meaningful, exciting interaction.

Creating an Environmental Ambiance

To enhance environmental mood, consider mood setting in three categories: sensuality, the bedroom, and props. Some of the more playful ideas will not seem as softly romantic as candles and gentle background music. Making love to Sousa marches, squirting each other's genitals with water pistols, having a pillow fight, or finger painting each other can also set a playful ambiance and be arousing. Allow the ideas to stimulate your imagination and creativity.

Sensuality

Sight, smell, taste, hearing, and touch are the five senses to maximize as you explore creating and enjoying a romantic ambiance.

Sight. Men's and women's enjoyment of the visual may vary, but it is important to both. The husband may love to see his wife's body, and an afternoon delight with the sun shining in brightly can be very sensual. His wife may prefer gentle light that softens and dims the body while the other senses are enhanced. Experiment with lighting and find ways to add variety. Flickering candlelight gives ambiance and a pleasant scent while leaving the bathroom door cracked may give just enough light to feel less exposed but visually connected. The partially covered is often more erotically stimulating than the fully exposed.

Couples often find strategically placed mirrors exciting. They can enjoy being aroused by all that is going on. Movement and choreography are fun turn-ons. Seductive behavior and dances that you do for the viewing pleasure of your mate can be very arousing.

Colors are visually sensual. It doesn't have to be the stereotypical red with black lace. Bright satin sheets, emerald green boxer shorts, soft peach teddies, a peacock feather—all contribute to the mood.

Go slow. Setting the mood is something you can enjoy without following through on making love. Tease and revel in your sexual feelings with the visual stimulation. Make the bedroom aesthetically appealing to eyes and other senses. (The bedroom is important enough that we will take a separate section to discuss it.)

Smell. Scents are an exciting part of creating a sensual mood. The mind connects sensations like perfume to erotic arousal and experiences. The wife's perfume may be paired in the husband's mind with her total person and especially her femininity and sexuality. Just a scent of it and he feels more in love and almost becomes aroused. Candles, incense, and scented lotions also add sensual pleasure and an ambiance to making love.

Taste. Taste is not always associated with creating sexual moods, but it is a stimulating form of sexuality. The mouth, tongue, and lips are erogenous zones with many nerve endings and a sensuality about them.

Lingering over a sumptuous meal is a very sensual experience. Candlelight and long conversations while having coffee and dessert are great mood setters. In the privacy of your own home, feeding each other food and placing favorite tastes in strategic places can be very erotic.

Hearing. Soft music or your favorite song creates marvelous atmosphere. Slow dance to songs that express the love and commitment you feel for each other. Take advantage of sexy talking and uninhibited groans and squeals of pleasure during sexual sessions.

Touch. Don't neglect to employ a whole variety of sensual touching experiences. Many women hate to be stimulated continuously in the same way. Try gently rubbing an ice cube over sensitive areas and revel in the sensations. Use a feather duster, satin gloves, a silk scarf, or some fur. Lotions add a different feel to the touching and caressing. Many couples find it very erotic and sensual to spread a covering out and get oily together.

Nerve endings and tactile senses can obviously involve more than touching with fingertips. Lightly blowing can create marvelous sensations on the chest, stomach, or genital area. Breathing gently into the ear can be profoundly erotic. Taking the hair or beard and tickling or teasing sensitive areas produces great sensations. The tongue lightly licking or the mouth gently kissing like a butterfly flitting around can create delightful effects.

The Bedroom

Romance and sexuality should pervade intimate companionship, and making love will be varied and should not be confined to the bedroom. Because of privacy and comfort, though, the bedroom will be the primary love nest. It is the place that can be made secluded and arousing, and it provides a place to store props like lotions and birth control. It can have special mood-setting qualities.

Aesthetics is defined as "the art of making something beautiful or appealing to one's taste." The bedroom needs to be aesthetically appealing to you. Live flowers in a pretty vase, potpourri, mood lighting or candles, sensuous linens, and the ability to control the temperature are sexual enhancements. You are pairing in your mind the bedroom with fun, sensual, erotic experiences. Just walking into the bedroom should create a different mood.

It helps to have a bed that doesn't squeak and a comfortable mattress. They may be necessary expenditures for your love life. Make sure the room is secure against children with a lock on the door. Train children to respect your privacy and a locked door. The bedroom is the central environmental setting for making love and creating mood. It probably has been neglected, so do some brainstorming as you spice it up.

Props

Candles, music, and lingerie stimulate ambiance. Flickering candlelight with soothing music in the background creates a totally different mood from that established by mirrors employed in an afternoon delight with some jazz on the stereo. Clothing can be endlessly varied: garters and black hose, red boxers with hearts, T-shirts and cutoffs, bathing suits, a dress shirt with nothing else, a tank top, robes and peignoir sets, teddies, matching bra and panties, a tuxedo, and the list can keep going. The creativity is not just in the clothing but how you choose to slowly take it off in sensual, seductive manners.

Couples sometimes worry that certain props (like sexy lingerie) are artificial and will detract from their natural lovemaking. God gave us our imaginations to create and enjoy various means of setting moods and enticing our mates, and props can provide new experiences and sensations. Props are simply a means to an end: creating a sexy environment and providing the tools to enhance lovemaking. The relationship and personal romantic creativity remain the foundation of great sex.

Pillows are great to lean against as you have intimate conversations or to use in positions of pleasuring and intercourse. They help make the bed the playground it should be. Purchase various shapes and sizes, and use them to keep backs, necks, and muscles from getting too tired. Pillows can be placed strategically to lie on and prop up the genital area for more accessibility. Pillows can also have certain appealing aesthetics in decorating the bed.

Keep handy items for loveplay, from feathers to fruit and lotions to satin gloves. Oils and scented lotions add sensuality to massage as you linger over skin and muscles and curves. Items like a feather duster or satin gloves give different and stimulating sensations. You are limited only by your imagination and creativity. A certain enticing perfume sprayed lightly over hair or aftershave applied after a quick shave can become quite erotic. You may need to get a locking carrying case for your love paraphernalia that you can store out of reach of children and easily take on vacation with you.

Time Out . . .

1. What is your best used sense: sight? smell? taste? hearing? touch? Select your least developed and try something in that area tonight.

2. If you were going to spend two hundred dollars to make your bedroom more sexy, what would you buy?

3. Think creatively with your mate and this week-end take a risk: buy a prop that you have thought about but not purchased yet. Start acquiring some props that can enhance your sex life and set the stage for more exciting lovemaking.

Don't be overwhelmed by this information on mood setting. Pick out one or two ideas in each section, and start building your ambiance-setting skills. Don't neglect the mental, emotional, or environmental atmosphere. Learning to be uninhibited, creative, and playful will help keep long-term sexuality out of a routine—and it's fun!

Chapter Seven

♡

The Joy of Fantasy

Our mind and the ability to think and imagine are a crucial part of being created human. This ability to enjoy mental imagery can be used to expand and enjoy all aspects of your life, including lovemaking. An active fantasy life can be wonderful for building a great sex life with your mate. But fantasy can also distort and damage a marriage.

Defining Fantasy

You use mental imagery and your imagination to enhance many areas of your life. You pray and build a meaningful concept of God by utilizing your mind and imagination. You become a wise steward of your time and relationships by building on positive experiences and mistakes. You use the mind's repository of information to achieve this. The only way you are able to create intimate companionship is to renew your mind as you heal past negative experiences and learn to anticipate pleasure with your mate. All of this is accomplished by employing mental imagery, fantasy, and the imagination.

Sex is no different from these other processes. All of them use fantasy and occur in the mind and imagination. Your mind, with the ability to create and store information, is the central part of imagining and experiencing erotic pleasure. That is what sexual fantasy is all about: your mind, imagination, and images that are paired with the sexual excitement.

First Peter states, "Therefore, prepare your minds for action; be self-controlled. . . . Do not conform to the evil desires you had when you lived in ignorance" (1:13–14 NIV). In James we read, "Each one is tempted when he is drawn away by his own desires and enticed. Then, when desire has conceived, it gives birth to sin" (1:14–15 NKJV). Romans 12:2 talks about being "transformed by the renewing of your mind" (NKJV). Ephesians 4:23 advises to "be renewed in the spirit of your mind" (NKJV). In applying these passages to fantasy and lovemaking, you need to recognize that sexual desire is never wrong—it is how you choose to use the desire. You can renew your mind and prepare your imagination for the action the Lord wants you to have sexually. You can banish ignorance.

These passages are encouraging for a great sex life. You can rid yourself of old messages that you must maintain control and never be passionate. You can unleash the playful and sexy parts of yourself as you romp with your mate with a renewed attitude. You can also purge your mind of any thoughts that might get in the way of uninhibited lovemaking with your mate—lustful thoughts of another person, a preoccupation with job or children, the idea that sex is dirty. You can enjoy mental imagery and not let it become evil. You need to renew your mind so that sex is permissible and, at the appropriate moment, make it a priority. You can prepare for action and have a creative sexual mind-set that will result in enticing, dynamic lovemaking.

It's 80 Percent Mental

Sex is perhaps 80 percent fantasy (imagination and mind) and about 20 percent friction. Granted, pleasuring erogenous zones (friction) is fun, but what truly creates the excitement is your mind. With your mind, you can creatively set the mood and build a mental repertoire of erotically arousing experiences and images, as well as utilize your ability to imaginatively play in the joy of the moment.

For simplicity, let's divide fantasy into two areas: (1) the stored sexual information in your mind, which was given its erotic excitement by associating it with hormonal and genital arousal, and (2) your imagination's use of your erotic repertoire to create sexual attitudes and imaginary scenes and stimulate activity and excitement.

An example of the stored part of fantasy is a warm kiss, which is often an important part of making love. The brain pairs over time the behavior of kissing with hormonal, emotional, and relational responses to stimulate sexual arousal. Kissing your spouse is a turn-on, but your heterosexual responses were learned and stored from former experiences.

Erotic cues and imaginative processes can also be explained by the psychological principle of classical conditioning that explains how things get paired.

Unconditioned Stimulus (hormones) ➙ *Unconditioned Response (excitement)*
Conditioned Stimulus (kiss) ➙ *Conditioned Response (excitement)*

FIG. 7.1. Classical conditioning.

Unconditioned elements create sexual excitement when a girl is with a boy. Over time the unconditioned stimulus gets paired with the conditioned stimulus of a kiss, and then the kiss elicits excitement. This is true of most pleasurable things. The response we make to a specific stimulus becomes linked with the mental image or the doing of the activity. Our unconditioned response thus becomes conditioned.

You continually add to that memory bank of erotic thoughts and behaviors as well as utilize it for enhancing lovemaking. When you get married, you and your spouse's minds contain all the sexual data you have read, seen, and experienced. Certain images and ideas are especially erotically charged because you have paired sexual arousal (a sexual relationship, masturbating, hormonal desires) with them. If a spouse continues to build up the sexual surge and collect new data from other visual experiences, however, you may feel excluded and your sexual fantasy will become distorted.

It is important that you erase or refuse to think about some of the sexual learning and experiences from your past. They will detract from your one-flesh lovemaking. Carefully choose the images and experiences you wish to store after you are married. The images should be about your mate and should make lovemaking more exciting. Especially guard how you use your stored repository and imagination.

A common plight of many men is that they build in their fantasy worlds ideal women with specific physical attributes, such as big breasted, tall, blonde, and blue-eyed. Yet often the wives they choose are the exact opposite. Men—and women, as well—need to keep storing new sexual information, especially about their mates, as they imagine sexy aspects of their anatomy and sexy scenes.

Fantasy Is NOT Reality

Christ in His teaching stated, "You have heard that it was said to those of old, 'You shall not commit adultery.' But I say to you that whoever looks at a woman to lust for her has already committed adultery with her in his heart" (Matt. 5:27–28 NKJV). The Greek verb *look* is in the imperfect tense, which is an action that starts in the past and continues into the present. It could be translated "continually look." Christ emphasized the importance of guarding the mental fantasy life. Fantasy is different from sexual actions and at times more complex to manage. He stressed that continual thinking is more likely to lead to an unfaithful heart attitude and sinful behaviors.

This passage offers essential lessons about fantasy becoming sin. The sinful destructiveness of fantasy is relative to the situation and the individual person's inner attitudes. To look at a woman in a bikini or a man in a muscle shirt is one thing. To continually fantasize about your next-door neighbor or a person at work is dangerous. That could much more easily lead to adultery. Christ also encouraged us to be careful how we build mental fantasies. Even though fantasy is not reality or as destructive as actual behavior, Christ warned that your thought life can develop in such a way as to betray your mate in your heart. The specialness of your love and commitment can be diluted; all fantasy is not innocent or productive.

Paul in Colossians (3:5) encouraged Christians to clean up their thought lives and make wise choices in mentally pursuing sexual cues. Christians should avoid "sexual immorality, impurity, lust, evil desires" (NIV). Everyone has sexual reactions triggered by cues in the environment. That is not wrong desire, but you can control whether you objectify a person or "continually look" to the detriment of your thought life and partnership.

It is not wrong for a man to praise the Lord for heterosexuality and the female form. Fantasies are not behaviors, and visual cues can unintentionally stimulate arousal. A male can tune in so much to external environmental cues that he forgets to notice his wife's feminine appeal and have a proper focus on his own special woman.

Similarly, a woman's sexual fantasies are stimulated by sensory data (e.g., a romantic movie, a good-looking guy, or an affirming comment on her femininity) that go through the pipeline of her nerves to her genitals and body. A woman's response might be more general and not so genitally focused as a man's.

Remember that fantasy is not reality, and the real thing is enjoyed only together in your companionship. Let God be in your bedroom, and He will help you keep it pure and growth producing—to help you keep your desires centered on your lovemaking.

Men and women alike will experience sexual arousal as a part of the sleep cycle with erections, lubrications, and dreams. This arousal is not unfaithfulness, and if you think about your dreams, they are probably based on your mental store of erotically arousing events or perhaps your emotional struggles at the time. You cannot control dreams, and again, fantasy is *not* reality. A great way to understand your dreams is to deal with the feelings behind them. By not being afraid of your dreams, but praying and exploring them, you can learn from them and make necessary changes in your life.

Gender Different

The fantasy lives of men and women are different. Stored erotic data can vary as well as the manner in which imaginations are employed around these images. Saying fantasies are different says nothing about male/female capacities for enjoying fantasy. Distortions also have nothing to do with gender differences. Double standards that are not based in Scripture allow and encourage boys to be more in touch with their sexuality and to notice sexual cues in the environment more, and these same double standards encourage girls to be seductive, fearful, and repressed.

Overall, men seem to be more focused on genitals and explicit sexual activity, and women tend to be more holistic with an enjoyment of sensuality and personality behind the body. But men and women should not be stereotyped. Some men appreciate gentle, romantic ambiance more than their wives do. Some women may be very visually stimulated by genitals and enjoy immediate, direct sexual stimulation. There seem to be some general differences, though, that can help you understand the effective use of fantasy in your lovemaking.

Women and men may enjoy different memories of the same sexual encounter. If a couple were given the use of a private house right on the beach for instance, the woman might remember that one night by moonlight they had made love on a blanket in the dunes between the house and beach. There was the gentle roar of the waves, and her husband had left some soft music playing on the cassette player on the deck. They were warm from the day's sun and sensuously rubbed lotion on each other and passionately built up to some great sex. He rubbed her tummy and legs, taking time to enjoy her body. Afterward, they lay together on their backs and talked as they looked at the stars. It was a very bonding and romantic experience.

A man, however, might state how exciting it had been to set up the romantic props of music and blanket. He had gotten an erection just thinking of the coming activity and how great his wife had looked in her bathing suit that day. He might reminisce about how that evening he slowly removed her shorts and T-shirt and the way her body glowed in the light with the highlights of tan lines and nipples and genital area. The lotion was so very sensual, and he remembered the manner she had undressed and caressed him. He might also be aroused by the illicitness of having sex under the stars as if they were sneaking in a special way to enjoy each other. (Of course, she also might have been aroused by that—husbands and wives are not always that different in their erotic arousal.)

In the above example, there are some differences. The man's attention was directed toward visual stimulation by specific physical attributes and touching of the genital area. The woman reveled in the relational and overall sensual atmosphere and her husband's "slow hands." But she does not want to be stereotyped because she, too, enjoys visual aspects of her husband's body. Fantasy makes for great sex but can be varied from husband to wife and from individual to individual.

Time Out . . .

1. Think of a sexual experience that you mutually enjoyed with your mate, and each describe it fully. How do you two differ? How are you similar?

2. Brainstorm with your partner how you could increase the use of your imagination. What three things could you do to stimulate creativity?

Mental Variety

An important question is whether it is wrong to have fantasies of other people and events. When does this become destructive or dangerous? Christians need to come to grips with this issue.

The answer is important to us. Human beings are created with a need for stimulation and variety, and sexual fantasy can help provide both. God has shown, though, that any thought or behavior that detracts from enjoying your mate sexually is wrong and outside His blueprint for building intimate companionship and a great sex life.

As it happens so often in applying God's principles to our lives, "all things are lawful for me, but all things are not helpful. All things are lawful for me, but I will not be brought under the power of any" (1 Cor. 6:12 NKJV). Is it destructive to see and be excited by environmental sexual cues? There are few times we can be in public—whether at the beach or the shopping malls—without getting sexually stimulated. This is not wrong. But not controlling our eyes, thoughts, and impulses can become sinful and destructive to our relationships.

You may want to become more selective in what movies and television shows you watch. Some movies may stimulate your enjoyment of your spouse. Others create sexual imagery that does not help you enhance your sex life. Certain types of romantic novels may be too detracting from your lovemaking and get your mind into potentially dangerous patterns of thinking sexually. So many plots are built on adultery and casual sexual encounters.

Is it wrong to fantasize having sexual activity with an imaginary person or an actor or actress on the screen? Is it okay to think back on past situations that were arousing? We as Christians have been reluctant to talk about this subject. Everyone has fantasies about other people, and they can be destructive to your commitment to building sexual intimacy. Fantasy is important, but it should be centered on your mate and the fantastic sex life you are creating together.

Fantasy gives your imagination the opportunity to add variety within your marriage without the destructiveness of sampling greener grass. You can go to Hawaii or the Riviera; you can make love on a secluded beach; you can enjoy all over again favorite times with your mate.

One woman was curious about what it would be like to make love to a different man. What she needed, however, was mental variety and a better sex life rather than a different man physically. She needed to remember that one body is pretty much the same as another. Her more basic curiosity was a special mood, some novel experiences, someone to touch her sexuality in deeper and exciting ways. An affair may very well not meet these needs and would certainly destroy the honesty and trust of her marriage. If she was willing to work at it with her husband, she could meet her needs wonderfully with him.

A difficult part of fantasy is that, like masturbation, it is at times an individual sexual activity. Christians don't have too much trouble with the mutual part of sexuality, but the individual part is harder to sort out. In fact, the personal fantasies that accompany masturbation often raise objections. If you are not comfortable with your sexuality and able to revel in your orgasms and feelings, you may feel unable to create the mood for you and your mate to be intimate. Fantastic sex is designed to be a mutual experience, and individual fantasy should enhance, rather than detract from, mutual lovemaking.

Enhancing Lovemaking

Sexual imagery and imagination should be used toward the goal of increasing the enjoyment and intimacy of lovemaking. Here are some rules of thumb that can help you maximize your mental fantasy life. They can help you, whether individually or mutually, to keep your fantasy skills and usage within God's sexual economy as it enhances lovemaking.

Keep environmental cues disciplined. It is great to be heterosexual and enjoy the opposite sex. But you can make choices about how this enjoyment can be controlled. You can enjoy and be enriched by variety and romance without detracting from your commitment to enhancing your sex life as you eroticize your mate. If this doesn't happen, and you are fantasizing about something else during lovemaking, you are diminishing your relationship and sexual partnership.

Keep intentional fantasies centered on your mate. One man who went to many conferences built a fantasy in which he met a sexy woman who seduced him in his hotel room. Unfortunately, he never took his wife to the conferences. You know the sad outcome of this story and what happened at a conference. You should keep all fantasies that you willfully (intentionally) create focused on your partner. Sinful diluting of intimacy and acting out sexually are encouraged by continual, intentional fantasies about a person or situation outside your marriage.

Keep the enhancement of your lovemaking the primary focus. Continued fantasies about women with big breasts or men with big penises are stupid if your spouse is small. The same can be said about not taking the energy to allow your mate to be erotically attractive to you and fantasizing you are making love to someone else. This can be very demeaning and destructive to your lover and your lovemaking. Create fantasies about you and your mate. During and after making love, notice and fantasize about aspects of your spouse that you find erotically attractive. Let them become a part of your increasing store of sexual memories. Turn your imagination loose on ideas that could make you a better lover and your sex life more exciting and intimate.

Keep creative variety. Fantasies can become as routine as your sex life. You need to continually add to your store of sexually arousing material and keep creatively utilizing it with your mate. Don't be guilty of a limited repertoire. Men, even more than women, can allow fantasies to be repetitious and boring. Some of them probably date back to high school. Allow your mate and dynamic lovemaking to stimulate your imagination and spice up your fantasy life.

Keep between the lines. Some people and ideas should have tight boundaries placed around them so they are never allowed to create erotic arousal. You may inadvertently get sexual feelings, but you can choose to stop the feelings as completely inappropriate.

A sense of the unusual, of newness and adventure, enhances sexual excitement and variety. The human mind is curious and loves mystery or new experiences. Your imaginative capacity and fantasy can help fulfill this in many ways. Keep an adventurous component in your personality. Fantasy with mystery and novelty can give your love life wings. Mentally making love with your spouse on your office desk may lead to your setting it up and seducing your mate there. Wives and husbands can imagine themselves wild and uninhibited and then practice some of these fantasy behaviors. These lovemaking sessions usually end up with much laughter and a bonding closeness. A great fantasy life and a dynamic sex life are indeed a state of mind. Unleash your childlike wonderment and curiosity as you discover new dimensions of play.

Enjoying Fantasies

You can take pleasure from your imagination in a healthy and exciting way to increase sexual intimacy. You can experience joy and variety by increasing your repertoire of stored sexual images and using them more creatively. You should romantically enjoy fantasy with your spouse.

Fantasy Lovemaking

Each mate should get a piece of paper and pencil and take the time to unleash your imagination as you write how you would program your lovemaking for maximum pleasure: How would you start? How would you create atmosphere? What props would you use? What things have you always wanted to include? This is fantasy and not reality, so let your imagination loose.

Block out at least an hour for discussion, creative brainstorming, and enjoying the following process.

One at a time, take your fantasy lovemaking sessions and describe them to your mate. Detach from your own feelings as your mate shares his or her ideal lovemaking. Don't interrupt, but let your mate develop the whole scenario. Sit back and just be an empathetic listener. Abandon your defenses and do nothing but validate your mate's ideas, needs, and feelings. Ask feedback questions to make sure you understand. Try paraphrasing what you are hearing. Don't assume or mind read, and above all, don't make any judgments.

After each of you has shared your fantasy sessions, have fun with the following challenges:

1. Share three items from your mate's sexual fantasies that sound particularly exciting to you. Embellish these three ideas with elements from your own fantasy life and have fun laughing, sharing, and fantasizing.

2. Describe three aspects of your lover's fantasies that you don't relate to or might have some problems enjoying. Be a good communicator and don't get stuck on semantics or content, but reveal your needs and feelings on a deeper level. Why would you struggle with those parts of the fantasy? Talk about it as you take risks and disclose more about yourself.

3. Be creative and compile a composite of your fantasies, but don't create just one big scene. Pull your ideal lovemaking apart and make up three different scenarios. Laugh and let your imaginations get on a roll. Increase your repository of sexual information and ability to fantasize new and different situations.

4. Use your ingenuity and plan when you will implement one of the above composite lovemaking sessions in the next week. (How might each of you sabotage accomplishing this task this week? This is probably a hindrance to your fantasy and sex life you need to resolve.) Which session would be good to save for your next getaway?

Acting Out Fantasies

One overburdened wife found vacationing especially romantic. The second honeymoon to Hawaii was a favorite source of her fantasies. She loved the moonlight walks, the sensuous dinner talks, the exciting hike to one lagoon and having no demands from children. About twice a year, her husband would surprise her with baby-sitting already arranged and meet her at the door in his Hawaiian shirt. They would have loads of fun recreating her fantasies about their honeymoon in their own home.

Husbands and wives enjoy their mates initiating exciting and different lovemaking. One wife was aware of her husband's fantasy of being surprised sexually as she sweeps him off his feet and enjoys his "irresistible masculine charm." She made reservations at an elegant hotel and made up a plausible story that got him to the hotel lounge at 6:00 P.M. that Friday. Unbeknownst to him, she got off work early and checked into their room where she took a leisurely bath and got some props ready. You can imagine the rest when she met her man in the hotel lounge. They did not leave their room until the 11:00 A.M. checkout time the next morning.

Time Out . . .

1. Think of your most common sexual fantasies (scenes, settings, objects, ambiances, styles) that could help your mate understand your sexual needs better and be a real turn-on. Strategically share appropriate ones with your partner as you discuss and perhaps incorporate some of them.

2. What three things do you need to do that would better unleash your fantasy life and help you be a better lover? (For example, take the courage to tell your mate some of your fantasies, become more child-like, and tune in to cues in your lovemaking.)

Should you share all of your fantasies with your mate? That probably wouldn't be wise. You may need to make some aspects of your fantasy life more mature as you conform to God's economy for a fulfilling sex life. But discussing fantasies can be arousing and enrich your love life. Not letting your partner into your fantasies can diminish your love life. It can be great fun to act out some of them as you increase variety and playfulness.

Distorting Fantasy

Fantasy can be distorted. As you allow yourself to enjoy fantasy, you must be wisely mature. What exactly gets your thinking outside God's guidelines for great sex and into sinful, destructive lust? The Bible warns that the Lord hates "a heart that devises wicked plans" (Prov. 6:18 NKJV), and it urges that "you put off...the old man which grows corrupt according to the deceitful lusts" (Eph. 4:22 NKJV). How can you as a Christian utilize your visual perceptions and the sexual thought processes that follow to sabotage healthy sexuality and intimate companionship? When are you guilty of "wicked plans"?

Destructive lust forgets that every person is special and three-dimensional with a body, soul, and spirit. Lust objectifies (makes a sexual object) a person and views the person as a detached body with only genitals and erotic appeal but no personality (soul). Lust can harm other people for personal sexual gratification because it has detached sex from a person and an intimate relationship.

Harmful sexual thinking is immature and practices poor impulse control. You constantly focus on sexual stimuli in the environment; sex becomes a mental preoccupation. Sex invades your total life, assuming too great an importance as you notice every little sexual cue. Sex can take on addictive proportions and sabotage a balanced life and caring relationships.

Damaging sexual fantasy keeps looking at and obsessing about a person or sexual situation outside marriage. This "lusting after" sets up a person until the thinking begins to encourage the likelihood of sinful behaviors and infidelity. Sinful lust is often a detrimental pattern that comes out of and perpetuates a series of poor choices.

Injurious lust diminishes your attraction to your mate and can be insulting to your mate, who comes to feel inferior, embarrassed, or neglected. It detracts from your commitment to building a more exciting sex life with your partner. Sinful fantasy adulterates your enjoyment of your partner rather than enhances your sexual intimacy together.

Poor Thought Control

The Roman Christians were exhorted, "Do not be conformed to this world, but be transformed by the renewing of your mind"; and "To be spiritually minded is life and peace" (Rom. 12:2; 8:6 NKJV). Paul also encouraged, "Whatever things are true, whatever things are noble, whatever things are just, whatever things are pure, whatever things are lovely, whatever things are of good report...meditate on these things" (Phil. 4:8 NKJV). God has given us as human beings the marvelous capacity to choose what we wish to think and fantasize about.

Men don't have greater sex drives than women. Men more often than women have poor thought control, though both are afflicted with this disease. Seeing an attractive woman at a restaurant and following her across the room as you mentally undress her is creating a sex drive, not a result of your higher sex drive. There's a difference between being highly sexed and allowing one's thought life to run along unchecked.

Lust is a fascinating and often poorly understood word. We have already established that we are not talking about enjoying sexual stimuli or creating a fantasy life. Lust is distorted fantasy and especially unchecked sexual thoughts—objectifying and using sexuality in a way that does not produce intimacy or a more fulfilling sex life. We are warned as Christians that "each of you should know how to possess his own vessel [body, especially the mind] in sanctification and honor, not in passion of lust" (1 Thess. 4:4–5 NKJV).

Diminishing Your Mate

The sexual verbs are *relate* and *connect*, and great sex is based on a fun and loving relationship. Your fantasy life, both old and newly input erotic data and the imaginative use of this information, should enhance your intimate companionship. Pining over the lack of breast size or focusing on the muscles of other men is diminishing your spouse and can lead to ineffective fantasies. If you choose to focus on supposed flaws, you will never build the kind of erotic enjoyment of your mate's body that you need for a great sex life.

When you fantasize, fantasize about your mate in exciting situations. Any time your fantasies exclude your mate, you diminish your mate's importance to your emotional and physical fulfillment.

Many mates at times think of something else when they are making love. Is this destructive? One wife confessed that she often planned her week's agenda during the Sunday night sexual session with her husband. Is this always wrong? Anything that diminishes your mate and your focus on making love is counterproductive.

Is it always damaging to bring erotic fantasies of someone else into married sex? It will not instantly sabotage your love life, but it will not maximize your lovemaking. It can drain off sexual energy that you could be using to eroticize and focus on your partner. You may be creating a private world in your head to the exclusion of your partner as you simply use the body. It diminishes your mate and could come to destroy your mate's erotic attractiveness. If you are feeling bored or turned off, you need to face that and deal with it.

Immature Patterns

Men often are less holistic in their sexuality than women as they fixate on some narrow focus, neglecting a broad range of fantasies and feelings. Men unfortunately are not alone in creating patterns that restrict God's plan of exciting sexual bonding in marriage.

One woman enjoyed dating, loved to kiss, and all her life had romanticized sex. In her mind, sex was gentle wooing and sexy flirting. After she married, sex became difficult for her. It suddenly involved physical aspects of making love, and she felt she lost all control. As she sought answers, she realized that she had an immature, limiting sexual mind-set that desperately needed an overhaul. Her repertoire of erotically stimulating images, settings, ambiances, and styles required expansion.

Spectating

Another variety of immaturity and ineffective use of fantasy involves *spectating*. Mentally, great lovers focus on and revel in the present experience. However, all of us at times mentally leave the scene and watch the lovemaking as if from afar. The wife, who thinks she is taking too long to climax and her husband is growing tired, all of a sudden becomes anxious, spectates, and loses all capacity for arousal. The husband who doubts his ability to get an erection or excite his wife mentally leaves the immediate lovemaking, anxious about his performance.

You can use your imagination in negative ways as you spectate and borrow trouble or create agendas in your mind rather than enjoy the sexual celebration. Effective fantasy utilizes imaginative capacity to enjoy the party and create new levels of excitement. Keep your mind on your lovemaking, and don't spectate!

Destructive Fantasies

"It all depends" does not apply to all of fantasy. Some types of fantasy are wrong, period. Any fantasy that involves children is wrong. We are responsible for protecting God's little ones, especially those He has entrusted to our care, and ensuring they are not sexualized destructively.

Time Out . . .

1. Each of us distorts fantasy in some way. Which examples and areas apply to you? What reward do you receive from that distortion that keeps you from changing it? The first step in changing this distortion can be sharing this secret with your mate or a friend.

2. What makes you detach and spectate? Discuss this with your mate, and both figure out how to do some prevention as well as ways to get back into the lovemaking (e.g., criticism causes anxiety and detachment; your mate's being more active would get you back into the activity).

Allowing your neighbors or friends' mates or associates or clients to be at all sexually arousing and the objects of fantasies is courting disaster. You are in constant contact with these people, and you need to avoid any complicating sexual overtones. Noticing an attractive person on the beach is different from checking out a friend's mate.

Fantasies that involve hurting another person, pain, or domination do not promote loving, growth-producing sexual relating. It is easy to confuse pain and pleasure, but they are obviously very different in their effect on a relationship.

Any fantasy that would lead to adultery is sinful and contrary to the goal of intimate sexuality. Fantasies that dilute your erotic attachment to your mate, even if they don't lead to affairs, are ineffective. The word *adulterate* means to "water down," and your personal fantasy should make your mutual sexual pleasure more exciting—not less.

This is a tough area of sexuality to sort through. There are no easy answers. Talk with a wise friend or your mate about some of the areas and specific behaviors that still have you perplexed. Talk through some of the ideas of this chapter. Please bring your faith into the equation and humbly ask God to shine truth into your life and thinking. God has a way of honoring that request through many meaningful and sometimes surprising avenues.

Do not be afraid of fantasy. It comprises too important a part of intimate lovemaking. Acknowledge the fact that all of us notice and think about a variety of sexual cues in the environment. These cues and sexual desires are not wrong. It is how you choose to discipline your thought life and bring your fantasies into enhancing your sexual partnership that separates sin from great lovemaking.

Chapter Eight

Sexual
Communication

Many loving couples never talk about sex together. They often haven't developed a comfortable sexual vocabulary or the ability to dialogue about their lovemaking. Perhaps sex was never talked about in their growing up experiences. Let's face it, sex is a difficult topic to easily discuss. Sexual discussion can get into constructive criticism, problem solving, and private feelings. This is difficult to deal with—especially for men who want to be perfect lovers. Sex can become an emotionally loaded topic, which is therefore avoided.

Lack of sexual communication can be disabling, though. It prevents couples from making needed adjustments for greater pleasure, it robs them of a great aphrodisiac because talking is very sexy, and it blocks them from sharing fantasies and creating erotic, romantic evenings. For many marriages, it is not just sexual talk but communication in general that suffers. Mates often have acute skill deficits in resolving conflict and negotiating tentative solutions.

This chapter tackles all of these areas starting off with four basic skills for effective communication and dialogue, then exploring the language of lovemaking from vocabulary to slang to love talk. The sections on initiating and refusing, as well as on coaching and problem solving, should help resolve and avoid conflict.

Four Basic Skills for Great Communication

Intimately connecting, feeling and enjoying a sense of partnership, is what a one-flesh marriage is all about, and dialogue is at the heart of this process. Sex is not the most crucial part of your relationship. Communicating and building a loving, fulfilling companionship are the core needs. The more you communicate, the more intimately connected you will feel.

Four Basic Skills

Dialogue. Dialogue is the essence of communication based on a relationship in which two people want the best for each other. Dialogue is lovingly and honestly focusing on receiving and sending messages with the goal of understanding your mate, resolving differences, and creating an intimate partnership. Dialogue simply collects data—abandoning the need to win, debate, convince, or make a point. One partner talks while the other truly listens.

1. **Actively listen to your partner.**

   • Focus. Eliminate distractions, make eye contact, and give focused attention.
   • Detach. Be quiet, suspend judgments, and step out of self.
   • Understand. Mirror back, invite information, clarify, and summarize.

2. **Empathize with your partner's message and deeper reality.**

   • Validate the content. Partner's message is realistic and makes sense.
   • Validate the feelings. Partner's feelings are valid, and you accept them.
   • Validate the needs. Partner's core needs are important, and you desire to meet them.

3. **Assertively send messages to your partner.**

   • Increase self-esteem and self-awareness. Become conscious of needs and feelings.
   • Express core needs and feelings. Discover the deeper message beneath the content.
   • Use assertive, positive "I" statements. Avoid aggressive or passive statements; risk conflict; own responsibility; don't blame or resort to negative statements.

4. **Communicate and manage conflict in the partnership.**

   • Stick to the topic.
   • Pick your battles and develop your timing.
   • Remain courteous.
   • Set limits.
   • Reconcile the relationship.
   • Negotiate tentative solutions.

You will also discover many fun spillovers into your sex life from effective communication. The more you talk and feel close, the more you will want to make love. The more you talk about sex and your love life, the more satisfying your lovemaking will become. Dialogue and these four basic skills are crucial to resolving sexual conflicts, too.

The four basic skills will make more sense and be easier to apply if you take the time to practice the exercises after each step. They are fun and sexually arousing. Before developing the skills, let's look at communication as dialogue. This summarizes and symbolizes all that we will explore in the four skills and represents so much of what we have already examined in this book about intimate one-flesh companionship.

Dialogue

You are in a special union that has at its heart looking after the well-being of your partner. You can rest comfortably and safely in your loving, trustworthy companionship. Each is truly in the other's corner, and each is willing to give as gifts the things the other needs. Dialogue promotes this intimate partnership and is the spirit of communication. Dialogue is trying to understand what your partner needs and feels so you can be nurturing—as each gives up the need to win, debate, convince, or protect personal interests. You lovingly and honestly focus on receiving and sending messages with the goal of understanding your mate, resolving differences, and creating an intimate partnership. In a true partnership everyone profits, and there is no need for protectiveness.

The process of dialogue can be simply defined as data collecting—giving and receiving information. Bottom line, one of you stays quiet and listens while the other talks, and then you change roles. Don't be afraid that when you are keeping quiet your needs and feelings won't be heard. This is not a monologue. When your turn comes, your partner will be totally focused on listening and understanding you.

1. Actively Listen to Your Partner.

Most books on communication develop the process of active listening. It is a simple concept but very difficult to practice. Often, other people's concerns don't seem as important as your own, and you don't focus on them very well. You are often preparing rebuttals rather than giving feedback and making sure you are hearing accurately.

Focus. This skill demands that you establish an atmosphere in which you are knee-to-knee and eye-to-eye as you are truly present for the other person. Eliminate as many distractions (television, children underfoot) as possible so you can focus your attention on your mate. You want to demonstrate that your mind and memory are in gear and you are truly trying to hear what is being said. Sometimes nodding the head or saying "uh-huh" helps.

Detach. You may not hear a given message because you are unable to detach from your own issues, feelings, and thoughts and the preparation of your rebuttal. Effective listeners learn to step away from themselves and focus totally on the communiqué coming their way.

Understand. Your mate won't feel listened to if you don't demonstrate an understanding of the message you are hearing. Mirroring back to your mate is the easiest way to accomplish accurate listening. This can be a simple paraphrase of what you just heard. It is always helpful to give an invitation for more information as you say, "Is that all?" or perhaps ask for repetition of a part you are not sure you heard accurately. Don't assume or mind read, but clarify. Brief summaries throughout the listening process are also helpful in keeping messages clear, and they allow your partner to give feedback about whether you are accurately listening and understanding.

Practice exercise. Take turns describing (1) how you feel during an orgasm or when you are very sexually excited, and (2) one thing you wish you could do more of in your sex life and why. Keep the feedback loop going, and paraphrase as you learn about your mate's differences and similarities. When you are the sender, stop every minute or two and give your mate time to mirror back what you have just said. Stay focused and detached as you collect data from your loving partner.

2. Empathize with Your Partner's Message and Deeper Reality.

Empathetically acknowledging your partner's message is actually the final step in active listening. Empathizing means walking miles in your mate's moccasins. Empathizing with, as you truly understand and accept (acknowledge and validate), another person's reality is perhaps the most essential part of communication. The foundation of effective empathy is deeply based in our Christian faith: unconditional love, respect, trust, and acceptance. First Peter 3:7 tells husbands, "Be considerate as you live with your wives, and treat them with respect" (NIV). True love and great communication are based on becoming a student of your one-flesh companion. In your partnership, you humbly acknowledge you don't have a corner on truth but want to empathize, share, and learn from your partner.

Empathizing means truly getting into your partner's thought processes and feelings as you live in your partner's reality. You will put on a new pair of glasses and see life differently. You will be required to say statements like these: "I haven't thought of it in that way, but you are right"; "That makes good sense to me when you say..."; "I, too, would feel...if that were done to me"; "You must need...; how can I help you meet that core desire?"

It is not enough to hear your partner's messages—you must acknowledge and validate them as you truly empathize and confirm the importance and truth of the communication. (You will have a chance later in the dialogue when you are the speaker to dispute the part of your mate's reality that you think is inaccurate. Right now you are empathizing and validating.) You must accept your mate's reality (content, needs, feelings) as being real to your mate and believe the message.

A validation or acknowledgment statement is a quick, empathetic summary (ten to twenty seconds and can be as simple as "you said..."; "you feel..."; "you need...") indicating you truly understand and accept the message. Your mate then knows you are not shooting back a defensive overreaction or overpersonalization. Validating does not mean you agree with what is said; it means you respect and believe the reality. You truly understand the content, feelings, and needs. Your mate will never feel heard unless the feelings and needs are also empathetically understood and validated.

Validate the content. You acknowledge that your partner's message is realistic and contains truth. It helps to use sentences like these: "You are reasonable when you say..."; "It is understandable that..."

Practice exercise. Tell your mate some of the things that are your favorite turn-ons as your mate makes validating summaries of the content of your message. These summaries may be only ten seconds in length.

Validate the feelings. You are being careful not to say your mate's feelings are right or wrong. They are your partner's feelings, and regardless of your opinions, they are valid to your partner. Right now you are simply validating and accepting them. You will discover a marvelous side effect of validating your partner's feelings—your mate will then have a clearer perspective of the feeling and resolve unrealistic elements of it. Validating statements like "Wow, you probably feel...." or "I would also feel...if I were in your shoes" are helpful.

Practice exercise. Let your partner choose a personal hot spot or an emotionally loaded topic in your sex life. You are not going to try to resolve it right now but practice short validation statements of the deeper feeling part of the message. Become the active listener as you take a deep breath, step back from yourself without defensiveness, and take your role as a detached validator. Truly hear and believe and validate what your partner is feeling. Now switch roles but you go into a new topic. Do not try to resolve anything or make rebuttal in this communication session—just validate your partner's feelings.

Validate the needs. From childhood on, each person builds a reality in which certain things become more important than others. Meeting certain needs is vital to feelings of well-being. In a loving partnership, you desire to help your mate have these needs met. Great communication validates these deeper needs that will underlie your companion's messages. Validating statements that help do this are "You probably need..." or "You really feel uncomfortable when you don't have...."

Practice exercise. Ask your partner to describe a lovemaking session that was very special. Put yourself in your mate's sexual reality, and decide what are some deeper needs: variety, tenderness, competence, challenge, affirmation, fun, comfort. These needs are probably evidenced in other parts of the companionship and need validation there as well.

3. Assertively Send Messages to Your Partner.

Increase self-esteem and self-awareness. The more secure you and your partner feel about yourselves, the more you will open up and talk to each other. It is difficult to risk self-disclosure and trust your partner when you dislike your body or feel uncomfortable with yourself. It is also difficult to manage communication with your partner if you do not understand yourself. Proverbs 16:23 states, "The heart of the wise teaches his mouth" (NKJV). Self-awareness of feelings and needs is crucial to communicating effectively and assertively sending accurate messages. You must take them out of your unconscious mind and be consciously aware of them. Then you can share them with your partner as you become intimate soul mates.

Practice exercise. Share with your mate something you are afraid of in your sex life. Tell your mate some things about yourself that make you the excellent lover that you are becoming. Let your mate mirror and then acknowledge these statements.

Express core needs and feelings. So many couples never slice to this deeper level of communication. Their messages stay on a very superficial plane with debating, nit-picking, rehashing, and inconsequential chitchat.

Practice exercise. Take a sexual argument about something one of you wants to do but the other doesn't. This time detach, empathize, and assertively get into the needs and feelings. Try to find ways to meet these needs without doing the thing you have argued so much about.

Use assertive, positive "I" statements. Being assertive means being able to be self-aware, straightforward, and confident in expressing needs and feelings. That is quite an order. Assertive communication is neither passive (sitting on needs and feelings) nor aggressive (your needs and feelings must be met regardless of your mate's needs and feelings). Which of the following nonassertive communication techniques do you allow to get in the way of effective messages?

Hinting occurs when you beat around the bush rather than say what you think, feel, or need. Often, it is done by asking a question ("Could we maybe make love this weekend?") rather than coming right out with a statement ("I'm really excited tonight and hope we can make love; I'll even come to bed early"). You phrase a question, "What do you think about taking a shower with me tonight?" rather than state, "I'm sure in the mood and would enjoy taking a shower together tonight."

Avoiding conflict is not that unusual. The problem is that you and your mate are unique male and female individuals and each will feel, need, and desire different things. This incompatibility will naturally cause conflict and differences. Healthy assertiveness accepts this reality and persists in expressing needs and feelings. Assertive people know their needs won't be met every time, and that is okay. They risk the conflict and confrontation, knowing they can be resolved.

Gunnysacking is a term meaning you take your needs and feelings and passively stuff them into a gunnysack on your back rather than let them out. Eventually, the gunnysack won't hold all the feelings, and it explodes. Not expressing sexual needs and feelings is dangerous because they have a way of bursting out in very destructive ways.

Fragile tiptoeing occurs when you walk on eggs around your mate. Both lose an essential ingredient of assertive relating. Sometimes this happens because one or both partners create an aura of being fragile in a given area: "Mention my lack of sexual drive and I will explode," or "I'm trying to be a good lover, but I just can't remember what you want." Good communicators toughen up and assertively confront all areas of their sexual relationship. Another aggravating way of tiptoeing is when one partner talks baby talk because of the hesitancy to confront the other or deal openly. Tiptoeing can be very annoying.

Positive "I" language is an excellent technique for assertively sending messages. Positive "I" language eliminates the words *never, always, don't,* and *won't* and replaces them with *I need* or *I feel*. With "I" language, you take responsibility for your needs and feelings and express them positively—rather than with negative, blaming "you" language. You say, "I feel irritated and think you have not listened to me; sex is not fun for me when we need to be at church in twenty minutes," *not* "You always want sex at the absolutely worst times." Assertive communication will run the risks of conflict—that is a normal part of a loving partnership.

Practice exercise. In a self-aware, straightforward manner, communicate to your mate what you would like sexually on the coming weekend—what you desire and how you would appreciate your desires being met. Take the courage to assertively express what arouses you and some of your feelings associated with those behaviors. Maybe complete the following sentence: "I wish sexually that you would..." Then dialogue about your answers. Remember you are nondefensively collecting data. Now try this: "I enjoy it when you..."

4. Communicate and Manage Conflict in the Partnership.

Both you and your partner are intelligent people with a lot of spunk and opinions. That strength naturally creates conflict.

Perhaps you and your spouse grew up arguing and enjoy the challenge or are afraid of conflict and avoid it or distance yourself when you feel attacked. Your arguments often end with nothing resolved and anger on both sides. Agree to practice fight management skills as you institute some rules. The guidelines apply to managing all of your communication more effectively, but they especially apply to conflict resolution.

Stick to the topic. Perhaps you have the habit of switching topics when you're losing. Sometimes one topic suggests another, but it is extremely confusing to get two or three going at once.

Pick your battles and develop your timing. Some things are not worth fighting about. If you have seven points of contention, pick your top two. Otherwise, in your nit-picking, you will not be heard when you really need to make a point. Choose carefully the things you cannot live with and accept—make a stand only on those items. Be strategic in timing your conversations and conflict. Don't sit on your feelings, but avoid times when you are extremely hungry, angry, or tired.

Remain courteous. Increased volume, power struggles, score keeping, and blaming "you" language are extremely ineffective. Passive withdrawal or aggressive attacking is discourteous and can create a negative atmosphere.

Set limits. Know when to stop, even if it means to agree to disagree for now. From midnight to 3:00 A.M. is seldom a productive time. You and your mate know when conflict has become counterproductive or is escalating out of control—stop right then! Remember to include humor and to include a short bathroom or snack break now and then. These help both of you keep your perspective and limit angry intensity.

Reconcile the relationship. Reconciling is different from agreeing or compromising on the issues of your fight; it is not letting "the sun go down on your wrath" (Eph. 4:26 NKJV). It is amazing what you can accomplish by saying, "I'm sorry you're upset,"

"I really do love you," or "Forgive me." Somehow, in the midst of conflict, they stick in your throat, but if you can apologize and affirm your love, these words have a soothing and healing effect. Humility and gentleness go a long way in managing conflict. Remember, your relationship is much more than this one fight.

Negotiate tentative solutions. The purpose of conflict and confrontation is to resolve differences, not to win or make your point. You and your spouse need to mutually seek tentative solutions and compromises. This may be to agree to disagree, or to put the issue on hold. It could be a behavioral solution negotiated around each mate's needs and feelings, a solution both are willing to try to implement. Don't just drop the argument—seek a tentative solution.

Practice exercise. Start working through one at a time the emotionally loaded topics in the sexual area of your relationship, those that have produced ineffective fights in the past. Both of you keep a list of the communication management skills in front of you. Set a limit of forty-five minutes to confront the topic. Practice sticking to the topic and remaining courteous as you work your way through to tentative solutions. Stop at forty-five minutes per session. Be courageous and wise as you look at tough areas (e.g., sex during the wife's period, managing the children, language you don't like, more spontaneity, birth control, and so on). Practice your active listening skills and give validating summaries of the content, feelings, and needs.

The Language of Lovemaking

Sex is a difficult, taboo topic. Couples can often make love more easily than they can talk about it. Assertively asking for what they need does not come easily for many people, especially in the sexual arena. Sexual problems and sexual ignorance, with unresolved anger and hurt, can also impede sexual communication. Each partnership needs erotic communication.

Vocabulary and Slang

Before getting into sexual vocabulary in general, let me comment about male and female slang. If the male genital slang is not funny, it is aggressive and harsh. The female slang, if not demeaning, is silly and suggestive. This is a sad and destructive distortion of God's gift of sexuality. Christians need to reclaim sex from the world and bring back to making love the beauty and joy that God intended. Slang is certainly an area where we can practice not buying into sinful, destructive values.

In developing a sexual vocabulary, you may be wondering if slang is ever appropriate. Of course, slang is permissible and fun and erotic. Your pet names for body parts and secret vocabulary shared by only the two of you contain a lot of slang. And as a couple you will find other words expressive and arousing. As Christians, however, we must be careful to avoid the very negative attitudes and ideas about sex that society over the centuries has incorporated into slang. We never want to be funny, aggressive, demeaning, silly, or suggestive.

The renowned semanticist S. I. Hayakawa said all language and words are symbols and we give them their meaning and impact. That is especially true of slang. Remember two points as you keep your language within God's guidelines:

1. You have the necessity of building an erotic vocabulary so you can enjoy the gift of making love with the comfort and flair God desires.
2. The vocabulary must enhance the loving, exciting process of making love. Each partner should be able to associate the same symbolic meaning with the vocabulary as it becomes playful and arousing. If any language is demeaning, offensive, harmfully aggressive, or cheap to either mate, it should be avoided.

You should know the correct biological terms for parts of the human body. That is a good starting point. One woman grew up in a home where sex was never discussed. She and her husband had some very frustrating times in the early part of their marriage. She did not have an adequate vocabulary, and neither did he. He had picked up some slang from the locker room and peers, but that did not help. She was not orgasmic when they married and was given to yeast infections, but they couldn't comfortably discuss these problems.

Time Out . . .

1. Turn to chapter 3 and read out loud to each other some of the information on sexual parts as you repeat the correct biological terms to each other.
2. Have fun the next time you are making love by creating some pet names for activities and body parts. Tell your mate of two slang words you find exciting and two that you feel would decrease your sexual enjoyment and arousal.

The wife bought a book on becoming orgasmic and began becoming more comfortable with her body and sex in general. She learned exactly where her clitoris was and how it functioned. They both laughed as they practiced vocabulary together because they had never said many of the words aloud before.

Learn to converse openly about making love without shame or embarrassment, and talk during sex. Expand your vocabulary, and adapt slang that both of you enjoy.

Nonverbal Signals

Build up a fun and useful repertoire of nonverbal language. Experts speculate that anywhere from 65 to 95 percent of communication is nonverbal, so it is no wonder that great lovers master this aspect of connecting. Try not to mind read or assume; check out or establish some of the nonverbal signals verbally. Perhaps gentle pressure with a hand signals the desire to shift into another position. Groans, sighs, and exclamations may signal degrees of arousal and when to proceed to another phase of lovemaking. Nonverbal communication helps orchestrate a sex life that will grow ever more comfortable and meaningful.

Develop nonverbal signals that indicate your desire for sexual activity. Without allowing it to completely lose its subtlety, make sure the nonverbal vocabulary is accurate and obvious enough. It may be a passionate hug or kiss. Sometimes an amorous look or a soft kiss on the back of the neck is all it takes.

Nonverbal communication evolves with most lovers. Don't just use it as a signal to orchestrate—get excited and involved as you express and increase your arousal. It is difficult for most people to relax control and truly get excited, not only in sex but even on a roller coaster or at a ballgame. Give yourself permission to be uninhibited and make noises during sex. Groan, breathe loudly, exclaim in excitement, purr with pleasure, squeal with delight, and allow your nonverbal communication to be truly expressive.

Remember not to get lazy or assume or completely rely on your nonverbal communication. Some messages need to be verbally communicated and feedback exchanged. Lack of communication can become amusing. A wife finally disclosed to her husband, "I wish you wouldn't stick your tongue in my ear during lovemaking." The husband quickly retorted, "I thought that turned you on. Why didn't you say something two years ago?" She replied, "I liked it two years ago." People change, and a continuing verbal dialogue is irreplaceable for true sexiness to flourish in intimate companionship and love lives.

Time Out . . .

1. What are some of the nonverbal signals you currently enjoy in making love? Think of one area you would like to signal your partner better about nonverbally, and add it to your bag of techniques.

2. Make love this week, but agree ahead of time that you will make more noise than is usual for the two of you—exaggerate and enjoy it.

Love Talk

How much do you talk before sex? during sex? after sex? Talking really is a great way to enhance your sex life. One couple stumbled onto the importance of talk one night as they were making plans for their summer vacation. It was after the wife had become more adept with her sexual vocabulary, and both felt less inhibited about sex in general. They were working through plans to go to the Caribbean and spend a long-anticipated week in the islands. She had bought a cute bathing suit and, after modeling it for her husband, asked how he would like to take it off on some deserted beach. They then digressed into how much they were looking forward to time alone and some fun sex.

The husband related how seeing the hotel room and Jacuzzi in the travel brochure had made him excited as he fantasized being with her on that king-sized bed after some time in the Jacuzzi together. She remarked how wonderful it felt after sunbathing to lie on cool sheets, bodies entwined. She even found it erotic the way their bodies perspired while making love during the summertime. As they sat there talking about sex, they could see that both were becoming very aroused. The evening concluded with his slowly taking off her bathing suit in the bedroom and their having a very enjoyable sexual encounter.

Each of three areas of erotic communication—before, during, and after making love—has its unique excitement and sexual stimulation.

1. Love talk before. This couple discovered that just engaging in sexual talk made them feel closer, more comfortable with sex, and aroused. They made a special effort to include the topic of sex at least once a week in their discussions. They tuned in to conversation triggers (a television show, a new bathing suit, a joke) more readily and just talked about sex more.

They discussed why they, like many couples, had seemed in the past to unconsciously avoid communicating about sex. Some of it was a lack of vocabulary, and some of it might have been an unwillingness to take the risk to be that intimate with each other. They realized that they did not trust each other or feel comfortable enough to discuss relational and sexual topics. Their closeness grew as they discussed her insecure perfectionism and his feeling he could never make enough money to satisfy her. One weekend they jumped into the topic of his getting a vasectomy, with many raw nerves being exposed, but they came to a much better understanding of the needs and feelings of both.

In fantasizing about the Caribbean getaway, they got into another great type of before-sex talk: sharing fantasies! It is fun to enjoy before the fact some of the things you would like to do. Often it is crucial to creating the ambiance. They also took the time, as suggested elsewhere in this book, to relate to each other their ideal sexual encounter and to incorporate some of these ideas into their lovemaking. The less inhibited they became in their sexual talk, the more fun they had. It did not have to lead anywhere, either. It was enjoyable to get aroused some and then go on to another topic.

She started to tease more and make sexually suggestive comments like the one about the bathing suit and a deserted beach. He would tease her in turn. He would say things on the phone to her at her job, and she would laugh in delight but be a little embarrassed, as if somehow her officemates could read her mind. They might be at a friend's house waiting for them to answer the door, and he would surprise her with a sexual comment.

2. *Love talk during*. During sex, the idea is to relax and let the talk be free-flowing on what you are feeling and sensing. Sometimes you and your mate will be on a common theme, and at other times each will pursue personal images—both can be connecting and stimulating sexually. The wife might say, "You sure are hitting the right spot inside me." And the husband might reply, "You feel so good, I wish I could do this all night." Or the husband might go off on his own tangent: "I'm glad you're feeling excited. That dance you did to seduce me tonight was unbelievable."

During making love, you can also tease and talk about fantasies. This talk can be very erotic as both get into creating the mood. Tell your partner what you want and need sexually in a given session. If something pops into your mind that you two haven't tried in a while, bring it up and both may enter into the activity with gusto. Erotic communication has so much potential.

3. *Love talk after*. In chapter 4 we discussed the resolution phase of sexual activity: the time after each partner has been satisfied and bodies and genitals are returning to their normal state. It is a time that is important for couples to connect and enjoy an afterglow, but this resolution phase is fraught with pitfalls. Wives often need to empty the bladder and clean up, while husbands feel so relaxed that they can tend to roll over and go to sleep. Both can end up feeling frustrated and ruin the warm connecting that just occurred.

Time Out . . .

The next time you make love, try practicing a stream-of-consciousness flow of conversation—both of you keep up a running commentary on what you are feeling and sensing. It will be tremendously exciting.

It should be a time of talking and warm reminiscing, of talking and reaffirming your love for each other, of talking and appreciating how truly close you two have become. You are perhaps closest to the Garden of Eden at this time in your intimate connection—like Adam and Eve, during your lovemaking, you have become naked without any shame.

Take the time and energy to discuss with your partner what kind of affirmation and talking (and holding) would be special and affirming for you in the love talk after sex. It's a different kind of love talk, but it's so bonding. Don't neglect this afterglow time of nonverbal and verbal linking. Even a simple "you mean so much to me" takes on special significance during this vulnerable, united time. Wives especially feel vulnerable and need this affirmation because they have both physically and emotionally opened themselves up to their husbands.

Coaching

A wife may think that her husband is supposed to know all about sex. Or a couple may wonder why they are the only couple in the world whose sex life has not automatically fallen into place. After all, if making love is supposed to be such a natural thing, why are they struggling? The truth is that, like marriage in general, two unique male and female persons getting together will have differences. No matter how technically skilled they are, their sexual relationship will be a blending of two unique bodies and varying attitudes and needs.

Coaching is all about assertively expressing your sexual needs and feelings, learning to problem solve around difficult areas, and helping your mate understand you. All couples have to gain skills in coaching, whether it is initiating and refusing sex or encouraging what you enjoy. Like other aspects of communication, these skills don't come naturally. You can't immediately know exactly all the things that pleasure your partner. Throughout the years together, the stresses of life, the aging process, children, and many other issues will give you new reasons for readjusting your sex life.

This section considers three areas of making love that will need some coaching. First, how do you initiate and refuse sexual activity graciously, without feeling pressured or pouting? Second, how can you maximize your sex life by talking about what you need, what turns you on, and what turns you off? Finally, what are some pointers on problem solving so stressors and difficulties can be worked through with no lasting roadblocks to a great sex life?

Initiating and Refusing

Consider these comments:

- "My husband is so uncreative in the way he approaches me for sex."
- "Why is it that every time I turn him down, and it isn't that often, he pouts?"
- "I would love for my mate to be more aggressive in initiating sex."
- "I love my wife, but I'm not always instantly ready to make love like she expects."

All successful lovers have to polish initiating and refusing. No couple is immune from some misunderstandings in this area of sexual communication and attitudes.

Think a minute about what is at stake that makes initiating and refusing become so symbolic and filled with disappointments and hurt feelings. First, initiating and refusing make one vulnerable to rejection and feelings of abandonment. Second, ineffective initiating attempts can make a person feel pushed, controlled, and treated like a sexual object. Third, much of initiating is nonverbal and therefore open to misinterpretation. Fourth, initiating, or the lack thereof, becomes synonymous with sexual desire and sexual appeal. Fifth, initiating or refusing sex means coordinating two unique people with different needs and priorities on a given day or hour.

No wonder this is a loaded topic that must be discussed with both partners open to coaching! Great lovers take the time and energy to understand their mates and make changes.

Time Out . . .

Switch roles. Take your mate's place, and demonstrate how you would like your mate to initiate and refuse. Remember you are not yourself but living in your mate's reality. Keep your partner's needs and attitudes in mind as you model initiating and refusing. In this positive way coach your mate on the things you appreciate and the things you would like to be eliminated. Practice both nonverbal and verbal techniques as you smooth the process and make it honest and loving.

Maximizing

In your sex life there are some things your mate does that really turn you on and others that really turn you off. You have to tell your partner what you want and what you dislike, including specific behaviors and attitudes that are appreciated or get in the way. You want to maximize your sex life? Talk! Emphasize and practice the positive!

Here are some important guidelines for giving helpful suggestions as you coach your mate and maximize your sex life:

1. Major coaching should be done fully clothed as you dialogue about your sex life; subjects could be poor hygiene, inhibitions, boredom, pushiness, and/or technique deficits.

2. Minor adjusting needs comfortable nonverbal and verbal language that can be done nonthreateningly. For example, you might say, "That hurts. Slow down. More. Shift."

3. Keep your coaching adult-to-adult as you teach without becoming parental or condescending. Stay humble and self-confident as you listen to criticism. Allow yourself to be in a nondefensive learning mode, and create dialogue. This is a partnership.

4. Potentiate the positive! The primary goal of coaching is not to correct what's wrong—it is to maximize the strengths, bring the best out of the players, and create a winning combination.

5. Great coaching employs many methods: demonstrate by doing it on yourself or guiding your mate's hand, dialogue and exchange data, buy books and use them as your assistant coaches, go to a sex therapist, and start with small changes.

6. Know thyself! Acquire wisdom! It is tough coaching if you are not sure what you need or want. Read; experiment; give yourself permission to be uninhibitedly sexual as you become truly self-aware. Great coaches know their sport.

Roadblocks

Quite often a couple feel that they are the only ones whose sex life isn't easy and effortless. However, probably 60 percent of couples have had some kind of sexual difficulty in the past year. Any normal marriage will encounter roadblocks to making love. It may be a lack of desire, temporary impotence, conflict around frequency, an inability to let go of control, problems reaching a climax, or an unresolved affair.

All the things you have already read about sexual communication especially apply to roadblocks. You can't sweep them under the rug because they won't go away. They can be embarrassing to discuss, and they are emotionally loaded. Communication skills really count now. Choose a setting where there is plenty of time and privacy. Keep clarifying the message as you focus and really try to understand your mate's needs and feelings. Detach from your anger and fear as you listen and validate your partner's assertive sharing of what is happening. Get a dialogue going.

Time Out . . .

Practice this assignment frequently. Fully clothed, sit with your lover and discuss what modifications you would like to make in your sex life. Be specific, and explain what you wish your mate would do more and less of. Arrange a time for a lovemaking session in which you institute and practice one mate's suggestions and a separate time for the other's suggestions. Be sure to use the six ideas for maximizing your sex life.

You may need some professional help, but first read an appropriate chapter in this book or another that deals with your problem and start talking. Sexual communication has some marvelous healing capacities. A central part of most sexual difficulties is anxiety (fears, worry, guilt) or anger (irritation, disappointment, disrespect, hostility). Talking about the difficulty and acknowledging its impact keep lovers from being so anxious and avoiding sex. The fear and guilt of impotence or climaxing too slowly can cause partners to wonder if it will happen again with each lovemaking session. Talking it through encourages enjoyment of the moment instead of panic.

Anger and disappointment can quickly distance lovers as hurt and disrespect grow. It is painful and tough at times, but there is no substitute for talking through the difficulty. This is true of an affair, a partner's ineptitude or inhibition, or any other problem. Talking defuses the tension, creates understanding and acceptance, and promotes changes. Yes, it may take professional assistance from a sex or marital therapist, but start with your own honest, open dialogue.

Time Out . . .

Pick a roadblock in your sexual relationship, and do some reading and research on the problem. Rehearse in your mind what you would like to say, and choose a strategic time for this discussion. Talk!

Great lovers have to be able to communicate. Don't forget the list of necessary communication skills and the importance of dialogue found at the beginning of this chapter.

Husbands and wives, especially husbands, need to take responsibility to learn effective communication skills. Develop a great sexual vocabulary, and enjoy erotic communication. Talk before, during, and after you make love as you enhance the entire experience. God has given you a wonderful aphrodisiac in your ability to communicate!

Chapter Nine

Sensuous Massage

This book stresses the importance of building a loving, nurturing relationship for lovemaking to flourish. Massage is a marvelous way to accomplish the goal of feeling connected and deepening your intimate companionship.

Massage has been shown to have profound effects on both the one giving the massage as well as the person receiving. It reduces stress, blood pressure goes down, and a relaxed, comfortable, nurturing atmosphere is encouraged within the friendship.

In this chapter you first learn an exercise called *sensate focus*, which is sensual touching for your personal pleasure. The following three sections explain and demonstrate sensuous massage with helpful illustrations: how to set the stage for massage, basic techniques to get you started, and massage on various parts of the body from face to feet with ways to increase the sensuous pleasure as you apply these techniques. The last section details ways to utilize massage as you incorporate it into more intimate stroking.

Sensate Focus

In chapter 3 we talked about sensate focus as a means of exploring erogenous zones. Remember what a marvelous gift God has given you with your skin and its sensory nerve endings? If you can learn to relax, get comfortable with touching and being touched, and focus on your sensual feelings, you can embark on a wonderful journey of pleasure and bonding. Your ability to enjoy touching can be the foundation for enriching your marriage and creating some fantastic lovemaking.

Sensate focus develops the art of sensual touching. It is often a prescribed part of sex therapy because it takes the focus off performing and places it on mutual sharing and sensuality. Sensate focus and massage will enhance your ability as a lover to be sensual and to give and receive nurturing touch. It also is very bonding and increases a shared sense of partnership and intimacy.

In this exercise, both partners are nude, and the temperature is controlled to a comfortable setting. The active partner is in charge of setting the ambiance (music, lighting, etc.) and choosing the place. The bed (in massage the bed is too soft and giving) is excellent for enjoying this experience of sensuality and touch. Do not touch the genitals or breasts as you learn to enjoy the whole body. This is a sensual as well as an erotic activity. To make this easy and comfortable to include in your repertoire of intimate activities, block out two fifteen-minute sessions in a week, and each of you be the active partner once. Sometimes you may wish to block out thirty minutes and each take the role of giver and receiver.

Mates will have to be able to assume two different roles as they enjoy the experience of sensate focus. To relax and revel in sensuality, do not have intercourse or manual stimulation of the genitals for the remainder of the day after sensate focus. Focus on touch and its sensual, erogenous nature.

The Active Toucher

The active mate touches the passive partner in ways that feel good to the toucher. This touching is oriented toward individual pleasure and sensuality, not attending to the partner. The toucher focuses only on personal feelings and enjoyment of the mate's body. There are no performance needs.

Experiment with a variety of touches and strokes on any area other than genitals and breasts. It is often helpful to start with the touchee lying on the stomach. Begin at the top of the head and slowly work your way down to the feet. Have the passive partner roll over, and work from the feet to the head. It is best to not have any communication at this point but to revel in individual sensations. If you are aware of areas of the body that your partner does not like to have touched, in love and respect stay away from these areas.

The Passive Touchee

The touchee lies passively and allows the active partner to touch the body. Often the touches that pleasure the active toucher give stimulation and pleasure to the passive mate, too. The passive partner can increase self-awareness by noticing which areas and types of touching give the greatest pleasure. These can be asked for and repeated while making love at a different time. The touchee is also learning about the lover— what kind of touching and strokes the toucher usually enjoys to give and receive.

Don't confine your touching when you are the active partner by this information. Do your active touching for yourself.

You will find this a very bonding and warmly connecting exercise. In other chapters, you have explored the need to get beyond performance and to selfishly delight in sensuality for yourself. Sensate focus will do this in marvelous ways.

Setting the Stage for Massage

Tools

There really are few preparations or necessary items other than some oil and a quiet, warm place to lie during the massage.

Oils. Natural oils like coconut, sesame, safflower, almond, soya, or avocado work well. Some natural oils like olive, peanut, or corn oil can be too thick and don't spread or absorb as easily. Adding some scent to these oils or buying already scented oil can add to this sensuous experience. Be sure to warm both the oil and your hands before applying. Use only enough oil so the hands move smoothly over the skin—don't saturate to a greasy feel. Two types of containers work well for storing the oil during the massage. You can put it in a shallow bowl and dip your hand in it. Even better perhaps is a plastic squeeze bottle that allows you to control the amount and won't spill if it turns over. You can place the oil on the skin and massage it in, or you can squeeze some on the back of your hand and massage it in while maintaining your rhythm.

Table or mat. A bed does not work well because it is too soft and will prevent firm, even pressure. If you have a table that comes to your upper thigh, find a mat or foam rubber or use blankets and towels to put over it.

You may not have a table of about thirty inches in height but don't let that be a roadblock. Put a mat or blankets and towels on the floor. You can get a mat or a piece of foam at a sporting goods store and create a comfortable pallet. Place a pillow under your knees to soften the floor as you give the massage.

Movements

Be sure to remove your jewelry and warm your hands. Massage is lovingly nurturing your mate's body, and these are common courtesies to enhance the experience. You may want to buy a flannel sheet to drape the parts of the body you are not massaging. Keep towels handy to roll up under the neck or other areas that need support.

Rhythms. A soothing and sensuous massage should maintain a smooth and even rhythm with strokes that flow into one another. It should have a relaxing, almost hypnotic, effect. One technique for accomplishing this is trying to always have at least one hand on the body at all times. You will become more adept as you practice. Don't worry, it will feel great regardless. As you practice, a natural rhythm will come more easily.

Pressure. A common mistake is thinking that massage, to be effective, must always be firm. Vary the pressure. Sometimes a light stroke or a hand lying on a body part will start nerves and skin to tingling and will feel very sensuous. The reason the table should come to upper thigh is that the pressure in massage should be given by leaning your body weight into the person—not straining your back or shoulder muscles. It is helpful to face the way you are stroking and be able to move around the person as you go from legs to back to abdomen.

Breathing and relaxation. Massage should be a stress reliever, both physically and mentally. Put on some relaxing music, and dim the lights. It helps to practice diaphragmatic breathing for stress management: draw deep breaths clear into your stomach and gently let them out. You can practice diaphragmatic breathing by resting a hand on your partner's stomach as your partner breathes deeply and slowly, causing your hand to rise and fall. The one giving the massage also needs to breathe deeply and be relaxed; the goal is to avoid communicating stress and tenseness. You will be amazed how relaxed you feel after giving a massage if you allow yourself to calm down and get into the sensuous flow. Slow down your mind and choose to focus on the sensuous massage rather than everything you need to be doing. This is a marvelous gift God has given you: you can mentally choose to relax and tune out the world's worries for a time.

Sequences. You will establish some sequences that will feel good to you and your mate. This chapter starts with the back and shoulders, then moves to feet and legs, then hands, abdomen, chest, and face. Because of time limitations, you may wish to do mini-massages in which you do shoulders and face, or you may wish to focus on the lower and upper back. Sometimes it will be meaningful and relaxing to stick to one part of the anatomy like feet or face. Create different sequences that connect and relax you as a couple. A full body massage could take at least an hour, so you will have to adapt your massage to accommodate your time schedule.

If there is a problem with sensitivity or ticklishness, try a firmer touch. If that doesn't work, move on to a less ticklish part; often you can come back later. The person being massaged often finds that the ticklishness is more mental and will go away as relaxation increases. Massage not only helps a person relax and enjoy a very sensuous experience but also is very beneficial healthwise. Massage accelerates the flow of blood in the body without straining the heart. The blood removes the waste from muscles and tissues and can promote healing and physical well-being.

Basic Techniques of Massage

Massage is not complex. This section develops basic movements that you will need to master to pleasure and relax your mate. Many other techniques of massage are simply variations. We will demonstrate on the back and arm so you can practice quite easily as you learn.

Stroking

You will use stroking the most in your massage as you glide your hands over the skin with modified pressure. You will use this technique often (e.g., applying oil) in a simple stroking motion as you rub an area with fingertips or entire hands. Remember the importance of a steady rhythm in which you vary the pressure and speed of the movements. Here are seven variations of stroking motions.

1. Fan stroking.

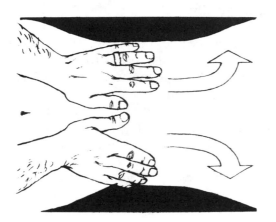

Start with hands together and move them upward, applying pressure with palms and heels as you lean into stroke.

Maintain gentle pressure as you mold hands to body and slide them up abdomen and lower back.

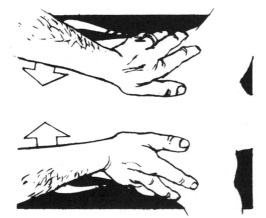

Fan hands out and lessen pressure as you glide them down and around the sides.

With light pressure move hands back into position to begin stroke again.

2. Circle stroking.

Make a continuous circular motion with hands rotating in a wide curve with firmer pressure on upward stroke.

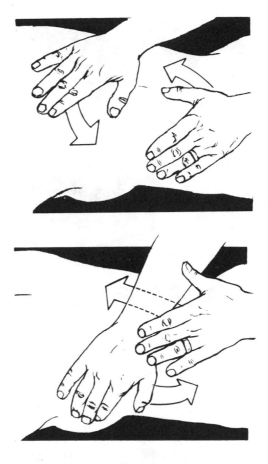

One hand does a complete circle, and the other hand crosses over in a half circle.

3. Alternate stroking.

One hand strokes upward while the other hand glides downward in alternating motions—the upward stroke can be firmer as you vary pressure.

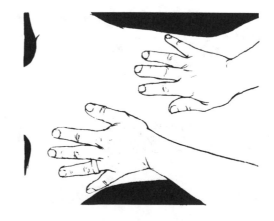

4. Sequential stroking.

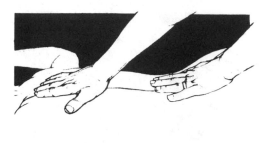

Stroke one hand soothingly down the area, followed immediately by the other in a rhythmic, pawing sequence as you lift the lower hand and begin again. Try with very light pressure as well as firmer.

5. Thumb stroking.

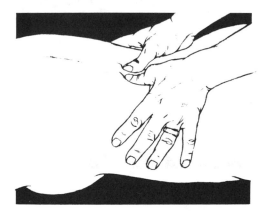

Place the thumbs on the side of the spine and slowly move them up and back down with firm, even pressure.

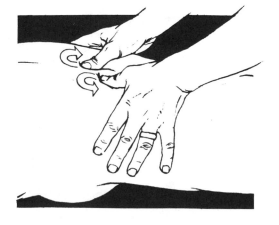

Apply pressure on an area with only the thumbs in small, firm circular movements.

Stroke upward with one thumb and fan outward as you begin stroking upward a little higher with the other thumb and fan outward, repeating sequence up the limb.

6. *Friction stroking.*

Circle leg with hands placed side by side and create friction with firm pressure and alternating hand strokes.

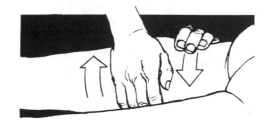

7. *Brush stroking.*

With fingertips or entire hand sensitize the skin by *very* lightly brushing an area of the body—often used at end of massaging a given part of body.

Kneading

Kneading is a technique that you can use on larger areas (the soft tissue of the lower back) as well as smaller fleshy areas (shoulders, thighs, and calves). It is much like kneading dough and relaxes muscles as it stimulates blood circulation. You can vary the pressure and rate of kneading as you wish to get deeper muscles or just sensuously stimulate the skin.

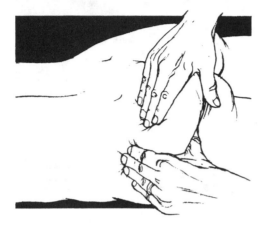

Place hands on area and squeeze and roll the flesh between the thumb and fingers of one hand as the other hand and fingers apply pressure.

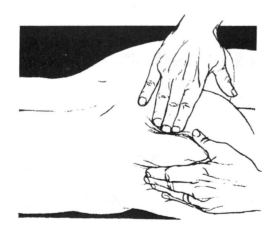

Glide the hand grasping the flesh toward the pressure of the other hand. Release; grasp the flesh with the other hand as you repeat motion with that hand. Rhythmically squeeze, push, and release as you knead with alternating hands.

Knuckling

In this technique the knuckles apply small circular strokes and create a pleasant rippling effect. This stroke is effective on back, shoulders, and chest. It can also be enjoyed on the palms of the hands or soles of the feet.

Curl your fingers into loose fists, keeping the middle joint of the fingers against the skin. Now ripple your fingers around in small circular motions.

Pummeling

The important part of this technique, whether you are using a loose fist or relaxed hand, is to use bouncy motions and not strike the flesh. Pull your hand away as soon as it touches the skin so there is no bruising pressure. It helps to keep the wrists loose and hands and fingers relaxed so you can hear them slapping together. The motion should be brisk as you rapidly stimulate. Sometimes pummeling might be better reserved for the end of the massage, though it can be relaxing if done more gently. It is great for fleshy areas like the back or thighs where there are heavier muscles.

Relax wrists and hands and apply brisk, alternating movements with your hands in a light, bouncy motion.

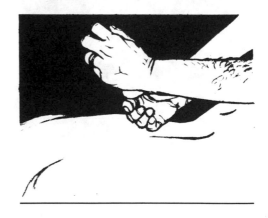

Passive Touching

You don't always have to be actively stroking or massaging a body area. Simply placing a hand on a spot as the partner's body feels the warmth or pressure (if applied) really feels good as tissue is stimulated by the passive touch. Passive touch also includes pulling or rotating a part of the body to loosen up and exercise joints without actively stroking.

1. Pressure.

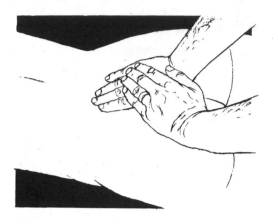

Place your hands over the tailbone area and leave them there lightly for thirty seconds—now lean into your hands with pressure but no movement.

2. Lifting, pulling, and rotating.

Lift your partner's arm up and down several times and gently pull up on it; now slowly rotate it in a circular motion several times and hold it a few seconds and then lay it down.

Sensuous Massage for Areas of the Body

Let's now look at areas of the body where you can bring tension release and sensuous pleasure to your mate with massage. The illustrations include a variety of techniques, but use your creativity as you improvise and create your own sequences. You won't believe what this sensuous nurturing will do for your friendship and love life. As you conclude the massage on each area, gently caress that area and hold your hands there a few seconds to seal the nurturing of that part.

Back Massage

1. Fan stroking.

Begin with hands on lower back with thumbs on each side of spinal cord. Apply firm pressure as you move upward and fan out to shoulders. Squeeze firmly and stroke down over sides and back to spinal column.

2. Kneading.

Begin with fleshy area of lower right side and knead up and include shoulder. Move over to left shoulder and knead down the left side and work across the buttocks area and back to right lower back.

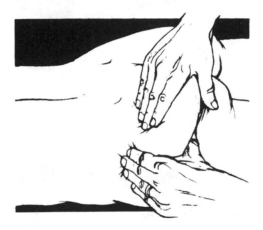

3. Passive touching.

Place hands over kidneys as partner feels warmth and tingling. Put one hand on tailbone and the other on spinal column under shoulder blades and gently press. Position heels of hands next to spinal column and press. Work your way up to neck—gently applying pressure every few inches. Leave hands over kidney area for a few seconds.

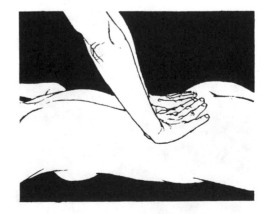

4. Pummeling.

Lightly begin pummeling with loose fists the fleshy area of back on either side of spinal column and the entire shoulder area.

5. Circle stroking.

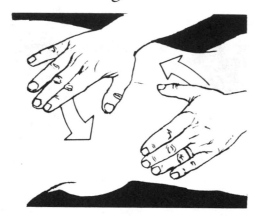

Start with broad circle strokes on upper back and work your way down. Do smaller circles as you thoroughly massage both left and right sides. Remember to lightly caress entire area and gently leave hands on middle of back for a minute to gently seal the nurturing.

Foot Massage

1. Stroking.

Do one foot at a time. Grasp it firmly as you stroke it from ankle to heel and down arch to toes. Hold foot with both hands and do thumb strokes on back of foot—stroke between the tendons and up over arch and around base of ankle.

2. Toe massage.

Grasp toes with hand and wiggle
and bend them. Massage each
toe separately; gently squeeze and
pull each toe. Hold the toes
between hands and rub rapidly.

3. Passive touching.

Grasp ankle and with the other
hand manipulate foot. Hold
foot and apply pressure with
thumbs at various points of the
arch.

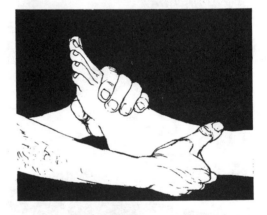

4. Knuckling.

Place one hand over the top of foot
and knuckle the arch from heel
up to toes. Gently caress and hold
foot a minute. Go to other
foot.

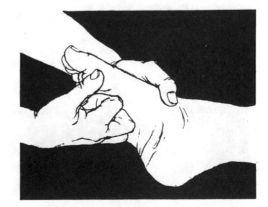

Leg Massage

1. Stroking.

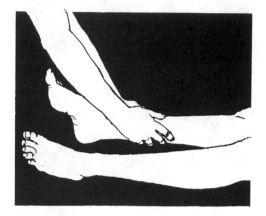

Begin at ankle, and using an alternating stroke, go up sides of left leg. Then repeat on right leg. Now with one hand having fingertips on shin and the other grasping calf, apply alternating friction strokes as you encircle and work up calf and thigh.

2. Pummeling.

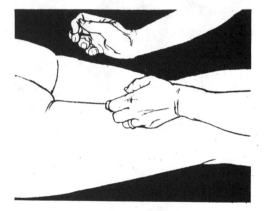

With partner on stomach, begin pummeling calf and work your way up to thigh. Carefully work on the upper thighs and buttocks area in a rapid motion.

3. Passive touching.

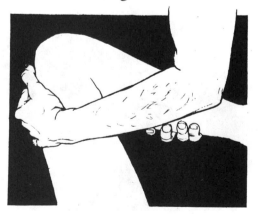

Have partner lie on back and place one hand under calf and the other palm on thigh as you softly apply pressure on calf and thigh. Lift leg and manipulate the knee and the hip joint with lifting and rotating.

4. *Thumb stroking.*

Grasp knee with both hands and carefully massage with thumbs, using thumbs in small circle strokes to deeply massage. Try the same stroke on upper thigh as you squeeze with hands, lightly caress entire leg, and gently hold calf and then thigh for a minute.

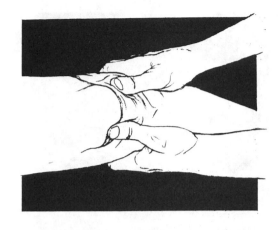

Hand Massage

1. *Thumb stroking.*

Lock your little fingers under thumb and little finger of partner's hand and massage palm from fingers to wrist thoroughly with thumbs.

2. *Finger massage.*

Grasp and stroke each finger as you also rotate and lightly pull. Take your index finger and thumb and rub at base of each finger and thumb.

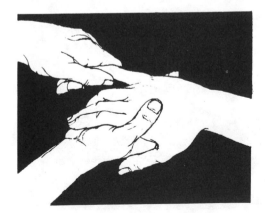

3. Passive touching.

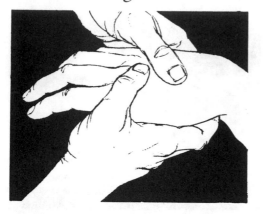

Holding arm just above wrist, manipulate and bend each finger and the wrist. Then grasp the hand between your hands and press and release and press several times.

4. Thumb kneading.

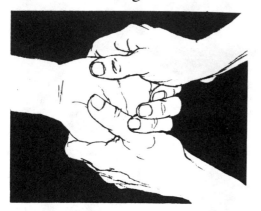

Focus on your partner's thumbs as you grasp and knead the fleshy palm and work your way up to joints. Gently tug thumb back. Conclude by caressing and holding hand between yours.

Abdomen Massage

1. Circle stroking.

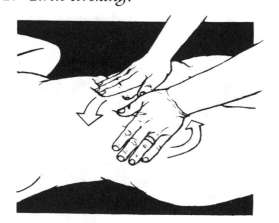

Start with circular stroking using the navel as center point and gently sweep in larger clockwise circles around the entire abdomen area, lapping over the sides.

2. Kneading.

Place yourself beside your partner. Start with the hip away from you and knead up the side to ribs, then work across upper abdomen and down side closest to you to hip and knead across lower abdomen. On areas of lesser flesh use fingers and thumb to knead in lighter fashion.

3. Passive touching.

Maneuver so you can place heels of hands on hip bones with fingertips touching and gently press on abdomen. Reach under back with fingers meeting on spine and gently press up. Go back to abdomen and press gently and relax and press again.

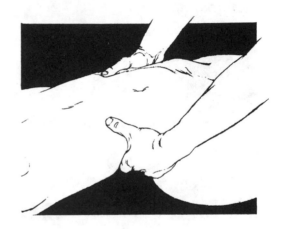

4. Sequential stroking.

One hand follows the other as you start stroking on the sides with long movements up over navel to other side. Change sides and repeat with a smooth rhythm. Conclude with caressing abdomen area, placing hands softly on stomach for a few seconds.

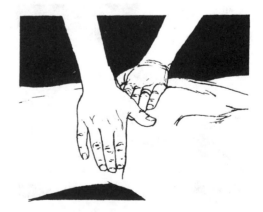

Chest and Neck Massage

1. Fan stroking.

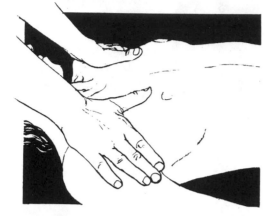

Position yourself behind head and place hands below collarbone. Press down chest, then fan across pectoral muscles to shoulders and bring fingers with pressure up back of shoulders and neck and back to original place. Repeat.

2. Knuckling.

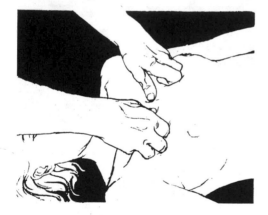

Using knuckling stroke, ripple muscles of chest and shoulders and back of shoulders and around back of neck.

3. Passive touching.

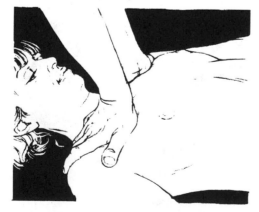

Place palms of hands on shoulders with fingers under shoulders and press down. Release and press. Gently hold head by placing hands at base of skull, and slowly without jerking, put traction by pulling on head, then rotate while neck is loose.

4. *Alternate stroking.*

Begin alternate stroking on chest
and work around to shoulders
and then back of neck and back
of shoulders. Conclude by
caressing entire area and resting
hands on upper chest for a
few seconds.

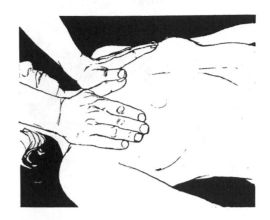

Face Massage

1. Stroking.

Take your hands and softly stroke
and cup the entire face—
reaching under the jaw, over the
cheeks, down the nose, and
across forehead and eyes.

2. Stroking with fingertips.

Do small circles with both hands
using fingertips on temples,
jaw, base of skull, and carefully
around eyes and forehead.

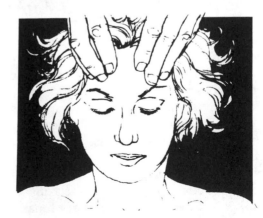

3. Passive touching.

With hands cupping face, gently press on temple area. Rest fingertips on eyes. Press on forehead with one hand over the other.

4. Alternate stroking.

Place hands on cheeks and do alternate stroking as you loosen mouth and stroke up into hairline and down to tip of jaw. Conclude by caressing face and gently cupping it between hands for a few seconds.

Massage to Enhance Lovemaking

Massage will help you as a couple feel more sensuous and close. By its very relaxing and nurturing nature, it will be an aphrodisiac to your sex life. Massage can't help teaching you to be more gentle and sensitive lovers and bring you as one-flesh companions into a more bonded, caring, and stress-free relationship.

Here are some suggestions for applying the massage techniques you are mastering to more erogenous loveplay. Please keep in mind that you can destroy the soothing, sensuous experience of massage if you keep it too erotically charged. Overall, let the occasional surges of sexual feelings that come with such an intimate activity be enjoyed but not acted upon. That is why it may be wise to strategically drape your partner's body as you focus on relaxing and nurturing. Designate the times when the massage will be a prelude or part of making love and when it will be separate.

In the following activities use plenty of warmed oil because the massage will be on tender areas of the body. All focus on nongenital erogenous zones and may be activities you choose to do in beginning loveplay as you increase arousal. Making love to your mate's body is such an exciting and varied process. Massage emphasizes this fact in fun and sensual ways.

Circular Sensuality

Begin a gentle, circular stroking of the chest area, starting at the collarbone and shoulder area. Use both hands in a wide circular motion. Slowly, an inch at a time, lower the circle and massage down over the abdomen, over the pubic area, until the movements are circling the genital area with the top end of the circle on the pubic bone and the lower end over the thighs. Now start the circle moving back up to the upper chest again. This can be very arousing visually and sensually as you allow your hands to follow the contours of the body with fingers and palms lightly caressing. Don't linger on nipples or genital area—just keep rhythmic sensual motions.

Kneading

Have your partner lie on the stomach, and begin with a kneading motion on the left thigh, starting at the knee and working up over the buttocks area to the lower back. Now sensuously knead the right thigh in the same fashion. Have your partner roll over, and knead from knee to pelvic bone. Do this softly, but squeeze the flesh in a full way that manipulates the thigh and genital area as you knead.

Intimate Fan Stroking

Have your partner lie on the stomach, and stand (if your partner is on a table) or kneel between your partner's legs facing the buttocks. Begin with the palms of the hands on the calf of the back of one leg (slightly shaded toward the inner part of the leg) and fingers pointing upward toward the buttocks. Slowly push up with the heel of the palm in a firm stroke and do a fan motion with your fingers up over the legs to outer side and back down. Slowly work your way up the thighs toward the buttocks an inch or two at a time as you repeat the fan motion until the top of the stroke is fanning gently down over the outer abdomen and hip area. Do the other leg.

Sensual Stroking

Sit or stand beside your partner, who is lying on the stomach, and do a sequential stroke beginning at the left knee and working your way up almost in a wavelike motion—gently stroking at the inner thigh in a hand-over-hand sensuous rhythm that is relaxing and erotically arousing. You can continue this sequential stroking in a sideways fashion up over the buttocks area and the back. Switch to right side and come back down to the knee. Have your partner roll over. Begin at the top of the chest and work down the side of the body over the abdomen, pubic area, and inner thighs. Switch sides and repeat from thighs up to chest. (Try this with knuckling for a different sensation.)

Skin Tingles

Have your partner lie on the stomach. Start at the base of the skull with one hand and slowly move it, hardly touching the skin, in one continuous brush stroke down the body to the ankles and very softly back up, conforming to the contours of the body. Repeat several times going down the right and left sides of the body. Now with fingertips, lightly stroke all over the body as the skin tingles.

Have your mate roll over on the back. Do small circular motions lightly with both hands over the whole body from face to feet for several minutes. Hardly touch the skin with very light strokes on chest, breasts, abdomen, shoulders, thighs, legs, hands—the whole front of the body. This exercise is very sensually arousing and can awaken and stimulate the skin. Finish by lightly stroking with the fingertips.

Let massage be another way of enjoying your one-flesh companionship. Don't get too technical but practice enough to become comfortable. You may wish to buy a whole book on massage and learn more specific ways to relax and stimulate various parts of the body. You may want to go to a bookstore, look over what is available, and pick one that meets your needs. Great lovers have mastered the art of sensuous touching. Massage is a marvelous way to develop that skill as you relieve stress and grow more intimately connected to your mate in the process.

Chapter Ten

♡

Making Love with Clothes On

Many couples earnestly search for a deeper intimacy in their marriage. They wish longingly to feel more in love and recapture some of the passion of their dating days. If only they could be playful soul mates and enjoy a fun companionship. Making love, of all marital activities, should be a powerful agent in creating this type of intimate bonding.

What happens to sabotage lovemaking so it doesn't create this loving closeness? I think the biggest culprit is that married partners forget the important concept of making love with their clothes on. In an exciting, intertwining way, sex should permeate the whole marital relationship. Perhaps the word *foreplay* should be banned. *Loveplay* more aptly describes what God intended for couples who are sexually bonding. It does not depend on having your clothes off and reaching a climax. Making love is so much more than intercourse.

In the Song of Solomon the wife speaks about her mate and making love in a beautifully poetic fashion:

> His mouth is most sweet,
> Yes, he is altogether lovely.
> This is my beloved,
> And this is my friend. . . .
> My beloved has gone to his garden,
> To the beds of spices,

To feed his flock in the gardens,
And to gather lilies.
I am my beloved's,
And my beloved is mine (5:16; 6:2–3 NKJV).

Kissing, cuddling, and giving long romantic looks with some lily gathering should be daily or even hourly activities as you keep your mate present in your thoughts and life.

Time Out . . .

Put a bookmark in your place, and after reading this exercise, lay this book down a few minutes. Close your eyes and get comfortable. Allow your imagination to take you back in time to when you first met and were getting to know and love your mate. Remember some of your first dates and times alone together. Recall your feelings and the many things that initially attracted you to each other. Fantasize about some of those early sexual feelings. Recollect and re-create those times when you intimately bonded with your clothes on and it had nothing to do with genital sexuality.

The goal of this chapter is to help you feel a deeper sense of intimate companionship as you learn to make love as a total part of your relationship. It reviews the important concept of pair bonding and the need to be sexually complex and balanced. A genital focus can be impoverishing to a fun love life. It then describes and encourages a sexual celebration for two that is not centered on the goal of intercourse. Creative techniques for erotic fun with clothes on close out the chapter.

When you were dating and putting your best foot forward, you abandoned your defenses and allowed yourself to be intimate and uninhibited. You may feel uncomfortable with the deep kind of intimacy encouraged in this chapter. In order to really feel in love and sexually alive, you will have to let down your walls and defenses and need for control all over again. This type of intimacy requires trusting and being vulnerable and living joyfully in the present moment.

Pair Bonding

Loveplay and intimate bonding are a great prescription for your sex life. Forget about intercourse and some of your other favorite sexual focuses. Create some alone time with your partner. Fix some popcorn, put on some music, sit on the couch with your sweetheart, and let yourself be transported back in time to your courting days. Recapture some of the magic of those days when just looking into each other's eyes and holding hands was a spiritual experience with a physical rush of feelings. Remember when you made love for hours with little or no physical touch and your souls communed.

Sociologist Desmond Morris addressed this important concept and process in his book *Intimate Behaviour* and called it *pair formation* or *pair bonding*. He observed humans in their courting behaviors and saw a process that often included all or most of twelve separate steps. Each step is progressively different and important. The needs of an initial step cannot be met by skipping ahead to another. Lovers often hope that genital to genital will instantly create intimacy. They fail to realize, to their great detriment, that intimate bonding is indeed a process.

I have taken the concept of pair bonding and applied it to the sexual enrichment of a marriage and the importance of making love with clothes on. Even though intercourse is an important part of married love, mates need to continually incorporate each of the twelve steps. Here is a simple summary from Desmond Morris's work of these important steps that can help you build or recapture a deeper romance and intimacy:*

12 Steps of Pair Bonding

Eye to body. Our senses feed our minds information about another person. This includes sexual information, but it is a more total observation. We sort and assess this information as we define attractiveness. We sum up and ponder in our mind the personal and physical qualities that are appealing to us.

Eye to eye. People usually watch one another privately and do not directly look at each other, or into each other's eyes. Strangers will often break eye contact because this is an invasion of privacy. A friendly smile or an inviting look is often the beginning of more intimate contact. The old song "Drink to me only with thine eyes" emphasizes a crucial bonding behavior.

Voice to voice. Often initial verbal contact is quite casual but furthers the bonding process. The connecting conversation allows more information to be exchanged. Accents, tones of voice, vocabularies, and styles of communication and thinking all give data to the pair becoming intimately involved.

Hand to hand. Hand to hand or arm may be more of a supportive behavior at first as one person assists the other out of a car or lightly supplies directional guidance. It may be a disguised intimacy and lead to more hand-holding if there is a mutual inclination and desire for closeness. Both partners are aware that this is symbolic of a bonding sequence that may in time involve richer intimacies.

Arm to shoulder. The previous steps can be more casual in nature, but this step

---

*Abridged from Desmond Morris, *Intimate Behaviour,* New York: Random House, 1971. Originally published in the UK by Jonathan Cape, an imprint of the Random House UK Group.

intentionally brings the partner into closer body contact. An arm around the shoulder communicates a message of close friendship and perhaps love. It draws the partners together and indicates a deeper level of intimate companionship.

Arm to waist. This is a more direct statement of sexual and romantic interest. The arm is around the waist and closer to the private areas of the body. Arm to waist is indicative of a growing intimacy and amorous bonding. Like the preceding step, it brings the trunks of the bodies into contact in an increasing intimacy.

Mouth to mouth. Kissing on the mouth with the accompanying behavior of a close, frontal embrace is a big step forward in pair bonding. This is the initial step that can create erotic and genital arousal, especially with prolonged and intimate kissing. The man and woman are becoming lovers and are enjoying sexual arousal with an intimate closeness developing.

Hand to head. Perhaps as an accompanying behavior to the intimate kissing, the hands touch and caress the partner's head. The defensive walls are let down and bonding occurs as fingers tenderly stroke the face, hair, ears, and neck. Sometimes the hands will lovingly clasp the head in a communication of caring and intimate possessiveness.

Hand to body. Intimacy deepens as the hands explore the partner's body with touching, rubbing, squeezing, and gentle fondling. The trust and bonding is deepening with caressing of the female breasts and further sexual arousal. Often couples who do not wish to proceed to completion in making love will stop at this step.

Mouth to breast. With this step the bonding behaviors have become private and a new level of intimacy reached. The first nine steps, with the exception of caressing the breast, might be expressed in public and the pair bonding developed without a need for privacy. The female breast is covered in most societies, and its exposure is symbolic of advanced intimacy. The mouth caressing and suckling the breast is the last of the pre-genital bonding behaviors. This step is usually the prelude of stimulation to an orgasm, rather than a more general step in loveplay.

Hand to genital. This is an advanced step in pair bonding. Touching the lover's genitals implies a sufficient level of trust and bond of attachment for deeper intimacies. This touching often begins in a teasing, caressing manner. As arousal increases, the partner proceeds to a tender, rhythmic rubbing that stimulates arousal. This step can include the intimate behaviors of stroking the penis, fondling the labia and clitoris, and inserting fingers into the vagina. Manual stimulation can also lead to the partners trusting each other in the sharing of a climax.

Genital to genital. The final stage of pair formation includes intercourse and the potential for creating a life. Each preceding step will have deepened the bond of attachment and intimate connection. The intimacy of intercourse is built on the earlier bonding behaviors that have created a partnership to provide for the possibility of pregnancy. The design is that the couple remain bonded beyond the satisfaction of the sex drive in orgasm. The couple will have created an intimacy deeper and more long-lasting than sexual arousal and consummation.

If you want to feel more deeply in love and expand into a full-time lover, devote some time to each of these steps. Let's take them one at a time and explore how each can enrich your sex life. Ralph Waldo Emerson stated that "foolish consistency is the hobgoblin of little minds." No one wants to be categorized as having a little mind and neglecting effective ways to enrich sexuality. Everyone at times gets into a destructive "consistency." That is why this chapter deemphasizes orgasm and intercourse in making love. You need to expand your sexual realities. Certainly you want to be a wise lover characterized by emotional depth and an enriching complexity.

Making love is an attitude from which exciting behaviors flow. There are great returns in practicing better body and mind control, in not being ruled by the heat of the moment. God intended His one-flesh concept to include a lot more than intercourse.

In the first three steps couples learn and share information that builds companionship and sets the stage for sexual connectedness. In these steps there is no erotic touching. Steps four through nine encourage a fun sexuality that is not genitally focused. They are less erotic in nature than the last three steps. As you practice these steps, you will find it exciting to make love with your clothes on.

1. Eye to Body

This step includes much more than observing or staring at select parts of your mate's nude body. Become a student of your spouse's body as you fall more deeply in love. No one perfectly meets Hollywood standards, but everyone has many endearing qualities. Examples are dimples, hairy legs, expressive hands, the face lit up with a smile, startling blue eyes, the shape of the nose, the calves, and the body intensity when sharing a story or working in the yard.

Practice exercise. Let the word *bedroom* trigger in your mind an opportunity to carefully observe. So often *bedroom* triggers the idea of sleep or a place for active sex play. The bedroom is actually a marvelous place to study your mate and notice some things you have passed over. Focus on noticing, accepting, and enjoying as you tune in to your mate's masculinity or femininity when putting on clothes, reading a book, or simply bustling about. Observe your mate one night peacefully sleeping and feel happy for this companion God has given you.

2. Eye to Eye

Do you two look into each other's souls anymore? Eye-to-eye contact connects two individuals in this special way. Romantic dinners are integral for staying in love. They are sensual feasts, and they create a context for much eye-to-eye bonding. In the busyness of life, lovers forget to make eye contact when they are talking—or for that matter, when they are making love. The eyes express so much: acceptance, excitement, a longing to understand, and sexual desire.

Practice exercise. Look into your mate's eyes whenever possible. See if you don't feel more connected and in love after a couple days of doing this. Communicate warmth, acceptance, and appreciation with this eye contact.

3. Voice to Voice

Isn't it amusing how much time adolescents can spend on the phone? Perhaps you remember when you and your mate first met and started dating—an hour-long phone conversation was not that unusual. Your voice and speech patterns are unique and can trigger warmth and enjoyment in your partner. The chapter on sexual communication noted how erotic talking about sex can be whether in bed or with all of your clothes on. Learn to love your mate's voice as you connect through intimate conversations. Husbands may have to work harder on just engaging in connecting chitchat and meeting their wives' greater need for conversation, which is a crucial part of intimate companionship.

Practice exercise. Stop reading right now and say to your mate, "I love you!" It may necessitate a phone call. Make contact voice to voice!

4. Hand to Hand

Holding hands has special meaning. This behavior symbolizes trust, protection, and caring. An excellent example is a child who holds an adult's hand almost instinctively. When lovers hold hands, they convey this idea of trust and togetherness as well as acknowledge sexual bondedness. Holding your mate's hand in public demonstrates the one-flesh companionship you two have created and are continually creating. Gently squeezing your partner's hand when you are in the car says you think of and value this love relationship. It's a fun way to make love without taking your clothes off.

Practice exercise. Unless you are different from most couples (if so, I congratulate you), you have quit holding hands enough. Make a mental note to hold hands the next time you are leaving church, driving to Mom's, or sitting on the couch.

5. Arm to Shoulder

Commitment is a vital component of fun sex. On the one hand, it is saying, "We can count on each other, and together we will build one great sex life." On the other hand, it is saying, "Forget about the sexual transmission of HIV, sweetheart, we're clean, and our fidelity will keep it that way." A partnership is comforting, and two can be better than one. It is great to feel an arm around your shoulder and have a lover to help you achieve your sexual potential.

Practice exercise. Commitment involves a series of daily choices that protect your marriage and your sex life. Have you made any poor choices recently? How about serving on that extra committee, working late, or not exercising? How could you rectify these destructive choices this week?

6. Arm to Waist

So many pop songs emphasize getting closer. This deepening of intimacy is a complex task. Intercourse and genital intimacy won't eliminate the need for preliminary buildup and loveplay. Remember a key concept of pair bonding—you can't meet the needs of one step by skipping ahead to another! Arm to waist provides a different closeness from genital to genital. This closeness can be exemplified by a full body hug as you pull your mate tight and revel in the warmth of each other's closeness. Sexually, this would be more like being on first base: sharing fantasies, caressing and holding, talking, and drawing close. These activities can be enhanced by keeping your clothes on.

Practice exercise. At least four times a day this week, embrace your mate in a bear hug, kiss the neck and express your love. You will be surprised what this arm-to-waist activity will do for helping you feel in love and increasing sexual desire.

7. Mouth to Mouth

Mouth to mouth creates a sensuous, experiential bonding. Emotions and minds and bodies connect in a special manner, and there is fusion in a romantic and erotic rush of feelings. You allow your partner deeper into your private spaces. You actually kiss and exchange body fluids; you experience a scary but exciting lowering of your ego boundaries and a melding with another person. There is almost no need for talking in this step: *Let me gaze into your eyes and passionately kiss your lips. You are mine and I am yours.*

Practice exercise. Married couples can forget the importance of kissing. Put on some soft music, wrap your arms around each other, and get body to body as you gaze into each other's eyes. Close your eyes and focus your whole mind and senses on slow sensual kissing as you bond.

8. Hand to Head

This is trust! You may not like people to muss your hair up, caress your face, or touch your head. But you feel safe with your spouse. Hand to head is very intimate.

Practice exercise. Place your head in your mate's lap so that you can be caressed and nurtured. It may feel uncomfortable at first but try to relax. Try some face massage (demonstrated in the chapter on sensual massage). You may discover you also don't know how to relax and let your mate nurture you during lovemaking.

9. Hand to Body

Start on top of the clothes and keep away from the erogenous zones. The husband can unbutton the wife's blouse or the wife can pull down the husband's zipper later. This is sensual exploring and relaxing caressing. Giving and receiving sensual pleasure are possible for every lover. Read the chapter on sensual massage and get creative in this hand-to-body bonding. You are nurturing and accepting this person you love. You are saying, "Your body is unique and I enjoy it. You are one sensuous person!" If you want to touch skin, unfasten belts and snaps, but don't remove your clothing. Your clothes will be a signal to go slow and build this hand-to-body experience. Pretend you are dating and making love with your clothes on.

Practice exercise. Get in your car and find a safe parking place (it may be in your garage). Have some fun hand-to-body contact or get steamy without taking clothes off or following through.

10. *Mouth to Breast*

Now the male can unfasten the female's bra and allow another level of pair bonding. What might the male be experiencing? Dependency and closeness, acknowledgment of his sexual needs, appreciation of her need to nurture, sexual arousal in enjoyment of this special symbol of femininity, and a desire to stimulate his mate. What might the female be experiencing? Intimacy and vulnerability in sharing a special part of her body, pleasure in nurturing her man, sexual arousal, and realization of the sexy power of her feminine self. This is fusion on a deeper level than simply nibbling on erotic tissue. Mouth to breast is symbolic! You are acknowledging the fact that you depend on each other to create this great sexual magnetic field of excitement. God's great design of complementary differences is being celebrated with male and female needing each other. The female can also enjoy the male body by nibbling on his nipples, neck, and stomach as she sensuously bonds by placing her mouth on his erogenous zones. He may feel reluctant at first, but he, too, needs the mouth-to-breast foreplay.

Practice exercise. When the mood is right, the wife can invite her husband to make love to her breasts. He can pull her blouse up, but the rest of the clothes stay on. Allow yourself to enjoy the pleasure and the symbolic nature of this loveplay. Salute your mutual ability to meet needs and merge into warm closeness. Then reverse roles.

11. *Hand to Genital*

This level of intimacy expresses that each is completely the other's to enjoy. To hold your husband's testicles in your hand with their sensual softness truly symbolizes his trust and sexual surrender. To tenderly and voluptuously slip your finger into your wife's vagina demonstrates her confidence in and love for you. Be sensuous and go slow as you become a total lover.

Practice exercise. Undo zippers and belts but again keep clothes on, and preferably do this in the dark. This is a tactile adventure and experience in sexual bonding. Loosen clothes as needed as you slowly touch and explore genitals in a renewed way. No orgasms—you are making love with clothes on. Your mind and emotions are tracing and memorizing favorite sensations through your fingers. You are strengthening attachment and trust.

12. *Genital to Genital*

We are to remember that "the two shall become one flesh" (Matt. 19:5 NKJV). Somehow we were created with an intense enjoyment of and need for this genital union. Never forget the emotional and spiritual closeness of this final step of pair bonding. Never forfeit the sheer sexual excitement of this lover's embrace. This step involves intercourse, even though this chapter is trying to deemphasize this aspect of making love. Allow this to be playful and focused as you keep as many of your clothes on as possible. Don't climax—this is genital-to-genital bonding. Isn't it exciting to think that you will repeat this act countless times over the coming years? The sexual potential and promise of an intimate marriage are amazing.

Practice exercise. Get each other excited with some face-to-face and hand-to-body connecting, then very slowly let vagina contain penis. Hold each other in this embrace for a few minutes. Stop for now and do something else companionable. This step obviously takes mutual resolve and willpower but will teach some important lessons on making love all the time.

Creating a Party

One man struggled in his sex life with retarded ejaculation, an inability to focus on his own pleasure and reach a climax. One day he developed a fascinating metaphor. He saw sex as a great party in which there were fun and orgasms. He saw himself in a raft on a river heading for the party, which he likened to some exciting rapids. No matter how hard he paddled, he always got stuck on snags, and he could never reach the party. He looked longingly down the river at the rapids that he was denied the pleasure of enjoying.

His wife had also gone through some of those feelings as she became orgasmic in the earlier days of their marriage. She had learned the hard way about loveplay and that curious paradox in sex: the goals you anxiously worry about and strive for are never achieved. The only way to reach most sexual destinations (e.g., orgasm, increased desire, less inhibition) is to forget about the goal and start enjoying the journey. She told her husband, "The party begins the minute we get into the raft and ease into the river. Forget about the rapids!"

She remembered trying so hard to reach an orgasm, only to end up frustrated. She finally relaxed and focused on the loveplay and her feelings of the moment. She achieved an orgasm only after she learned the skills of playing, enhancing feelings, focusing on fun sensations, and expecting the journey to be a fulfilling experience. She learned to party!

The husband quickly identified with the idea of enjoying the journey. He and his wife loved to raft, and some of their most memorable trips had been floating down a river with no rapids above a Class Two category (ones in Class Five are adventurous and usually take a guide). He remembered sunny Saturday afternoons with occasional lazy paddling to maintain their position in the river as they relaxed, ate, drank, and talked. They would spontaneously pull into an island and swim, or pull over to the shore and jump off a rock with other people sharing their raft. One time they were on a mountain river while the mountain laurel and rhododendrons were in full bloom. On the same trip their guide had them all get out of the raft on a calm stretch and float. The water was so cold it took the breath away at first, but the adventure was one of the most exciting memories of the trip.

The husband started hitting the rapids again as he began to enjoy the journey. Laughter, variety, spontaneity, and excitement returned. His wife helped him polish up his party skills. They made love with their clothes on and off in a creative, uninhibited manner. In a childlike fashion he began anticipating and expecting their lovemaking to have a lot of little thrills (Class Two rapids) and got truly excited about them. In awe and wonder he noticed sensual delights and unexpected pleasures. Rafting was fun once again.

Loveplay versus Grabbing or Controlling

"I wish we could hug without him grabbing me." One wife related how she and her female friends at work were laughing in frustrated amusement about how their husbands' hands were "homing devices." This irritating male habit is certainly not consistent with the idea of making love with clothes on. Couples, wives especially, need physical affection and warm nurturing gestures that are not always focused on the breasts or buttocks or genitals.

Making love with clothes on and pair bonding include hand-to-breast but should have a lot of general hand-to-body contact. Perhaps you did not grow up in a home in which physical affection was demonstrated freely. Hugging, holding someone's hand, rubbing a back, and patting a shoulder are such affirming gestures. You need to know that you can physically nurture your mate without its being overtly sexual.

Time Out . . .

After your mate has had a shower, you take a towel and dry off your mate's body. Massage the scalp, rub the back, pat the face, and nurture your mate. Like other "making love with clothes on" gestures, the emphasis is not on visual stimulation but on touching and enjoying with a cloth boundary. Let it be a subtle sexual experience.

Perhaps it is not fair to pick on men. Some women also have trouble allowing easy physical affection without its heading in a sexual direction. Some women are preoccupied with the husband's body and detrimentally focus on genital sexuality and orgasm. More often, however, the female counterpart to grabbing is needing control. Making love with clothes on can be hampered by always wanting exactly the right time and place. Yes, it can be a nuisance when you are intensely involved in a project to stop and get romantic. And yes, when you are busy, sex may be the farthest thing from your mind. But part of making love all the time involves relaxing control and enjoying your mate.

Romantic Fun with Clothes On

This section offers more suggestions for making love without the urgency to head for the bedroom and get nude. These activities further underscore the spirit of erotic fun with clothes on—subtle, pervasive, spontaneous, tantalizing, and sensuous loveplay.

Sensuous Exploring

How do you think Marco Polo felt enjoying marvelous new experiences daily? Great lovers have the qualities of a famous explorer: curiosity, adventure, and a desire for more knowledge and new discoveries. Your mate's body can be your undiscovered territory if you are willing to enjoy eye-to-body and hand-to-body bonding in innovative ways. This exploring can be done nude, but doing it clothed has special excitement. It allows you to concentrate on exposed parts like face, hands, and feet without genital distraction.

It is easy to build the attitudes of a sensual explorer, letting your fingers do the walking. Gently explore curves and crannies; feel the beauty of the human body and the softness of a cheek or firmness of a shoulder. Drink up your lover's uniqueness as you touch and memorize some of your favorite sensations. Close your eyes and focus on hand-to-body contact as you lightly run fingertips over your partner.

Part of the fun of making love with clothes on is the sensuous texture of fabric and the way it alters the feel of the body under it. Gently stroke your mate's back with a T-shirt on, and feel the soft warmth of the flesh underneath. Wife, stroke your husband's genitals with his underwear on, and revel in a similar sensation. Now repeat, caressing the body with a more silky fabric—the experience is entirely different. Stand up facing your mate and massage his upper arms with his suit coat on. Husband, lightly touch your wife's hips and buttocks with a slip or pantyhose over them. Expand beyond erogenous zones and become a sensual explorer!

Dressing Up

Clothes are fun erotically. They stimulate the imagination and increase anticipation. Imagine what is under a robe or a strategically draped towel. Use your creativity and dress up for your mate. Flatter your strengths, and flaunt your masculinity or femininity. Build a private wardrobe designed for making love and increasing sexual attractiveness.

Clothing doesn't have to stimulate erotic thoughts to enhance your ability to make love to your mate all the time. Maybe you enjoy dressing up for a wedding or a night on the town. Making love with clothes on is getting excited by your mate's appearance in evening clothes, admiring that new tennis outfit or colorful top, appreciating a particular piece of jewelry, and delighting in the love and joy of eye-to-body pair bonding. Dress up for your mate, and watch your intimacy grow deeper.

Unexpected Treats

Variety and the unexpected do indeed create spice in life. Part of the fun of making love with clothes on is spontaneously enjoying hand-to-body, hand-to-genital, and genital-to-genital encounters while clothed. Unzipping pants in the privacy of a car or home in order to share some quick contact is tremendously exciting. Stay loose, and don't get goal oriented—just enjoy the short encounter.

So much of your time is spent clothed—plan treats for your mate. Buy an outfit with convenient buttons or zippers. Let the erotic and romantic pervade your relationship. Encourage that occasional foray beneath the clothing as you keep the unexpected alive.

A Striptease for One

Be intimate and trusting and allow yourself to be totally naked and unashamed with your mate. Falling deeper in love is a marvelous process. In the context of this safe relationship of marriage it is bonding to do some stripteasing and self-disclosing. Baring your soul is usually more difficult than taking your clothes off, but both are important. Orchestrating your private striptease for your mate can be another playful aspect of making love with your clothes on.

I am talking to both husband and wife, and I am not encouraging you to get completely nude. Wife, put on your husband's shirt over a funny T-shirt and wear some sexy lingerie under that. Take your time in slowly pulling off various garments as you eat supper or do some other activity together. Right now in your closet and drawers you have all the garments for a fantastic show. Maybe include a fancy dress, your bathing suit, and the lavender bra and panties. Get creative and have some fun being silly together.

Husband, find out what garments are sexy to your wife and what aspects of your body trigger erotic thoughts. If it is your hairy legs or muscled shoulders, start off with them covered and dress to show them off as the striptease proceeds. Buy a muscle shirt or brightly colored gym shorts. Be subtle, and arouse your mate with innuendo and hidden secrets. Maybe do the unexpected by buying a crazy-for-you item of apparel and setting the stage so you can slowly strip to it. This is pair bonding and loveplay. You are building that deeper intimacy you have been searching for. Throw caution to the wind, and let the clown and entertainer in you take over.

Section Three

Delighting in Each Other

Chapter Eleven

Mutual Pleasuring

Making love is one adult activity that encourages mates to focus on fun, be lighthearted, enjoy curiosity and enthusiasm, and step out of their controlled, dutiful attitudes. In sex, lovers are supposed to step back from their everyday routine and create a bonding, pleasuring experience together.

This chapter focuses on the sensual pleasuring of your mate's genitals, without a demand for intercourse or orgasms, as a bonding part of making love. Nondemanding genital pleasuring does not mean you must exclude intercourse and orgasms. It simply means that bonding, affectionate sex can be hampered if it is always goal-oriented toward rushing into intercourse or producing a climax. The chapter starts off with describing the concept of pleasuring and works through feelings about masturbation. It develops two comfortable positions for you and your mate to pleasure each other and enjoy genital sensuality. It concludes with some suggestions for including nondemanding genital pleasuring as another way to make love.

Pleasuring and Masturbation

Pleasure is an interesting word. Somehow it almost does not seem to fit within Christian values. It feels self-centered and sinful. The truth of the matter is that God gave us our sensuality to enjoy. The sin is not in experiencing pleasure but in calling pleasure sinful and not allowing ourselves to enjoy God's many gifts, including genital sensuality.

Pleasuring

Many Christians think they don't deserve pleasure, sexual or otherwise. Perhaps it does seem very self-centered and contrary to our hard-working, self-sacrificing American Christian ethic. The truth is, however, that God created humans with the ability to experience and enjoy pleasurable feelings. And marriage enables mates to help each other overcome inhibitions and enhance the ability to become aroused and feel sexual joy.

Enjoying genital pleasuring that is slow and bonding without pressure and demands is critical to a truly intimate, nurturing, and exciting sex life. You need to be able to make love for half an hour to a couple of hours at a time. You have already explored the enjoyment of sensual massage. Pleasuring is a more focused sensual massage. It requires that you notice and give yourself permission to enjoy your sexual feelings. Tell your mate what you like and don't be afraid to ask for more. As a part of pleasuring, find relaxed and comfortable positions that enhance the process. Luxuriate and focus in on your sensuality and sexuality.

Masturbation

The word *masturbation* conjures up all kinds of taboos and guilt. Myths existed even in medical textbooks into the 1930s about masturbation causing psychoses, "lunacy," blindness, and many other mental and physical problems. Supposedly, people could tell self-abusers by the way they walked and their stunted physical development. Obviously, this is not true, psychologically or medically.

In terms of morality, the Bible is silent on the topic of masturbation. It does not say the behavior is right or wrong to do. Like some other sexual behaviors, we keep it in line with God's economy by applying general scriptural principles. Its becoming destructive and sinful depends on the individual and the relationship. We will discuss some of these guidelines at the end of this section. Why, then, has Christianity been reluctant to deal with masturbation and even fostered some of the myths?

One such myth is denouncing masturbation by calling it onanism and saying Scripture is clear on this point. This is a gross misinterpretation of the Genesis account. Onan's brother died, and the custom was for Onan to impregnate his sister-in-law so she could have children to carry on his brother's name. Onan apparently wanted the inheritance for himself and his own children, so he practiced the withdrawal method of birth control: "But Onan knew that the offspring would not be his; so whenever he lay with his brother's wife, he spilled his semen on the ground to keep from producing offspring for his brother" (Gen. 38:9 NIV).

Some of the prohibition against masturbation seems to have evolved from the early church doctrine on birth control. Within marriage, masturbation was viewed as a form of preventing conception. It also was seen as promoting uncontrolled lust and self-centered sex.

Married couples need to establish a definition of masturbation. Most couples are fine as long as they are stimulating each other to an orgasm, manually or orally. Many consider this loveplay and pleasuring, not masturbation. It becomes more questionable if it includes pleasuring or touching yourself, even if your mate is present and participating. It often is considered wrong if done alone or in the presence of your mate without your partner's active involvement.

Because of the excessive baggage the word *masturbation* carries with it, I prefer using the descriptive words *genital pleasuring*, which is a behavior that can be done to yourself and to your mate. We have already established that great sex is built on enjoying your own feelings uninhibitedly, which also arouses your mate. Sometimes in the excitement of making love or the nature of some lovemaking positions, it will be natural and arousing to increase the stimulation of your genitals by stroking yourself.

Mates who have never stimulated themselves have forfeited an opportunity to learn about their arousal patterns and what type of stroking feels best on which areas of their bodies. Going through this discovery process and learning to celebrate sexual feelings more fully will also be a fun part of the mutual genital pleasuring. And sometimes pleasuring through to an orgasm can be a helpful release when a partner is unavailable for a variety of reasons.

Christians should be able to experience joy and pleasure. We have often short-circuited this by viewing pleasure, especially sexual pleasuring, as somehow carnal and dangerous. I am encouraging us to challenge the negative view of masturbation as we allow ourselves to enjoy nondemanding genital pleasuring done within God's guidelines.

I include three different aspects of genital pleasuring from which I have banned the word *masturbation:* (1) pleasuring each other's genitals is a vital part of making love and enjoying arousal that leads to a climax; (2) stimulating yourself during sex can be an exciting and sharing part of the process, and your mate can be aroused by your enjoyment of sex; and (3) arousing yourself apart from your mate can be a way of learning about yourself and releasing sexual tension (this area will have to be thought through more carefully).

There is nothing biblically wrong with the behavior of genital pleasuring. Is this carte blanche approval? Of course not. Like most behaviors, sexual and otherwise, some attitudes and circumstances can make them very destructive (sinful) for a given individual or couple. Here are some guidelines for genital pleasuring:

1. Enduring sexual pleasure is ultimately based on an intimate companionship. The sexual verb is *relate.* Any sexual activity that undermines the loving connecting of mates will be more hurtful than helpful. This is true of coercing your partner into behaviors you may find exciting but offend your partner's sensibilities, like using certain slang words or insisting on oral sex. It also can apply to genital pleasuring that excludes your partner and does not promote intimacy. Genital pleasuring as a solitary activity can create a secret world that diminishes your mate and excludes you from a more exciting love life.

2. The apostle Paul wisely wrote, "All things are lawful for me, but all things are not helpful. All things are lawful for me, but I will not be brought under the power of any" (1 Cor. 6:12 NKJV). Any sexual behavior that becomes a habit can

be detrimental to and narrow your sex life. It is true of getting locked into a routine that excludes spontaneity or focuses only on intercourse. It is also true of genital pleasuring, especially the solitary variety, which can create a habitual kind of sex that detracts from making love and locks in a type of erotic arousal that your mate cannot duplicate.

3. In any type of sexual pleasuring, especially self-pleasuring, you must guard your fantasy and thought life. In chapter 7, we explored the importance of keeping sexual desire and fantasy within God's guidelines. The bottom line was allowing sexual thinking to promote intimacy with your mate and not have your partnership adulterated by fantasizing about other people. This point is vital if you use self-pleasuring as a solitary activity to release sexual tension while separated from your mate.

4. Sexually compulsive or addictive persons should never pleasure themselves alone. Chapter 26 discusses sex addiction. A simple definition would be someone who exclusively uses sex to destructively control and alter feelings, much as others use alcohol or food. Self-pleasuring becomes an isolating activity and builds a secret world, separate from the mate, in which sex becomes a drug to combat boredom or relieve stress or alleviate guilt. As with any drug or surge of adrenaline, sex outside the concept of a loving relationship takes bigger doses and can lead to destructive behaviors like exhibitionism, voyeurism, and hours spent watching pornography.

Positions for Genital Pleasuring

Here are two relaxing positions that lend themselves to nondemanding genital pleasuring of various kinds. In each position, you may wish to lie on pillows or use the back of the bed to prop up and get comfortable.

1. Sitting or Lying with Legs Overlapped

You can experiment with which legs are better on top in the overlapping process. Size and whether you are the pleasurer or pleasuree can make a difference. The pleasuree may wish to lie supine with knees bent and focus on personal pleasure, while the pleasurer props against the back of the bed with pillows in a sitting position. Both may wish to face each other sitting. This position lends itself to communicating and exchanging nonverbal signs of pleasure.

2. Sitting with Back to Chest

This position has the pleasuree sitting comfortably between the legs of the pleasurer, leaning back against his or her chest to be cuddled and pleasured. The hands of the pleasurer have access to the chest and genitals of the partner. The pleasurer can be propped up against the back of the bed for comfort. An important part of nondemanding genital pleasuring is feeling close and connected as you give your mate pleasure and in turn sensuously enjoy your mate's body. This position allows special closeness as you cuddle up close to your partner and enjoy the delight of the hands. Another important aspect of mutual pleasuring is feeling supported and comfortable physically. This position helps prevent aching backs and sore knees.

Making Love with Genital Pleasuring

One couple valued the sexual part of their relationship. But the longer they were married, the more neglected and routine it became—although it still was enjoyable. Their biggest disagreement sexually was about the husband's greater need for sexual release and the wife's feeling pressured to perform. Both wished they could put more of the sparkle of earlier years back into their lovemaking.

Practicing genital pleasuring became a key source of making changes as intercourse was deemphasized. The wife did not want to have an orgasm every time they made love. The husband felt that he wasn't a very good lover or did not have as much fun unless she wholeheartedly entered the process and he brought her to a climax. They started off with genital exploration and slow sensual massage of the genital area as they got back into the habit of taking more time to play and build excitement. It was done in a nondemanding fashion so that the wife could relax and not climax unless she so desired.

Genital Exploration and Massage

They began by sitting with legs overlapped, and through sensual touching, they explored each other's genital area from top to bottom. With the wife lying back, the husband started with her outer vulval lips and moved to the inner lips and the clitoral area and finally into her vagina. He did this gently, with plenty of lubrication. He found his index finger most sensitive in the nerve endings. During this entire process, they communicated with each other about what felt most sensitive to her and what was particularly sensual to him as he experienced her body. A part of the time he closed his eyes so he could focus on his sense of touch and revel in her softness.

The wife then explored her husband, beginning with the base of his penis between the scrotal sac and the perineum at the external point of the prostate. With fingers and whole hand she then caressed his testicles and proceeded up to his penis where she explored the shaft, top, and bottom. Extra care was taken for the head of the penis with its ridges and sensitive nerve endings.

They took their time doing this exercise, stretching it out over most of an hour. They repeated it in the same week. They later discussed that it was an entirely different experience to explore each other's body the second time. They were becoming more aware of each other's skin and softness. The touching seemed more sensual and exciting.

In the coming weeks they progressed to genital massage. He enjoyed having her sit with her back to his chest as she propped her knees up and leaned comfortably back.

He had easy access to her genitals while he held her warmly to him. It also allowed easy nongenital caressing, too. She liked to kneel between his legs facing his genitals. She could easily use both hands and seemed to get less tired. They adapted their own fun routine.

At first, the husband's ego was a little offended when she offered to show him what felt good to her, and he kept his hand too rigid for his wife to guide. As he relaxed it, she was able to demonstrate some of the touches that she found most arousing. She took his relaxed index finger and placed her index finger over it as she caressed her clitoris. He showed her places on his penis that were especially sensitive and placed his hand around hers as she massaged his penis to help her learn the firmness and rhythms he appreciated the most.

They liked to use coconut oil as a lubricant even though it was not water soluble. (You as a couple can experiment about what feels and smells and tastes best to you—depending perhaps on the type of genital massage you wish to engage in on a particular occasion.) Both were pleased that the genital exploration and massage increased the wife's pleasure and desire for sex. She felt more attended to and loved the closeness. The husband developed greater sensualness. Both welcomed it as he expanded his repertoire for erotic arousal to include some very stimulating touching.

Nurturing Through Orgasms

This husband often wanted more sexual activity than his wife did. And she did not desire to become actively involved on some evenings when she was fatigued. The following technique revolutionized their sex life. At least once a week, she pleasured him to an orgasm without her active participation.

She would slip off her nightgown and gently hold his testicles while he stroked himself to a climax. She did not mind his fondling her breasts, and she appreciated the pleasure she brought him even with the minimal involvement. Sometimes she would place her hand over his and in other small ways would be supportive. She snuggled close to him and afterward used a warm washcloth to help him clean up. Often that type of sexual activity would not take over ten minutes, but he found it nurturing and fulfilling. They still felt like they were making love.

They grew closer as they eliminated one of their nagging problems and the husband felt sexually satisfied. His wife promised him that once a week she would whole-heartedly engage herself in making love. But at other times she would focus on meeting his needs. She was happy to be able to nurture without thinking about birth control (they used a diaphragm) and cleaning herself up afterward. At times she was tired and did not feel up to active lovemaking. Sometimes as he began getting aroused, she decided she was in the mood, and she inserted the diaphragm. At those times she might not be as active, but some of the fatigue would melt away as they made love.

For other couples, the husband may pleasure his wife when he is not in the mood or feels tired. Nurturing through orgasm can be a loving compromise in a sexual partnership.

Overcoming Anatomical Differences with Genital Pleasuring

The greatest source of male sexual arousal is the head of the penis, while female arousal is centered in the clitoris. During intercourse the penis is being constantly stimulated—but the clitoris isn't. The pleasuring position of sitting with legs overlapped allows a better match-up of the most sensitive parts of male and female anatomy. It is an exciting, connecting, and very accessible position for pleasuring both partners. The hands are free to caress and massage both genital and nongenital parts of the body. You are eye to eye and mouth to mouth, so verbal and nonverbal communication is facilitated with long, sexy looks and interchanges of how you are feeling. Again, be sure sensitive tissue is lubricated. Here are two variants of this position that sensuous, playful mates find exciting to include in their repertoire of genital loveplay:

1. Sit with legs overlapping. You, the wife, are the pleasurer. Start with caressing his face and chest and connecting with him physically. As you continue to do this with one hand, take your other hand and play with his testicles and penis. Now direct your full attention to the penis. Have him close his eyes and revel in the sensations as you run fingers up and down and stroke the shaft and head. Build the excitement as you use the stimulation that can create a climax. As he approaches an orgasm, stop your active stroking of the penis.

Now direct your attention to yourself as you use his penis as a wand to stimulate your genital area. Lovers find the penis is a marvelous tool for stimulating the clitoral area. He may lose some of his arousal, but that is good as you prolong this pleasuring session. He will enjoy your continued penile touching as well as your participation in arousing yourself. Go slow at first, and stimulate your whole vulval area as you keep coming back to the clitoris. Bring yourself to a climax first if you so desire. When you have enjoyed your genital stimulation enough, focus back on his sensations and build him to an orgasm.

2. You, the husband, are the pleasurer in this exercise. Start with a hug, and caress her back and face, sucking her fingers and lightly kissing her arms, running fingers teasingly over her breasts and stomach as you approach and back off from the nipples. You are arousing and connecting with your lover before approaching direct genital stimulation. As she becomes aroused and desires more genital excitement, have her lie back with her legs continuing to overlap yours. Arouse your penis to a full erection, and use it to slowly stimulate the whole vulval area as you spread her lips apart and lightly caress.

As she becomes more aroused, use your penis to increase the stimulation of the clitoris. Let her guide you in what area feels best and what motions are more arousing. As you use your wrist and arm to create vibrating sensations, you can also stroke the shaft of the penis as a part of these motions, continuing to also increase your sexual buildup. Be creative as you vibrate faster, then slow down some; apply lighter pressure and more direct pressure; run your penis down to the vagina and back up to the clitoris. Entice and tease as you take plenty of time to enjoy each other and slowly build to a climax. After she has had an orgasm, you can bring yourself to one, also.

Coaching the Pleasure

Teaching your mate what feels sensual and arousing to you can include guiding hands and fingers to create the touch you desire. Utilize several of the pleasuring positions as you alternate blocks of pleasuring time. This will challenge you as a couple in many growth-producing ways. It will require you to tune in to your own pleasure as you instruct your mate about what you desire and find stimulating. It will perfect your coaching techniques: verbally, in talking about what you desire; nonverbally, in guiding hands and illustrating motions. You will become more comfortable in asking for what you want and demonstrating your desires. These are vital skills for a great sex life over the next fifty years.

The Pleasure of Oral Stimulation

In the same way that kissing and intimately sharing mouths bring erotic arousal and intimate bonding, oral stimulation of the genitals can build trust and be exciting for mates. A quick bath and good hygiene are crucial for this genital pleasuring. If seepage bothers you, keep a warm washcloth handy and gently wipe as needed. Don't worry about his climaxing in your mouth—you as wife are assertive and can ask for what you do and don't want. Actively share your needs and sensibilities.

Remember that Scripture is silent on the topic of oral sex. This does not make it right or wrong. You as mates will have to sort and pray through certain behaviors as you choose what to include in your repertoire of lovemaking. Never make your mate feel guilty or inhibited because he or she does not feel comfortable with a given behavior. The object is to be playful, lovingly connected, and creatively varied. This can be accomplished without oral pleasuring of the genitals.

Trusting your genitals to your mate's mouth is warmly intimate. The genitals are called the "privates" for a reason. Husbands are very protective of the penis and testicles. To allow the partner complete access is an important commitment as they feel very vulnerable and in turn arousingly close. Wives have sometimes bought into the notion that somehow they are dirty down there, or they have left their genitals as an unknown area. To have the husband intimately scrutinizing and enjoying this part of the body takes special trust and openness.

Here are a few suggestions for wife and husband to enhance this variety of genital pleasuring:

Wife, use your lips as buffers for your teeth in order to prevent damage to sensitive tissue. Use tongue and mouth to tease as you manually stroke the shaft of the penis and create firmer stimulation. Allow your mouth to create a vacuum effect—the stronger the sucking action, the more pleasurable feelings produced. The head of the penis is the most sensitive part—don't worry about trying to take more of the penis in your mouth.

Husband, tease with your tongue as you flick it lightly over the vulval area. Kiss and gently suck the entire area. If your tongue gets tired, hold it firm and create rubbing sensations by moving your entire head side to side. You can also create sucking motions with your mouth over the clitoris to produce a climax. Keep teeth covered, and employ variety until she actively approaches an orgasm.

Oral sex can be interspersed with other types of genital pleasuring in a non-demanding, emotionally connecting manner. It can be more exciting at times if combined with simultaneous manual stimulation. While enjoying oral sex, keep your hands active, too, as penis and testicles are stroked, fingers are inserted in vagina, back is caressed, buttocks are massaged, and skin is teased. Inhibition vanishes and control is relaxed as partners revel in each other's sensuality and sexuality.

Genital pleasuring may not come easily to you or feel comfortable. You may need practice in tuning in to the pleasurable sensations of your body and allowing excitement to build.

Listen to your body and enjoy the natural sexual feelings God meant to be aroused by pleasuring the genital area. Respond to rhythmic stimulation, breathe more rapidly, and allow your automatic responses to flow without inhibitions. Let go of your embarrassment, need for control, or fears and relax in the excitement of mutual pleasuring. You are creating a special intimacy.

Keep balanced in your lovemaking, and don't just focus on intercourse and orgasm. This may seem odd advice when the next chapter is completely focused on intercourse, but you need variety. Always keep in mind that sex is not the only facet of your companionship. Enjoy your wonderful marital partnership as you play together in various ways.

Chapter Twelve

Creative Intercourse

Unleashing a childlike curiosity, becoming delightfully uninhibited, trying new things, and being playmates are all part of this vital component of exciting intercourse. Your minds and relationship can take these uninspired techniques and bring them alive. The imagination with some practice and experimenting can create great variety and immense romantic pleasure.

Playful, Creative Sensuality + Knowledge + Practice = Creative Intercourse

FIG. 12.1. Equation for creative intercourse.

You as a lover provide the fusion, sensuality, and excitement to intercourse. You as a couple can choose when and where you want to enjoy these positions, whether on a soft mattress, under the stars, or in the shower. You control the candlelight, music, lotions, lubrication, and ambiance.

Playful, Creative Sensuality

Enjoy the total array of your senses and lovingly enhance touch as you employ the suggestions and encouragement of earlier chapters. Go slow and build tension as you sensuously progress through the lovemaking process. You can enjoy intercourse in different ways during the arousal and plateau phases of the sexual cycle. Let intercourse and various positions be interspersed throughout the arousal activities as you warmly connect as well as build tension. Each position will offer a new variety of ways to stimulate, touch, and take pleasure from each other's body. Allow your hands and mouth to keep actively caressing and stroking throughout intercourse. Focus on yourself and your partner.

Knowledge

Figure 12. 2 shows the physiology of intercourse with the penis in the vagina with the man on top. Stimulating intercourse is developed through a knowledge of male and female bodies. Notice where the penis touches in the vagina. Six o'clock, twelve o'clock, and the outer third of the vagina are most sensitive. The head of the penis and the coronal ridge create the greatest arousal in the male. The vagina or the penis is angled differently for every individual, and each couple need to find those positions that feel best for them. Never put up with physical discomfort, but make necessary adjustments to receive the most pleasure.

Becoming a great technical lover in intercourse is more than just knowing physiology and the various positions. The actual entry of the penis into the vagina can be new and exciting every time. Intercourse and the bonding one-flesh experience of lovers joining bodies should be an emotional and mental rush. Slow your mind and focus on the actual physical feelings of entry; don't take it routinely. As one partner separates the outer vulval lips and guides the penis in, each can delight again in the other's body. Over the many years together, this scintillating connection you enjoy can have a delightful electricity every time you experience it anew.

Make sure the lubrication (artificial or the seepage at the tip of the penis) has been gently spread over the head of the penis and the vaginal lubrication has wet the mouth of the vagina. (Dry skin chafes and hurts; be sure the vagina is lubricated.) The husband should take care not to simply shove in and start vigorously thrusting. Part

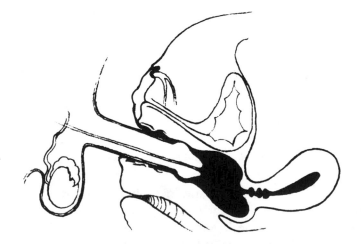

FIG. 12.2. Penis in vagina with man on top.

the outer lips with their pubic hair, and position the penis at the mouth of the vagina or allow the penis to sensually slide down the inner labial channel to the vagina. Slowly and gently push the penis in, reveling in the sensations. Slowly thrust part way in a time or two with tender gentleness as lubrication is spread, and revel in the feelings. Perhaps lightly shove the penis all the way in and stop thrusting, while the husband wiggles his penis by using his PC muscle and the wife tightens her PC muscle; feel warm and close in this one-flesh embrace. Allow the vagina to lovingly contain its partner.

Practice different rhythms of coital thrusting with pelvic muscles as both partners push to meet each other or one controls a given movement. The outer third of the vagina is particularly sensitive—the husband can practice quick, shallow thrusting at the mouth of the vagina, flicking the penis in and out. It is a myth that deep, strong thrusting is the greatest turn-on, though it can be very exciting for both partners, especially as excitement builds. Intermittently varying rates and depth of thrusting is a crucial skill of the mature lover. Intercourse thrusting might be charted like this: slow deep, rapid shallow, stop, rapid deep, stop, rapid deep, slow shallow, slow deeper, stop, rapid shallow, and so on.

Luxuriate in developing a variety of rhythms. When the wife is on top and in other positions, she can control penetration and pace the movement, bouncing and moving in ways that produce great feelings for her and her mate. Take care of muscles and ligaments; most of us are not gymnasts. It may be helpful to read the last section in chapter 18 on increasing arousal and becoming orgasmic during intercourse.

As excitement builds and orgasm approaches, the movements and rhythms of both partners will probably increase in intensity and rapidity. Again, movements do not have to be rough or painful. Muscle contractions, facial grimaces, exclamations of excitement, and rapid breathing will be a part of intercourse. Throughout the activity and especially toward orgasm, the wife can enjoy contracting the PC muscle. Remember, it is not abnormal for a male to climax in two or three minutes if actively thrusting. Throughout the process, practice stopping and starting, occasionally slowing down, and squeezing the male PC muscles (see chapter 22) to prevent premature ejaculation.

The stimulation and arousal caused by the angle and depth of the penis penetrating the vagina will vary from woman to woman. Talk and experiment. Varying the position will create different angles or allow deeper penetration. Enjoy what is exciting to you. Some find a lateral or scissors position, with the side of the vagina being stimulated, very arousing. The twelve o'clock (toward the belly button) and six o'clock (toward the anal area) parts of the vagina have many nerve endings and the G spot. Positions that stroke these areas (man-on-top; rear entry) are often physically exciting to the woman.

With intercourse, as with all of sexual activity, enjoyment and passion will be enhanced by your imaginations and stored erotic stimuli. Certain positions can excite the visual sense of the husband, and others the romantic, connecting needs of the wife. Invent a fun repertoire together. Celebrate the bonding, nurturing, and excitement of intercourse. It is indeed a fun playground activity for the loving, creative couple. At times forgo any movement and just lie in each other's arms, basking in the warmth of one-flesh togetherness.

You as a couple should consider seven items in finding positions of intercourse that provide variety, meet different needs, and enhance your lovemaking:

1. Are you comfortably supported so muscles don't grow weary and neither partner feels squashed or smothered?

2. Does the position allow for good penetration—not too deep or too shallow—with the penis, and is it hitting the right spots in the vagina?

3. Is there visual contact and is it sexy—with the husband and wife enjoying a view of each other's genitals and body with penis and vagina thrusting, and both appreciating eye-to-eye connection?

4. Does the position allow manual or oral contact with the body, breasts, or genitals? Can you kiss, cuddle, and caress—stroke scrotum or clitoris while thrusting?

5. Are you positioned with enough leverage to create easy, thrusting movements so that husband or wife or both can produce exciting friction?

6. Does it encourage creative lovemaking? Can you enjoy it in the shower? Can you accomplish it partially clothed? Does it allow either partner to take a more dominant role as desired?

7. Are there special needs? Can it work in pregnancy, can it work with a partial erection, can it lessen pressure on hips or knees, or can it help control the depth of thrusting?

Practice

You know the old saying that "practice makes perfect." Any new position will be awkward at first and perhaps not as fun, warmly connecting, or erotically arousing as ones you are used to. Practice is important so that you as a couple can quickly begin to enjoy different positions in an adept and relaxed manner. They say that if you use new vocabulary words three times in your conversation, they are yours for life. Do this with positions of intercourse, too.

Practice the following positions in two different ways. First, do some preliminary learning with the book beside you as you learn the position and try it out. Second, incorporate the new position into your lovemaking over the next week or two as you truly make it yours.

Be playful and creative as you make up some of your own variations to try. Also practice shifting into a new position from an existing position without removing the penis. This creates fun moves and erotic loveplay.

Eight Types of Intercourse Positions

The rest of this chapter develops eight basic types of intercourse positions. Under some types, two or three alternate positions are described. Relax and play at acquiring this knowledge. Learn what fits you two, but be creative and try some new positions. Consider when a given position would most enhance your lovemaking. Men and women have different physical and psychological makeups and will have differing preferences about what is exciting to them. Remember that as you take this knowledge and give it playful, creative sensuality.

1. Wife-on-Top

The wife-on-top positions are favorites for several reasons. For the husband who has a bad back or knees, this position takes the pressure off and allows his wife to be the active participant. It is also the needed position for a couple with disabilities who want to press into the vagina the flaccid penis of the husband. The positions are visually very arousing to the male, and the female is more in control of her own stimulation. Many women find being on top positions the vagina and clitoris to achieve orgasm more readily during intercourse. The husband's hands are also nicely placed to stimulate the clitoris as needed.

Kneeling

The wife kneels while she straddles her husband. She can use a number of angles: a backward tilt as she supports herself with arms straight and hands on his legs or the bed, a 90-degree upright stance with bouncing motions or a 45-degree forward tilt with weight on arms or forearms propped on pillows. This position allows the woman to control the depth of penile penetration and orchestrate the movement of the penis in the vagina with the clitoris against the pelvic bone. It may be easier for her

FIG. 12.3. Wife-on-top, kneeling.

to guide the penis into the vagina. It is also pleasurable to simply lay the penis on his stomach and, with proper lubrication, rub the clitoral area back and forth with a rocking motion across the erect penis without vaginal penetration.

The husband can also thrust with pelvic motions. This position is fun for the husband because his wife's breasts are near his face and mouth, and the pubic area is very visible. The wife can enjoy the easy access her husband has to massage the clitoris with his thumbs. For variation and different sensations, the wife can kneel facing away from the husband.

Prone

The wife lies comfortably on top with her legs straddling his body or between his legs, finding leverage with her feet and knees. She may also wish to prop her shins and feet insteps on top of her husband's lower legs and hold her feet against his feet to gain leverage for giving thrusting motions. In this prone position, as well as others, it is easier to insert the penis in a corollary position (wife kneeling) and then ease into the position desired. The woman-on-top position allows the wife to take the lead in a fun, selfish way, using her husband's body for her pleasure.

2. Side-By-Side

Couples enjoy side-by-side positions because bodies are comfortably close and facing each other for cuddling and kissing. Bodies are well supported, and both partners can control and contribute to coital thrusting while they caress and stroke.

Relax and enjoy the total experience of intercourse. Look at each other and delight in your mate's arousal and in the beauty of the body. Gently caress skin and revel in texture. Talk and give verbal and nonverbal exchanges of love and excitement. Close your eyes and focus on the specific pleasure of the penis in the vagina—go slow with light, feathery motions, rapidly thrust with penis touching only the outer inch of the vagina, try deeper penetration—stop and lie in each other's arms for a minute. Creative intercourse is making love, not just building to an orgasm.

FIG. 12.4. Side-by-side, wife straddling husband's leg.

Wife Straddling Husband's Leg

The husband lies comfortably on his side, with his bottom leg extended straight, his other leg bent at the knee, and his foot on the bed. The wife lies on her side and straddles the top bent leg, with her lower leg between his legs and her top leg thrown over his torso. This positions the penis at the vagina (with proper shifting) for easy access with either partner guiding it in. Again, pillows under heads or sides increase comfort.

Couple Embracing Chest to Chest

The wife lies on her side with the husband facing her in a mutual embrace. This may be most easily achieved by rolling over onto the sides from the wife-on-top or husband-on-top positions. The husband's top arm and hand are free to caress his wife's buttocks and back. This can be a fun, bonding embrace as you adjust the underneath arms for greatest comfort and both supply movement.

3. Husband-on-Top

This has often been called the missionary position because, according to legend, the Hawaiians did not employ this position. They were surprised to discover that the missionaries to their land used it exclusively. It may be an apocryphal story, but this standard position is often thought of as uncreative or elementary. Actually, it is pleasurable in various ways. It allows deep penetration, active thrusting by the husband, and a total body hug.

Legs Between

The husband lies on top of his wife and supports his weight with his knees and elbows or arms. His legs are together between her legs and give leverage for easy pelvic thrusting. Variations of this position are the wife's raising her legs and scissoring them around the husband's torso or raising her legs to rest on his shoulders. Be gentle. This position offers perhaps the deepest penetration of any position.

Legs Straddling

It is easier for the husband to start with legs together and the penis inserted in the vagina. Now, with the penis remaining inserted, he can gently shift one of his legs outside one of his wife's legs as he straddles that leg. For different sensations, he can shift his other leg from between to outside as he straddles with both legs outside his wife's legs. This allows his wife to clamp or scissor her legs together and produce greater friction on the penis in her vagina. The husband has an easy swinging motion of the pelvis and can raise up on his knees and elbows to relieve any excess pressure on his wife.

The husband-on-top position gives an ability to be body to body in a special one-flesh hug. Try just lying there in an intercourse embrace, remembering your commitment and love for each other as you rest warmly, savoring your togetherness.

4. Crosswise

Both crosswise positions are great for freeing hands to stimulate the clitoris and caress bodies. While the husband is thrusting, the wife can caress his testicles or scissor two of her fingers around his thrusting penis to increase stimulation. She can also stimulate herself or hold his hand as he stimulates her clitoral area. The husband can maneuver his body (collapsing the + into an X), while keeping the penis in the vagina so that he is able to nibble at her breasts and enjoy kissing, too, in these positions.

Wife's Legs Over

The husband lies on his side facing the wife, crosswise on the bed. His wife lies on her back and creates a cross of their bodies by resting her legs over his thighs with one leg toward his waist and the other leg toward his knees, allowing easy penetration by the penis. The husband creates the thrusting motion with pelvic movement.

Scissors

The husband lies crosswise on the bed with his head to the wife's right, and she lies on her back. This time the wife's right leg is propped over her husband's thighs, and her left leg is scissored between her husband's legs. If the husband is left-handed, he

Fig. 12.5. Crosswise, scissors.

scissors her right leg placing his head on her left side. This leaves manipulation and penetration of the penis to be controlled easily by the husband.

Scissors is an ideal position for using the penis as a wand to stimulate the vulva and clitoris. The husband can hold his erect penis and, with his wife's instructions, learn the right rhythms and pressure and placement to help her achieve an orgasm. If the wrist grows tired, he can use more of the entire arm, like painting, to vibrate and massage the clitoris. This can be interspersed with vaginal thrusting to keep the whole area lubricated. As she approaches a climax, the husband may wish to switch to vaginal stimulation alone.

Either crosswise position works well during pregnancy. From the scissors position, the couple can maneuver into the next position without withdrawing the penis. The wife rolls on her side with her back toward the husband. The husband gently unscissors her leg, then slides his legs so they are behind hers in a spoon position as he thrusts against her buttocks.

5. Rear-Entry

The rear-entry positions, especially the lying down spoons or both kneeling by the bed, are great during pregnancy. The wife should be comfortably supported with pillows as needed, and thrusting should be as gentle as desired.

FIG. 12.6. Rear-entry, spoons.

Spoons

The husband faces his wife's back, like two spoons cradling. The penis can be inserted with the husband separating legs and outer vulval lips, while the wife guides the penis into the vagina. Male pelvic thrusting bumps softly against her buttocks as the penis stimulates the front of the vagina and the G spot.

The husband can enjoy caressing his wife's stomach and breasts and stimulating her clitoris with his free hand. The wife often likes this angle of the penis with slow or vigorous thrusting that is exciting but not too deep. Both are comfortable with less demand on muscles and joints—a great position for aging bodies or for a break from more active loveplay.

Kneeling in Husband's Lap

The husband kneels with knees together and back upright. The wife kneels with her back to him, straddling his legs and propping herself in his lap—carefully inserting the penis as a mutual effort. He can place his hands on her hips to help control movement as she moves up and down, and he can create some pelvic thrusting. She may wish to bend forward and brace herself with her arms. This position leaves the husband's hands free to caress, while the wife can control depth and positioning of the penis with pelvic and leg movement.

Both Kneeling

The husband kneels behind his wife who is kneeling, bent at the waist with forearms and head resting comfortably on a pillow or the edge of the bed. The husband separates the outer lips from the rear and gently inserts his penis into the vagina. This position may seem awkward to the wife, but it is very visually stimulating to the husband. He has an exciting view of waist and hips and his penis penetrating the vulval area. It also allows easy thrusting motions from slow to vigorous and stimulation of the sensitive twelve o'clock part of the vagina.

Another variant of this position is for the wife to slide down into a prone position on the bed, with a pillow under her stomach propping her buttocks and genital area up. The husband lies down on her back with his legs between her legs and inserts his penis. He can get leverage for thrusting with his feet and knees as he hugs her from the back.

6. Standing

The standing positions encourage creative intercourse without the need for a bed. They are fun for rooms of the house other than the bedroom.

From the Back

This is similar to both kneeling, only both partners are standing. The wife bends at the waist and supports her weight with her hands on a bed, a table, or shower fixtures. The husband stands or crouches behind her and, separating outer labia with one hand, inserts the penis. This can be a fun position for a quickie in the kitchen or a romp in the shower.

Facing with Wife on One Leg

The wife faces the husband and raises her left leg, which he cradles with his right hand, and they mutually insert the penis. If the husband is much taller than the wife,

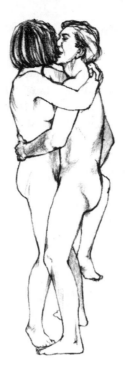

FIG. 12.7. Standing, facing with wife on one leg.

she may need to stand on a small stool or pillow. This position permits eye-to-eye contact and a chance to mutually hug and caress.

7. Face-to-Face

These face-to-face positions will remind you of the wife-on-top and the rear-entry kneeling (only reversed) positions of intercourse. The fun comes in as you stay creatively sensual and are willing to experiment. As playfulness and curiosity take over, you can create many hybrids on your own.

Husband Sitting and Wife Kneeling

The husband sits upright with his back propped against pillows, while his wife kneels astride his lap facing him with her legs around his thighs. This position allows for fun hugging and kissing and provides close body contact but not much leverage for thrusting. Movement can be assisted by the husband's hands under his wife's buttocks and bouncing motions. The penis can be mutually inserted, and since this position allows for deep penetration, care must be taken for comfort. This is a good position if the husband has back problems because he can be comfortable with his back propped with pillows.

Wife Supine and Husband Kneeling

The husband kneels and his wife, lying on her back, places her legs over his thighs with knees bent and feet flat on the bed. It may help to prop a pillow under her head and shoulders or position a pillow under her buttocks to position the penis better. This is a good position for using the penis to stimulate the clitoris. If the angle is too much to allow easy penetration, the husband may wish to bend forward and cradle his wife's legs with his hands under her buttocks or waist so access is more comfortable. This allows pelvic thrusting as well as adjustments and movement with his arms. This position can be gentle on the wife's arthritic or damaged knees. Again, husband and wife are face-to-face so they can enjoy each other visually. (For variety, have the wife flip over on her stomach with the insteps of her feet on the husband's shoulders—use imagination and creativity.)

FIG. 12.8. Face-to-face, wife supine and husband kneeling.

8. Partners and Props

In the chapter on setting moods, we explored the utilization of props, from candles to showers to pillows. These positions use the furniture around your house as props as you increase your erotic playing together.

Sitting on a Chair

The husband sits up straight on a chair that allows the wife to sit in his lap facing and straddling him. The penis is inserted with mutual effort. It is helpful if the wife's feet touch the floor or are propped up on pillows to ease insertion and to help create movement. This position, like other face-to-face positions, allows visual contact and kissing and holding and whispering or breathing in ears. The hands are free so the husband can caress back and buttocks. He may try cradling her buttocks in his hands to help produce movement with his arms. A variant of this position is to have the wife turn around and face away. Again, it is helpful if her feet can touch the floor. The husband can stroke breasts and clitoris while she reaches down and stimulates his penis with her fingers.

This position, like some of the other sitting positions, does not allow a great deal of thrusting motion. It can be quietly erotic; the connecting of intercourse does not always have to lead to rapid movement or produce a climax. Sitting positions can be playful, and they add variety.

Wife on the Edge

This position is important for men with bad backs or women during pregnancy. The bed is a comfortable object for the wife to be on the edge of, but don't limit creativity. Dining room tables, kitchen counters, couches, and easy chairs work well, too.

The wife is positioned at the edge of the bed, sofa, or table. Her legs are around her husband's torso, resting comfortably on his thighs, with his arms supporting and clamping them to his body. The husband kneels or stands depending on the height of the object the wife is on, so his penis is accessible to her vagina. He has an easy thrusting motion, and the wife may not be fully reclined but propped up on the pillows of an easy chair and have access to stroking and caressing herself and her husband.

This position is very visually stimulating to the husband: he can observe the vulval area and the penis thrusting in and out. It is exciting to the wife: she can observe her

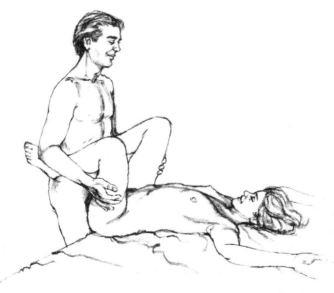

Fɪɢ. 12.9. Partners and props, wife on the edge.

partner's arousal by her body as well as experience her own visual excitement. Her vagina and clitoris receive excellent friction in this position. The wife-on-the-edge position works well during later stages of pregnancy or when the fatigued wife wants her husband to take the active role. It lends itself to all rooms of the house and provides some fun variation because it can be enjoyed without removing or wrinkling clothing.

You now have a good working knowledge with the basic positions and many variations. Now it is up to you to bring them alive in your lovemaking. Be curious and experimental as you take the risks to try new positions, and learn them well enough that they become comfortable. Truly frolic and laugh and love as you enjoy making intercourse a fun part of your sex life. Create your own variations and become lovingly at ease with a wide variety of moves and rhythms.

May God always be in your bedroom as you grow increasingly comfortable with His gift of erotic play. May you enjoy the specialness of one-flesh union as symbolized in intercourse. Use your God-given imagination and sensuality as you seek out positions especially suited to your bodies and those that can be very arousing to you as a couple. You have been given a rich and exciting treasure in the complexity and simplicity of sexual intercourse. Celebrate!

Chapter Thirteen

Making Love to Your Wife

You want to understand your wife, but you may be hampered by common male myths and attitudes. You are trying to be a great lover, but certain skill deficits and gender differences are getting in the way. Your wife at times may be a real mystery to you, and the great joy God intended for you and your partner is sabotaged. Let's try to solve this mystery so that making love to your wife can become more exciting for both of you.

Uniquely Female

Begin this journey by trying to walk in your wife's moccasins as you foster understanding. You have to get inside her head and see sex from a completely different perspective.

There are more similarities than differences between men and women. Some of the differences may be learned behaviors and not necessarily God-given, as we discussed in an earlier chapter. There is a uniqueness, though, that is helpful to understand.

Warmly Connected Soul Mates

The saying that "men give love to get sex and women give sex to get love" seems so manipulative and distorted. It is true that many men allow themselves to become more quickly emotionally connected through sex, while most women allow affection and other avenues to produce emotional attachment—they don't rely on sex so exclusively to create closeness.

It is also true that women seem to be more holistic in their sexual expression. They want to be affectionately connected as well as sexually connected. They want to have feelings of sharing another person's soul, of being truly included in the other's life and thinking, of accomplishing what the Bible describes as "becoming one flesh." In a wise, biblical way, women don't divorce sex as easily from the relational and emotional aspects the way men can. For women, fun sex flows out of an intimate companionship.

A woman wants to feel cared about and emotionally connected before sexual activity can have appeal. But conveying this feeling is not something you can do quickly an hour before you want sex. The atmosphere of intimacy and affectionate connecting involves daily and hourly choices. It begins in the kitchen and permeates your life together. More than likely, you more easily demonstrated these behaviors in your dating days as you let your defenses down and allowed yourself to be warm and passionate. Your wife's sexual fantasies may include this aspect of love, being admired, feeling supported, and being surprised with extra attention.

Build her up and affirm the many things you enjoy about her as you truly pay attention to her. Talk more, and share many positive experiences as lovers and friends. As you do, you'll feel closer to each other. Learn that sex has more to it than just physical arousal.

Your tenderness may be more erotic to your wife than great techniques. Time spent in loveplay draws her closer than time spent producing orgasms.

Consistently Inconsistent

You may wonder why your wife is physically inconsistent. On one evening she may like oral arousal or enjoy her breasts being caressed, and at another time she may not want that particular stimulation at all. Her body and reactions do not stay consistent, and you get confused. The fact is, she does change in what is arousing to her. Sometimes her clitoris is more sensitive than at other times, and a particular stroke is more irritating than exciting. A firm, rapid stroke might feel good later on in a lovemaking session but is annoying for her initially. Your penis is very consistent, and most times it responds to firm stimulation. But your wife's body does not function in this way.

A wife likes variety in the strokes and approaches to lovemaking. She needs you to vary the rhythms and ways you caress her: long strokes, light strokes with fingertips, circular, teasing, and firm. If you do something the same way every time, she is less likely to enjoy it. She needs flexibility and the skill to appreciate her body in consistently inconsistent ways. It can't be rote or mechanical if you want to truly be sensual and passionate with her.

Develop a series of strategies for making love. Become adept at smoothly switching gears, from strategy A to strategy B, depending on where your wife is in a given lovemaking session. Ask her to say what she wants. Sometimes she may just want to nurture you, and you may climax as quickly as you want to. At other times she may desire gentle massage of nonerogenous zones or her breasts. Expect inconsistency and revel in your fast footwork and improvisational skills. Become a skilled lover as you vary approaches and rhythms and types of stimulation. She will love your spontaneous variety.

Your wife may not have the same consistent desire that you do. This may be hormonal, and you can enjoy certain times in her menstrual cycle. It may also be relational and environmental as you help make changes to alleviate stress and create romance. Talk about it and negotiate.

Vulnerable to Distraction

Your wife may be more easily distracted by the environment and her inner attitudes. When she is fatigued, struggling with body image, or feeling hurt, she may be unable to focus on sex, and her sexual desire is dampened. Fearing that children might interrupt or hear lovemaking may be another major distraction.

Your wife, more than you, may have to fight distractions during actual lovemaking as she focuses on her own arousal. The wise husband minimizes distractions. Be sensitive to her concerns. Install a good lock on the door so she need not fear the children's intrusion. Keep tissues and lubrication handy.

A part of overcoming susceptibility to distractions is that you probably want to make love without the mood having to be exactly right. As you are more supportive and involved, she may be in the mood more often. Your wife may find making love more appealing and restorative in spite of the distractions.

If your wife is fatigued, sex can sometimes be restorative. As you are more supportive and emotionally involved with her, she may be in the mood more often.

Making Love an Emotional Choice

Your wife is more likely to willfully choose when she wants to make love—it isn't the more immediate, hormonal surge that it can be with you. Wives love surprises and being spontaneous, but they are usually not crazy about quickies or jumping into bed the minute the vacation destination is reached. Maybe it is a learned response. Women have most often had to take the responsibility to prevent pregnancy, and there has been the double standard, which says that men try to score and women are the gatekeepers. But it may be deeper than that, based on the need to feel mental and emotional connection before making love. Out of a bonding feeling of emotional connection flows the choice to be physically united. It may also be a need to have making love be a meaningful experience, with the children and other duties taken care of. Sex is more purposeful, romantic, and intimate with a woman; you can learn a lot from this emotional choosing.

Sex is an emotional decision stemming from a companion, and it often involves some anticipation and preparation for a woman. Plan fun romantic evenings for your wife. The sex seems to be more exciting and easier to engage in when she can save energy and enjoy the build-up. Not always but often, she appreciates when she can plan for sex with a sense of appropriate timing.

Husbands often learn quickly that if she wants to make love, she has made a choice and is ready. Perhaps you have had the experience of staying in front of the television to watch the last quarter of the game, then rushing into the bedroom ready to go, only to find her fast asleep and the opportunity lost.

Your wife has to want sex and choose to make love in ways that are consistent with how she is feeling, with emotional and affectionate attachment. The timing must be appropriate with plenty of loveplay as her body is "primed" and allowed to respond in a passionate way to her choice.

Gentle and Teasing and Slow

The husband can easily be an inept and insensitive lover. And a wife may complain of clumsiness, speed, or predictability. There may be a real skill deficit in the art of touching softly, approaching gently, and keeping a teasing variety in lovemaking.

There can be too much pawing and grabbing and immediate sex. Your wife may feel frustrated and sometimes inadequate. You may wonder why she doesn't light up with ecstasy as you expect her to—from your education in the locker room and movies and novels.

Especially in initial loveplay, your wife may prefer gentle, teasing caresses, and she may like for intercourse to start off with easy, shallow thrusts. You can practice touching with just the soft pads of your fingertips, teasing with light tracing movements of one finger, gentle massaging with the palms of your hands, and using your penis as a wand rather than a battering ram.

She may like to flirt, to start making love with clothes still on. She may love it when you tease her body and softly blow in her ear, kiss her neck, and do not immediately head for her breasts or genitals. The pleasure will gradually grow, and will be exciting when you take the time to playfully torment her by coming on, then backing off. Take a lot of time to become aroused and then lose some of the arousal, only to be aroused again.

Slow is the operative word in fantastic sex. Teasing arousal by its very nature takes time. Lovemaking will get vigorous and fast in the later stages, but a gradual, unhurried, leisurely pace will be greatly appreciated by your mate. Masters and Johnson's research indicated that a woman in her subjective arousal took longer to achieve an orgasm. Your wife may sometimes feel turned off by your quick arousal and your desire for immediate stimulation of your penis. She may enjoy direct stimulation of her clitoris in a vigorous manner but not at first. Sometimes she may fear she is taking too long and you are getting tired. She may need reassurance that stimulating her is arousing for you.

Going slow demonstrates to her that you love her, and it enhances her romantic connection to you. The tenderness and loveplay are important. She may not always need an orgasm to feel fulfilled. Orgasms may not be so equated with ultimate sexual pleasure in her mind. But being gentle and teasing and slow can revitalize your lovemaking.

Multiorgasmic

Women are multiorgasmic; men are not. After a man has had an orgasm, he has a recuperative time and often does not want to be stimulated for a period of time—from minutes to hours to days as he grows older. A woman can have a series of orgasms, one right after the other. A woman may experience five or more separate orgasms in a couple of minutes with a short pause or rest between each.

Some women report a sequential orgasm with a series of spasms or orgasms as a part of the same experience and no pause between. Masters and Johnson's research stated that mild orgasms in males and females have three to five muscle spasms and intense orgasms can have eight to twelve spasms. The sequential orgasm can be explained as a more intense orgasm with more spasms in a single experience.

Women often report varying intensities in their orgasmic experiences—perhaps both a physical and a psychological response. Sometimes the climax feels more like an intense reaction, and at other times it feels like a more generalized wave of sexual feeling spreading throughout the body and lasting longer. Another phenomenon with some women is a gushing of vaginal secretions upon orgasm almost in an ejaculatory fashion, which can sometimes be a part of intense arousal. But don't get hung up on numbers or multiple orgasms! Help your wife enjoy her orgasmic potential, but let go of any need to create more or deeper climaxes. She won't be keeping score as long as you are being an increasingly skilled lover. The intensity of the orgasms will follow.

Erotic Symbolism and Sensuality

What do women find sexy in men? Eyes and gentle or sexy or attentive looks are turn-ons. Stomachs and buttocks that are kept in shape are high on the list, along with grooming in general (haircuts and showers and aftershave). Many women notice hands and find them sensually arousing—maybe imagining them caressing their bodies. Women notice voices and what they represent in loving, nurturing interchanges. Talking and being vulnerable are important; the ability to express feelings is very attractive and arouses erotic feelings. Minds are often considered sexy, and men are pleasing who can be passionate about life or a cause.

Your wife may enjoy smells and sounds and touch in ways you never thought to appreciate. Making love can become much more interesting and arousing as you learn from her sensual temperament and incorporate a wider range of erotically stimulating symbols.

Vive la Romance

People are not born romantic. Romance is a combination of skills and attitudes that are learned. I remember in my inept dating days when I was still learning those skills. I was so embarrassed one evening. I jumped out of the car I had parked, and I was fifty feet across the parking lot before I looked back and realized my date was still in the car waiting for me to open her door. She had been well-trained by her mother, and I forgot to employ some of my father's everyday behaviors toward my mom: respect, attentiveness, and personal interest.

What is this romance that women yearn for and need to have included in their sex lives and relationships? The words *special sweetheart* describe the attitude your wife desires from you. Your passionate focus on her as if she is the only woman in the world and your many little gestures make her feel special.

Women are vulnerable to the seduction of romancing: having dinner by candlelight; receiving surprise gifts, cards, and flowers; and trusting them with sharing one's soul as inner needs and feelings are disclosed. Women desire unsolicited attention and the feeling of being special.

Women especially need romantic affirmation after making love. Make time to hold your wife and quietly caress her and show her how much she means to you. Create an afterglow so she can revel in the close bonding you have just experienced. Affirm her feminine vulnerability in opening herself up to receive you into her, and show her that you love her and are trustworthy. Celebrate and extend the excitement you have delighted in together and how meaningful it is to share her sexual arousal. Mention something you particularly enjoyed, and tell her you love her.

Women are certainly on target in demanding romance as a necessary component of making love. *Vive la romance!* Great sex does indeed originate from your imaginative creativity and romantic inspirations—and the discipline (time and energy) to carry them out.

For Men Only

Men constantly sabotage their efforts to be the world's greatest lover. In this section we will consider how easy it is for men to objectify women and sacrifice depth in sexual bonding. We need to truly love our wives with passion and depth. This leads into the need to expand our erotic repertoire and truly be connoisseurs of sex and of our lovers. Great lovers are sensitive, and we will discuss some methods for improving sensitivity. Finally, we will explore the concept that women are excited by passionate, confident men who can lead.

3-D Women

Men have a difficult time letting women be three-dimensional, with a body, soul, and spirit. The preoccupation with the body aspect of sex actually puts a damper on the true fun God intended. I am not saying that God gave the female form with its wonderful curves and sexual allure to be ignored and not enjoyed. I am simply encouraging men to consider that any time they look at a woman, whether on film or in life, and think of her only as an object for sexual arousal, without a personality or a connection with God (3-D), they are sacrificing ultimate sexual enjoyment.

Becoming truly monogamous will help you as a husband stay three-dimensional. When you are attracted by the physical beauty of another woman, tell yourself: "God has given me my own partner for sex; this woman is someone else's partner and not mine to enjoy." Cultivate this one-woman attitude, and your intimacy as well as your ability to enjoy women as people will blossom.

Do you want to be a great lover? Learn to notice women holistically, and sometimes look at them only from the neck up. Forget sexuality completely. Pay attention to competent women in the workplace, and maybe read books by female authors as you challenge your stereotypes. In women you observe, be aware of depth, with a personality and needs and feelings and flaws. Men, myself included, want the one-dimensional feminine beauty to be flawless—we don't want to see warts, scars, or sags. When you see a sexy woman (not in magazines where they have touched up the photos), look for fatigue or cracked fingernails or a mole—anything that makes her a real person. This skill in seeing women as three-dimensional will spill over into your marriage and sex life in several important ways.

You will truly learn to love and appreciate femininity in general, and your wife in particular, in new and exciting ways. You will begin to notice more physical dimensions like ears, hands, and eyes rather than just breasts and genitals. You will better observe your wife as playful or intense or intelligent. You will notice the way her friends and family enjoy interacting with her. Your mate will experience more acceptance and admiration, and your lovemaking will have more soul to it. Your sex life will have a new depth and added dimensions.

Let me warn you about something that I hope you haven't already done. At some point you will find some aspect of your wife's body that does not appeal to you and you will obsess about it. *Don't*—I repeat, *don't*—talk to your wife about it. It will only hurt her and come back to haunt you.

Work out these obsessions with a good friend, a therapist, or on your own, and pray about it. Focus on her sexy, strong points, and the supposed flaws will come to have less importance. Quit comparing your wife to fantasies as you accept, love, and enjoy her.

A Sexual Connoisseur

I don't want to make a sweeping judgment, but I imagine right now you are in a boring sexual routine. You may not know it, but you need to expand your repertoire of erotically arousing stimuli. Most men have a very underutilized imagination and have forfeited real sensuality by getting locked into a couple of scenes and situations that they have allowed to become erotically charged.

Reread chapters 6, 7, and 10 as you better understand the importance of being sensual, playful, and creative in your sexuality. We men have the reputation of being sexual experts, and I know each of us would like to be a sexual connoisseur. So often though, we get locked into knowledge and erotic arousal that date back to high school. God created the one-flesh concept of making love for a husband and wife to enjoy sex in an ever-new and refreshing manner. You need to know effective technique, but much of being a great lover is your attitude of being willing to continually learn and incorporate new ideas into your sex life.

Our wives have legitimate complaints that we can be uninspired and mechanical in our lovemaking. Sometimes we need to have a better memory and remember and incorporate things they have told us they enjoy—and change irritating behaviors. We can be too immediate sexually, with a short attention span, which stops us from being slow and teasing. We don't take the time to create romance and ambiance. *But* men have a bad rap for being stubborn and unwilling ever to change. I disagree.

Men are intelligent and flexible in using new knowledge once we start trying. Please work at broadening your sexual repertoire as you become more sensual, imaginative, and romantic, and incorporate some of the strong points of the feminine sexual reality. Step back and at least ponder the idea that you, like most men, are living out a very restricted sexual existence presently.

Male Mythology

Probably the most prevalent male myth concerns the size of the penis. Look at your penis in a full-length mirror. When you look down, it always looks smaller, but when you look across, it is more in perspective. But this is irrelevant. Do some self-talk and get over any feeling of inferiority. It's not the size but how you use it.

Along with the size-of-penis myth is the idea that a woman is turned on by hard, deep thrusting in intercourse. Clench your fist and try tapping your cheek and jaw with it, using a little force. Now try softly patting the tender tissue of your face with your fingers—it feels better, doesn't it? Your wife will enjoy and be more turned on by softer, smoother motions in intercourse as you make love to her tender genitals. Another variant of this myth is that a really sexy wife will want her husband to take her immediately and then will go into fits of ecstasy as his penis fills her vagina.

Another devastating myth is that men know all about sex and are always ready to go sexually. On a recent television show, someone stated that sex is all men think about. That simply isn't true. We have our knowledge and desire deficits just like women, but we often feel guilty admitting them. All of us, as lovers, feel very deficient and inhibited at times. Where do men come up with such distorted ideas? The locker room, peers, movies and magazines, popular music—and the belief that women think and feel the same way as men.

You have heard stories in high school or at work of some woman who wanted sex all the time. I call this the nympho myth. Psychological research shows that people's characteristics, like their intelligence or sexual desire, can be charted on a bell-shaped curve.

Most women and their sexual desires are average (see fig. 13.1). Sixty-eight percent of women will fall in the category of quite moderate sexual interest, 14 percent will have somewhat higher or lower interest, and only 2 percent will fall in the extreme of very low or very high desire. Many women's sexual barometers are not shaped by hormones or genetics. They vary from strong desire to lack of desire because of environmental influences and their mental and emotional attitudes. These factors (e.g., lack of experience, a need for safety, sexual abuse, fatigue and children, or anger) can often be overcome with love and an intimate relationship, some work, and perhaps therapy. Those high on the scale of sexual desire may also need to work

Inhibited   Strong

Fɪɢ. 13.1. Women's sex drive.

through what sex means to them. Is it a way to get love or maybe an effect of not liking themselves because of abuse? They may be trying to satisfy other needs through sex.

Start letting go of your myths. Your wife is probably quite average in desire, and you don't have to be a sexual machine. Don't assume that problems are all hers or yours. Look at ways that you both might be contributing to a lack of sexual frequency and other concerns you have in your lovemaking.

Let's talk briefly about anal sex. Many Christian men have allowed this to become an obsession detracting from the rest of their lovemaking. They obsess about this behavior as a symbol of variety or adventure. The vaginal tissue was designed by God for intercourse and the anus was not. With hemorrhoids and the fragility of the rectal area, it is better not to make it an area of sexual arousal. It is so easy to sustain tears and lesions in the rectal tissue. Also, many bacteria in the anus can interfere with the bacterial balance in the vagina and cause infections.

This may be an area of your fantasies that you need to let go of. A great lover is always empathetic to the needs and sensitivities of his mate. Because your mate finds certain types of sexual behavior uncomfortable or completely unappealing does not make her in any way inhibited or less adventurous. You may be the one creating barriers by remaining obsessive about one symbolic area. Search out your sexual mythology. Challenge and erase some of those myths and obsessions from your mind. You will be a better lover.

Macho Sensitivity

Your wife will be able to blossom as a woman and as a lover as you are able to sensitively understand and affirm her. You may need to start with affirming yourself and your body image and sexual self-esteem. Accept the size of your penis, trust your ability to acquire whatever skills you need to be an adept lover, and exercise your romantic creativity. You have the intelligence to understand and remember sexual moves she enjoys. You can learn to be very sensitive and attain skills to empathize accurately, respond gently, be more self-disclosing, and enjoy feelings. Maleness and sensitivity are not opposing concepts. Here are some ideas to practice that can help you be a sensitive, focused lover:

Get a Ph.D. in "My Wife." You should get a doctorate for the study of your wife. Continually learn new things, and detach from the way you think and feel so you can truly understand your mate. Maybe you could do your dissertation on her sexual needs and how you think you could affirm her femininity and increase her sexual pleasure. Listen to her, observe her, increase your attention span, ask questions, try different things as you collect data, and be willing to make changes to please her.

Gain a working knowledge of feelings. Sensitive people have to recognize various feelings in themselves and others. They also need to become comfortable in expressing and receiving a whole range of feelings. What feeling are you most comfortable with now? Maybe start there and expand into some that you are less comfortable with. It is especially important sexually that you learn to empathize and express excitement, dissatisfaction, gentleness, joy and happiness, contentment, discomfort, and pleasure.

Cultivate softness, humility, gentleness, and love. Paul exhorted the Ephesians, "Be completely humble and gentle; be patient, bearing with one another in love" (Eph. 4:2 NIV). Learn to have a light touch and a soft empathetic approach. Practice gentle responses and the strategy of going slow. Cultivate this feminine side of your masculine personality. It is a vital part of being a sensitive and adept lover.

Learn the art of empathy. We talked about empathy in regard to communication skills (see chapter 8). You will never be sensitive unless you can learn to understand and validate your wife's reality, which will be much different from your own. Learn to speak a different language and deal in a different dimension. In the same way you desire her to put herself into your head and do things that will turn you on, she needs you to be gentle, easy, and slow. It will take time and practice, but it is an amazing catalyst for intimacy.

Passionate Leader

Most wives want husbands who are strong and confident and can provide nurturing. They would like men who are not always predictable but have spontaneous energy and mystery. They desire men who have sexual expertise but who are also able to implement suggestions without pouting and shutting down. They love men who are secure enough to appreciate and encourage their taking the sexual lead—leaders who enjoy being seduced, yet who can competently stimulate their arousal. I see no reason why all of us cannot achieve this goal of being a passionate guide for some great lovemaking.

It is probably tough for you not to take constructive criticism or suggestions very personally. Try not to take any comment on your lovemaking as a personal put-down. Learn to give and take constructive suggestions and express what you need—or you will never be a competent lover. Encourage communication; mind reading is impossible.

There may be times you feel embarrassed because you initiate sexual activity and your mate does not desire to participate. *Don't continue the behavior and hope your wife finds it stimulating.* She won't! "Stop," "no," or "that hurts" means exactly what she says. Don't pout, either. That is especially easy to do when you really want sexual activity and she just is not in the mood. Practice gracefully initiating and refusing. Don't fall into the common male pattern of being prickly or moody if you are not making love as often as you'd like. Confront and discuss as you and your wife problem solve.

Let's talk expertise awhile. It is not fair for your wife to expect you to know all about sex or to have an instant erection. You are not a programmed machine. But she enjoys your acquiring the necessary techniques and skills to be an efficient lover. That is fair, and that is what this chapter and book are all about. She desires you to lead and to arouse her. Remember, she is not predictable, and you will have to have four or five alternate ways of stimulating her and building the tension toward orgasm.

Learn to encourage and accept her suggestions. You can do this in a confident way as you increase your leadership and expertise. She will expect you to remember what she taught you about her needs and preferences.

If you can succeed in your career, with its many demands and needs for varying skills, you can become a self-assured and expert lover. Don't be predictable. Surprises bring a jolt of energy to the relationship as you increase your image of being mysterious, romantic, and passionate. She may think she has you figured out, but keep her off balance with impromptu romantic flourishes. Mystery and variety are very sexy to your wife. Keep humble and secure and nondefensive as you evolve into a passionate leader.

David's Sling and Harp

David was a man after God's own heart as he tried to remain within God's guidelines and humbly welcome the revelation of new truth in his life. He made some serious mistakes but repented and made changes. He was a strong leader as he protected Israel with a sling against Goliath.

David was a man's man and a part of that was his great sensitivity. The powerful warrior and king played a harp. He was passionate as he built relationships, danced before the ark, and loved deeply. With his harp, he would soothe and entertain with an empathetic touch.

Your wife needs you to be her David with a sling as you provide a protective covering of attentiveness and romantic leadership. She desires you to be sensitive and to gently soothe her, to entertain and to be playful. This will not always be an exciting job.

Having a great sex life and being a strong and sensitive leader are built on some mundane but important things. Prioritize them into your behavior and make your wife feel special. Remember David's sling and harp. Emotional connection and nurturing precede sexual readiness and arousal. The following activities can make your wife feel tremendously in love and alive.

The Art of Kissing

Women enjoy variety in kissing, and the mouth can be extremely sensuous.
Butterfly kisses. Lightly kiss all over her face and body, keeping lips soft and gentle.

Kiss her eyelids, behind her ear, her neck, between her breasts, all over her stomach and thighs. Be light and teasing, like a butterfly flitting about.

Gently sucking. Practice this kiss by taking your fingertip and placing it between your lips and lightly touch your tongue to the fingertip—now pull your finger out of your mouth with a gentle sucking motion. Try this on your wife's nipple, her fingers or toes, her neck, or her lower lip.

Warm, connecting ones. Plant a warm, juicy kiss on your wife's cheek or forehead as you walk by. It is almost like the family kiss that communicates greeting, love, and "you're my special person." It lets her know you enjoy her companionship and not just the sexual relationship. Hugging her, rubbing her shoulders or feet, and holding her hand in public convey this idea in warm and emotionally connecting ways, too.

Deep kissing. There is something passionate and intimate about sharing mouths and tongues. Here, as in all of sex, good hygiene applies. Bad breath is out. Brush your teeth before you go to bed. Don't fill her mouth with your tongue or shove it down her throat. Long exciting kisses where you have to come up for breath should vary between playful tongue contact (don't immediately go beyond her teeth), warm and easy nibbling of her lower lip or earlobe, and deep, passionate sharing of tongues and souls. Breathe heavy and allow yourself to become aroused as you make kissing a drawn-out affair.

Practice long hugs, also. It is amazing, at first, how long a thirty-second hug can seem when compared to an ordinary hug. You will be pleasantly surprised how bonding they will become. The dutiful hug or quick peck on the cheek does not accomplish what a longer hug or kiss will for creating the feelings of being in love.

Making Love to Her Breasts

Breasts and nipples are very symbolic of femininity. They are erotically charged and an important part of the sexual anatomy to both you and your wife. Compliment, appreciate, admire, and enjoy them—don't grab, squeeze, or instantly rub.

Making love to your wife's breasts, like all of making love, should teasingly progress from light touches to more direct stimulation. Lightly brush your hand over the entire breast and her stomach without lingering on the nipples. Take a finger and move lightly in circles around the nipple and move the circle out to include the complete breast, and then move to the other breast. Avoid contact with the nipples at first. Put your fingertips together and place them on the nipple. Open your fingers and slide them over the breast until the palm is resting on the nipple.

Lightly rub the palm of your hand on the erect nipple. Now progress to more direct stimulation with light tongue movement and soft, nibbling kisses. Enjoy the closeness as this moves into warm sucking and intimate arousal. Caress her face and body as you continue making love to her breasts.

Private Intimacy

Part of the beauty and bonding nature of making love is choosing to allow another person, your special mate, into the most private areas of your life and body. Your wife allows you, her husband, to explore and enjoy her vulva, vagina, and clitoris in ways she has probably never even done herself. You need an intimate understanding of her body, especially her clitoris.

The clitoris is the central organ for stimulating sexual arousal in your mate. Expecting your wife to have an orgasm through vaginal stimulation alone (without carefully stimulating the clitoral area) is like her expecting you to climax by rubbing your testicles (without stimulating your penis). The clitoris is another part of the female anatomy that will need an indirect approach. Don't head for it immediately.

Again, the art of teasing comes into play. With a soft, extremely light touch, caress thighs and stomach and outer lips and pubic hair—varying the motion from circles to pats to gentle, long strokes. Don't focus yet. Keep teasing. Try closing your hand and forming a V with your index and middle fingers. Gently walk these two fingers over her torso and legs, like a horse slowly and playfully galloping in a teasing manner. Stiffen the same two fingers and run the V softly over her outer lips, starting down at her vagina and up to her navel—then reverse and back down again and gently up again and gallop some more.

As she gets more excited, take thumb and middle finger, and rub the outer lips together over the clitoral area as you stimulate her more directly. Remember that the clitoris needs to be kept lubricated during lovemaking. Vaginal secretions, saliva, seminal fluid, or artificial lubricants can be used. It is very sensitive tissue and can be irritated quickly, which is obviously a turn-off. Unlike in the vagina, the lubrication does not appear naturally.

Women vary in the way they desire clitoral stimulation. Learn what your wife appreciates the most. Let her place her hand over your hand as you relax it, and let her guide your fingers as to the amount of pressure and rhythms she finds most exciting. It may be direct as she gets aroused or remain quite indirect. You can feel her clitoris get hard as you caress the top of the clitoral hood—it feels like a small electrical cord under the skin. Some women experience a more intense orgasm through external stimulation of the clitoris without the penis in the vagina. You may wish to vary the way you bring her to a climax and sometimes just pleasure her without intercourse until she has climaxed.

The mouth and tongue can stimulate the clitoral area in a very sensual manner. Oral sex, like many other enjoyable techniques, depends on a couple's sensitivities. In fun and loving sexual activity, you are always sensitive to your mate's likes and dislikes. This is especially true of oral sex. There seems to be nothing contrary to Scripture in having oral sex unless you engage in it to the exclusion of all else or force it on your mate.

There are three positions of intercourse that your wife will find especially exciting because they enable you to provide direct stimulation to her clitoris:

(1) the scissors position; (2) the husband in back in the spoon position; and (3) the wife-on-top position. (For details, see chapter 12.)

The G Spot

In the early 1950s, a German physician, Ernst Grafenberg, described a place within a woman's vagina that has since been named the Grafenberg or G spot. The G spot is located about an inch or two into the vagina at the twelve o'clock position toward the navel. It is about the size of a nickel and seems analogous to the prostate in the male. When stimulated, it can become smoother and firmer than other vaginal wall tissue. Whole books have been written about this phenomenon, though many sex therapists think it has been greatly overrated.

The fact of the matter is that the vagina is sensitive and certain parts like the G spot can create more intense physical sensations. That is why different positions of intercourse feel different as the penis rubs various parts of the vagina. An excellent exercise for husband and wife to conduct every now and then is genital exploration. After your wife is relaxed, take a finger and explore her vagina as she tells you what areas are most sensitive. Try to find the G spot. Often six o'clock toward the anus and twelve o'clock toward the clitoris are very sensitive with many nerve endings.

God has given you a precious gift in creating for you your own special woman and putting you into a one-flesh companionship with her. Together you two can enjoy excitement and intimacy! Maximize His gift as you humbly and wisely become a skilled and passionate leader and lover.

Chapter Fourteen

Making Love to Your Husband

Many times you have probably been amazed at the way your husband thinks and acts sexually. From the male perspective, there are few situations where sex doesn't add some spice and enhance the relationship. He can seem so obsessive and physically direct.

Making love is perhaps the primary means your husband uses to feel connected to you. He may allow emotions to come out and himself to be physically close in a special way during your lovemaking. He also utilizes his sexual feelings to create variety and excitement in his life, perhaps letting sex have too prominent a place in his thinking and needs. As you read the following pages, you will discover he has a different sexual reality from yours. You may have to make some changes in the way you think, feel, and act to please him and improve your love life. But it is interesting that you are probably more similar sexually than you are different.

You both were created to enjoy your sexual feelings and have fun with erotic loveplay. You will find that his desire can be dampened by fatigue, conflict, anxiety, or a fear of losing control, just like yours. He actually doesn't always want sex and can become very balanced in expressing feelings and being intimate without having to be sexual. His feelings will get hurt, and he will shut down emotionally and sexually sometimes, just like you. You may have more desire than he does right now, and he will have to work through his fear of intimacy or whatever is blocking the excitement.

Uniquely Male

Are men different or simply more immature sexually than women? Women overall seem to be more holistic with their sexuality than men. They value emotional involvement and are not so genitally focused. Some of your husband's actions and attitudes may stem from immaturity, and he indeed may need to make some changes. Many of them, though, are due to the fact that you and he are wired differently. This section explains some of these distinctions.

No Menstrual Cycle, More Apparent Desire

Female hormonal fluctuation is tied in to the menstrual cycle. Obviously, men do not experience this cycle. The hormone operating primarily in the male, testosterone, remains at a steady level within the male body until aging has some effects. Though this is not always true, many women find some of their sexual desire tied to the hormonal cycle. Men do not experience this phenomenon, and their testosterone (the hormone that creates desire in both men and women) creates a fairly consistent desire.

That the male desire is apparently (more visible but not necessarily) stronger may be more a psychological than a biological occurrence. Because of the double standard in our society, boys are given a freer rein to their sexual curiosity and experimentation. They are encouraged to tune in to sex more as they, at an earlier age, build a strong visual arousal to sexual cues. Their genitals are also more visible as they hold the penis each time they urinate. No wonder they are genitally and sexually more aware. Much of this sexual proactiveness is certainly learned behavior rather than physiological.

Because men use making love as a primary way of connecting with their mates, their sexual desire can seem greater because the sexual part of the relationship may carry the load of maintaining intimacy. The need for more sexual activity can stem from an inability to connect in other ways, like conversations and nonsexual touching. Some men are so afraid of intimacy that they cannot let themselves connect, even sexually. Some wives are surprised their husbands are not the sexual dynamos they expected. Men are not sexual machines always switched on. They can be angry or stressed out or have defensive walls up that can sabotage their ability to relate sexually.

Your husband's sex drive is probably more apparent than yours, and it does affect the way he interacts within marriage. Enjoy it as you give freer rein to your sexual desire and he learns to find more avenues for enjoying companionship.

Visually Specific and Genitally Focused

You can't have helped seeing how your husband is prone to noticing parts of the female anatomy. Research has shown that both men and women are aroused by visual stimulation, but they have different styles visually. A woman can drive by a cute male jogger, notice his strong physique, and immediately forget the visual stimulus. A man can see a female jogger and almost drive off the road trying to see in the rearview mirror what her breasts are like. He is more specific and obvious in his pursuit of visual sexual cues. He may even fantasize further about the cute jogger as he mentally tunes in to other sexual cues.

Men, in general, need to learn to discipline the thought life better and tune out some of the sexual cues in the environment. They can more easily depersonalize sex as they tune in to erogenous zones more quickly than their wives do. They can stay one-dimensional and see an erotic body without noticing the personality. That can lead to objectifying a woman and seeing her as a sexual object rather than as a total person. But there is a positive side to this trait.

Focusing visually on sexuality can also be exciting as your husband appreciates and affirms your femininity. His excitement and arousal can be contagious. You may find yourself tuning in to sexual cues more readily and learning from his openness to sexuality.

If you have shared fantasies with your husband and discussed what you really enjoy sexually, you may be amazed at the differences. Your fantasies of past vacations likely include a lot of ambiance and tender relating along with lovemaking. You may recall the wonderful bed and breakfast and feeling so relaxed being away from the children. Perhaps you woke up to see him bringing you a cup of coffee, looking so cute in his green boxers with the hearts on them. Maybe you started to fool around and the sex grew into a passionate forty-five minutes of exciting lovemaking.

He may remember the bed and breakfast too, but his fantasies likely include your seductive movements and the way your bodies came together in exciting sexual passion. Your husband may remember fondly the lace see-through lingerie and your sexual surprises before breakfast and dinner. His would be a visual, genitally-focused reality.

Great sex is built on going from general arousal to stimulating specific locations. You naturally tend to enjoy the general and teasing arousal, while he more enjoys the excitement of specific locations. It is fun to combine these different styles. You will find that a part of you enjoys a focus on erotic zones, and he can appreciate a more general, sensual approach. Each of you may find similarities you didn't know existed.

Immediate and Quicker

Your husband has a tendency toward immediate gratification with his visual arousal and genital focus. You may enjoy an occasional spontaneous, quick encounter but not as much as he does. You probably seldom notice your husband getting out of the shower, but he usually appreciates your naked appeal. The problem is that one half hour before needing to be at an office party is hardly the time to make love. Often, what he sees he also wants to touch. Don't overreact. He'll probably be satisfied with a long kiss and a few caresses. You may feel that his quick responses are a bit of a nuisance when you go away for a weekend if as you arrive at the hotel he wants to make love right away and you want to unwind or sightsee or reconnect. An understanding of each other's reality helps to reach a compromise.

In sexual cycling, you will take longer to reach an orgasm. Sex researchers

Masters and Johnson found that men climaxed in less than two minutes if actively thrusting and women took a longer time psychologically for arousal (up to eleven minutes) and orgasm. And after an orgasm, he'll need a longer recuperative period between orgasms. This difference in quickness may also require some accommodation.

Wives may sometimes wonder if their husbands have remained sexual adolescents (even though it adds zest to their lovemaking). He thinks about sex a lot; he tends to forget consequences and jump into pleasure, whether it means being late to a party or messing up her lipstick; he touches and grabs at what he likes; he loves the excitement of the moment, even if brief, and then savors these incidents to talk and think about later. He often has a short attention span sexually and will skip to something that seems to offer more fun. You probably love these qualities in your mate, even though sometimes they drive you crazy.

Predictable

What turns you on physically today might vary tomorrow. Sometimes you want direct clitoral stimulation, and sometimes you do not. But your husband is very predictable. If you appeal to him visually or rub his penis, he gets excited. He has to work harder than you do at creating a broader repertoire of erotically arousing stimuli and to be able to change gears in the middle of lovemaking. Nevertheless, he does not want sex all the time and does not have an instant erection.

In another very important way men are predictable. All men at some time or another will have trouble getting an erection. It may be fatigue, stress, or anger that has precipitated the loss of erection. You can be a great help by not panicking with him. Tell him it is normal, and move into another aspect of feeling close. Don't work too hard on that given night to try and get the erection back, but tell him it will be okay the next time. Your reaction is very important. Be truly loving and supportive. (You may want to read chapter 22.)

In some ways it can be fun that your husband is an easy read. When you take risks and initiate something silly or different, it will seldom flop. Try to remember to include visual stimuli, some immediate gratification, and friction on specific locations. You have a lot of power in a fun way sexually because he responds so predictably.

Turning Yourself On

Every wife should be able to tune in to and enjoy the wonderful gift God has given her of femininity and a capacity for sexual pleasure. You may be wondering, in a chapter devoted to turning your husband on, why a whole section is now being devoted to turning yourself on. The answer is easy: your husband is sexually excited by the sounds and sights of you tuning in to your sexual pleasure and intensely enjoying the whole process. You want to turn him on and be a great lover? Learn to be intensely turned on yourself!

Permission for Pleasure

God has given us a sexual celebration in marriage. The sad fact is that in Christianity, sex has often been suspect. Part of the distortion and confusion is created because of the silence rather than negative messages. Anyone becomes suspicious about a topic that is constantly avoided. You may have to erase some mental tapes going around in your head to truly enjoy sex and let it be a celebration.

Time Out . . .

With a female friend, discuss the messages you have incorporated into your sex life and where they came from. Look at your mother's attitudes on sex, your childhood, your high-school years and your first sexual experiences, any traumas, and your marriage. Which attitudes will you choose to alter?

Judeo-Christian heritage and values can be a safe platform for a more exciting sex life if you let them. From self-love, honesty, and commitment, you can launch a spectacular love life. Spirituality and sexuality are truly intertwined, as we saw in discussing God's boundaries for great sex. The mature Christlike woman will be able to celebrate her sexuality in ways that others can't—with a deeper love and joy and trust.

Women often struggle with relaxing control and abandoning themselves to pleasure. Some of this may be due to unfortunate double standards. The brunt of maintaining sexual control in dating relationships is placed on girls. God, in His sexual economy, makes both sexes responsible for healthy boundaries. The unhappy truth is that so often boys try to score, and girls slap hands and try to keep from getting taken advantage of, hurt, or pregnant. Wives can have a difficult time relaxing control and giving themselves permission to enjoy sexual pleasure, even in a committed and loving marital relationship.

One possible way of relaxing control and giving yourself permission for pleasure is to talk during sex. Express what you need and what you are feeling in a verbal and nonverbal manner. Most women find as they talk and abandon themselves to pleasure, their bodies respond in a marvelous, God-designed fashion. Lovemaking is enhanced.

You may desire that your children grow up with different attitudes about sex than you acquired. You can help your daughter be more open about sexuality. Demonstrate an open, loving relationship with your mate. It is great sex education for a child to see Mom and Dad kissing and being in love. Be comfortable discussing sex. You may want to practice with close friends or your husband before she asks tough questions. Here is another vital key: teach her to be sensual and to revel in pleasurable experiences! Nonsexual sensual lessons spill over into the sexual arena when needed. If your child knows how to play and have fun, if she can enjoy flowers and perfume, she will someday be a better lover for her husband.

You may need to practice what you want to teach your children as you truly give yourself permission to enjoy pleasure and sensuality. Go out and buy yourself a beautiful article of clothing with the accessories and underwear to go with it; worship God with real joy; keep some cut flowers in your bedroom and notice their sensual colors; sing lustily along with the songs on the radio; observe your lingerie in a mirror and feel its texture. Teach your children, whether boys or girls, to delight in sensual and pleasurable experiences.

Sometimes you may not allow your sensuality to spill over into your sexuality. One husband stated that his wife could be sensual in many ways like enjoying flowers and appreciating music but that sexually she was a "cotton person." She had cotton undies, wore jeans and sweatshirts, and had a favorite flannel nightgown. Maybe your husband wishes you would bring your initiative and intelligence into being more erotic. A sexy lover doesn't just happen, and you won't fall naturally into uninhibited sensuality.

Tuning in to Cues

From boyhood on, men seem to tune in to sexuality more overtly and, in an unfair way, are regarded as the sexual experts. Girls are taught psychologically to control sexual impulses and do not tune in to sexuality as readily. The environment also takes a toll on sexual desire. In the midst of busyness and children, husbands often fear their wives could go days without sex being that much of a priority.

Time Out . . .

Where in your sex life do you need to relax control and become more abandoned? Think through how you will start talking the next time you make love. You will be amazed how it turns you and your husband on.

God gave each person responsibility for her own body and for learning to experience sexual pleasure. But perhaps you are disappointed that lovemaking hasn't fallen into place as easily as you expected. Don't be too hard on yourself. Take control of your sexuality and tune in to cues more readily—for your pleasure and for your husband's. Give yourself permission to have pleasure.

For you, lovemaking may always be more of a choice, flowing out of your emotional relationship. But you can choose to create a greater sexual awareness and more immediate desire. This fun desire to enjoy your mate sexually is not usually caused by hormones; rather, it is caused by your uninhibited focus on making love.

Here are ten conscious choices that you can make to tune in to sexual cues and keep lovemaking on the front burner of your marriage:

1. Budget in and spend a certain amount of money each month on your sex life.
2. Every now and then wear a sexy piece of lingerie all day and allow its unusual feel to remind you of sex constantly.
3. Don't wear any underwear to a social gathering, and tell your husband on the way out the door. You will drive him crazy while you keep aroused.
4. Plan a sexual surprise at least once a month in which you try to blindside your husband in an arousing sexual way.
5. Keep a mental note, and regardless of fatigue or low interest, initiate sex at least once a week.
6. Have fun with your husband's visual arousal, and flaunt your nude body at unusual times just to enjoy his reactions.
7. Take a bubble bath and indulge in other sensual delights at the end of a tiring day—it is a great aphrodisiac and tunes you in to your body.
8. Create romantic sexual fantasies about your love life while driving in the car and share them with your mate at the end of your day.
9. Use a special perfume that you have associated in your mind with making love, and wear it on the evening or the day you anticipate sexual activity.
10. Practice Kegel exercises.

Kegel Exercises

These popular exercises are named after Dr. Arnold Kegel who developed them in the fifties to help women with urinary incontinence. The exercises involve the pubococcygeal (PC) muscle, which surrounds the opening of the vagina and anus. This large muscle connects from the pubic bone in front to the coccyx, or end, of the tailbone in back. It is one of the muscles that contracts during orgasm and increases genital awareness. To locate this muscle, you can practice stopping the flow of urine; it can quite easily, in this fashion, be distinguished from the buttock muscles. You may feel it by inserting a finger in your vagina and trying to squeeze down on the finger.

Through childbirth or disuse, the PC muscle, like any muscle, can lose its tone and may need to be strengthened. Why bother with the PC muscle? It increases sensation in the pubic area and the vagina, which can increase your pleasure. It will tune you in to your sexuality. Many women report an increase in the intensity of their orgasms. In a sexy and exciting way, your husband will enjoy the extra stimulation as he can actually feel you contract this muscle around his penis.

Kegel exercises also help you become more familiar with and appreciate your body. It is important to cultivate a healthy body image and enjoy your femininity and genital area. I asked a wise, mature Christian leader if he thought the hesitation with oral sex was because Christians thought it was somehow homosexual or wrong scripturally. He stated he did not think those were the reasons. He thought people viewed their genitals as embarrassing and unappealing. Be honest—do you enjoy and appreciate your genitals?

Here are three different types of exercises that you can practice to strengthen your PC muscle. They are easy to practice while in the car, while on the telephone, or while watching television.

1. Get familiar with your PC muscle as you contract and immediately relax it. Do this rapidly five times as you inhale and then exhale. Repeat five times.

2. Tighten the PC muscle for a three-second count (1001, 1002, 1003) as you inhale and then exhale and relax. Repeat ten times and then rest. Try to practice several times a day as the muscle is strengthened.

3. Pretend your husband's penis is at the mouth of your vagina and you are trying to suck it into your vagina by pulling with your PC muscle. Pull for three seconds and relax. Repeat ten times and then rest.

Assertive Demands

You as a woman may enjoy a slower pace than your husband and need different strokes. A basic part of turning yourself on is assertively expressing your needs. Sometimes you may want to cuddle and be held tight and have it lead nowhere. You may not like to always be the one to go first in having an orgasm. Now and again you may enjoy the intensity of a type of thrusting in a particular position of intercourse. Become very direct in your requests, especially in the excitement of the moment as you become a comfortable coach of your own needs.

The more demanding you become about your sexual needs, the more you may turn on your husband. Both of you can gain skills in sexual self-awareness and assertive communication.

Passionate Power

You have tremendous power to arouse your husband. He needs and desires you even if, from fear of intimacy or environmental pressures, his desire is low presently. This attraction can be a lot of fun, and you should learn to flaunt and enjoy your power.

You may be reluctant to use your feminine power, not wanting it to degenerate into destructive manipulation. But healthy power and productive sexual manipulation result in a win-win situation, not the win-lose interaction of harmful sexual games.

Correctly using passionate power is *not* meeting him at the door in see-through lingerie so you can manipulate a designer dress out of him when you honestly cannot afford one. That is a lose-lose or at most a lose-win situation—not a win-win interaction. Actively seducing your husband or playing on his visual nature is a manipulative use of sexual power in which your love life flourishes, he grins all day, and you delight in your femininity—a definite win-win. Healthy flirting and teasing increase the playfulness and fun in your sexual companionship.

Openly Visual

Trying to be more openly visual to turn on your husband will be at first like writing with your left hand when you are right-handed. It will have to be a conscious act of will. Remember, men are aroused by seeing the female form, and the more obvious sexual parts (e.g., breasts, genitals, hips) are more powerful. Views and actions that would do nothing for you will have amazing results on your mate.

Constantly play on his attraction to your femininity. Go upstairs in front of him and put an exaggerated swish in your hip action, knowing he is noticing and getting excited. Alone with him in his office or at home, assume a less modest sitting position—flashing him images of things to come. Lean over when you're near him and then wink when he sneaks a peek down the front of your dress.

In lovemaking, remember to increase his visual excitement. Certain positions are more stimulating, like when you are on top. Encourage his exploration and enjoyment of your genitals. In this process, your appreciation for and arousal by visual stimuli may increase, too.

Part of the fun is being playful as well as being visual. Easily combine the two, along with some surprises. As you get into his male mind-set, you can create fun bonding and intimate companionship.

Immediate and Balanced

Your husband wants to touch what he visually enjoys. Work out some appropriate compromises in which he allows you to be seductive and visual without its leading to immediate gratification. Sometimes he may be content to have a quick caress or some immediate contact.

Satisfy his need for immediate gratification, but keep balance in your sex life. Enjoy quickies, and seduce him when he does not expect it. Also teach him to postpone pleasure and not leap right to intercourse. Give him full body massages and include other activities to increase his sensuality. Make his immediate pleasures memorable, but encourage prolonged and exciting lovemaking.

Teasingly Seductive

It is hard to beat the metaphor of a romantic dinner at a fancy restaurant for teaching about great sex and seductive teasing. You eagerly anticipate the evening as you make reservations several days in advance. When you finally get there and are seated, the table has been beautifully set and the red rose is gorgeous, creating a wonderful ambiance. They begin by tantalizing you with appetizers and slowly progress through the courses as you become satiated. There is no goal of chowing down; it is a process to be savored. Two hours fly by as you are continually seduced by a new flavor or an artful arrangement or a special dessert. What come-ons! Who cares about the entree?

Isn't it fascinating that in adolescence we are taught not to tease? Now I am telling you that teasing is a basic concept for great sex. Actually, I am not disagreeing with the dating context of not being a tease and promising something sexually that you have no intention of delivering or using your sexuality to manipulate. In marriage, though, teasing is seductive, exhilarating, and intimate.

Tantalize him by telling him in the car on the way to dinner what you hope to do later on that night with him. The sexual tension will build during the course of the evening. While making love, your teasing comments will be met by increased arousal and excited orgasms. Seductively initiating sex and meeting your mate's needs will keep your intimacy alive in a refreshing and passionate way.

Rebekah's Well of Water

As a sex therapist, I have always liked the Old Testament characters of Isaac and Rebekah. Genesis 26:8 states that he was "showing endearment" to his wife, Rebekah, in an intimate sexual manner so that King Abimelech knew they were not brother and sister. Out of fear, they had been trying to pass as siblings, but Isaac and Rebekah couldn't keep their hands to themselves. Earlier when Isaac was trying to pick a wife, he prayed to God for a sign of an open, giving woman: "Behold, here I stand by the well of water, and the daughters of the men of the city are coming out to draw water. Now let it be that the young woman to whom I say, 'Please let down your pitcher that I may drink,' and she says, 'Drink, and I will also give your camels a drink'—let her be the one You have appointed for Your servant Isaac" (Gen. 24:13–14 NKJV).

Proverbs encourages husbands to drink sexual water from their own springs and rejoice in the wives of their youth (Prov. 5:15–19). Sometimes you may feel that you have exceeded Rebekah's giving behaviors and that you have watered him, his camels, and his sheep, too.

To be Rebekah with a fresh jar of water can also be a fun, exciting, and mutually fulfilling undertaking. Consider the following suggestions for activities that can enhance your lovemaking. Enjoy your one-flesh companionship. Men, though predictable, are not always easy to live with sexually. They are wired in some seemingly crazy ways, but you can enjoy your sexual power with your husband. You have a wonderfully refreshing well of water; teach him to drink deeply.

Focusing on Your Husband's Body

Because men are usually more easily stimulated physically and visually, couples neglect to focus attention and energy on the husband's body. Your husband may feel uncomfortable at first, but throughout the loveplay, keep your hands on him. It should not be a focus on his genital area. Hold and caress and stroke his body. You will probably find he ejaculates less quickly as you touch and hold more.

Men, and women, can be very uncomfortable at first with hugging and touching if their families were not physically demonstrative and they have not practiced both giving and receiving physical nurturing. These are skills you and your mate need to learn to be great lovers.

Don't let your husband get away with focusing only on your body! Reread chapter 9 on sensual massage, and help him learn to enjoy back rubs and facials. Use some scented lotions and expand his repertoire of experiencing sensuality. Practice five-minute embraces. Don't neglect caressing during intercourse. Holding his testicles lightly or massaging the prostate or reaching down and placing your index and middle fingers like scissors at the mouth of your vagina to grasp his penis going in and out can all bring extra delight. Assertively insist on nurturing him physically. Like so many things in life, as he tries it, he will like it.

Special Stimulation

Making love to your husband's penis is crucial to turning him on. The penis is a part of your husband's anatomy that he is proud and protective of, but it is not fragile. Rapid and firm strokes are usually more stimulating. Develop a rhythm and pressure that he enjoys.

Orally stimulating the penis is very exciting for most men. Remember that fun sex is based on keeping sensitive to your own and your partner's needs and enjoyment sexually. Although the Bible is neutral on oral sex, many women are not comfortable with it. Some say that they are turned off by the secretions or they are afraid the husband will slip up and climax during the process. Sex is a partnership with trust and cooperation. Your husband can prevent himself from climaxing, or he can warn you so you both are ready. Take a warm washcloth and wipe off the penis before engaging in oral sex. Keep tissues handy. In this and other exercises, try them and you may find you truly like them or can relax with them for pleasuring your mate. Never berate yourself, though, if you choose not to engage in some sexual behavior. Lovemaking is much more than one method of erotic arousal.

In oral sex, probably your mouth and lips are not strong enough to give sufficient stimulation for building toward an orgasm. The fun is more in the teasing and the intimacy of his entrusting his penis to your mouth. Manually stroking the shaft while focusing on the head of the penis with your mouth can bring real enjoyment. Greater sensation exists in the head of the penis. Shield your teeth with your lips pulled over them as you orally stimulate with tongue, lips, and mouth.

Try these methods. Place the head of the penis in your mouth and suck like a vacuum as you pull it out of your mouth; repeat the process. Or stimulate the penis with licking motions lightly and firmly around the ridge and over the top with the head of the penis in and out of your mouth; wrap your hand firmly around the shaft of the penis to retain the blood in the head as you do this to increase excitement. Or tease the underside of the penis with flicking motions of your tongue or gentle sucking. The underside of the penis is very sensitive, especially on the line of skin that runs vertically up and connects at the ridge on the head of the penis.

In intercourse, practice your Kegel exercises with your mate's penis in your vagina. That can be arousing for both of you. Allow him to feel your PC muscle enclose and tighten on his penis. Have him do this with just the head of the penis as he gently thrusts into the mouth of your vagina as you tighten the PC muscle. Play and experiment—sex is fun.

Sexual Flooding

Many husbands dream about being ravished by so much sex they couldn't stand more. At a time when you are feeling relaxed and rested—it may have to be on vacation—tell your mate that he is free to initiate sex whenever he desires and that you will be disappointed if it is not very frequent.

Help him out by planning some sexual sessions that appeal to his specific visual orientation. Place him on the bed, or wherever, and let him get aroused with some anticipation as you get your props (lingerie, music, etc.) ready. Then overwhelm him with sexy apparel, sexy movements, and sexy sights of your body clothed and nude. Plan exciting surprises of your own during this time. Create a flood of sexual activity.

An Exciting Climax

Men and women experience differing types of orgasms. Some are a gentle rush, some are a fizzle, and some seem like volcanoes erupting. Men experience greater and more satisfying orgasms with increased arousal over a period of time. Some researchers think this might have to do with a greater accumulation of semen that gives a stronger feeling of ejaculation. It may be more psychological.

Talk with your partner and discuss how he can enjoy a stronger experience of climaxing. Part of it is, of course, bringing him to the point of ejaculation and backing off as you stimulate him for a longer period of time. Utilize the techniques discussed here. Tease him manually and orally as you help him build up close to an orgasm but not fall over the edge. Keep him on an exciting plateau: approach and back off, then approach as you increase his pleasure and excitement.

The prostate is located in the body with the external pressure point located between the scrotum and the anus. Take a finger or thumb as your husband gets aroused and gently stroke with pressure the area at the base of the penis behind the scrotal sac. Let him direct you as you find the exact spot and desired pressure and rhythm that feel most exciting. You can experiment and see if this increases orgasmic enjoyment for your husband. It may at least give pleasant stimulation to a new area.

Part of the secret is focusing on the orgasm and at the point of climax expelling the pent-up tension with force. Encourage your mate to make loud noises and exaggerate the muscle tension and spasms. He can use his PC muscle to expel the ejaculate with force. Refuse to let him be inhibited. This is a stimulating and fulfilling part of making love. Vary the climaxes in the positions of intercourse you use as well as occasionally climax externally with manual stimulation. Tension buildup and strong release are exciting parts of making love.

Power Positions

Be sure to read the chapter on creative positions for intercourse. While enjoying intercourse, remember your husband's penchant for looking and touching. Learn to flaunt your body as you exercise your power to turn him on. Encourage him to caress and explore. It is an intensely sensuous experience for him to run his penis or a finger over your clitoris, gently down to your vagina, and slowly into it—the warmth and moistness and unique femininity are very arousing. You have tremendous power with your femininity—exercise it during intercourse. Most women, as they get comfortable with their capacity to be seductive, find themselves aroused by this ability.

Another turn-on for a man in intercourse is for him to know you want and need him inside you thrusting—throw in a little playful admiration and flattery, too. You will be surprised how excited he will get when you say, "You are so firm, I need you right now," or some variant on this theme. Your husband will be stimulated by the fact you need him.

Quickies

If you initiate a quickie, unless there are other problems, your husband will rapidly make it a mutually enjoyable experience. Men relish quickies, and you will keep him smiling by initiating them quite often—a special sexual dessert for him in an otherwise great sex life. The unexpected surprise and thoughtful attention are very arousing.

Men may appreciate this more than women, but many wives have come to greatly enjoy the quick dessert, too. Others just enjoy nurturing their mates and seeing the flood of excitement created by a 3:00 A.M. encounter. Remember how much power you have and the quickie will certainly confirm it. Short, refreshing drinks from Rebekah's well can be amazing.

May you have courage, spontaneity, zest, love, and a whole lot of fun as you turn your man on. The rewards of learning new skills are great. Take a walk on the male side of life. You will find yourself enjoying your sexuality a lot more and your relationship reaching new depths.

Chapter Fifteen

♡

Making Love When You Have a Disability

Disabilities are a part of many couples' lives and relationships. They do have an impact on lovemaking, but a good sex life is highly possible. A committed, loving relationship is still the most important part of making love. All people have erogenous zones, a mind as the key sexual organ, and a need to develop fulfilling sexual sensations, attitudes, and techniques.

The frustrating news for the person or couple with a disability is the same for any person or couple—you will have to work to learn skills, build erotic fantasy, and tailor your own warm, unique, and exciting lovemaking together.

This first section explores five needed skills to enhance lovemaking. The second section considers temporary disabilities, the nondisabled spouse, the effect of medications, preparation for lovemaking, and pregnancy. Section three lists practical suggestions for increasing sexual enjoyment, and the final section looks more specifically at three categories of disabilities: birth defects, accidents and injuries, and illnesses.

Five Necessary Skills

Every person with spina bifida, muscular dystrophy, or cancer has not faced the same journey. Disabilities and varying levels of severity present different challenges in roles and attitudes to males or females. But there is much commonality in working through a disability to a fulfilling sex life. Certain skills are vital to learn and employ consistently. This section develops five of them.

1. Creating a Positive Sexual Self-Image

Everyone struggles at times with body image and the comfortable enjoyment of masculinity or femininity. Please don't let physical problems or disabilities color yourself as a lover. You have a special personality and the ability to play and be very sexy and romantic. It is an exciting phenomenon that we have the ability to become what we think we are. Our attitudes and beliefs about ourselves are crucial.

Two men can have gone through a similar set of experiences and be in wheelchairs. One likes himself and thinks he is an interesting and attractive man. He comes across that way and is appealing to the opposite sex. The other man is insecure and angry. He does not think he is special or sexy. He also comes across that way. Being sexy has to do with an attitude and not the way the body looks.

Granted, the disabled person faces unique challenges. You may have to be in a much more dependent role than you desire. Mobility and autonomy may be limited with someone helping to attend to your bodily functions or your spouse assuming a more active physical role in making love. Unless you expand your concept of masculinity or femininity, you will constantly be threatened.

The character traits that are important for a great lover include the ability to be playful, honest, gently loving and nurturing, and self-disciplined. These characteristics are essential for becoming an accomplished sexual partner and truly sexy, whether disabled or nondisabled. Real masculinity or femininity is based on your creation in God's image and goes way beyond body parts or disabilities.

Sex is also much more than intercourse, certain physical activities, or the ability to have an orgasm. You can kiss and have stimulating arousal strapped into a hospital bed. Persons who have a paraplegia, a hearing impairment, a visual handicap, or a similar disability can be intensely sensual and develop differing senses in ways that others don't. Making love is a marvelous personal and relational quality that doesn't have to be lost through physical problems. Challenge your attitudes and develop your tremendous potential in new and creative ways. Do some self-talk as you work through to a positive self-image.

2. Communicating

Dealing with bodily wastes, handling menstrual cycles, or choosing when to pass gas is often taken out of your hands and made a public matter. If you want to live as a comfortable friend and lover, you will have to learn to communicate with your spouse about the loss of personal control and many other emotionally loaded topics.

Talk to your mate. Become excellent sounding boards for each other. Learn how to dialogue. In dialogue, one partner keeps quiet and carefully listens while the other partner assertively expresses needs and feelings. The one who stays quiet and becomes an effective listener focuses on the message being communicated. The listener detaches from his personal feelings or the need for a rebuttal—trying to clarify and really understand the message. The one sending the message puts it into assertive, responsible, and courteous "I" language ("I feel hurt when you don't initiate making love to me, and I wonder if I'm still attractive to you") and not blaming "you" language ("you don't ever make love anymore—you must hate me").

As a part of becoming a great listener, make sure that after you have focused on and understood the message, you empathetically validate that message. A validation statement is only about twenty seconds and tells your mate that you are acknowledging the reality. You are not saying that your mate is right, but you are validating the message. Validate three separate areas: the content, the feelings, and the needs. Here is an example: "It is logical that you wonder about my attraction to you when I neglect to initiate making love" (content); "You probably feel hurt, insecure, and disappointed" (feelings); and "I know you need me to be more consistent in initiating" (needs). Only after you have validated your partner's message can you then start a new dialogue process in which your partner becomes the listener: "I have been tired. I really do find you attractive."

You will often hear some of the same feelings, needs, and struggles. Remain an active listener as you help your mate work through grief and other issues to a better sense of resolution. Especially express and process your feelings. You are having to deal with some very tough and private issues, which will be intense with anger, despondency, excitement, sadness, helplessness, and hope. Understand and work through them to a deeper sense of intimacy.

Take the time and energy to talk about the structure of your sex life. You are into a new and challenging era that will take some creative problem solving. Provide courage and romantic creativity for each other as you find different ways to make love. Talk through possible ways to adapt moves and brainstorm on solutions to overcome the disabilities. You will find good communication vital as you determine not to lose God's wonderful gift of sexuality in your intimate companionship.

3. Expanding Your Senses and Knowledge of Sexuality

So many adults have a body and mind that God created to enjoy pleasure, but they use only about one-third of their full sensual capacity. Individuals and couples need to more fully allow their bodies to take in sensual pleasure—which so easily spills over into their sexual lives. Look more carefully and take in colors, textures, and the visual joy around you. Or go to an antique shop or a botanical garden and revel in the sights. Or stop and listen, with your eyes closed, to the world around you. Or surround yourself with music, take a course in interpretive reading, or go to a stock car race and hear the power permeating the air. Or eat more slowly as you notice the tastes and smells. Or visit coffee shops or bakeries, buy some potpourri, eat ethnic foods, or enjoy a new perfume or bubble bath. Or go through your house and touch the objects with your mind focused on your fingertips. Or enjoy smooth and rough, cold and hot, soft and hard, oily and dry.

We are still learning how the brain takes in and stores data. It is exciting how when one sense is disabled, another expands. The person who is blind develops a keener sense of hearing and touch. The person who is paralyzed from the waist down takes on greater sensuality with chest, neck, and face. A part of this is the concept of phantom feelings or the power of the mind. The person with an amputated arm still feels itches and pain on occasion. In a similar way, the person with no sensation in the genital area can experience a phantom orgasm within the sexual cycle as excitement builds. Different sexual behaviors and parts of the body can take on new meaning—creating a warm closeness or exciting arousal.

All lovers have to continually work at staying out of routines and expanding their sexual behaviors and mental store of erotic images. Mates with disabilities need to expand their sensuality and modify behaviors as their lovemaking grows in its excitement and joy. Become more creative, sensual, and varied. Your lovemaking can surpass in its meaning, variety, and enjoyment that of the nondisabled couple who take so much for granted.

4. Choosing Optimal Times

Understanding medications and using medical advice. Medications can help you feel more like making love. The person with arthritis or other types of disability might want to have sex when the medication is having maximum effect. The person on dialysis will feel better right after the treatment, before the toxins have begun to build up again. This can be a much better time to enjoy sex. Creatively discuss and work through your special situation as you as a couple increase your ability to make love meaningfully.

Medications can also have a negative effect, creating less desire for sex or ability to perform. You must learn to minimize the negative side effects of some medications (e.g., antidepressants, blood thinners, and blood pressure treatments). With some medications, making love right before taking them will lessen their effects, or perhaps it is possible to periodically reduce the dosage (e.g., before a vacation).

Check with your physician and ask specific sexual questions about what is permitted physically and what is not. Ask for and find pamphlets on your particular disability. Be an informed lover and determine what physical sensations and types of sexual activity are possible as you maximize lovemaking.

Planning that enhances romance. You will enjoy sex more when you are rested, relaxed, and able to focus on your sensual feelings. You will have to consider more than medications. For the person with a heart problem, the optimal time might be the middle of the night. For the person with spinal cord injury or with spina bifida, it will be necessary to plan around urination and catheterization. For the person with a paraplegia or quadriplegia, if your mate helps you dilate the rectum and allow bowel movements, wait several hours and allow that to be separate from being lovers and making love. Like any couple with a dynamic marriage and sex life, you will have to use your creativity and common sense to find optimal times for lovemaking.

5. Grieving

Elisabeth Kubler-Ross and other psychological researchers have demonstrated that people go through various stages and feelings when they are grieving a loss. You and your partner have experienced multiple losses: the marriage as it was, autonomy, dreams and expectations, sexual self-image, and mutual health—to name a few. The one-flesh companionship has been shaken up in many ways, and the sexual part may be most obvious.

The first reactions in grieving are usually shock and denial. You can't believe this is happening to you. Then come anger, bargaining, and depression as the reality settles in. The anger will be at God and any available target. You may bargain with God and ask God to take away the disability and you will make drastic changes. Withdrawal into isolation may occur as the issues are worked through. Eventually, the disability is accepted and equilibrium returns. However, life has a way of triggering the losses over and over again, so flashbacks into the grieving process are likely.

Sometimes Christians get stuck in the grieving process as they wallow in self-pity or hope for God to miraculously cure them. There is no way around this grief. The point is to work your way through it to acceptance and healing and new alternatives. If you repress the tears and anger, they will come back to haunt you later. The nondisabled mate will have to find time and space to grieve, too. You cannot stay strong for your partner throughout the whole process.

Both of you will need to build a solid support network that you can lean on. Christ designed the church to fulfill this role of being a healer. Allow your loving brothers and sisters to take you up in their arms and hold you while you angrily yell at God and uncontrollably give in to your tears over the injustice that you are experiencing. With sin in the world, bad things happen to good people, and that is what God gave us the grieving process for—to slowly work our way through the pain and hurt of life's unfairness until we heal.

Important Areas to Consider

Most couples will experience temporary disabilities and the side effects of medication, especially as they grow older. Both partners have needed roles.

Temporary Disabilities

Most couples will encounter some physical disability during the course of their marriage. Some of them—a complicated pregnancy, pneumonia, broken bones, yeast infections, a heart attack, or surgery—are temporary in nature. But unless you make the necessary adjustments in your lovemaking, these temporary conditions can completely shut down your sex life to the detriment of your marriage and intimacy. Sometimes the temporary disabilities can create long-term effects in the love life of a couple.

Much of this chapter, which is primarily addressed to persons with permanent disabilities, will also apply to you with temporary disabilities—as you creatively enjoy different but satisfying lovemaking sessions. You will have to adapt and try to focus on sexual activities other than vigorous intercourse and the pursuit of orgasms as you learn to caress and hold each other and be close. Don't assume that you must forgo sex for the duration of the temporary disability. Talk to your physician and learn about your physical condition, whether it is high blood pressure, a hysterectomy, broken ribs, or poison ivy. Don't be embarrassed to ask specifically about making love; plan on being as sexually active as you can—despite the temporary disability.

The Nondisabled Partner

The feelings of the nondisabled partner will range, much as those of the partner with the disability, from despair to optimism (sometimes false around some possible cure), from anger and discouragement to joy and pleasure. Sometimes it may be difficult to switch from the role of nursing or helping your mate with the disability to being a passionate lover.

As the nondisabled partner, you will probably have to assume a more active physical (not emotional) role sexually. You may be asked to do things, like dealing with bowel or bladder accidents or perhaps trying types of oral stimulation, that you might have found unpleasant in the past. New behaviors will be required as you pleasure your mate. As lovers, learning new and effective lovemaking techniques is seldom comfortable or smooth, whether you are disabled or not. It may be helpful to talk to a therapist regarding any problems. But whatever you do, don't treat your partner as fragile. You need to process your feelings, too, as you work through to practical solutions in your lovemaking.

Stay creative and pray for extra strength. Your stamina and hope will be needed commodities, especially if your mate is adjusting to a recent disability and is reeling from the blows to self-image. Create an effective support network for both of you as you affirm your sexual partnership.

Medications

Many sexual problems are often caused not by the disability but by the medication required because of the disability—or perhaps by the medication required to deal with the depression caused by the reaction to the disability. You cannot just stop taking the medication, but you should be aware of possible sexual side effects. Check with your pharmacist or physician so that you can be informed of any negative side effects. Every medication reacts differently with various body chemistries, and a given medication may not negatively affect you.

Common sexual problems are loss of or decreased sexual desire, impotence in the male or inadequate lubrication in the female, less physical sensation in the genital area, more difficulty in achieving or decreased intensity in orgasm, delay or pain in ejaculating, and priapism (a sustained erection to the point of being painful). Some common drugs that have side effects are certain tranquilizers, antidepressants, hypertension medications, blood thinners, stomach and digestive treatments, and chemotherapy.

Sometimes one medication can be exchanged for another that will have fewer side effects on a given individual. There may be a period of time before taking the medication that is more conducive for making love. Over time a person may grow beyond the need for a medication like an antidepressant and eliminate the negative side effects. Often a couple will have to be creative and minimize the effects of a medication because not taking it would be life threatening. Creating atmosphere and being rested can increase libido. Increased length of time of stimulation can offset lack of genital response and the male can still have an orgasm and ejaculate without an erection. Like other challenges to a great sex life, they must be met with knowledge and creative alternatives.

Preparation for Sex

The couple with a disability will have more things to remember in getting ready to make love. Like other couples, you will have to plan through things like birth control and artificial lubrication. It is wise to have towels and other cleanup needs handy for those inevitable accidents that will occur. You will also have to sort through timing and use optimum minutes or hours that can enhance the lovemaking.

Don't neglect having a water soluble lubrication available (and use it liberally). Women with spinal cord injuries or diabetes will have nerve or circulatory problems that prevent natural lubrication. They can be more susceptible to vaginal and urinary tract infections and subsequent problems with intercourse. Stress, grief, pain, and other aspects of a disability can also prevent enough lubrication.

A real concern will be taking care of bladder and bowel needs prior to making love, especially if intercourse is involved. Often in today's medicine if there is an indwelling or Foley catheter, the condition is such that intercourse perhaps should not be attempted. If a condom catheter is being used, that can be removed immediately prior to intercourse. In the case of spina bifida and some other disabilities in which intermittent catheterization may be needed, it is important for females to catheterize and empty the bladder both before and immediately after intercourse. This step can help prevent cystitis and other infections.

Bowel needs can often be taken care of well in advance of making love. An ostomy bag cannot be removed but you can drape a towel over it if you prefer. Don't forget as you prepare to make love that sexiness originates in the mind. Create a mood and revel in your sexual power and attractiveness as you look forward to making love with your mate.

Pregnancy

A disability does not usually affect fertility. It is necessary to be careful with birth control and guard against an unwanted pregnancy. Sometimes the disabled person can have a greater physical sensitivity and reaction to rubber condoms or anti-spermicidal chemicals, so caution must be exercised.

Practical considerations must be faced with the mind and not the heart. With the disability, will there be a way to adequately provide for a child's care? If it is a life-threatening illness, is it fair to bring a child into the world who is likely to be raised by a single parent? Can you as mother-to-be go off certain medications without serious threats to you emotionally or physically? Will you be subjecting yourself to undue physical risk? Is there a high genetic risk to the child that the disability will be passed on? This is often actually a very low probability, but could you raise a disabled child?

The woman with spina bifida or spinal cord injury is capable of conceiving and carrying a child through pregnancy. Careful care as to medications and health concerns must be exercised with kidney and bladder functions monitored and infections avoided. Having damaged nerves doesn't mean that tissue and organs are not functioning healthily. The woman with spinal cord injury may not be able to feel the beginning of labor pains, but a monitoring device can be utilized to signal when they occur.

The male with disabilities may not be able to father a child because of lack of ejaculation or infertility caused by fever or testicle damage. With a lack of erection (e.g., from diabetes), an ejaculation can sometimes occur, and artificial insemination can be done in which the semen is placed in the wife's vagina at the mouth of the cervix. There is also a technique called electroejaculation in which the doctor takes the semen out of the body with electric stimulation. With spinal cord injuries and prostate surgeries, occasionally retrograde ejaculation occurs: the semen goes back into the bladder instead of out through the penis. It is sometimes possible to separate fertile sperm from the urine and use them with artificial insemination.

If you want a child, carefully think through what childbearing and child rearing would mean. Explore the possibility of fertility and take advantage of modern medicine.

Practical Suggestions

Making love as a couple with disabilities will necessitate creativity and knowledge. Here are some further words of advice and points to think through and discuss.

Love Through the Pain

Sometimes your mate may want to make love despite feeling some pain. Learn to enjoy together times that may be less than optimal. With careful communication, you can be sensitive to your mate's needs and know when to engage and when to stop. You may have to do more of the stimulation, but it can still be mutually enjoyable. Sometimes your disabled mate may want only to be held or lovingly caressed, which still gives opportunity for closeness. At other times your disabled partner may wish to nurture you but not become fully involved. Learn to recognize those times when it is important to make love as you play through the pain and discomfort.

Acquire Adaptive Creativity

Sex will be different, but don't assume that there is a different set of lovemaking techniques for disabled couples. Much of what is discussed in this book, especially the ideas of utilizing your imagination and learning new ways to be sensual, applies across the board to lovers. If you are more recently disabled, don't abandon all that you used to do. It might take some creativity and adaptation, but you may still enjoy those exciting or warmly connecting techniques. Don't accept a label and think you are incapable of "normal" sex—whatever that is. Like any couple, enjoy your sensuality and cultivate a whole repertoire of exciting behaviors.

Develop Expectations and Humor Around Accidents

You will pass gas sometimes while making love, or you will have a bladder accident. But then, so do couples who do not have a disability. Expecting and preparing for accidents helps you prevent an overreaction when they occur. Making love demands that you keep a sense of humor because the unusual and funny will often happen. You can get frustrated, or you can laugh and allow the intimacy to go on unbroken. Great sex is built on being playful companions who can laugh over the accidents and mistakes.

Overcome Dual Disabilities

Sometimes both partners will have a disability. Each should avoid prejudice against the other's disability. It is unfortunate but true that sometimes a disabled mate can have more difficulty dealing with a partner's disability than a nondisabled mate. Much of what is written in this chapter applies to a marriage with dual disabilities. There will be a need for extra creativity and a willingness to reach out strategically for help from people outside the marriage. With maturity and wisdom, each can be an even more empathetic source of encouragement and motivation for the other than a nondisabled mate.

Three Categories of Disabilities

Most disabilities can be listed under three broad categories:

1. Birth defects: spina bifida, cystic fibrosis, cerebral palsy, mental retardation, sensory deficits (blindness, deafness)
2. Accidents and injuries: spinal cord injuries, traumatic brain injury, loss of limb or mobility, sensory loss (sight, hearing)
3. Illnesses: cancer (mastectomy, prostate, hysterectomy), endometriosis, heart attack, stroke, arthritis, depression, diabetes, muscular dystrophy (genetic but often doesn't appear until adulthood), and multiple sclerosis

Gather information about your specific disability. There are videos, pamphlets, and associations dealing with many of these disabilities like spina bifida, cancer, deafness, endometriosis, depression, and spinal cord injuries. Following is a sampling of disabilities within each category and the possibilities of warm, connecting love-making.

1. Birth Defects

Being born with a birth defect does not make a person asexual. All people have sexual feelings and at puberty will undergo normal development into adult sexuality. The disabilities create special social and sexual challenges.

Children with birth defects or constant illnesses are often not allowed to develop a sense of modesty as nondisabled children do. The genital area is not treated as private but is a part of caregiving with bladder and bowel care and medical exams. To develop a comfortable understanding of nudity and privacy, the personalness of genitals and sexuality, they require a careful approach to the subject.

Children with spina bifida often go through puberty early. And many individuals with spina bifida do not have any sensations in the genital area.

During intercourse, a woman with spina bifida has to take special care with lubrication, which does not occur even with sexual arousal. Her damaged nerves do not signal for vasocongestion (blood rushing to the genital area, which becomes swollen, with lubrication sweating through the vaginal walls as a part of this sexual excitement phase of arousal). Without artificial lubrication every three minutes or so, it is easy for the skin to break down. With tender tissue, twenty seconds of dry rubbing could create an abrasion.

She also may be prone to cystitis and urinary tract infections, so care should be taken to empty the bladder both before and after intercourse. A primary cause of cystitis and infection is *E. coli* bacteria, which reside in the colon. She should be cautious to prevent any contact of waste material with the vagina. She may not be orgasmic, but she can be a sensitive, sensual lover who enjoys her sexual feelings and the interaction with her husband.

Whether spina bifida, cerebral palsy, or blindness, the individual will have to work on overcoming developmental deficits in social skills and building a healthy self-concept. The individual will need friends and family who can see the whole person, not just the disability.

Gender identity, a good sexual self-image, and sexual feelings will be affected by the disability. Some sensations (maybe even genital feelings and orgasms), sexual techniques, and experiences will be impossible. Creative adaptability will be crucial as the individual and couple become sensual in other ways (sight, oral, holding and cuddling, enjoying nipple or facial stimulation).

2. Accidents and Injuries

Though spinal cord injuries are not the most common disability, they do bring about changes in a couple's sex life in a more dramatic way than some of the other disabilities.

There are four parts to the backbone, and the spinal cord (nerves) runs through the middle of it. Usually, there is a loss of sensation and movement from the point of injury on down if it is a complete lesion (severing of the spinal cord nerves). There are seven cervical vertebrae in the neck, and an injury to these bones with a complete severing of the spinal cord can cause quadriplegia (paralysis from the neck down). If the injury occurred in the lower, thoracic vertebrae, of which there are twelve, it can cause paraplegia. Below the thoracic vertebrae there are five lumbar vertebrae and one sacral bone (tailbone) at the lowest part of the back.

There are two types of erections: *psychogenic* and *reflexogenic*. Psychogenic erections occur as a result of the mind thinking about something sexual and conveying arousal to the genital area through the nerves. Injuries in the middle and higher parts of the spinal column prevent men from experiencing psychogenic erections.

Reflexogenic erections result from direct stimulation of the penis or are perhaps caused by a full bladder or bowel. About 90 percent of men with higher spinal cord injuries are able to get reflexogenic erections though there is still no sensation in the penis. The problem is that these erections do not always occur when you are making love, or they don't last long enough. Manual or oral stimulation can help, and a technique called stuffing, in which the wife-on-top position of intercourse is assumed with the wife pushing the flaccid penis into her vagina, sometimes creates an erection.

The impairment of ejaculation is true of most complete spinal cord injuries. This does not mean that the husband is unable to experience the pleasure of sexual arousal and the plateau phase, as well as the enjoyment of resolution after making love. He may be able to experience some of the old sensations of an orgasm with what is called a phantom orgasm.

Nipples and neck and chin can become particularly sensitive to touch and sexual arousal. Couples can become more sensual with fingers and mouth.

Other types of injuries, in addition to spinal cord, can affect the ability to enjoy making love. Loss of a limb or one sense (e.g., hearing) may have much more of an impact than you might have thought. You might not have realized how much you depend on hearing your mate's nonverbal groaning, heavy breathing, and talking for pacing the lovemaking or becoming aroused. You will have to use new senses and develop a new style. This is also true of the loss of a limb with certain positions and methods of stimulation needing adaptation or change.

Traumatic brain injuries don't as often affect sexual arousal and behaviors. The impact is on the relationship with less impulse control and angry outbursts that damage loving feelings and respect. Things may improve as time goes by, but psychotherapy or marriage counseling may be necessary to heal the relational damage. The medications required to work with emotional and physical impairment may have a negative effect on sexual desire and physical ability to experience arousal. Like medications in general with disabilities, they will have to be worked with and regulated as best as possible to limit their negative side effects on lovemaking.

Injuries do not shut down sexual desire and the ability to become sexually aroused and make love. Certain behaviors or physical responses may not be possible, and you will have to develop new sensations and techniques.

Both partners will have to take time to adjust to the changes as both reestablish sexiness and the ability to comfortably make love. Communicate and work through the feelings.

Spinal cord injuries will vary in the effect, depending on whether they are complete or partial lesions and where on the spine they occurred. Higher injuries will allow reflexogenic erections in the male but usually no ejaculation; the female will not lubricate; neither will be able to experience an orgasm. The mind enhances sensitivity in other areas of the body, and there can be sexual arousal and pleasure in making love. Sometimes a person will experience a phantom orgasm at the place in the lovemaking cycle that it used to occur. Pregnancy is possible in most females, but the males usually cannot ejaculate—electroejaculation is possible in a small percentage.

3. Illnesses

Because of nerve and vascular damage, a man with diabetes may have problems getting and maintaining adequate erections for intercourse. To minimize psychological anxiety, he and his wife may go to other activities in their lovemaking and not make erections and intercourse the be-all and end-all.

They may work with blood sugar levels and lessen fatigue as they choose optimal times for lovemaking. If the man's testosterone levels are at normal, hormone replacement will not help. But oral medication may improve blood flow. Or injections into the penis of papaverine or prostagladin may increase blood flow and cause erections firm enough to permit intercourse. However, the positive effects of the injections may lessen over time as the nerves and blood flow in the genital area become worse.

Then the man may want to learn about vacuum pumps. A vacuum pump placed over the penis creates a vacuum pressure that draws blood into the penis, creating an erection. A tension ring is then placed at the base of the penis to maintain the erection during intercourse.

If impotence becomes permanent, a penile prosthesis may be a possible solution. A semirigid rod or a mechanical pump is surgically placed within the two corpora cavernosa of the penis. With the semirigid rod of coated wire, the penis stays firm and is kept down with special underwear. The hydraulic pump has the fluid pump surgically placed in the scrotum and two inflatable cylinders placed in the two corpora cavernosa of the penis. The erection is achieved by pumping a bulb in the scrotum, which fills the two cylinders and can then be released when desired.

Diabetes does not have to diminish the man's sexual desire and the enjoyment of his wife's body and femininity. He can refuse to let illness dampen the closeness with his wife as a lover and sexual companion. They can work together to make good choices as they discuss the next part of their journey through impotence and disability.

With aging come increased chances of heart problems, arthritis, and other illnesses that can affect a couple's sex life with permanent disabilities. Become a student of the illness, and find ways to minimize its detrimental effects on your sex life. Seek reliable medical advice, and ask questions until you receive answers. Keep creative and romantic as you remain sensual lovers. It can be wise to keep caregiving separate from your lovemaking and sexual enjoyment of each other. With illnesses, always keep an eye on effective timing.

Cancer can have particularly devastating consequences on making love. A wife's mastectomy can affect both partners. A beneficial approach is to learn about cancer, the surgery, and the healing process. An attitude restructuring may need to precede the discovery of new and exciting ways of arousal and sexual enjoyment.

Cancer surgery can sometimes damage nerves, which leads to lack of erections or lubrication. New surgical techniques have led to fewer problems with prostatectomies (prostate) and hysterectomies (uterus and perhaps ovaries). Sometimes radiation therapy may affect sexual desire or physical arousal, but over a period of months, nerves may be regenerated.

Even a man dying of prostate cancer may evolve into a sensual lover. Despite his impotence, the love for his wife and their intimacy may reach a depth they never knew existed.

Sometimes he may be too tired to make love, and he may just want to be held. But when they do make love, there may be a tenderness, a sensuality, and a passionate connecting that were never in their sexual relationship before. Their senses may be finely tuned to pick up touches, sights, and smells. And each may gently caress the other's face and back, allowing passion and connection to build, totally focusing on the moment of being together.

Being ill, even with life-threatening cancer, can be a time of discovery about making love and building a better sexual relationship. Timing, taking initiative, following medical advice, and separating being nurse from being lover are important.

Creatively seek solutions to new obstacles as you patiently allow for healing and medications to take effect.

Chapter Sixteen

Sex After Forty

So much of making love depends on our attitudes. Some couples think sex will drastically change when they reach forty-five or sixty-five, and for them it does. Other mates know life changes with aging but determine to continue to enjoy making love. They gracefully adjust to change and create an active sex life.

Throughout life, an interesting phenomenon is that the more frequently you make love, the more frequently you will make love. A sex life in motion seems more likely to keep in motion. Keeping intimacy and communication open and thriving may be the reason. Maybe any behavior gets awkward with disuse and neglect. If you see yourself as sexy and expect to make love, whether you are twenty-five or eighty-five, it often happens with consistency and enjoyment.

The first section examines the physical changes that come with the aging process in males and females. This includes some common physical problems in aging that affect sexual functioning. The second section explores relational changes with maturity, as environment and needs alter. The third section expands on the concept that sex over forty can be more exciting and fulfilling than in earlier years. You can create a second honeymoon as your lovemaking broadens into new horizons.

Physical Changes with Aging

Both men and women struggle with the aging process and their sexuality. Though it shouldn't be true, our culture discriminates against the aging person. A man's ego is affected by performance. Concepts like strength, stamina, production, and physical prowess are valued. A man will naturally get concerned as he experiences aging and normal changes in sexual performance. He may wonder about his erection not being as firm and about taking more stimulation to achieve it. In youth he could look at a nude body and instantly get firm. Occasionally now he is impotent, he cannot experience an ejaculation, or his aching back and muscles prevent some activities. He begins to question if he will continue to enjoy sexual pleasure and be able to bring true enjoyment to his partner.

A woman may experience even greater discrimination than a man and have difficulty with her self-concept. I think older women are very sexy, but a female friend once told me, "Men are allowed to age gracefully with graying hair a sign of maturity, but women just get old."

It is a distorted and very limited way of thinking to believe that only the young are beautiful. This is putting too much of attractiveness into tight skin and firm bodies. A wise definition of beauty includes tolerance, wisdom, character developed through suffering, enjoyment of life, the eyes and the voice, achievements, and social adeptness. Age has a positive effect on beauty and sexiness.

Male Sexual Changes

As you get older, there are normal wear and tear on your body with its nerves, muscles, and blood supply, which can affect sexual functioning. You may have to ease off on certain positions. There may be some leakage in an erection as the blood going into the penis is not held there as firmly. That does not make you impotent or sexually inadequate. With a better understanding of yourself, you'll have the freedom for greater enjoyment with less anxiety. Be reassured that sex will continue to be good.

Here are seven common changes a man experiences with the aging process:

1. Erections will need more direct physical stimulation of the penis. In younger years, visual or mental sexual stimuli could bring about an erection. That doesn't mean you are losing your sexual desire because your wife's breasts or genitals don't create the same quick reflex action. Sometimes this can mistakenly be seen as impotence because both partners expect spontaneous reactions as in the past. When enjoying loveplay and wanting to engage in intercourse, you and your partner will have to touch and play with the penis. If while you focus on pleasuring your wife you lose some or all of your erection, it will take direct stimulation to get the penis firm again.

Like other aspects of aging, this does not have to be a serious problem. Your wife must not interpret the lack of instant arousal as any reflection on her attractiveness. It is physiological, and she can simply make a note to engage in more manual and oral stimulation of the penis. Both of you can be erotically aroused as you make adjustments and, in a loving, sensual way, creatively stimulate the male organ. Throughout this chapter, you'll learn that sex over forty can add new dimensions of sensuality. You and your mate can experience a new level of intimacy and connectedness.

2. The penis may not achieve the same firmness with erections. With aging, the blood supply can be diminished, and the valve system that keeps the blood in the penis can leak. The penis therefore will not achieve the same hardness as before. This change can evolve into more of an attitude problem than a real issue. The penis does not need to be extra firm; it simply needs to be hard enough to insert and thrust.

Don't let your attitude get in the way. The firmness of erections does not make the man; it is not the symbol of a great lover. The surest way to become psychologically impotent is to worry about erections rather than enjoy the moment. Some lovemaking sessions you may not achieve an erection, or you may achieve only partial firmness. Don't worry about it. Chalk it up to fatigue and distractions, and know the erection will come back. (You may want to read the section of chapter 22 on working through impotence.) Your wife can be helpful in reducing your anxiety. You can mentally destroy your lovemaking by worrying about your firmness.

This point affects only a man who has not been circumcised. With aging, the skin of the foreskin may lose some of its elasticity and tighten. With full erections and intercourse, the skin may split rather than stretch as it used to. These skin tears will be small and will heal quickly, but they can be painful. This condition can often be prevented by pulling back the foreskin at night before going to sleep. During the sleep cycle and nightly erections, the skin will be stretched and be less likely to split during subsequent erections.

3. The waiting time between erections and ejaculations will increase. Men are different from women and need what is called a refractory time to rest between orgasms. Women are multiorgasmic even into older age and can be stimulated to a climax several times in a row. When you were nineteen, your refractory period was less than a minute, but it may be a day or more as you get into your sixties. Both partners need to remember that so you don't panic or create feelings of anxiety or failure by attempting to create another erection and orgasm before the body has had enough recuperative time.

Remember that making love does not depend upon an erection or an orgasm. Enjoy each other, but if an erection is difficult to achieve, your body may be recuperating. Be creative and enjoy intimacy as you help your partner achieve her climax. If you have not climaxed and you are focusing on your partner and lose your erection, this is not a refractory period. Apply direct stimulation and you will most likely regain your erection.

4. Climaxes will be needed less often. As you age and get into your sixties, you may need to climax only once a week or once or twice a month. That does not mean sexual closeness with your wife two or three times a week will be impossible. You should not push yourself to climax every time there is intercourse, you can have pleasant intercourse and enjoyable thrusting without a climax and ejaculation. Putting pressure on yourself to perform and achieve certain results can result in anxiety and loss of erections.

5. The pleasure of intercourse can be longer. This is a pleasant outcome of needing less ejaculation and fewer climaxes. You can last longer and even with active thrusting can pleasure your wife with added endurance.

You may want to use some positions (e.g., wife-on-top) that let your wife be more active. This is a great time to experiment and play at this aspect of making love. There are advantages to growing older.

6. Ejaculation is less strong, and erections disappear more quickly. With aging, you may not feel quite as much like a volcano going off at your climax. The muscles that expel the semen are less strong, but that does not have to affect the pleasure of an orgasm. Part of feeling like an explosion is in your head and has nothing to do with the expulsion of semen. Stronger orgasms are created by building greater sexual tension, accumulating more semen, and letting yourself mentally focus on your orgasm as you abandon yourself to the feelings.

After you climax, you may find yourself losing your erection faster than in years past. Don't let that affect the afterglow as you hold each other and share closeness. If your penis doesn't stay in her vagina, caress and hug and hold as you tell her how much pleasure she brings you sexually. Learn not to worry about seepage of semen from the vagina but sensually and emotionally enjoy each other in intimate ways.

7. Testosterone levels will be lower. Testosterone is the hormone that produces sexual desire in both males and females. Women need only a very small amount for sexual desires, while men have higher levels of testosterone produced by the testicles in addition to the adrenal gland (females). However, this does not mean men have a higher sexual desire. This hormone is also used for masculinizing, producing beards and heavier muscles, while the ovaries are producing the feminizing hormone, estrogen. Testosterone does help create sexual desire and the ability to get an erection.

If there is severely limited desire or persistent impotence or inability to ejaculate, have a hormonal check. If a low testosterone level is discovered, you would be a good candidate for testosterone replacement, which can be in pill form or with injections. The injections, administered about once a month, are considered more effective and long-lasting. You should begin to see some improvement in erections within a two-week period. It is important to be under the care of a physician because there can be certain side effects like water retention. Certain conditions, such as prostate cancer, would contraindicate the use of hormonal therapy.

Remember that there are other physical causes of impotence: diabetes (affects the blood supply), certain medications, and nerve damage from surgery. Depression and certain antidepressant medications can also affect erections. Alcohol is a depressant and can create temporary impotence. Even if testosterone levels are low, hormone replacement doesn't always resolve impotence. The erection difficulties may be caused by physical problems with nerve or vascular deterioration. Testosterone replacement won't affect these problems.

Female Sexual Changes

Menopause is the time in the life cycle that the female stops having her menstrual cycle and the possibility of pregnancy is over. Because of a hysterectomy (removal of the uterus and possibly the ovaries), this process is entered earlier by some women. Menopause is occurring later for women today, with many approaching fifty rather than the early forties of their grandmothers. Some women enter into early menopause in the late thirties to early forties and begin experiencing the signs of estrogen loss. In menopause the female hormone estrogen is drastically reduced, which can have some immediate and long-term side effects.

Immediate effects of loss of estrogen. Emotionally, you may experience irritability, depression, and mood swings. Physically, you may experience hot flashes with possible headaches as your body adjusts to the changing levels of hormones in your body. In any period of stress there can be insomnia and fatigue, and this time will be no different. These effects vary among women but can be quite painful and intense. The adjustment may last six months to two years.

Fortunately, you do not have to experience all the discomfort of acute estrogen loss. These symptoms can be quickly relieved with estrogen replacement.

Long-term effects of loss of estrogen. Estrogen helps maintain the sexual organs, and its loss brings about some changes. The vaginal walls thin so they will not have the same elasticity and soft padding. The vagina may shrink, with its mouth becoming narrower. Because the vagina has lost some of its cushioned effect, some women will experience urethritis (sometimes called the honeymoon disease, it is an irritation of the urethra and bladder from the penis hitting them during intercourse). The loss of estrogen can affect lubrication, too. It may take longer to lubricate, and the amount may be less. In the past it may have taken seconds and now may require several minutes of loveplay to create arousal and sufficient lubrication.

Intercourse may need to be more gentle at first and care taken on entry. Artificial lubrication can be more liberally used to counteract some of these changes. Estrogen replacement therapy can minimize long-term effects and make intercourse more comfortable. In addition to seeing your gynecologist, you may need to consult an endocrinologist who specializes in hormonal treatment.

Loss of estrogen does not diminish sexual desire and the ability to experience orgasms—multiple if so desired. The hormone of sexual desire is testosterone, not estrogen, and this can remain steady during menopause. With some women there is a loss of testosterone, but it can be replaced with a simple implant under the skin. The nipples will still become erect, and the clitoris will become hard and be sensitive to sexual stimulation. It may take more stimulation and time than in the past for your organs to become vasocongested, but your ability to enjoy arousal is undiminished.

So much of sex is in the head. This can be a rich time for you sexually; you have lost some of your earlier inhibitions and know more what arouses you. Pregnancy is no longer a fear. You may have to engage in some self-talk about your sexiness as your body loses its firmness and its skin tone decreases. Again, maturity can be associated with greater skills and more comfortable attitudes. Older women make great lovers.

Estrogen replacement therapy. Not every woman going through menopause or a hysterectomy (which does not always produce menopausal symptoms because one or both ovaries are not always removed) needs estrogen replacement. At one point, researchers were concerned that the treatment increased the danger of uterine cancer, but that was dealt with by altering the hormones estrogen and progesterone to more closely simulate a woman's natural cycle. In fact, estrogen replacement may help prevent cancer, osteoporosis, and heart problems.

Hormone replacement usually consists of a combination of estrogen (Premarin and other brands) and progesterone (Provera and other brands). The estrogen is usually, though not always, taken the first twenty-five days of the month and stopped for the last five or six days. The progesterone is added from day sixteen to day twenty-five. Hormone replacement therapy may be contraindicated if there are heart or lung problems, breast cancer, or liver disease.

Physical Problems in Aging

There are a lot more creaks and groans from the body in general as you grow past your forties. Some specific illnesses like arthritis, ovarian and uterine problems, heart disease, bladder incontinence, prostatitis (inflammation of the prostate gland), some types of headaches, and lower back pain will become more common. Health changes will have an impact on your sexual performing—and attitudes—if you are not careful.

A hysterectomy or surgery following a heart attack will naturally take the focus off the sex life for a while. Sometimes a hysterectomy, after physical healing, enlivens making love, now that the fear of pregnancy and the monthly cycles are gone. But some diseases, like the threat of another heart attack, can dampen sexual desire and contact. The mate having the heart attack is fearful of excitement, and the partner can be overprotective. It is a time for believing and following medical advice.

It is also good to check out the side effects of drugs being employed to treat medical problems. Some tranquilizers, antidepressants, and hypertension medication can affect sexual performance with loss of sexual desire, decreased sensitivity in the genital area, and impotency.

Certain problems are perhaps more common than you realize, and they deserve mentioning. Prostate enlargement and cancer can require the removal of the prostate. That can but does not necessarily produce impotence. More likely it can cause retrograde ejaculation with the ejaculation going into the bladder during orgasm. That doesn't destroy sexual pleasure, however. Peyronie's disease is an upward bowing of the penis, which can make intercourse painful. Consult a urologist, but the condition does not usually preclude sex in other forms. After childbirth the vagina can be stretched or torn, making it very loose and not as pleasurable for either partner. Surgery can correct this problem.

One couple had a double dose of problems hit them as they grew older. Arthritis ran in the wife's family, and even with her medication, it was very painful as she approached sixty. Joints ached and some positions of intercourse that she had enjoyed were not possible anymore. The husband experienced lower back pain with a deteriorating disc and muscle aches. He was glad his heart and blood pressure were fine and there were no prostate problems. His physician did not think the back problems warranted surgery, but there would be chronic pain on some days. He found it difficult to be sexual when the pain was there, and like his wife, he found that certain positions weren't comfortable.

They loved each other and had built a very mutually satisfying sex life. They refused to give it up. Making love kept them smiling and connected in wonderful ways, and an exciting intimacy had grown over the years. No matter what the circumstances, they were determined to enjoy making love on a frequent basis the rest of their lives. They had never allowed inertia to set in, but they were troubled by their present disabilities.

They also had other ingredients of a great sex life that helped them do some effective problem solving. They were creative, flexible, sensual, and passionate. In spite of the effects of aging, they still liked themselves and their bodies and sex. Here is the list of solutions they began to implement:

Heating pads and warm baths. Loosening arthritic joints and stiff backs before making love helped. Baths could also be quite sensual; shared, they became a part of loveplay. The couple came to associate relieving rubs with erotic arousal. Rubbing his back often preceded fooling around and some fun sexual times. She was careful to wash her hands before touching sensitive genital tissue after nearly sending him through the ceiling one time with Ben-Gay on her hands.

Maximizing medication and heeding medical advice. There were windows of time when both felt better after taking pain medication or an arthritis treatment. During those times, they found it easier to focus and enjoy each other sexually. A possible side effect of one of the medications the wife was taking was decreased sexual arousal, and she asked her doctor to change the prescription. They also got regular medical checkups and advice. They learned about their physical problems and what would or wouldn't hurt his back or her arthritis. They were surprised how much freedom their physician gave them medically, and he encouraged them to maintain an active love life.

New moves and selected positions. The husband found he could sit propped against the headboard of the bed with pillows and heating pad on the lower back and be comfortable. The wife could then sit between his legs with her back against him or lie back with her genital area in his lap. These positions allowed her to be pleasured with less wear on their bodies. They practiced the positions of intercourse that allowed them to lie down and stay less active. They enjoyed the crosswise positions, and certain rear-entry positions were easy. She missed the wife-on-top position, which had been a favorite, but her knees would not permit that. She substituted a side-by-side position that allowed her to have some active participation. She also found that, when her hands ached, oral stimulation was a good alternative. It pleasured him in fun ways and let her feel very sensual, too.

Lubrication. They made sure to have lubricants handy. When her arthritis was bothering her, she had more difficulty focusing on arousal and becoming lubricated, so they quickly utilized artificial lubrication. That took the burden off both of them. They bought extra pillows to prop up and get comfortable. Soft music helped set a soothing atmosphere.

Playing through the pain. They had heard of athletes who said they would play through the pain. They found that if they never made love except when both felt good, it would seldom happen. They increased their communication and trusted each other when one expressed a desire to make love. At first both had a difficult time tuning out the winces and grimaces of pain and not losing their arousal. They got better at knowing when to adjust or even stop loveplay. Both were pleasantly surprised to find that sometimes making love and having orgasms actually diminished their pain.

Attitude readjustment. There were losses with aging and physical illnesses but so many gains, too. The couple learned to adapt and focus on the positive side. Part of grieving was crying over the loss of a favorite position but not allowing it to become an obsession. They enjoyed sex and intimacy. They did some self-talk or sharing together when self-pity or obsessing began to take place. They reveled in how much they were learning about sensuality and a deeper intimacy. Once she had to sternly lecture him when he thought he was losing his grip as the world's greatest lover. She affirmed that sex was much more than firmness of erections or vigorous thrusting.

Relational Changes with Maturity

Have you had your mid-life crisis? You may respond, "But I didn't know everyone had to have one," or "But I'm only forty-one, and that seems a little early to be into mid-life." Actually, the phenomena of "mid-life crises" occur throughout life. They might be better titled "identity" or "purpose in life" struggles. They all involve struggles with personal meaning and identity crises, mortality and advancing years, realizing goals and dreams, and creating deeper intimacy. Areas that are usually included are sexuality, relationships, spirituality, career and life pursuits, and meaningful leisure distractions.

Sex after forty has to consider not only the physical changes but also the mid-life relational changes that occur in the crucial years leading up to and including retirement. Middle age keeps getting pushed back, so I am not sure what middle age is anymore. For this chapter, a definition of mid-life is not crucial because we are examining the sexual cycles of a couple's life from forty to eighty (or more) where much reevaluating goes on. During these years, we constantly reassess many parts of ourselves that have great impact on our sex lives: intimate companionship, sexual passion and variety, career development and retirement, and children in later stages of leaving the nest (notice I said stages of leaving the nest because I don't think they ever do completely).

Sex is different as we age and marriages mature. That does not mean we give sex a lesser priority or lose our intimate passion. This section explores two aspects of relational changes that affect sex as we mature and grow older: (1) our environment, and (2) our individual and relational needs.

Changing Environment

Children are stressors as they enter the teenage years and there are struggles for independence. Parents incur the expense of their children's college educations. Eventually, the nest is empty. This can have a positive and a negative impact on a couple's sex life. On the positive side, there is more time to be together with greater privacy and flexibility. The negative emotional stress is the feeling of loss, especially as children become adults and launch out on their own. Parents can lose a sense of purpose and, in their grieving, lose touch with each other.

All of these environmental factors take time and energy away from making love and focusing on the marital relationship. Sometimes parents get too much identity from their parental roles and have a difficult time readjusting to being best friends and lovers. The greater time together is scary. The excuses for lack of intimacy and infrequent sex have to be faced head-on.

The forties and fifties bring many career decisions to the forefront: Will my dreams ever be realized, and will I achieve the level of success that I had hoped for? This can bring on a full-fledged mid-life crisis. You may have to grieve over some of your goals and change gears.

Mid-life career changes and whole new career directions are common in today's marketplace. The wife may be back in the job market after full-time homemaking, and she faces many new decisions as she revs up a vocation she put on hold for the sake of mothering. The husband may be in the most productive and busiest time of his career—fighting for time to keep everything balanced and to enjoy making love.

All of that affects intimacy and a thriving sex life. The husband is entering a time when he has less sexual energy but a greater desire for intimate connecting. The wife is entering a time of more sexual enthusiasm with greater independence and openness to explore and enjoy. As their bodies begin to age, their circumstances are a kaleido-scope of changes and challenges. Sex can be ignored and intimacy put on the back burner as the husband stays later at work and the wife works at varying jobs from taxiing children to balancing her own career.

The fifties and sixties face even more changes with easing into retirement over the coming years. Retirement can be structured differently for every couple. It may be going into early retirement and a new career or easing into more leisure time with relaxation and pursuit of hobbies. It may be a shock and a complete loss of purpose as mandatory retirement is reached and there is nothing to fill the vacuum. Grand-parenting can bring special meaning and enjoyment. You may have to throw into the equation a major illness and the recuperation time involved. This is also the time in life that you start dealing with the loss or needs of your aging parents. You may have to make difficult decisions and adjust your living situation.

One couple had some major adjusting to do when the husband was forced into early retirement at age fifty-two. It was a financial crisis because there were still college bills to be paid for their last child, and his field did not offer an immediate lateral shift. It was also tough because they were just adjusting to their last child's leaving the nest. The wife grieved more over her empty nest than she expected but launched into a part-time job that helped fill the need for personal identity and fulfillment. Her father passed away after a struggle with cancer. It was expected but still left a hole in her life.

The husband got depressed, and the whole relationship suffered. But they rallied together. The wife grieved through her losses and started healing. She was able to get more hours at work, and he shifted into a less well-paid but personally gratifying job. They had some major decisions a year later when an opportunity came up in his original field that would necessitate a move geographically. He turned it down, especially for his wife's sake. She enjoyed being near her daughters and liked what she was doing. They had already moved three times because of his job over the years, and both felt a deeper need for roots and stability. They had also bought some land in the country where they were going to build a cabin and get away from the rat race. Both found nature very therapeutic to their souls, and the cabin was a mutual goal for their sixties and seventies.

The couple valued their intimacy and worked to lessen the toll of the environment on their companionship. There were some lean sexual times during his depression and job fluctuations. Their marriage slowly changed—but for the better—during these times. She became more independent and he less driven, and sex came back to its place of priority.

Changing Individual and Relational Needs

Couples find their marriage and sex relationships different at age fifty-four from those of age twenty-six. Their marital intimacy has changed over twenty-some years of togetherness. Both husband and wife may find greater independent enjoyment within the context of deeper mutuality and intimacy. A couple will need to learn to expose impasses and not be afraid of confrontation and honest discussion. Unfortunately, all couples do not work hard at exposing impasses, resolving problems, and deepening companionship. Some give up and seek meaning outside the marriage. This may be through having an extramarital affair or sinking time into the grandkids or a hobby instead of bonding with the mate.

Let's take a minute to look at the overall progression of a marriage. An excellent Christian book called *Passages of Marriage* develops five stages mates mature through.* Aspects are based on the aging process and not just the exact years of a marriage. I am taking these cycles of passage and adapting them to the sexual part of the marriage in particular.

1. Young love (one to two years). The couple become a unit and work through control issues. They will feel like resisting change and running away, but they hang in there and learn. This is a time of sexual discovery, of dealing with disappointed expectations. They need to seek out good information and try to avoid setting ineffective sexual patterns. They will have some of the excitement, joy, curiosity, and energy of exploring something new. They will also feel misunderstood and get their feelings hurt as sex does not evolve exactly as they had anticipated.

2. Real love (three to ten years). This is a time of surfacing hidden agendas and sorting through some of the motives (they will not all be high and holy) for marrying—getting away from home or working through unfinished business with

---

*Frank and Mary Alice Minirth, Brian and Deborah Newman, and Robert and Susan Hemfelt, *Passages of Marriage* (Nashville, Tenn.: Thomas Nelson Publishers, 1991).

parents. It is dealing with children and working through the seven-year-itch with new contracts and commitments. Sex can become routine. It will need some erotic emphasis on fun vacations and renewal with a greater focus on exciting and nurturing each other. Everything can become too realistic, and attention to setting moods and being romantic is crucial. Frequency in making love should not be neglected, or lovemaking will get lost in the shuffle.

3. *Comfortable love (eleven to twenty-five years)*. There will be a search for individual identity with a need to learn to practice forgiving and the skills of grieving over losses. Teens complicate the picture. There can be some panic as you wonder if you have missed the perfect mate and maybe it is now or never. You desire the deeper intimacy of mid-life. Don't think that you know your mate perfectly or that there are no new horizons sexually. You will want to revive mystery and plan sexual surprises. Like the last stage, you will not want to get into routines and neglect frequent and passionate lovemaking. It may take getting out of town to overcome this. Husband and wife may switch roles with the wife having an increased desire for sexual activity and the husband wanting intimate closeness. Be selfish sexually as well as nurturing as you individually put some pizazz back into your comfortable sex life.

4. *Renewing love (twenty-six to thirty-five years)*. Circumstances will hit the relationship with grief and losses. You may wonder if it is too late to establish a deeper level of intimacy, but you have tremendous opportunity for renewal. You are entering the years where the blessings and curses of the aging process become more apparent. There indeed is exciting and more intimate sex after fifty, and you can achieve a level of affirmation and togetherness as you celebrate this part of your relationship. Learn your limitations and flourish within them. You know each other so well from head to foot physically, but old dogs can learn new tricks—be creative and experimental, too.

5. *Transcendent love (thirty-six years and beyond)*. You are into retirement and facing the fact of losing each another eventually as health deteriorates. It is a time that suffering can build character as you transcend yourself and let go of control. You may fight through some new boundaries as you set up new ground rules around leisure routines and chores. Don't isolate or become too codependent. Sexually, the older body will creak and groan but don't let inertia set in. Continue to enjoy sexual closeness even if it doesn't frequently include intercourse—though it may. Fight for your privacy if your children are keeping you and enjoy the fruit of many years of bonding and sharing. Say nice things to each other, and hold each other close. You will start to fear losing each other, and it will be okay to desperately clutch the other one close now and again. Sex can have a transcendent beauty that is admirable for younger couples to emulate.

What did the couple in our example need as they matured into middle age? He wanted and valued a deeper sense of sharing and connecting with her as he risked his feelings and was tender and playful. She desired this, too, but she also wanted an autonomous identity—to feel competent and in charge of herself. Her job helped create this feeling, and her greater sexual initiative was affirming. They had passed through "comfortable love" and were into "renewing love." It was a time for reevaluating self and the relationship. They needed healing and a grieving through to acceptance of the many losses they experienced. Sexually, relating was an important part of the healing.

Neither minded living with ambiguity and uncertainty as much as they used to. They trusted their intimacy and could connect, separate, and reconnect more easily. In fact, sometimes the wife needed this process as she launched into her own career and endeavors. Both also wanted to know they were heading toward a stable retirement and there were some things they could count on. Sex evolved into something very special in helping to meet these varied needs and staving off environmental pressures. They entered a second honeymoon.

A Second Honeymoon

Making love can become a healing agent, a strong glue, a special form of nurturing, a statement of our independent selves, deep and intimate communication, and a celebration of life. God created us to age and did not mean that as a curse. Sex can become even more special after forty and fifty and eighty. Mature men and women are even better equipped, mentally and emotionally and physically, to bring their partners and themselves greater pleasure.

Nurturing Each Other

In aging, bodies do not respond with the same reflexive arousal but need the attention and nurturing of a partner in special ways. Older mates feel a greater sense of mutuality and power in their lovemaking. A husband may need his wife to stimulate his penis into an erection and help him reach a climax in ways he did not in earlier years. This can be very exciting and bonding to a wife as she enjoys being more aggressive and playful in her sexuality. Her husband involves and counts on her more, and she enjoys this form of nurturing. A man may acquire greater tenderness, sensitivity, and patience that make him a much more adept lover. Couples have fun feeling needed and engaging in mutual nurturing with a deeper sense of connection. They appreciate being skilled and sexy lovers.

Having Prolonged and Frequent Lovemaking

A woman likes to be stimulated in a slow, arousing style. As a man ages, he becomes less self-involved as his body slows down, and he can focus on his partner more easily. He can engage in longer loveplay and active thrusting without climaxing. Both mates have the possibility of greater passion and prolonged intercourse and lovemaking sessions. The roles may change some, and the wife has to learn that it is okay if her husband does not climax every time they make love.

With the children growing more independent, making love can be scheduled in more and last a little longer without interruption. Frequency can pick up rather than diminish, and afternoon delights on the weekends or, with retirement, during the week can become more frequent. Even with the children getting older, there will always be plenty of activity, with jobs and church involvement and grandchildren, to keep you too busy. This is a time when the importance of intimate connecting will increase with a redefinition of the relationship. Regular vacations can become more possible and important. Frequent lovemaking can become a marvelous means for fortifying, renewing, and sustaining your intimacy.

Affirming the Body and Life

As you grow older, you are reminded of your mortality and the changing nature of life. A significant part of personal identity is masculinity or femininity and feeling attractive and sexual. Aging causes you to redefine your sexual attractiveness as skin and muscle tone change. A continued enjoyment of your body and your sexiness becomes a very important quest at this point in life. You need a sense of self and a sense that life has meaning.

Consistent and active lovemaking can confirm for the older couple that their bodies still function and bring real pleasure. Being sexually alive and intimate can help provide that sense of identity, meaning, and a renewed zest for life.

Enjoying Adventure and Pleasure

Why should adventure, excitement, and intense pleasure be confined to the young? A healthy outcome of mid-life reassessment is that people refuse to abandon curiosity, risk taking, new experiences, and personal pleasure. No one can afford to completely lose the child and adolescent within.

One wife refused to let her husband's mid-life crisis permanently scar their long-term marriage. Some of his ideas were more like those of a teenager, but she went to midnight movies and rock concerts, sailed to Aruba and bought a bikini, and surprised him with sexually uninhibited behavior. In general, she let him know how lucky he was to have her around. She drew the line at swimming nude in Australia, but she was astonished to discover how much she was enjoying being a little wild and crazy. Growing older and more mature did not have to be boring. In fact, they had the time and resources to kick up their heels and go places they couldn't afford in younger years.

Pleasure can become more special as you grow older with your lover. Caressing your mate after fifteen or thirty years of working at a relationship and building a history of fun events together is different from a dating relationship. Romance can explore new dimensions, and you can enjoy a more profound sensuality as you age.

Maintaining a Healthy Sense of Control

Aspects of aging bodies and retirement can make us feel very ineffective and powerless. This is where an intimate and active sex life is invaluable. In bed with a mate who loves you, you feel like a king or a queen. You are chairman of the board of directors of your love life, and you control your own destiny.

As you lie with your mate and experience the intimacy of holding hands, caressing faces, hugging close, and stimulating sexual excitement, you are energized and affirmed. Making love is a safe haven that you can delight in despite the environmental pressures. As you age, this becomes even more important, and your sex life is symbolic of your ability to still be in charge of your marriage and your destiny.

Deepening and Protecting Intimacy

God has bestowed something precious in the ability as husband and wife to connect and bond sexually. Intimate companionship is the framework for expressing many powerful and exciting emotions like joy, love, trust, and playfulness. It also dissipates and defuses negative emotions and behaviors.

After forty, you especially need God's gift of sexuality to heal losses, reaffirm your sense of self and attractiveness, encourage playfulness, and express love. Not only is this deepening of intimacy important to bind wounds and protect the relationship, it is exciting to realize that it is much more likely to be achieved as you mature with your mate. Aging brings greater flexibility, knowledge, the ability to prolong pleasure, and a desire for intimacy.

Your fifties, sixties, seventies and beyond are something to look forward to with your intimate companion. Your fulfilling partnership can achieve a level never before experienced, and your lovemaking can be an integral part of that whole process.

Section Four

Jumping
Common
Hurdles

Chapter Seventeen

♡

"I'm Not Very Sexy"

Nobody is born a great lover who is sexually mature. Techniques and attitudes are learned. Sexual expertise and sensuality have to be gained through hard work at times.

I think women, more than men, are afflicted with a lack of sexual esteem and a poor body image. Society creates such stereotypes of what is sexy. The cosmetic surgeons are kept busy making breasts bigger or smaller, removing wrinkles, and eliminating sags. I am not always against such surgery, but I worry about the inner turmoil and terrible body image of so many people. How we feel about ourselves definitely affects our ability to relax and enjoy making love with abandon and pleasure. Great lovers have grown to be comfortable and confident with their bodies and sexuality.

In this chapter, you will start out by considering the concept of body image. You will seek to better understand how you feel about your body and where these ideas originated. And you will learn how to create a positive body image. You will explore what you can do to become a more secure lover. You will have to forgive the past and deal with shame and guilt. Finally, you will discover the importance of building attitudes and behaviors to remain forever sexy.

Body Image

Where do we learn about ourselves and what is sexually attractive? How do we build up body image, both positive and negative? Many women and men dislike their physical features, while others flaunt them. Older women and men are often intimidated by youth. God made us all so unique. It's a shame that we have to categorize and label. How do you feel about yourself?

Exploring Self-Perception

The people and ideas that most commonly help you form your attitudes about your body are listed. How have these influences affected the way you think and feel? Take particular parts of your body and sort through how each one has affected the way you perceive yourself. Think about your feet, your legs, your chest, your mouth, your body shape, and your genitals.

- The media—television, movies, videos, songs, books, newspapers, and magazines
- Parents and family—family values, comments, body shapes, interaction with opposite sex, interaction with same sex, siblings versus parents, and grandparents
- Peers—friends, schoolmates, work associates, opposite-sex influence, and same-sex influence
- Church and religious beliefs—sermons, comments, type of dress and conduct, and biblical interpretations
- Significant adults—Scout leader or youth minister, teacher, neighbor, boss, and friend of family
- Dates or romantic interests—group dating, individual dates

Which of the above affected you the most in your attitudes about your body? Where do you think the people who have influenced you acquired their attitudes and values? Are you aware that no one in the world has a perfect body? Your body gives you and your mate pleasure regardless of whether it is perfect.

Trace the silhouettes in figure 17.1 on a separate sheet of paper.

1. Using crayons or colored pencils, color the appropriate silhouette the way you feel about your body. Light, happy, favorite colors could represent the parts you like about your body. Darker colors or ones you dislike can shade in the parts you are unhappy with and wish you could change.

2. Now color in the silhouette of the opposite sex, not doing your opinion of your mate. Color in the parts of masculinity or femininity you notice first, the aspects of the body that affect your attraction and sexual reaction.

Why do you like the parts of your body that you have colored positively? How did you get the feedback that they were strong points? Who influenced you to dislike the parts of your body you see as imperfect or unacceptable? Observe the silhouette of the opposite sex. How did you come to find those characteristics appealing or sexy? Would it help you enjoy your mate more if you broadened your repertoire of arousing physical attributes? Think of one physical characteristic of your mate that could become very exciting if you chose to notice it more.

Talk over and process this exercise with your mate. Discuss the manner in which

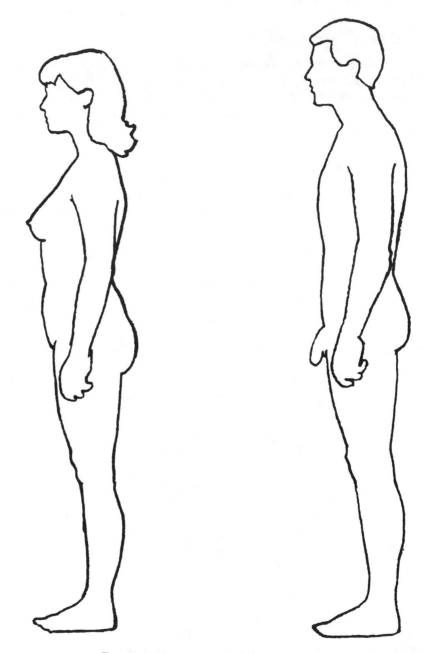

Fig. 17.1. Male and female silhouettes.

*Jumping Common Hurdles*_____

you have colored in your silhouettes. Start with yourself and explain what you like and dislike about your body image. Tell your partner how you think these opinions evolved and how your mate has helped or hindered your positive body image. Discuss the opposite sex silhouette and how men and women differ in their appreciation of physical characteristics. It is time for some healing and affirmation. Remember that body image and appreciation of yourself include more than just body parts—they affect also how you use the body parts. They can influence your posture, the way you walk, your smile, the way you laugh, voice tone, or some favorite mannerism.

Time Out . . .

1. Tell your mate three things you truly enjoy about your partner's physical appearance and body image. You must now brag on yourself. Do not disagree with what your partner said but accept the affirmation by adding to what was said about the three characteristics. You must further expound, "My smile is appealing; I like the way my eyes light up," or "My pubic hair is sexy; I like the curly thickness of it."

2. Tell your mate three things about your mate that you have sometimes noticed and enjoyed but seldom pointed out. It might be aspects of the opposite sex you usually do not focus on. It might be a body part, hands or lower lip or calves or earlobes. It might be a chuckle, a wrinkle of the forehead, or posture in sitting.

A final exercise in exploring your self-perception and body image is designed to increase your self-acceptance. Psychological research has shown that proximity and exposure create acceptance and attraction. Let me explain. If you ride on an elevator with a stranger every day for a week (being in the same proximity and being exposed to seeing him), you will begin to accept and like him. We can apply this idea to eggplant, which is a vegetable I do not like. If I did want to like eggplant, what would I do?

Proximity and exposure mean that I would need to buy several of them and leave them around my house so I would see them every day (exposure) and be close to them (proximity). It would be helpful if I picked them up and held them as I noticed their texture and beautiful color. I might cut one open and examine it further or cook it but not eat it. The more I was around eggplant, the more I could accept and even start liking them. Being familiar with something builds acceptance and attachment. That can also happen with your body.

An excellent place to start this process with your body is in the tub or shower or in the bedroom when you are dressing. You usually are nude but probably unobservant. Start to notice your hands, stomach, thighs, feet, and other parts of your body. Do not make any judgments; simply observe the skin texture, hair, wrinkles, and proportions.

Now schedule in some time specifically for observing (exposure and proximity) your body. Stand in front of a full-length mirror and look at yourself. If it is too threatening at first, do the observing with a towel or clothes on, but it is important to progress to the nude. Start with the top of your head and slowly go down your body to your feet. Turn around and observe the back side, using a hand-held mirror if needed. Notice what you are seeing, but detach from your usual knee-jerk reactions to your body. Close your eyes for a minute and try to picture in your mind what you are seeing. Tune in to your feelings as you do this mirror exercise.

After your first mirror session, ask yourself questions to help you sort through your attitudes about your body. How do you emphasize or hide parts of your body? How does your body image affect your sexuality and lovemaking?

Continue with your observation and mirror sessions over the course of several months. It will be interesting and affirming to see how your self-acceptance and attraction grow with exposure and proximity. You may also need to dispute some negative attitudes.

Disputing Negative Images

Certain ideas of Albert Ellis and the rational-emotive school of psychotherapy are useful. One very interesting device is the *A-B-C-D* way of viewing life and the concept of a rational and an irrational way of living life.

> *A* = the activating event
>
> *B* = personal belief system
>
> *C* = the consequence of an event
>
> *D* = disputing the irrational part of the belief system

You have been observing yourself in the mirror, and you have seen your stomach. This is the activating event *(A)*, and this information is then passed through your mind and attitudes and belief system. Your belief system *(B)* thinks rounded tummies are not sexually appealing. The consequence *(C)* of the activating data running through your belief system results in more self-hate and the refusal to be nude unless the lights are out. Another person looks in the mirror and sees the rounded stomach *(A)*, but the partner loves it and finds its feel and softness sexy. The self-image *(B)* creates a happy ending with a nude parade around the bedroom, showing off waist and stomach and ending in making love *(C)*.

It is not the activating event, but your rational or irrational belief system that creates the positive or negative consequences. In the next section, we will discuss how God created each of us unique and special. That is a rational belief system, based on the opinion of the Creator of the universe. How does this belief system get distorted? That is what we have been discovering. Women often think their breasts are too big or too small. Men believe their penises are an inadequate size. Where did they get these attitudes? Some people think they have too much or too little body hair. Where do we get the need to shave? How do we come to conclusions about this or that being more aesthetic? An especially troubling belief is that there is *one* right body shape for each sex. For women, it is an hourglass with a slim waist, and for men, it is a wedge with broad shoulders.

Please let go of your idea that there are any perfect bodies. Better yet, let go of the idea that there is any ideal body image that you have to measure up against. You can give and experience sensual pleasure regardless of body size or shape. You are worthwhile and sexy because God created you that way.

Think about the *D* part of the concept and the need to search out and dispute or change irrational, ineffective attitudes. Go back to your silhouette and pick out two areas that you dislike about your body. There are at least three ways you should learn to dispute irrational thoughts:

1. Search out the rational truth. The truth, if you will believe and act on it, has a way of setting you free. Where did you come up with the idea your _____ is too big or too small or ugly? Were your sources wise and accurate? What is God's opinion? Do you have a wise friend to consult with?

2. Create positive self-statements. You have many messages in your head that you need to erase. One great way to do this, once you have identified the truth, is to create a positive statement that counters the false belief: "My thighs are sexy and uniquely mine"; "My stretch marks are a reminder of my wonderful children and my maturity—I am a better lover than I used to be"; "My penis is the right size to create tremendous excitement and passion in my wife"; "My nude body is sexy and able to experience such great pleasure." List your statements and repeat them often as you change your belief system. Say them to yourself with conviction as you look at yourself in the mirror or record them on tape and play them back while you are dressing in the morning.

3. Use mental imagery. God has given you the marvelous ability to imagine how something would be even if it is not accomplished yet. You can imagine an activating event (walking across the bedroom nude) and bypass your current irrational beliefs as you imagine positive consequences. This is a great way to dispute your old belief system and advance the possibility for positive consequences. Try some more positive imagery scenarios as you close your eyes and utilize your imagination. Imagine looking in the full-length mirror and accepting and appreciating what you see. Imagine what your silhouette would look like if God colored it. Imagine your eyes, voice, and waist being seductive and arousing your mate.

Keep working on disputing irrational thoughts and beliefs. You, not the activating event, create the consequences of what happens in your lovemaking and body image. It is also important to understand God's opinion of you and to affirm that.

Affirming a Positive Body Image

Every person is created by God as a special and worthwhile individual. The psalmist David said that God knew him even before he was born and carefully made him a unique creation in his mother's womb: "I will praise You, for I am fearfully and wonderfully made" (Ps. 139:14 NKJV). Your body is fearfully and wonderfully made. You need to accept this and agree with God's opinion.

God did not intend for you to feel compelled to measure up to some arbitrary standard. He did not create youthfulness as sexy and older bodies as unappealing. He affirms your body and wishes you could, too.

Do you have a difficult time complimenting and affirming yourself? Learn to brag on yourself and affirm your sexiness:

1. Stand in front of the mirror and start with the top of your head and make affirmation statements about every part of your body: "This is my hair, and it is great hair"; "This is my nose, and I love my nose"; and "These are my legs, and they support me well." When you get to your genitals, name each part as you affirm even the body parts you cannot see. Proceed to your feet.

2. Get a sheet of paper and write on it the same affirmation statement twenty times until your knowledge starts to connect with your feelings: "My body doesn't need to be perfect to enjoy sexual pleasure"; "If I believe my body is sexy, it is"; or "My penis/vagina is marvelous, and I love the excitement it gives my mate." Think up some more affirmation statements that will heal your damaged body image and your inability to feel sexy.

God also holds you accountable to help your mate be the most secure and confident lover possible. You have a tremendous opportunity to help your partner feel great about body image. It is not always natural to give compliments generously to another person, but that should be one of your goals with your mate and your children. You should lavish praise and affirmation. This is tougher for some men to do than for most women. Men may tend to be less self-disclosing and more one-dimensional. That is, men often separate the *body* from the personality and a loving relationship, which can make them very critical.

Your mate will be much more involved and sexy knowing that you admire and appreciate the body and sexuality. If you exclaim over arousing nipples, cute legs, seductive eyes, gentle hands, an overwhelming penis or vagina, making love will blossom. Continual compliments as you see your mate step out of the shower or while you romp around the bedroom will pay great dividends. You have the power to make a real difference in your mate's self-image. There is one hitch, though—you have to learn to take compliments and believe what your mate says about you. You have to allow your mate to affirm you and increase your positive self-image and the way you think about your body.

Insist your mate learn to take a compliment and feel affirmed. Ask for feedback and an acknowledgment. Keep giving affirmation statements until they sink in and are believed.

Time Out . . .

You and your mate do this at the same time. Get pen and paper and write a short paragraph bragging on your partner as the most fantastic lover. List all the physical characteristics you love, personal appeal and charm, the activity that really arouses you, and so on. You may want to try it on a weekend away so you can fall into bed together and enjoy the exciting ambiance created by affirmation as you share your lists.

Attitude Readjustment in Lovemaking

Couples must learn to talk openly about sex as they readjust their attitudes. Discussions can clear the air and help a marital partnership create healthy attitudes. Here are some practical ways you as mates can help each other build effective attitudes and behaviors as you create a more comfortable, intimate sexual companionship.

Affirming Sexiness

In any relationship it is good to start with what you are doing right and what feels good. What are your existing strengths and positive points? You can then rest secure and confident in the fact that there are many ways in which you already have a great sex life and have a foundation from which to improve. As you do this, you will also begin to identify some of the changes in attitude and behavior that need to take place.

Identifying Old Fears, Messages, and Irrational Beliefs

There are many common fears about lovemaking: letting yourself go, losing control, making a fool of yourself, making noises or appearing silly, being inept and clumsy. Identify where some of these fears came from.

One wife realized that her fears were based upon a variety of old messages: "Nice

Time Out . . .

Create at least a half-hour window of uninterrupted time and share with your mate what you enjoy about your lovemaking. Describe what you are aroused by and how different things turn you on. Share when you feel very sexy and what creates passion and feeling excited. Name things you find sexy in your mate, and say how much you are looking forward to making love together for a lifetime.

girls are very careful about being overtly sexual"; "Never make a fool of yourself—it is safer to be seen and not heard"; and "If I'm embarrassed or made fun of, I'll just die." Her greatest catastrophe was to lose control of herself and make a real fool of herself. She dreaded that her husband might find her funny and make a critical comment when she was opening up a very personal part of herself—her sexuality.

One husband who was reluctant to initiate new things into lovemaking identified how critical his father had been whenever he did chores around the house. The worst thing that could happen to him was looking dumb and lacking the requisite skills to be good at something. He seldom took risks unless he could practice privately and perfect his skills before trying them out. He realized he did not completely trust his wife and feared that she might be critical and he wouldn't measure up. His core irrational belief seemed to be: "If I make a mistake, I am a failure."

Time Out . . .

Zero in on one specific part of your lovemaking that seems to lack comfort and passion for you. It may be having intercourse, initiating, stimulating genitals, trying a new skill, or achieving a climax. What old messages and experiences from the past might be interfering? What is the worst, most embarrassing thing that could happen? Discuss what you fear your mate might say or think. What do you think is your core irrational belief that needs to change before you can comfortably experience more pleasure in this part of your lovemaking? Dialogue and learn to trust.

Disputing and Changing Irrational Beliefs

As a couple, work on disputing and changing some of the old messages and irrational fears and beliefs that are affecting your marriage. You will be pleasantly surprised by feeling more trusting and in love. Intimacy is built upon honest sharing and nurturing each other. Your attitudes will begin to get readjusted in advantageous ways as your relationship grows.

Time Out . . .

1. Dispute your irrational beliefs by helping each other make up positive statements that are more in accord with God's ideals in lovemaking: "I am human and will make mistakes, and this is a natural part of learning"; "I can look foolish and still be accepted and loved"; "God wants me to enjoy my feelings of pleasure and be wild and abandoned in my lovemaking." Repeat these statements back and forth to each other as mates. Try practicing the ones designed for your mate; they will be helpful, too, and may uncover some more of your irrational beliefs and core fears. Look your mate in the eye and offer affirmation in areas of core fears (e.g., "I love you and you need not fear looking stupid with me").

2. Try behaviors that will make you violate your irrational beliefs so you have to deal with the fears. Affirm and support each other in what can be scary and uncomfortable behaviors (e.g., simulate an orgasm with wild abandonment, make love trying three new behaviors, practice kissing). Together you can realize that no catastrophes occurred, and you are growing and changing personally and sexually.

Skill Building

Each partnership has areas of lovemaking that could benefit from new and better skills. An ability to communicate about sex and try new things without embarrassment and fear of failure really helps in implementing these changes. To overcome insecure lovemaking, carefully evaluate your sex life and pinpoint specific areas that need to be addressed. Technique is not the be-all and end-all, but feeling knowledgeable, experienced, and confident bolsters overall sexiness. Remember to relax and play at trying these new behaviors.

Time Out . . .

Step away from your fears and defensiveness and carefully assess your sex life. Think through the way your average lovemaking progresses. Brainstorm together and pinpoint the exact areas you would like to improve: initiating, foreplay, kissing, intercourse, easier orgasms, slower ejaculations, smoother birth control, mood setting, greater variety. Focus on one specific area. Now research and try some new behaviors. It will take time and practice to incorporate new behaviors.

Healing the Past

Guilt and shame are emotions God gives you to motivate changes; they are never meant to be long-term. They are catalysts for change. Godly guilt is a feeling that energizes you to be repentant and make changes to rectify a wrong thought or behavior. Guilt helps you flag your mistakes when you have violated your values. Shame, on the other hand, is a result of imperfections and immaturity. It is a feeling that is intended to drive you toward God's wholeness and to work on overcoming inadequacy. Both guilt and shame can be harbored in a destructive manner and never be utilized to motivate change. Long-term guilt and shame become a black cloud that dampens your sexual freedom and enjoyment and creates fear and anxiety.

Learn to use the skills of confession, repentance, forgiveness, and making amends to heal guilt and shame. Don't let destructive behaviors and attitudes (which shame and guilt are flagging), whether past or present, cripple your lovemaking.

Following are some basic concepts for handling unfinished business from the past and healing destructive guilt and shame:

- Use godly guilt and shame. Act on the guilty conscience signal that an important value has been violated and the shameful conscience signal that an imperfection has been exposed—and make necessary changes.
- Confess. Expose the wrong behavior or attitude to God's truth, and break the secrecy and drain the sexual sin of its power, feeling cleansed and resolving

guilt as the sin is acknowledged and changed and you see yourself as worthwhile, accepted, and restored by God and the person hearing the confession.

- Repent. Recognize and accept responsibility for your sinful, destructive thoughts and actions, and choose to make necessary changes.
- Forgive. Let go of long-term guilt and shame, release hurt and resentment, and free up emotional energy to deepen intimacy.
- Make amends. Restore trust and self-esteem as restitution is made for destructive behaviors—bringing resolution and healing.

I'm Okay—We're Okay

It's a crazy dynamic in a relationship—you can get on either a positive or a negative roll. Insecurity and inadequacy feed on themselves and grow worse. Believing you are not sexy becomes a self-fulfilling prophecy. Confidence and greater skills create a platform for launching a couple into an even better sex life. In God's gift of one-flesh intimacy, sexual bonding and pleasure are available to every marriage. Every individual and couple should be okay and sexy.

Sexy Attitudes and Behaviors

Which comes first: the attitudes or the behaviors? Do you initially need to think you are sexy and then build a repertoire of sexy behaviors? Or do you practice sexually stimulating behaviors and from these actions derive increasing confidence and a sexy attitude? You can't eliminate either the attitudes or the behaviors. They go hand in hand. Inadequate knowledge could hamper the most positive attitudes of feeling sexy. An inferior, self-conscious perspective could hinder great technique. The truly sexy couple have to work on both.

Some people are convinced that, for them, their attitudes and the way they feel about themselves have to be the starting point of being sexy and truly enjoying lovemaking. They begin by appreciating and accepting their bodies. As they give themselves permission to be sexually proactive, not embarrassed or afraid of looking foolish, they are able to enjoy pleasure more. They relax their need for control and feel freer to experience God's gift of exciting lovemaking. Attitude readjustment makes a tremendous difference.

Other mates become sexier lovers and in turn help their mutual lovemaking by improving technique and behavioral skills. Reading some books that emphasize romantic sensuality and various techniques for arousal and then implementing these ideas dramatically improve self-confidence. Ego is very much tied up in altering skill deficits.

There is a fundamental rule for staying confident with lovemaking in an intimate marriage: the truly sexy couple are forever changing in both attitudes and behaviors. Life is constantly in flux. The forever changing couple must be characterized by openness, flexibility, the ability to take risks, and a zestful enjoyment of life.

Forever Sexy

Inhibitions, routines, and laziness don't become a great sex life for the forever sexy couple. Get on a positive roll and keep it up for the rest of your marriage. Concepts like abandon, seductiveness, admiration, playful curiosity, frequency, and power must replace embarrassment, timidity, control, naiveté, and boredom. "I'm not very sexy" is constantly disputed in minds and behaviors. Make love with vigor and confidence.

Be realistic enough to know that there will be some relapses and slumps. That is what healthy guilt and shame are for as warning signals. Marriage and lovemaking will always have some peaks and valleys. Old scars and attitudes might continue to haunt, and daily routines will sap energy. Covenant together to sound the alarm when either of you recognizes that sex is lapsing into ineffective patterns. Don't panic, but kick into gear the skills that helped you make changes in the past.

Never take your sexual comfort and aliveness for granted. Continue to work on aligning your attitudes with God's guidelines for great sex. It can be so much fun feeling and acting sexy together. There can be sexual tension and excitement in the air that add an energizing dimension to your daily interactions. Thank God for your ability to give and receive sexual pleasure.

Chapter Eighteen

Women Becoming More Easily Orgasmic

Does this sound familiar? You thought sex was a part of marriage that would fall into place naturally. You love your husband and find him very romantically attractive. But no matter what he tries to do in stimulating you, you cannot achieve an orgasm. Every time you make love now, the focus is on your achieving climax, and this has become very frustrating.

Anxiety has now crept in. It is an unfortunate sexual saboteur that makes existing sexual problems worse. It can be a real killer of sexual arousal. Instead of relaxing and enjoying lovemaking with sensuous abandonment, you worry about the process and are upset that you are not orgasmic.

Let me reassure you. You will overcome this hurdle like so many women before you, and you are definitely not alone! This is a very common issue with wives.

Understanding Orgasms

Perhaps you are wondering if you have had an orgasm. Sometimes during lovemaking you feel tingling and physical excitement. If you wonder, you probably haven't. A climax includes muscle contractions and is usually easily recognizable. The pulsing and tingling you feel in your vulval area are probably strong arousal that precedes an orgasm but not the actual climax.

The Nature of an Orgasm

The sensation of an orgasm begins with a pause in time as if your body is on the brink. Then occurs a rush of delightful feelings and sexual sensations centered in the clitoris but experienced throughout the pelvic area and, if an intense climax, throughout the body. These sensations are immediately accompanied by muscle contractions in the pubococcygeal muscle, which can be felt in the vagina and uterus. An average orgasm will be three to five contractions, and an intense one may be twelve or more.

Women greatly differ in their descriptions of their climaxes. As a woman gets more acquainted with her pubococcygeal (PC) muscle and vaginal contractions, she is more likely to describe the experience as containing pulsing and contracting sensations. Often it is described as a flooding or warm, shivery, tingling feelings that begin in the genital area and spread throughout the body. Sometimes it is likened to an explosion or a wave sweeping over the body with an abandonment to the bodily sensations.

Orgasmic Hindrances

The reflex action of an orgasm is created by increasing two types of sensory input: (1) bodily, and (2) mental. The body has to receive stimulating friction to the erogenous zones, with a special focus on the clitoris. It has to be done in a manner that feels erotic to the woman and builds adequate sexual tension. The mental, though, is the usual culprit. It is not easy erasing some girlhood messages and becoming openly erotic and sexy. Focusing the mind on sexual arousal and allowing sexual tension to build are skills learned through practice.

The rest of this chapter contains three specific plans that mates can work through to help the wife become more easily orgasmic. The first the wife accomplishes on her own as she becomes orgasmic with self-stimulation, learning about her sexuality and responses. Then she and the husband incorporate her knowledge into her becoming orgasmic in their lovemaking with him as the primary stimulator. Finally, the wife learns to be more easily orgasmic during intercourse.

Becoming Orgasmic with Self-Stimulation

The following plan contains five steps. Please take the time to carefully complete each step. If you skip ahead, you will sabotage the process.

You may wonder why you can't allow your husband to do the touching and pleasuring. You have never pleasured yourself in your life, and you feel uncomfortable trying. In these exercises, the goal is to help you explore and understand your sexual responses so you can share this pleasure with your mate. Your personal excitement and orgasms are bonding and stimulating to you and your mate. The goal is not to create isolation or self-centeredness; it is a means to an end: enjoyable lovemaking.

As you begin these exercises, please release yourself from a focus on orgasm. Allow your mind and body to learn to enjoy pleasure and focus on the immediate sensations. Enjoy your body and sexual feelings with increased fun and excitement. Allow yourself to delight in the sexual tension that is building.

As you work through these exercises, block out at least *three* thirty-minute to one-hour sessions per week. This will take planning and perhaps baby-sitting, but you will become frustrated if you do these steps sporadically. It will take time and focused attention to make changes. Structure in enough time and privacy. These months will pass quickly, and in addition to becoming orgasmic, you will enjoy many spillover benefits in your attitudes toward yourself, sex, and making love.

Step One: Self-Exploration

Before exploring your body and genitals, start this journey by exploring and understanding your attitudes about your body and sexuality. Take at least a week with three sessions to sort through your attitudes about sex and yourself. It would be helpful to take a pen and paper and write answers in a free-flowing style. Writing makes things more real and connects your head with your feelings.

Exploring Your Attitudes

Session One

1. How was the topic of sex treated in your family? What messages were conveyed around nudity, reproduction, menstrual cycles, the different roles of boys and girls? Were you allowed to discuss sex, and were your questions answered?

2. Were your parents affectionate with each other? with you? What do you think their personal attitudes were toward sex? How did your siblings affect you sexually?

3. What place did your religious convictions and church involvement have in developing your sexual values? Which messages do you think were helpful, and which were negative in your sexual development?

4. What part did your peers and friends play in the formation of your sexual attitudes?

Session Two

1. What are your earliest sexual memories in which you realized that boys and girls were different or experienced genital pleasure? Are these memories positive or negative in content?

2. What are your memories in elementary school of sexual experiences? Did you play doctor or masturbate?

3. What happened as you approached puberty? As you began menstruating and developing breasts, how did you feel differently about your body?

4. When did you begin dating, and how did that affect your attitude toward yourself and your femininity? Did you have any sexual encounters in the dating experiences? Where and under what conditions did they take place? Were they enjoyable, awkward, pressured, or fun? What was the most confusing and troubling part in this process?

5. When did you begin touching in the erogenous zones? Was it arousing? How was your first time with intercourse? How did it develop from there as a part of your sexual activity?

Session Three

1. If you were picking two positive and two negative experiences that affected your sexuality as you entered marriage, what would they be?

2. How did your sexual relationship develop before you were married? What activities did you engage in? Were they comfortable? Did both of you have an active sexual desire? Who initiated? Were there any traumatizing events?

3. How were the honeymoon and the first year of the marriage sexually? Was there a time in the beginning of the marriage that sex changed in any way?

4. If you could make three changes in your sex life right now, in addition to becoming orgasmic, what would they be?

Exploring Your Body

This part of the self-exploration step is becoming familiar with your body and its sensuality. You will need a private, comfortable place to practice, body lotion or oil, and a hand-held mirror. It would be better to have an hour for each session and repeat each session twice or until it becomes comfortable.

Session One

1. Sensual touching is an important part of sexual enjoyment and arousal. Lying back or propped up on the headboard of the bed with pillows, gently begin with your face and head and slowly work down your arms and hands and torso and legs to your feet. Use lotion as you desire as you lightly rub and sensitively explore all the skin of your body that you can reach.

2. Go back to several of the more sensitive areas (breasts, stomach, thighs) and now practice different types of touching: soft, firm, long, slow, rapid, changing directions, using fingertips and palms. Just enjoy and focus on the sensations it creates in your body.

3. You now have a better understanding of the types of touch and areas that are most sensitive. Close your eyes and focus on these parts of your body as you revel in the sensual feelings. Experience the tingling and warmth and stimulation you are able to produce in your skin and nerve endings.

Relaxation exercise. A part of becoming orgasmic is relaxing and eliminating anxiety. You will feel very tense or anxious sometimes in going through this process. Take in a deep breath through your nose and hold it a second or two, then slowly let it out through your mouth; repeat. You may need to actually calm your mind for a couple of minutes and take a break. Lie back, get comfortable, and go to a place in your imagination that is soothing and safe (perhaps a favorite place in nature)—gently breathe in and out as you put yourself into the scene. Feel a breeze or a relaxing waterfall or whatever sensations are a part of your scene. Let your body and mind calm down. It may help to consciously relax your muscles as you lie back and go limp—allow the tension to subside as you calmly breathe and feel safely comforted for a minute or two. You will occasionally need these relaxation breaks if anxiety builds.

Session Two

1. Lie down or prop up or sit comfortably so that you can easily see your genitals with your hand-held mirror. Begin with the pubic hair, then explore your inner lips and how they meet at the clitoris. Examine the clitoris and pull the clitoral hood back. Find the opening of the urethra. Pull the lips back and carefully examine the vagina. Notice colors, contours, skin textures, and shapes.

2. Write a description of your genitals. What do they remind you of in shape and texture? Look over your description. What is negative? How could you phrase it more positively?

Session Three

1. Begin with your nipples and proceed to your genital area and carefully explore, only this time pay attention to sensations and what area is most sensitive to the touch. Use your mirror as you look and slowly touch and caress each part, paying special attention to the vagina and the clitoral area.

2. Lie or sit back comfortably and this time close your eyes as you focus on the feelings in your genital area. Stay in the present experience as the nerve endings relay to your mind what feels most sensuous and pleasurable. The goal at this point is not to stimulate or build tension but to discover the pleasurable points of your erogenous zones and the types of touch that feel best.

Step Two: Kegel Exercises

Kegel exercises can sensitize the genital area. The exercises involve the pubo-coccygeal (PC) muscle, which surrounds the opening of the vagina and anus. It is one of the muscles that contracts during orgasm. To locate this muscle, you can practice stopping the flow of urine; it can quite easily, in this fashion, be distinguished from the buttock muscles. You may feel it by inserting a finger in your vagina and trying to squeeze down on the finger.

Why bother with the PC muscle? This is an excellent way to tune in to your genital sexuality as you progress toward orgasm. It increases sensation in the pubic area and the vagina, which can increase your pleasure. These exercises can be easily practiced throughout your marriage, and many women report an increase in the intensity of their orgasms with a strengthened PC muscle.

Turn to chapter 14 and practice the three different types of Kegel exercises listed there. It would be helpful to practice them in ten-minute sessions two to three times a day for a week.

Step Three: Self-Pleasuring

These two sessions concentrate on stimulation of the clitoris—the organ that helps produce orgasms. Don't start with the clitoral area as you enjoy your increasing understanding of your body. Sensuously begin by rubbing other parts of your body (breasts, thighs, etc.) that you have discovered are sensitive and produce tingling sensations.

Remember, this is not the time to try to produce orgasms, but relax and focus on your sensations. They may seem mild at first or not feelings you expect would lead to a climax. Please do not worry about arousal, but experience whatever sensations are there as you slowly blossom in your ability to enjoy stimulation. Allow yourself to appreciate all your feelings without overanalyzing or resisting them.

You will want to have some oil or lotion for lubrication. Eliminate distractions so you can focus entirely on your body and its feelings. Don't worry about what you should feel or allow frustrations or fears to encroach. You may want to try each session three or more times (allow about thirty minutes each time) as you learn about your bodily responses and encourage the sexual tension to build.

Session One

After you have done some sensual warm-up, focus on stimulating the clitoral area. Remember the clitoris has three parts to it: the clitoral hood formed by the inner labia, the glans, which is pealike in size and under the hood, and the clitoral shaft, which extends back from the glans toward the pubic mound. Women vary in whether they want direct stimulation on the glans or more indirect on the shaft or edges of the labia. This step continues with exploration as you try to find the right touches, rhythms, pressures, and places to increase pleasurable stimulation. Move from place to place in the clitoral area as you enjoy erotic sensations. Some touches will feel more arousing, and you'll want to repeat them.

Session Two

Do some warm-up stroking of your body as you relax and focus. Utilize the knowledge you have acquired on stimulating your clitoris, and in this session concentrate more on repeating the touch and pressures and locations that felt best. The glans can become more sensitive with arousal, and you may want to continue a given rhythm but not as directly. When aroused, the shaft becomes hard and can be felt under the skin as if you are rubbing across a small cord. Continue to experiment as you find a rhythm that can begin to build sexual tension. This session focuses on building excitement. Again, don't worry about orgasms, but enjoy the feelings. After your session, lie back and relax with some deep breathing as you inhale through your nose and exhale through your mouth.

Step Four: Renewing the Mind and Fantasy

The mind is a marvelous tool that God has given you. Unfortunately, it can record both positive and negative sexual messages. This step works with your mind to erase ineffective sexual programming and replace it with positive statements and create romantically stimulating fantasies. The first session focuses on positive self-statements. The second session develops erotically stimulating fantasies and allows you to relax control as you delight in your sexual feelings.

The usual style of psychotherapy in making sexual changes is called cognitive-behavioral therapy, during which you understand and change your attitudes and ways of thinking (cognitive) while you work on learning new, more effective behaviors. Step three was very behavioral as you learned to stimulate your clitoris and tune in to pleasurable feelings. Now renew your mind as you work on some cognitive changes. Each part of this step will take at least a forty-five-minute session.

Session One

Create positive self-statements. There is power in affirmative self-statements and positive thinking. We are encouraged in Scripture, "Whatever things are true, whatever things are noble, whatever things are just...if there is any virtue and if there is anything praiseworthy—meditate on these things" (Phil. 4:8 NKJV). Use the following self-statements to create your list of at least ten positive affirmations:

- The negative things I learned about my body and sexual feelings as a child no longer apply to me as an adult married woman. I am learning new feelings.
- I enjoy the way my body is sensuous and gives me pleasure.
- God created lovemaking and orgasms for my enjoyment.
- My breasts, clitoris, and vagina make me a woman, and I appreciate being a woman. They bring a lot of pleasure to me and my mate.
- I've started my journey to becoming orgasmic, and now it is just a matter of time.
- I know other women who enjoy their bodies and sexual feelings, and I am no different from them. I can enjoy my sexuality with my husband.
- My genitals are beautiful and respond delightfully to sexual stimulation.
- I feel the part of me that was uncomfortable with sex and had to keep control starting to change. I am more feminine and sexy than I have ever been.
- I am not trapped by my growing-up experiences and deficits. I am a marvelously sexual woman, and in an exciting way I now control my sexuality.
- There is nothing sinful or unnatural about sex. I rejoice in my body and its sexual feelings.

Here are four important ways to implement these affirmation statements (or ones you make up) in your forty-five minutes of practice and in future sessions:

1. In the privacy of your bedroom or bathroom, stand in front of a mirror, look yourself in the eye, and state them with conviction.

2. Take the three that you especially want to emphasize, and write each on a sheet of paper at least ten times. Writing somehow helps connect a statement from the head to the heart, and you start to believe it.

3. Use a cassette recorder to record the messages over and over again for about ten minutes of listening. Relax and get comfortable and listen as you let them affirm and change your attitudes.

4. Get in a place that you feel comfortably supported and relaxed (chair or bed). Now take a deep breath and slowly let it out as you practice some of your relaxation exercises. As you feel relaxed, imagine yourself achieving your goals in your affirmation statements.

Session Two

Fantasy is a significant part of sexuality. In this forty-five-minute session, you will try three different exercises to increase your ability to fantasize and enhance your erotic arousal. Women can easily enjoy fantasy and can be visually aroused by erotic symbols. Romantic and sensual imagery can enhance sexual focusing and physical stimulation.

1. A fantasy doesn't have to be explicitly erotic to be sexually arousing. Get comfortable and relax as you create in your imagination a warm and romantically sensual scene with your husband. Imagine him holding you gently and whispering to you how much he loves you. He is softly caressing you in a setting (Hawaii, a hot tub, the Ritz honeymoon suite) that you find very sensual. Now try caressing yourself sexually as you focus on this romantic scene.

2. Now proceed to more explicit sexual fantasy and pleasure your clitoris as you use your imagination and enjoy making love with your husband. Picture sexual activity and arousing interaction. Discover and create images that are sexually exciting for you as you allow your mind to respond with your body. It may help you to increase your knowledge by talking to a friend who is more comfortable with her sexuality or reading some of the other chapters of this book.

3. Complete your fantasy session by developing a complete ideal lovemaking session with your husband. Bring the romantic sensuality and some of the specific images into the lovemaking as you caress your clitoris and body. Let your imagination take flight and picture his hands touching you and stimulating your sexual arousal. Let your mind build a repertoire of sexually arousing images that are associated with your lovemaking, which can excite and increase sexual tension.

Step Five: Building Tension

The last step is designed to help you achieve an orgasm if you have not already done so. You may have to practice each of these last sessions many times over several months. You may want to rotate through sessions one, two, and three as you practice your affirmation statements and relaxation exercises before each session. Remember that an orgasm is a reflexive action and you cannot force it to happen. It occurs as you enjoy your bodily and mental stimulation. Allow your body and pleasurable feelings to take over.

Session One

An orgasm occurs as you relax, focus on your feelings, and continuously build sexual tension in your body. Start with an affirmation statement or two and get relaxed, then begin stimulation of your clitoris in the ways you have found build tension. Make a special point to concentrate on your sexual feelings as you tune in to your body and give in to your growing arousal. Enjoy some fantasy if it helps you focus and increases arousal. Keep a steady, continuous stroking, and don't stop even if you feel a tingling or warm feeling. Remember, an orgasm is the contracting of the PC muscle, and you may be on the verge of an orgasm and need to keep the stimulation going through to the actual orgasm. Don't exhaust yourself, but play and enjoy this continuous stimulation for a half hour.

Session Two

In this session, you simulate an orgasm. The physiological and other signs of arousal may be described as orgasmic triggers as they are a part of and can help produce a climax. Your body will increase (1) muscle tension in your legs, thighs, stomach, and arms. Your (2) breathing will become heavier and more rapid. Your (3) pelvis may rock or thrust up to meet the stimulation of the clitoris, and there will be other (4) writhing motions of the body and a desire for more rapid stimulation. Your (5) face will contort with pleasure and excited grimaces. Your (6) noises and verbal exclamations increase, and you express sexual arousal with squeals, excited moans, and "wows!" Practice each of these separately before role-playing your enjoyable and exciting orgasm.

Session Three

Combine sessions one and two as you relax, focus your feelings, and begin to build sexual tension by stimulating the clitoral area. As the tension mounts, more vigorously stimulate the clitoris and begin to incorporate some of the orgasmic triggers. Tense your muscles and allow your breathing to become heavier. Rock and express verbally and nonverbally your growing excitement. Keep the tension growing, but don't exhaust yourself. Stop after thirty minutes.

As you rotate through these last three sessions, keep practicing your Kegal exercises and incorporating affirmation statements as you change your attitudes. If an orgasm has not been achieved after three to six months of steady practice, you may need a sex therapist. If you are guilt-ridden over previous events you may need to work through these issues with a counselor. You may have been raised in a very sexually repressive home or church setting and need to sort through this for healing. Your marriage may have produced some scars if your husband in his frustration pressured for sex. Many women have been victimized by sexual abuse, and these traumas may especially require some professional help to resolve. These roadblocks may need some work before or in conjunction with this growth program.

Becoming Orgasmic with Your Mate

This section develops your husband's stimulation of you to an orgasm. The final section explores techniques for helping you experience a climax during intercourse. This process will be very exciting and bonding as you share your orgasms with your mate.

Four concepts are the backbone of helping you generalize your orgasms from individual pleasuring to mutual pleasuring and on into intercourse. As you understand these concepts, you can further improvise and incorporate them on your own. The last part of this section gives three specific exercises to help you implement the change you desire—becoming orgasmic with your mate.

Understanding Change Concepts

You and your husband need to read this section because it is important that he become a skillful partner in your pleasuring process. Two are better than one, and if both of you can understand the rationale of what is happening, you will more effectively implement it.

1. Desensitizing. With each of us, some sexual behaviors are sensitized (that is, they quickly elicit a strong response) with many uncomfortable feelings like fear, shame, embarrassment, hurt, and inadequacy. Desensitizing means taking the negative feelings out of the sexual experience and growing more comfortable or used to that activity. You have already desensitized yourself to experiencing pleasure and stimulating yourself to an orgasm. Now you must desensitize yourself to having your partner participate in pleasuring you.

Desensitizing requires starting slowly and building up to the full experience. In the first exercise, your husband will pleasure himself to an orgasm, trusting himself to your observation so you can learn from him. Then you will switch roles. Desensitizing may mean starting the process of self-pleasuring without achieving an orgasm the first time your husband is watching. It may mean starting even slower and having your husband in the next room, knowing what you are doing. The next time he may come into the bedroom part way through your arousal as you become increasingly desensitized to his presence and participation.

2. Approximating. Approximate means "to approach being the same, to closely resemble something." Approximating takes steps that duplicate as closely as possible the previous stimulation until you create the desired results. Approximating would be using two fingers in self-pleasuring manually as you duplicate the feel of your husband's larger finger caressing your clitoris. Approximating is placing your husband's fingers over yours as you teach him to closely resemble your types of stroking.

Another excellent example of approximating is trying to achieve an orgasm with intercourse. The first step may be individually pleasuring yourself to an orgasm with your finger in your vagina to approximate the sensation of the penis in the vagina. The next step may involve your husband's finger, then his erect penis with no movement, building up to achieving an orgasm with intercourse.

3. Building and switching. Often in behavioral changes it does not work to immediately try to make sweeping changes and expect them to succeed. Your husband won't immediately bring you to an orgasm, or you won't immediately have an orgasm through intercourse. You have to build up a series of steps until you achieve your goal.

Switching is a process that takes advantage of a series of steps that have already built up to the goal (e.g., orgasm). You begin producing the goal by the process you have already learned, and then when you are almost to the goal, you switch over and produce the goal with another type of stimulation. An example of building and switching would be using the steps you have gone through to achieve an orgasm by yourself manually. Right *at* your orgasm, quickly switch to your husband's manual stimulation to produce the climax. Next time, switch to manual stimulation right *before* the orgasm and so on as you make changes with building and switching.

4. Conditioning or pairing. Great lovers are always expanding their repertoire of sexual techniques and ways to stimulate their sexual arousal. In chapter 7 on building fantasy, we discussed how much of sexual arousal is built on conditioning or pairing one already sexually arousing stimulus with another stimulus. You have already paired sexual arousal with your self-pleasuring. In this section, you further pair your husband's physical stimulation with sexual arousal and orgasm. In the final section, you pair the stimulation of intercourse with achieving an orgasm. This pairing occurs physically, but your imagination and mind create the conditioning.

You have come far, so don't become discouraged. Practice some of your affirmation statements and don't *work* at these changes—laugh and play at them. It takes a sense of humor and a lot of creativity to implement sexual changes and learn new skills. You will make mistakes and will feel silly and will lose something of the erotic charge as you build and switch from one stimulation to another. You also will enjoy the desensitizing process as you pair new thrills and experience many fantastic connecting moments through this process.

Implementing Change

Talk through each session with each other before setting out to accomplish it. What will be tough to do and why? How can you overcome these barriers to progress and not sabotage the process? Each session should be repeated at least twice, and do your own improvising as you approximate and build.

Session One

Begin this session by both being nude and doing some gentle, connecting massage of each other's body. Let the wife get into a comfortable observation position and the husband in the position he feels best for pleasuring himself to an orgasm. Each may feel self-conscious. This exercise will take trust to let your mate into your private world of sexual arousal. Be a teacher and allow questions within limits that don't destroy focusing and building arousal. It may be helpful to save questions until after the first session or do more teaching in a repeat of this session. The husband will go first and employ the stroking and rhythms that best create sexual tension buildup in himself as he produces an orgasm.

Wife, now demonstrate your process in pleasuring yourself to an orgasm. Go slow if needed. Feel free to pleasure yourself to an orgasm with your mate in the next room or across the room, more indirectly observing. Perhaps it would be easier to allow him to quietly come in and observe, as you maintain your focus, after you have begun self-pleasuring. Set a thirty-minute time limit and enjoy the pleasuring and shared experience without worrying about orgasm. This is a learning and teaching experience. Let him observe only—no touching yet. It may help you to be less self-conscious and desensitize by simulating an orgasm for your mate as you employ the orgasmic triggers. Don't fake, but tell your mate what you are doing. Repeat this session until you are able to achieve a climax with your mate present.

Session Two

This session utilizes the procedures of approximating and building and switching to enable your mate to bring you to an orgasm. Begin by doing your own pleasuring, and allow your husband to be an active participant as you teach. One excellent technique is to place his fingers over yours or your fingers over his. Help him learn to duplicate the strokes, pressure, and rhythms that you use to build sexual tension. If your arousal decreases, practice building and switching. Stimulate yourself closer to an orgasm or right to the point of your climax beginning and quickly switch. The gymnastics of this teaching may be amusing as you rapidly pull these switches off, but you are playing and learning together.

Limit these sessions to a half hour as you build to an orgasm with your mate. Husband, learn from her. Keep your hand and fingers loose as she guides the motions. Try to approximate the type of stroking and procedures your wife enjoys. You can improvise and expand your techniques later. It can be exciting for your wife for you, the husband, to demonstrate some sexual arousal yourself, with muscle tension, heavier breathing, verbal and nonverbal excitement, and more rapid movements.

Enjoy and play at this session until you as a couple have approximated and built and switched to an orgasm. Don't get discouraged after several attempts. You are aware that the tension is building, and you will break through. Practice affirmation statements and keep enjoying the process.

Session Three

This session expands your repertoire of methods for creating orgasms. It also begins your journey of becoming multiorgasmic as it encourages you to achieve two orgasms.

1. Husband, get comfortable with your back supported in a sitting position on the bed and your wife sitting between your legs, leaning back against you. Use your hands to caress and massage her face, back, and outer arms and legs. Progress to her breasts and genital area as you begin arousal. As you advance to direct clitoral stimulation, practice what you have learned from your wife in the past sessions. Don't worry about an orgasm but enjoy nondemand genital pleasuring. If after twenty minutes you haven't achieved a climax, move on to part two of this session. Once you have achieved an orgasm, move directly to part two.

2. Take a few minutes to cuddle and kiss and delight in your sexual closeness. Husband, get into a sitting position and let your wife's legs straddle yours, genitals to genitals, as she comfortably lies back. She will not have lost all of her arousal but use lubrication as needed. After getting an erection, stimulate her genital area with your penis. Use it to arouse her as you focus on her clitoris. Let your penis become a tool

for pleasuring as you gently but vigorously build her sexual tension toward an orgasm. As she gets closer to a climax, briskly increase the rapidity of your wrist and arm movements.

Wife, coach what feels best because your genital area will already be sensitive and some touches will feel better than others. Lie back and focus on your sexual feelings. Let yourself build again to a climax. In time you may desire many orgasms in a single session. After climaxing, feel free to have your mate continue to stimulate you to another orgasm if you so desire.

Becoming Orgasmic During Intercourse

It is fun to enjoy sexual variety and be able to share sexual excitement and stimulate orgasm in different ways. Experimenting and working at becoming orgasmic during intercourse for playful and intimate reasons sound great. Here are two techniques that can help you achieve the goal of being more easily orgasmic during intercourse. The first includes direct clitoral stimulation and the second focuses on vaginal stimulation. Many wives do not regularly have orgasms during intercourse, so don't make this the sign of great lovemaking.

1. Apply direct stimulation to the clitoris. Self-pleasuring by the wife during intercourse is sometimes more easily accomplished than the husband's trying to apply friction. Certain positions of intercourse give better mobility. The wife-on-top and scissors positions allow the husband to more easily apply manual stimulation. The clitoris may be particularly sensitive during intercourse and need more indirect stimulation.

Apply the principles of desensitizing, approximating, and switching to achieve orgasm. You may want to start approximating by having a session in which orgasm is achieved (1) with the wife's finger in the vagina and (2) then the husband's finger and (3) then two fingers and (4) then the penis being contained with no movement. The wife may need to pleasure herself to an orgasm initially when there is a finger in her vagina and then switch to the husband's stimulation as it progresses. As you move into intercourse and more rapid thrusting, don't worry if the husband cannot always contain himself. Chapter 22 gives helpful tips to prevent premature ejaculation and you can practice some of them.

Allow your mind to make this an exciting, erotic experience. As you start to put a finger in your vagina and approach orgasm, use your imagination and fantasize your husband's penis in your vagina producing the orgasm. Sensitize your mind and pair arousal with his penis as you eroticize this thrusting type of friction. Let it ignite sexual arousal for you as you approximate up to and include intercourse, maintaining clitoral stimulation as needed.

2. To increase sexual stimulation without caressing the clitoris directly, sensitize the vagina and train the mind to focus on different erotic sensations than just clitoral ones. Center feelings in the vagina with the clitoris only receiving indirect pelvic stimulation. As the vagina and vulval area are sensitized, they can build sexual tension enough to trigger an orgasm.

The orgasmic platform, the outer third, is the most sensitive part of the vagina with greater nerve endings in the PC muscle. Tightening the muscle during intercourse can create vaginal stimulation that helps build toward orgasm.

This exercise is based on the build-and-switch technique and conditioning as you gradually pair vaginal stimulation with sexual tension and more easily achieve an orgasm through vaginal stimulation alone.

- Begin intercourse with a position that allows you to practice PC muscle squeezing and experience pleasure with your orgasmic platform as well as stimulate the clitoris. Stimulate the clitoris to build to an orgasm, and switch to vaginal thrusting alone at the point of climax. Again use your mind and imagination to picture your husband's penis and thrusting producing the orgasm in an exciting fashion.
- Now build and switch just short of the point of orgasm so that the final building is done with vaginal thrusting alone. Use your fantasy. Enjoy the feelings and focus on your climax as you allow all the orgasmic triggers to be present.
- Continue building and switching more quickly until you are able to build all or most of the sexual tension needed to trigger an orgasm with vaginal stimulation alone. If tension subsides occasionally, include some clitoral stimulation and then switch back to vaginal alone. Some positions of intercourse will give more indirect stimulation of the clitoris, which can be helpful. As with any new learning, the more consistently you practice, the more likely you are to master the skill.

As you build greater sexual enjoyment and practice new skills, please don't lose sight of making love and playfully enjoying each other. Becoming orgasmic, alone or with your partner, can become a quest that evokes feelings of anxiety and inadequacy. The goals should be pursued with playfulness as you enjoy the trip regardless of the destination. Keep in mind that orgasms are reflexive actions, and you simply set the stage for them to occur. If you have still not broken through to a climax alone or with your mate, keep trying the suggestions of this chapter. It takes time. You also might consider finding a competent sex therapist and getting some extra help. Relax and let your lovemaking be much more than orgasms.

Chapter Nineteen

"We Haven't in Six Months"

An inconsistent and unsatisfactory sex life plagues many marriages. Being Christians does not make mates immune to the problem of sexual infrequency or a lack of sexual desire. In the first section of this chapter, the primary enemies of a great sex life are briefly presented. Most couples have a few of these saboteurs at work. The last four sections discuss the four common types of sexual infrequency: lack of priority, temporarily stalled, inhibited desire and arousal, and blocked initiation and enjoyment.

Common Saboteurs of a Great Sex Life

Here is a list of the top enemies of great lovemaking. These saboteurs help create the four types of sexual infrequency. Go through and check off the ones that may be potential adversaries of your sex life as you detach from your fears and defensiveness.

Need for Control

You may be a perfectionist and need to feel your life is scheduled. Sex can seem messy and out of control. Your partner wants sex at inopportune times, and it is difficult for you to surrender to pleasurable feelings. Making love isn't much fun if you do not trust anyone enough, even your spouse, to allow yourself to behave in an abandoned, carefree way.

Emotionally and sexually, you can feel overwhelmed. Even if you don't regard your spouse as threatening, you may like to keep things to yourself. Some people pride themselves on their ability to keep calm regardless of what is going on around them. They suffer from the need to keep control in their lives to the detriment of their sex lives. Sex is by nature a little wild and crazy, with trust essential and uninhibited feelings abundant.

The Environment and Cold Buckets of Water

Busyness and fatigue. No couple is immune to this modern plague. It decimates the time to be lovers and friends, leaving mates exhausted—feeling separated and lonely. Between careers, children, church involvement, and leisure activities, couples don't have the time and energy for sex.

Having privacy and minimizing stressors are vital aspects of managing the environment. The luxury of focusing on each other in a private time together does not come easily. Sex is more exciting and fulfilling when you have forty-five minutes and are rested rather than fifteen and are exhausted. Couples have to learn to streamline their lives and practice stress management as they leave work at work and say no to new commitments. They have to make deliberate choices and set priorities to combat the saboteur of busyness.

Infertility and medical problems. Struggling to get pregnant and then perhaps experiencing a difficult pregnancy can throw buckets of cold water on your sex life that have nothing to do with your attitudes or behaviors. Unless you have been through infertility, it is impossible to imagine how consuming the process can be. Christian faith can help you see hope and comfort in the midst of trials and tribulations. But the physical exams and sex on demand take a definite toll on your lovemaking.

Illness can make sex the farthest thing from your mind. Recurrent yeast or urinary tract infections create discomfort and times when sex is not possible. They can keep you from building sexual momentum, and inertia can set in as you go through another round of treatment. Endometriosis, backaches, and a host of physical ailments cause similar problems. You are forced to work your sex life around these occurrences.

Loss, grief, and depression. Grief has a tremendous impact on intimacy in general and lovemaking in particular. A bout of depression causes loss of energy and libido. Any serious loss can cause a couple to feel very isolated and distanced from each other.

Drinking and drugs. Alcohol consumption seldom seems like alcoholism to the one who is drinking. It may be impairing sexual functioning and the health of the companionship, though. If you are having infrequent sex and are drinking heavily, you may have discovered a big part of your sexual problems. Certain prescription drugs (e.g., antidepressants and blood pressure medication) can also affect sexual performance and desire. Consult your physician as to possible side effects of any medication you are taking.

Extramarital affairs and other distractions. It doesn't take great insight to see that an affair will have a negative impact on your sex life with your mate. Affairs are prevalent and destructive even in Christian marriages. Infidelity destroys trust and honesty and committed playfulness, which are vital to inspired lovemaking. Other distractions can include children, addictive hobbies like jogging or renovating your house, and aging parents. It is tough to manage your environment and keep the cold water from completely extinguishing your sex life.

Personal Wet Blankets

Religious and societal prohibitions. Sex is a gift from God, but you couldn't prove it by one young woman raised in a Christian home. Sex was never talked about and was treated with such hesitation and avoidance that she was afraid of it. She confessed that if bananas had been given the same treatment, she would never allow a banana in her home today. She was ashamed of her desires in high school, and she tried to repress what she considered lust or sinful feelings. She never was helped to work through effective values; she was simply told to remain a virgin. Later she came to realize that her understanding of sexual sin was not based on Scripture. In the meantime, she had tuned out most sexual cues and was afraid of her sexual sensations. Just because she got married did not mean she could turn her mind back on and instantly be sexy.

Inability to play and experience pleasure. A perfectionist or workaholic, among others, will struggle with being playful or relaxing. A fancy word for this condition is *anhedonia,* or "the inability to experience pleasure." Instead of the husband's pointing a finger at his wife's uptightness, both partners need to enjoy the feelings of excitement and pleasure. Both need to relax and give themselves permission to enjoy sexual playfulness.

Homosexuality. This can be a complex problem. For some mates, through abuse and early experiences, there can be a pattern of arousal by same-sex fantasies and erotic stimulation. They are more homosexual in their arousal patterns than heterosexual. They got married because as Christians they wanted to be straight and not gay. They hoped that with marriage, their feelings would instantly change. Sometimes initially they do, with the newness of the marriage and the novelty of intense and frequent sexual activity. There are also the attraction to and love for the mate, which spill over into the sexual relationship. As time goes on, though, the homosexuality emerges and must be dealt with.

With other individuals, the homosexuality is more vague and built on a desire to be masculine or feminine and perhaps experience a closeness with the same sex. It is less developed in fantasies and behaviors, but it causes an inability to enjoy the opposite sex and to make love easily. Some people are bisexual, attracted to both men and women. This can be very upsetting to the mate, especially if acted out in a homosexual encounter. The fact that the partner has homosexual thoughts and attitudes is often suspected by a mate feeling sexually deprived. This is usually not the reason, but in some relationships, gay thoughts and feelings will dampen sexual arousal and performance.

Expectations. Some women expect sex to be a lot more romantic and less animalistic (physical) than it turns out to be. They may wish that perspiration, secretions, and odors were not associated with being aroused. They may be disappointed that their husbands aren't the knights they appeared to be in dating days. The husbands may not be very playful or sensitive to the wives' needs for romance and ambiance.

Some men are surprised to discover that they are uncomfortable with their wives' sexuality after a baby arrives. Being a mother and being sexy seem two opposing concepts. Psychologically, when this sabotaging attitude is pushed to the extremes, it is called the madonna-prostitute complex: moms adore their babies, but wanton women long for sex. This is obviously a crippling expectation.

Expectations, attitudes, and myths can be real wet blankets sexually. You have to search them out and erase them from your mental tapes.

Turn-offs. Lack of attraction can be a great saboteur. So many partners during the course of a marriage will obsess about some picky physical or personality feature to the neglect of all the beauty of their mates. Expanding the repertoire of sexual turn-ons and focusing on sexy traits can change the situation.

Some turn-offs are just personal preferences that you can negotiate and change as needed: "I would prefer that you not stick your tongue in my ear, but I tingle when you breathe in it lightly." Sometimes these preferences change, and you have to be sensitive to your mate's new needs: "I don't enjoy getting hickies on my neck anymore."

In fairness, there are also legitimate expectations in lovemaking, and the only way to eliminate these turn-offs is to confront them and change your behavior or attitude. These changes usually improve you, and you should make them for your own sake as well as for your mate's.

All sex lives have turn-offs. Search yours out and negotiate or change.

Poor Sexual Self-Image

This point could have been included in the previous section, but it deserves a section of its own for emphasis. Perhaps the wife doesn't like the extra pounds she is having trouble taking off after the baby's birth. Perhaps the husband thinks he is an inadequate lover and secretly wonders about the size of his penis. Sexy is a mind-set. A couple can hamper their lovemaking as they buy into the stereotypes of what a sexy body and lover are. The size of waist and penis has nothing to do with being sensual and pleasuring themselves and each other.

A couple's negative attitudes about their sensuality and ability to create sexual ambiance and stimulation may become a self-fulfilling prophecy. Their sex life can become routine as they doubt their sexiness. Instead of creating some great lovemaking and reveling in the ability to turn each other on, both may feel very inadequate and quit trying to be seductive and sexually exciting. They may stop affirming each other's sex appeal and complimenting the other's body. Ceasing to think and believe in their sexual glamour and allure becomes a vicious cycle.

Sensuality and seductiveness are never based on body shape, youthful firmness, occasional slumps in lovemaking, vast experience, or fatigue. They come from attitudes and sexual self-esteem. You have a crucial responsibility to help your partner feel sexy and valued as a tremendously appealing lover. Forget your age, experience, size, or fatigue. Hold your head up and know that you are sexy!

Disruptive Feelings

Anger and resentment. It is not much fun trying to make love to someone you dislike and resent. You have to resolve the anger before you can draw closer to your mate. There is a saying in marriage therapy that "sex is the first thing to go and the last to come back" in an angry, conflict-ridden relationship. This may not be true for every couple, but overall it fits. Angry resentment distances lovers and disrupts companionship. God designed making love to include the total person—body, mind, and emotions—and a good relationship.

Disappointment and hurt. Perhaps below the anger and resentment are deeper feelings that create the anger. Try to understand anger by hyphenating it. Is it angry-hurt or angry-disappointed or angry-afraid? Disappointment and hurt are the real land mines that explode into anger unexpectedly. Disappointment and hurt come when expectations and needs are not met satisfactorily—when you feel neglected or taken advantage of. They can crop up as you feel your sexual initiative is snubbed and not valued. When you are disappointed and hurt, you feel you are constantly walking on eggs and don't know what to expect. All sense of a nurturing partnership is gone, and sex becomes unappealing or not worth the risk.

Fears. The fear of pregnancy can undermine sexual relationships. The fear of appearing inadequate can quickly dampen sexual initiative. The fear of aging and its effects on the body can cause someone to try to be a sexual athlete. Fear puts unrealistic expectations and debilitating anxiety on mates that sabotage lovemaking.

Anxiety. This general condition of being apprehensive and uneasy is based on fears. Sexually, performance anxiety creates the phenomenon of spectating and watching what is going on rather than enjoying the process. If you are anxious about having a climax or getting an erection, anxiety usually ensures that what you desire won't happen. Relaxing and being playful and staying focused in the present are important to combat this sabotaging feeling.

Guilt and shame. Guilt has to do with a violation or supposed violation of personal sexual guidelines and values. Shame has to do with feeling inadequate about your deeper self in some way. There are legitimate guilt and shame as well as a destructive expression of these feelings that impair an exciting sex life.

Skill Deficits

As you and your mate explore your lovemaking, you may discover some skill deficits. Curiosity, playfulness, a willingness to learn and experiment, and a trusting companionship can go a long way in overcoming a lack of technical ability. Perhaps that is because both of you are humbly and playfully picking up new skills as you go and learning from each other.

Skill deficits in addition to technical ability (positions, effective friction, etc.)

include character traits (enthusiasm, curiosity, a humble openness) and relational skills (effective communication, romance, time). All are needed for great lovemaking, and the character traits and relational skills can help in your quest to be a better technical lover.

Communication and the ability to gracefully initiate and refuse making love are crucial skills. Deficits in these areas can undermine great technique. You are not born romantic; you must learn to create ambiance and make your lover feel special. An absence of certain character traits and relational skills is a serious deficit and affects sexual desire and frequency.

Don't underplay the importance of technique, though. Great lovemaking can be undermined by a lack of sexual knowledge, which can include everything from knowing where the clitoris is to finding arousing positions of intercourse to varying the strokes and approaches to the female partner.

Inertia

An object at rest tends to stay at rest, and this is certainly true of lovemaking. It is true that a slow sex life settles into ever more sluggishness and embarrassing awkwardness. Earlier chapters offer some solutions to this problem.

Relational Land Mines

Parental models. Your parents teach you about sex and relationships. They model abilities to be affectionate and affirming. They openly and subtly impart values to you about sex and trust and self-esteem. Your relationship with your primary caretakers in growing up has an ongoing impact on your current sexual relationship.

Someone may grow up thinking something is wrong with sex because of the way discussion of the subject was avoided in the home. Someone else may have trouble trusting others because of a real fear of intimacy learned from the relationships at home.

The verb for great, continuing sexual enjoyment is *relate*. Consider this couple. Both came from families in which their parents were affectionate toward each other and their children. They did not get much formal sex education, but they saw their parents in a loving relationship. They both acknowledged it was good sex education. They were able to nurture and be nurtured easily, which helped in their lovemaking. Their parents were proud of them and told them so openly. It helped them take risks and trust their judgment. They liked sex and being closely connected.

Fear of intimacy. Fear of intimacy may be based on a fear of being rejected or hurt and a discomfort with being close. Trust is absent, and there is an inability to let walls down. Intimacy is kept at bay, with a need to be detached and keep control. This can be manifested in the struggle of allowing sex and love to be combined.

Conflict and distance. Anger, fear, hurt, and anxiety have a way of creating relational conflict and emotional distance. They will hamper a potentially great sex life. It is not true that men are unaffected by hurt feelings or anger and are always ready for sex. It may be true that they compartmentalize their angry or hurt feelings more easily and allow their sexual desires to overcome the effects of a fight more quickly. Continued power struggles or unresolved issues will eventually have a negative impact on sexuality. A couple's sex life is a window into the rest of the marriage. Their lovemaking will reflect whether they like each other, are intimate companions, or have many unresolved conflicts.

Traumatic Sexual Experiences

Sometimes we think of sexual trauma only as rape or incest that includes physical molesting. A better definition of *sexual abuse* is "anything that disrupts healthy sexual development, bringing distortion and inhibition to personal sexuality and married lovemaking."

Estimates are that one out of three women has experienced a traumatizing sexual event by the age of seventeen, and the statistics for men are not much different. It may be a pushy boyfriend, an uncle who makes crude gestures or comments, a horrified beginning of the menstrual cycle because of lack of information, or a guilt-evoking same-sex encounter. It may be date rape, a terrifying or confusing molesting occurrence, being made sexually aware at too early an age, an abortion, or a sexual encounter with a person in power like a pastor, teacher, or boss.

Traumatic sexual experiences often require the chance to work through them in counseling. Some events may already have been recognized and resolved, but there may also be unrecognized incidents tying up much emotional energy and blocking present lovemaking. Sexual traumas obviously sabotage comfortable and intimate sexual relating until resolved. Chapter 24 carefully explores this area with suggestions for healing.

Lack of Priority and Frequency

Environmental Stressors and No Structure

You and your spouse can have a pretty good sex life, but you just never get around to making love often enough. When you do, you enjoy the pleasurable activity and connecting and wonder why you do not make sex more of a priority. The demands of children, occasional illnesses, and stresses of the workplace sap much energy. However, the truth is that you let everything else take precedence over sex and you stay tired. Schedule in weekly lovemaking sessions, start taking regular vacations, and overcome the toxic plague of busyness.

A Complexity of Issues

With some honest introspection and exploration, you may conclude that the lack of sexual frequency is more complex than just busyness. The environment and fatigue may become excuses to keep from facing many more confusing issues, such as skill deficits, poor body image, and a fear of intimacy.

It will not be an overnight revolution, but the frequency of sex will improve as you resolve these long-standing issues. You'll be surprised and helped as you discover lack of frequency involved more than busyness; real avoidance and other problems were at work. Making love will be more fun as you add skills and techniques and improve your body image. Overcome intimacy fears by creating playtime together. Carefully set goals with behavioral objectives, and make daily choices to keep your love life a priority.

Temporarily Stalled

Raining on the Parade

Life and external forces can have a way of interfering with a sex life. One couple did not expect to have problems conceiving a child. Although the wife had always had irregular monthly cycles, she thought that problem could be quickly worked around. But sex became a chore in order to have a baby; its joy and playfulness were gone. She had severe morning sickness in the first trimester. Then she was in bed most of the last two months of her pregnancy with false labor and other complications. After childbirth, her episiotomy did not heal quickly and prevented intercourse for over two months. The couple had barely become sexually active again when the husband's dad died and the husband went through an intense grief process.

Over the past three years, the husband had just established the friendship he had wanted with his dad since childhood. They went fishing together, and his dad had come through in marvelous ways for him and his wife during the problem pregnancy. The death was a terrible blow the husband couldn't seem to recover from. Depression set in and made it even more difficult to find the energy for the things he enjoyed doing. A vicious cycle shut sex down completely, even after he started emerging from the depression. The couple eventually applied the ideas offered in the next section and got back their fulfilling sex life.

Overcoming Inertia

How do you rev up a sex life that has come to a screeching halt? Here are some things that may work:

1. Start with rebuilding the companionship, and do some playful, nonsexual activities together first.

2. Don't start with intercourse. Start by getting nude and doing some massage and giving full body hugs. Don't put any expectation on the process other than starting to tune in to sexual sensations and feelings once again.

3. As with jumping into cold lake water, eventually, you must hold your

breath, psych yourselves up, and jump into having intercourse. Go into it with no expectations other than breaking the ice. Orgasms aren't necessary. Set a date night to relax and choose to make love.

4. Try to reinstitute the lovemaking process over the next few weeks, setting aside some relaxed time. Focus on the wife's pleasure at first and together help her enjoy satisfying climaxes. In the following lovemaking, bring the husband to orgasm with a focus on his needs and special turn-ons. This is bonding and will begin to reconnect you sexually as you enjoy and nurture each other.

5. If possible, plan a vacation at this time and include a lot of sexual activity. You are now ready to start setting some sexual goals on frequency and variety to maintain your gains.

6. If there are residual emotional problems from the reasons that stalled your sex life, talk them through, or get counseling.

Inhibited Desire and Arousal

Sexual Repression

One wife wasn't sure if her conservative Christian upbringing was more of a help or a hindrance sexually. She appreciated missing some of the sexual scars her more permissive friends had acquired. But she also knew that she had repressed many legitimate expressions of sexuality. She had tried so hard to remain a virgin that she had not acquired any real sexual values, and she was afraid of or turned off by the physical aspects of making love. She was great with sex as long as it stayed more romanticized and did not require her to be an active participant. Her Christian teaching never helped her think through dating sexuality. She felt her church believed that everyone was like Adam or Eve—marry immediately and everything will be beautiful and fall into place.

She had never masturbated and had been taught that it would lead to sexual sins. Pleasure through physical sexuality was taboo until she married, and then she figured it would somehow blossom. She felt so guilty about her sexual feelings in high school when the tingles would come. She prayed God would keep her pure and holy for her husband. (She has come to realize that it wasn't an inappropriate prayer but that God also wanted her to not fear her sexual feelings and to explore them carefully.) She wondered what an orgasm felt like.

She knew that her penchant for structure and organization did not help. Her husband called her a "fastidious neatnik." She liked things to be under control, and the messy, ambiguous parts of life were tough on her. She found parts of sex very messy and out of control. Her husband seemed to her to have an insatiable drive, and there was nothing neat about birth control and secretions. She kind of dreaded as well as longed for a climax. She feared getting out of control and letting her feelings go, but she knew there must be more to sex than what she was experiencing.

Disappointed Expectations

The husband's criticism and disappointment, which he tried to hide, did not help. She knew he was disappointed with her lack of sexual desire and inability to participate comfortably. The criticism hit at her core personhood and her femininity. She took it very personally and felt diminished and inadequate in a vital part of her life. Sex was a primary process like eating—she thought everyone was born with certain innate abilities, and making love in marriage was one of them. They both had many shattered expectations, which made it tough to be lovers. She thought the whole process would be more neat and romantic. She did not understand why men could not be more like women.

He, too, struggled with trying to understand female reality and gender differences. At first he thought it was only his wife, but then he heard his buddies talking about many of the same things. He knew he got too impatient, but he had waited for exciting sex in marriage and felt very cheated. Maybe he was unrealistic to expect his mate to initiate and want sex for herself. Sometimes he thought it was all her fault, and then he realized he had problems that perhaps were bringing out the worst in her.

Two to Tango

They both recognized that though she had a great need for control, she was much more playful with the children. He kept a level emotional state that prevented him from being high or low, with little real excitement or downheartedness. Sometimes it was nice, but it could make him a little boring. He also had a quiet intensity, which made it tough for him to relax. He worked at being more playful with his wife. He thought that maybe he could help her bring her playfulness into sex if *he* could just loosen up.

He had masturbated since early adolescence and felt comfortable with his sexual feelings. He began to see that he did not know women and their sexual reactions very well. As he read about and practiced new skills in their lovemaking, he discovered there were gaps in his skills as a lover.

Skill Deficits

The toughest part in overcoming his skill deficits was letting go of his male ego—both in acknowledging his inadequacies and in not assuming that his wife would writhe in ecstasy if he were the perfect lover. His male need to provide made him want to fix everything. She told him that she would have to work on becoming orgasmic on her own and that she would have to take responsibility for improving her ability to experience sexual pleasure.

She had to work on enjoying sensuality and creating sexual pleasure by faith. She trusted that if other women had become orgasmic and could relax and revel in their sexual feelings, so could she. It was a tough journey for her. It took her many practice exercises to sensitize her clitoris and give herself permission to focus on her erotic arousal. She slowly came to associate semen and vaginal secretions and birth control with sexual excitement and lovemaking. The messiness became more bearable, and it became much easier to make sex a priority. (In other marriages, the husband is struggling with inhibited desire in perhaps a similar way as this wife.)

The Negative Snowball

It is tough getting rid of all of the negative baggage that can accumulate in a marriage. If you neglect a problem long enough, it eats at the core of the best of relationships. Work at renewing your mind and changing old attitudes and patterns of behaving. Here are some of the things that can help:

The truth shall set you free. It is healing just to gain insight into problems. You understand better the causes of your inhibited sex life. It is tremendously freeing. Just knowing what is going on helps you start making needed changes. Now you can wisely plan strategies to implement change. Review in your mind and make notes of some of your key saboteurs.

Tune in to feelings. You may be surprised at how much of both the negative and the pleasurable feelings around sexuality you have blocked out. They are there under the surface, but you may never have tuned them in. It is cleansing and healing to feel and accept any anger, shame, and confusion you felt about sex in growing up. It is tough work to dig up the feelings and acknowledge their reality. Focus on any anxiety that the physical aspects of sexuality arouse in you. Tune in to any resentment that has grown in you and your mistrust of excited, playful feelings or your mate.

Work on giving yourself permission to feel pleasure and passionate arousal. Make feelings more of a priority in your life and conversations. You will find yourself slowly getting beyond the numbness your mind has created around anything sexual. Even your genitals may have to learn to respond to pleasurable friction. It is exciting and fun to awaken sexual sensations and feelings that have been shut down.

Undertake renewing your mind. You will discover how many unrealistic expectations, distorted messages from growing up, and poor attitudes you possess. Begin to restructure and change the thoughts and beliefs. Some of this is done by understanding the erroneous messages and challenging them with truth. Do a lot of self-talk. You might say, "Relax . . . you can do it . . . it's okay . . . enjoy . . . play at it." Create positive affirmation statements: "God created sexual pleasure"; "I am capable of change"; "If I enjoy sex, it does not mean I will lose control"; "Sex is fun, and I don't need to feel guilty anymore."

Practice these change statements by writing them over and over, saying them out loud to your spouse or to a mirror, and repeating them before you begin behavioral exercises. Slowly, you will restructure your thinking, and your new attitudes will begin changing your feelings. This will take awhile. It will be worth the effort as you make love and actually begin looking forward to it. When you can abandon yourself to an orgasm, you will know you have arrived.

Remember that actions speak louder than words. You may believe you can make needed changes, but you will have to take positive steps to learn new behaviors. This is probably the most difficult but the most rewarding part of the process.

Give yourself permission to experience pleasure. You may feel like quitting sometimes, but persevere until you achieve your goal. The behavioral exercises give many opportunities to work through feelings and keep changing attitudes. You will come to enjoy giving your spouse massages and focusing on sensual feelings. Try to initiate sex at least once a week as you endeavor to tune in to sexual cues better. Buy several books on sex and utilize some of the suggestions in your lovemaking. You will become a more intimate companion and have fun playing.

Blocked Initiation and Enjoyment of Sexual Activity

This sexual problem differs from having inhibited desire or being temporarily stalled. The sexual desire and ability to be aroused are present in both mates. The blocks and inability to make love as comfortable companions are not temporary but have haunted them throughout the marriage. Occasionally, there may be satisfying lovemaking, but it never lasts.

A couple may start off on the wrong foot sexually on the honeymoon. The wife may be unable to relax. The husband may feel inadequate and confused, so he becomes reluctant to initiate sex.

After the honeymoon, the couple may not be able to talk through the problems. The husband may continue to feel inadequate and anxious, even though the wife has learned to relax and enjoy her sexual feelings and lovemaking.

He may not initiate making love because of the terrible beginning of their sexual relationship and because of his dislike of doing anything unless he can be good at it—and he does not feel that way making love.

The husband may not know how to ask for things and to get his needs met. He may not have the skills to negotiate and be close to someone and comfortably keep his own space. The wife may be better at expressing her needs and feelings. But when she does ask, he may feel pressured.

For other sexually blocked couples, different scenarios may be played out. Sexual abuse or addiction, anger or disrespect, pain in intercourse or impotence—all can stymie successful lovemaking. You may need to confront a fear of intimacy, poor communication, or a mistrust of the opposite sex. You may enjoy the challenge of the chase but not sustained intimacy.

Sex over the course of a long-term relationship is a very demanding process with much giving and receiving. It requires self-disclosure, the expression of feelings, and an ability to nurture and be close. A close sexual companionship means commitment and work.

If you want a meaningful sexual relationship, here is a list of tasks to accomplish as individuals and as a couple that can help you resolve your blocks to enjoyable lovemaking:

1. Learn communication skills. Learn how to dialogue, resolve conflict, and engage in light conversation.
2. Express needs and feelings effectively. Identify feelings, take risks to self-disclose, ask for what you need, and refuse what you do not want.
3. Learn to nurture and be nurtured. Put your head in your spouse's lap and enjoy gentle caresses, learn to nurture yourself and create the space you need, and become comfortable with sexual nurturing.
4. Create separateness and togetherness in a solid companionship. Blocked lovemaking often evolves into a serious relationship problem. Learn to be close and depend on each other as well as create individual hobbies and downtime. Make time for each other and encourage time for individual pursuits.
5. Resolve scars from the past. Work through feelings about your growing up, and resolve any traumatic experiences. Get counseling if needed to work through addiction or deeper intimacy problems and scars.
6. Create a safe harbor through commitment. Make constant choices to trust and take your wall down. Commitment will grow deeper, and you will revel in the permanence of your relationship. Bite your tongue and do not nit-pick. Strongly commit never to allow adultery in your marriage as you build trust. Do not compare or judge your mate as you work on unconditional acceptance and love.
7. Make love more frequently. It may take some effort and a few failed attempts to get back to a more consistent sex life. Start with sensual massage, tune in to sexual sensations, and then include a lot of loveplay before intercourse.
8. Build a mutual erotic repertoire. Build in plenty of variety. Learn some great moves, and create some magic in your lovemaking. Read some books and come to feel competent in your sexual skills. Combine love and sex in a fun way.

Don't feel discouraged if you can't work through your lack of sexual consistency on your own. Difficulties with desire and frequency are complex and may need some therapy to help you discover needed changes. Your natural inclination will be to continue to avoid dealing with the issues. Don't! And don't settle for an infrequent and dissatisfying sex life! Many couples suffer from this problem and work through to satisfying lovemaking.

Chapter Twenty

Relational Ruts

All couples and marriages occasionally fall into relational ruts. Certain feelings—hurt, anger, apathy, and anxiety—can be the scourge of great lovemaking. Remember the formula for a great sex life?

An Intimate Marriage + Mature Lovers = A Fulfilling Sex Life

Even though it is tough to maintain, God made an intimate marital relationship crucial to fun sexual connecting. Without the playful, loving companionship, sex becomes just another arousing activity that could lose its perspective and have increasingly diminishing returns. A one-flesh marriage allows sex to be ever new and exciting. Sex is a means to an end and never an end in itself. Making love unites and excites, but the relationship gives the context and meaning. Without the intimate relationship, sex becomes an activity that rapidly loses its dynamic appeal. When your marital companionship is damaged or suffering under the onslaughts of destructive feelings, your sex life will automatically suffer.

Unfulfilled and Angry

Two changes are usually required if you want your marriage and lovemaking to improve. You must learn to be efficient at connecting conversation. Women usually have less trouble with this than men. It involves sharing yourself and what you are experiencing in your day-to-day life. Otherwise your spouse may feel excluded. You must be aware of and disclose your feelings.

The second necessary change is to spend more time together in fun, companionable activity. Lessen the fog in the relationship and start enjoying each other again. Try to understand your spouse's needs better and tailor some of this time to include what your spouse considers connecting.

Some people may be upset and think this is unfair. They defensively reason, "The quality of my sex life depends on skills I'm not good at. I don't know if I can express my feelings and learn connecting chitchat. Why isn't great lovemaking based on hard work and practical problem solving?" But if you can put a swing set together, cook a meal, or handle the daily challenges of your job, you have the intelligence and ability to learn relational skills and become romantic.

Both partners contribute to the dullness of a relationship. Resentment is crippling. You must love your spouse into change. You can't angrily nag a person into being a better partner. Don't let anger rob you of some of the fun things that originally attracted your spouse: impulsive adventures, enjoyment of the outdoors, and a curiosity about everything.

Diffusing Anger

When so much fog and anger are in the relationship, companionable activity seems impossible. The angry, destructive arguments as well as the confusion and hurt around sex take a toll. The husband may refuse to engage in more of what he considers fruitless talks, and he may passively withdraw. The wife becomes more furious and unconnected. As she gets angrily in his face, he shuts down more. They are into a very common pattern of angry wives and passive husbands with both partners feeling hurt and thinking changes may be impossible.

This pattern destroys the companionship, especially through ineffective conflict. He might mention sex, and then she confronts all that is wrong in their relationship as she recalls incidents all the way back to when they met. As her anger builds, he withdraws and feels she is impossible to deal with. This reaction, of course, makes her pursue him with even greater anger.

One way to break this escalating conflict and get out of the roles of distancer and pursuer is really quite simple. Go back to your dating days and recall the character traits and behaviors that attracted you to each other and kept you dating. You chose each other, and many of those reasons are still there, just hidden behind a lot of fog. As you reminisce about these positive points, you will see tension relax and the fog settle. Then "act" loving: practice the old "fake it until you make it." It will feel a little contrived and awkward, but actually, you aren't faking it because you do love your spouse.

You will be amazed how acting loving can start to affect your attitudes. You're starting to associate home and the relationship with love, trust, and a true partnership once again. The same way that the angry fog seemed to take over, the sunshine of acting loving will begin to permeate your marriage and mind-sets—creating tremendous change.

You may wonder if these exercises will help as you learn to express feelings more. They will not resolve all the problems in the angry circular dance you have gotten into, but they will give you a foundation upon which you can build further changes. Until you lessen the fog, you can't see very clearly to make the needed changes. You also need to reaffirm your commitment and sense of partnership.

Closing the Hatches

In the midst of all the conflict and lack of lovemaking, you may begin to wonder if you can make the marriage work. Maybe you made a bad choice and are truly incompatible. I have never met a truly compatible couple. God has made each partner a unique individual with different gender, personality, and family background. Your incompatibility can bring a richness to your relationship if you will understand each other better and rub some of the rough edges off. Much of the problem may not be core personality but immaturity—things you need to change and allow God to transform, regardless of your mate. God has given you a potentially great partnership, but you will have to reaffirm your commitment.

Time Out . . .

To recapture the feelings and behaviors from your courting days and early years of marriage, list five things you need from your spouse and then write what you think your mate will list. Exchange and discuss lists. During the week, as a part of acting loving, do a couple of things from both lists as well as little loving behaviors. Be nice to each other, and pay attention to the behaviors in the relationship that you would like to continue.

A friend likes to compare marriage to a submarine: if you leave the hatches open, eventually, it will sink. I love this illustration. Don't just think of major hatches like divorce and affairs. Mates can leave many small hatches open that allow the intimacy to be dampened and the seawater of distractions, fatigue, and distance to pour in.

If you both love each other, commit to the process of being consciously aware and slowly start closing all the hatches. The husband might strive to avoid conflict less, express feelings, become more comfortable with intimacy, and spend less time in solitary hobbies. The wife might focus on minimizing the children's demands, enjoying sexual feelings, and working through and expressing anger better. Like acting loving and lessening the fog, closing the hatches will not resolve all the problems. It will give you a foundation to work from as your anger dissipates and you identify the changes that need to be made.

Healing Conflicts

Many couples get into opposing roles: distancer and pursuer; amplifier and condenser with an emotional and a calm/passive partner; miser and spendthrift; and controlling and rebellious. Initially, the opposite poles attract, but they can create conflict and division as mates try to balance each other.

Time Out . . .

Brainstorm with your mate and discover at least three areas where you are polarized and take opposite roles in the relationship.

Three things help you and your mate break out of the polarization of roles and become healing agents for each other:

1. Consciously become aware of the roles and power struggles that you engage in, and identify more clearly unfinished family business or personal need. How did the poles evolve? Become more adept at picking out roles by dialoguing about the problems in the relationship. The problems most easily identified in marriages are the role or pole of your mate that is opposite to you, such as spendthrift, passive, angry overfunctioner, and so on.

2. Bring God into your relationship. Begin to rub the rough edges off your role in polarization. Quit blaming and be willing to take responsibility for your own changes. Honestly look at your rough edges, and begin to grow up with greater love and competency. Genuinely communicate and believe what your partner is saying, and validate your partner's feelings by making changes.

3. Make movement to the middle, and try to include behaviors of the opposite pole. As you change the polarization and heal the conflict and deficits of childhood, the marriage will become less foggy. You will start to trust each other again and give as loving gifts what your mate needs for healing and balance. It is a tough process, but it works.

Overcoming Distorted Thinking

Once conflict and anger build up steam in a marriage, they are constantly fed by the partner's distorted thinking. You have to identify some of these immature thought patterns and change them before you can resolve some of your anger and gain a better perspective.

A poster proclaiming, "Stop Your Stinking Thinking!" is a graphic statement of the scriptural injunction to "renew your mind" as you grow into greater maturity.

Here are five common illogical and immature ways of thinking all couples will fall into on occasion:

1. All-or-nothing thinking—simplistically thinking that everything is black or white with nothing in between: "We must resolve it right now, or it will never get resolved"; "How can we make love when I am not in the mood?"

2. Mind reading and assuming—believing you know what your mate is thinking or expecting, without discussion, or assuming your mate knows what you are thinking: "We would love to do that"; "My mate should know I don't like sex before going to work."

3. Inflating or catastrophizing—inflating the consequences of events whether bad or good: "Now I will never be able to trust the marriage again"; "Great sex can resolve all fights"; "He always/never wants sex."

4. Overpersonalizing—taking behaviors as directed personally against you: "She's stopping for directions to show me up"; "He's doing that to hurt me"; "You don't want sex because I'm not a good lover."

5. Irrational labeling—arbitrarily, perhaps from personal hurt or bias, reaching a conclusion about a person or event and attaching a label. Over time you begin to believe the label: "He is an insensitive bully"; "She is frigid"; "Our lovemaking is boring."

As the relationship grows back together with less conflict, you will have greater perspective and be able to recognize more quickly when your thinking is getting distorted. You can become consciously aware of and dispute some of these destructive thought processes and the erroneous messages they create. The wife might say to herself, "My husband is not always insensitive, and he isn't doing it just to hurt me." And the husband might say, "My wife is angry, but that doesn't mean we will never have sex again. She has reason to feel isolated and hurt, but she loves me. I do need to make some changes." Recognize and challenge your distorted, immature thinking.

Conversational Connecting and Expressing Needs and Feelings

Some conflict is due to normal gender differences and being a man or woman. Whether by birth or by training, many men are not as adept with feelings nor do they have the same style as women. Women must do a lot of communicating just to connect. They typically ask questions to get closer and share feelings. Men ask questions to get information. It is amusing to note the differences. Her asking, "Are you tired?" is meant to start conversation about how the day went, ask if he is considering going to bed early, or find out if he needs extra attention. His question,

"Are you tired?" is meant to be answered yes or no, and if it's yes, he will begin turning out the lights and get the house ready for the night. He is more content-oriented in a businesslike way, not trying to feel connected.

A man may think what a woman wants is idle chitchat, but he comes to see that it is connecting chitchat and a sharing of feelings. As she gets to know him more intimately, they become supportive and establish consensus. She needs him to talk so they can really share feelings and be a partnership. The process of better communication skills and an actual format in which to validate her feelings and needs really help. A woman comes to realize that not only may a man be very unaware of his feelings in communication, he may not naturally tune in at all to the feeling part of a message as she does. Both gain a lot from trying to summarize each other's messages by validating the deeper needs and feelings involved.

A man learns that as he listens to and validates what a woman is saying and feeling, the arguments slow. He also becomes less defensive as he comes to realize that she does love and approve of him despite his relational shortcomings.

It is marvelous how sex improves as the relationship gets better and both act loving and recreate the partnership. Anger and conflict dissipate as both communicate and hear each other finally. Both partners can make changes as loving gifts to each other and choose to stop the polarization. A wife can consciously work at building her husband up and showing her respect and approval. A husband can validate her feelings and reality as he helps her feel connected and secure. He becomes more adept with expressing and dealing with feelings, and his response enhances their lovemaking. Both mates see the marriage blossoming sexually and now understand how the impaired relationship and the negative feelings of anger and hurt had taken a tremendous toll on their sex life.

Out of Love

People often think feeling in love is some mysterious chemistry that they don't control. It is either there or not, and if it's lost, it's lost forever. If you are feeling out of love or have never felt in love, you have a choice to make. Do you want to be in love? If you do, you can.

The reasons that got you married are seldom all the ones that keep you married. If you desire, today can be the beginning of your new marriage.

God has given you a marvelous capacity in your rational mind to think and make choices. You can mobilize your will and choose to follow through on behaviors that will create loving feelings. You can rework your past attitudes and learning. Attitudes and behaviors are the bases of feeling in love and not some mysterious chemistry of feelings that you can't control.

Generating Feelings of Love

You may be thinking that you have desperately tried to get the loving feelings back but have been unsuccessful. Here are some ideas that can help:

- Actions often precede and even produce feelings. If you want to feel in love, act loving. Begin doing things that are fun and companionable. Start with being friends, then ease toward being lovers. Be nurturing, and close the hatches as you do intimate things together. Converse lovingly. Appreciative, caring conversations are excellent actions that produce similar feelings.
- What would happen if you were in love? Down deep do you really want to feel in love? Maybe you are halfheartedly trying because you fear getting hurt again or being trapped. What might be some of the reasons and blocks that are keeping you from being in love?
- Fantasize about and focus on feeling in love. Like the athlete who psyches herself up and imagines doing a perfect skating routine, imagine yourself being in love with accompanying actions. Visualize in your mind's eye what being in love with your mate would be like. Fantasize as you feel and get comfortable with the feelings.
- Persistence usually pays off. Anytime you are making difficult changes, it takes months and even years to alter old patterns. Build a support network that can encourage you as you persist through to becoming loving, intimate companions.

Healing Intimacy According to God's Plan

Sometimes couples need to clear the air before they can consciously act and think lovingly. God gave a special set of skills that are important for healing damaged relationships. The effects of sin and destructive choices constantly creep into companionship, and there are scriptural methods for cleaning out garbage and healing short-circuited intimacy.

Confrontation. The apostle Paul told Timothy that he should learn to "convince, rebuke, exhort, with all longsuffering and teaching" (2 Tim. 4:2 NKJV). Christ taught that when someone offends you, you should confront the issue first with just the two of you and see if you can resolve it. Then if the person persists in denial, get some witnesses to corroborate what you are saying and hopefully break through (Matt. 18:15–16). Mates and people who care about each other must help confront and polish up personal rough edges. Confrontation shines the spotlight of truth on attitudes and behaviors, examining whether they are in accord with God's economy.

Confession. James wrote, "Confess your trespasses to one another, and pray for one another, that you may be healed" (5:16 NKJV). Confession breaks the secrecy and helps you overcome guilt, allowing for cleansing and increased self-esteem. Confession allows you to demonstrate love and acceptance for each other as all the secrets are out in the open and being worked on. Mates realize they are much more than their sins and secrets.

Repentance. Repentance is a frequent topic in the New Testament: "I hold this against you: You have forsaken your first love. Remember the height from which you have fallen! Repent and do the things you did at first" (Rev. 2:4–5 NIV); and "Godly sorrow produces repentance leading to salvation, not to be regretted" (2 Cor. 7:10

NKJV). Repentance recognizes and accepts responsibility for sinful, destructive thoughts and actions, choosing to make necessary changes. Follow through on repentance and seek out all the destructive thinking and behaviors damaging your marriage and change them. Recapture your first love and move on to an intimacy you have never experienced before.

Expression of feelings. Listen to this advice: "A soft answer turns away wrath, but a harsh word stirs up anger" (Prov. 15:1 NKJV); and "Rejoice with those who rejoice, and weep with those who weep (Rom. 12:15 NKJV). Feelings are the deeper part of communication and yourselves. Mates must tune in to and validate anger, grieving, excitement, love, and jealousy as each encourages the other to heal and move into resolution and rebuilding. Help each other recognize and work through a myriad of feelings as you rebuild love. Especially help each other grieve over losses and work through hurt and anger.

Forgiveness. We are told, "Judge not. . . . Condemn not. . . . Forgive, and you will be forgiven" (Luke 6:37 NKJV); and "[Bear] with one another, and [forgive] one another, if anyone has a complaint against another" (Col. 3:13 NKJV). Forgiveness lets go of resentment and shame, freeing emotional energy to deepen intimacy and rebuild love. Realize forgiveness is a process that slowly unfolds over time as you remember and let go of the hurt and anger of various incidents. Forgiveness does not condone what has happened, nor does it create instant trust. Trust, like love, will be built over time.

Making amends. After repenting, Zacchaeus told Christ that he was going to make fourfold amends to those he had cheated as a tax collector. Christ saw true penance in the act (Luke 19:8–10). Ezekiel 33:14–15 encourages that if a person "turns from his sin and does what is lawful and right . . . gives back what he has stolen, and walks in the statutes of life without committing iniquity, he shall surely live" (NKJV). Making amends restores trust and makes restitution for harmful behaviors, bringing resolution and rebonding into the marriage. It is not vengeance but doing what the mate needs to restore intimacy.

Becoming Lovers

What can you do to become more mysterious and passionate for your spouse? Be less predictable. Strange as it seems, you have to work on being more spontaneous. In the romantic and sexual area, plan a surprise at least once a week. It will take some creativity to take your mate unaware. It can't be flowers or dinner out every other time.

Learn to assertively unleash your feelings. You will be surprised to discover how passionate your spouse finds this. After a fight in which one husband stood up for a point as he tried to explain his needs and feelings, his wife told him she loved him and was finding him more exciting. Play a practical joke: it is not the joke so much as the playfulness that will surprise your mate.

Consider writing love letters. When you think about something and then write it down, it helps get your feelings out. Try this assignment: write a page about how glad you are to have each other as mates. Mention three things you are really looking forward to as you grow older together. Start leaving little notes around affirming your love and appreciation. Include a passionate note in your mate's lunch bag. Learn techniques from your married friends. There are many creative behaviors that can increase your joy of being lovers.

Don't panic if you don't feel in love all the time. You have a whole repertoire of behaviors and thought patterns you can use to encourage those feelings to return. You will be pleasantly surprised by the chemistry that will occur.

Anxious

Anxiety puts a damper on any relationship, but it can destroy a sexual relationship. Anxiety has a very harmful cycle in a companionship. Let's look at one couple who found this out as they struggled with normal marital concerns.

When they married, the wife had never experienced an orgasm. That is not unusual, and her husband reassured her that they would work on their lovemaking so that she could enjoy it fully and be able to climax. The problems began to occur when she started trying to read his mind and feeling anxious that he must be getting tired of all the effort. She also got upset with herself and felt she must be the only woman at her office and in the church who couldn't achieve an orgasm. Rather than talk it out with her husband or her best friend, she sat on it and increased her worry and anxiety. She became irritable with life and her husband, and the companionship suffered. Of course, that negatively increased the sexual problem, and a vicious cycle was in the making.

Any sexual problem that creates performance anxiety seems to end up in spectating. Spectating occurs when a person mentally leaves the enjoyment of lovemaking and anxiously critiques what is happening. The spectating and increased anxiety then undermine the very thing the person wants to happen. It may be the man who is worrying about his expertise and wondering if he can be a satisfying lover for his mate. He loses his passion and excitement as he ends up evaluating his performance rather than being involved in the pleasure of the lovemaking. When a man is under a lot of pressure at work, he might have times when he cannot achieve an erection. This may make him very anxious.

Women who experience pain in intercourse because their vaginal muscles tighten up become more afraid and anxious. This becomes a vicious cycle as they worry about pain and tightening up and escalate the tension that causes more tightness that causes more pain. The anxiety, spectating, and increased problems with sexual performance take a toll on the rest of the relationship.

How do mates break out of the anxiety trap? How do they get their sexual relationship and marriage back on track? Here are six anxiety-reducing techniques. Some of them, like disputing distorted thinking, have been emphasized earlier in the chapter.

1. Loveplay and a Sensual Focus

A key part of playing and fun lovemaking is enjoying the pleasure of the moment—celebrating the party without thinking you have to wait for erections or intercourse or orgasm. Relax and begin to immediately enjoy your mate, and focus on the sensual loveplay you are experiencing. It becomes loveplay once again and not foreplay as you resist anxious spectating. Immerse yourself in the beauty of making love and the mutual celebration of the sexual moment.

You may especially enjoy sensual massage. The exercise of sensate focus is an immediate antidote to anxiety. It shifts your focus back to the fun of each other's body. Massage is tremendously relaxing and short-circuits anxiety. You are able to delight in the totality of your physical relationship and feel much more bonded and in love.

Initiate Get-Your-Mate-Excited lovemaking sessions. In these playful times together, your spouse is free to selfishly focus on personal feelings. The receiving partner can center on the pleasure the body is feeling and revel in the mounting sexual excitement. Focus on *p* words: *present, pleasure, personal,* and *playing.* The sensual focusing really works.

2. Affirmation Statements and Disputing Distorted Thinking

Many people are preoccupied with faulty thinking: (1) inflation ("I always have erection problems"); (2) irrational labeling ("I'm a failure"); and (3) mind reading ("My husband is really tired of dealing with this problem"). These distorted messages just increase anxiety. Learn to do self-talk and dispute these negative statements with positive affirmation statements. Here are some examples: "I am capable of having erections when I relax"; "Making love is so sensual and exciting with my husband"; "Orgasms are not the goal of lovemaking"; and "I am a sensitive and joyful lover." Put appropriate messages on a cassette and play them to yourself with headphones at night while relaxing. Repeat them with conviction to yourself in the bathroom mirror. While making love, when you catch yourself spectating, say to yourself, "Relax and enjoy...relax and enjoy." The affirmation statements make a difference and greatly decrease the anxious, distorted thinking.

3. Effective Communication

Talking to your spouse can be a tremendous antidote to anxiety. It eliminates mind reading and reassures you that your mate is in your corner and finds you a very sexy lover. As you talk more about sex and making love, you will become more aroused and closer to each other. Start incorporating more verbal interaction while you make love; you will find it very sexually stimulating. Discuss what is exciting for each and things you would like to try to do. Of course, anything that is arousing keeps your mind away from anxious thinking and spectating. Talking helps.

4. Interventions in the Anxiety Cycle with Solutions to Stressors

Think through the anxiety cycle in which some stressor in your life or lovemaking produces anxiety and diminishes sexual performance. Then anxious worry creates more anxiety and sexual dysfunction. Look for specific causes of anxiety (stressors) and what behaviors might intervene in the anxiety cycle to eliminate stressors. A wife might worry that she is taking too long, that her husband must be getting tired and bored. But when the husband either verbally or nonverbally expresses his excitement in the process, she is able to relax and quit worrying. One husband stated he got more stressed out and less creative when he and his wife did not have enough time to relax and enjoy each other. The couple started taking at least a half hour to make love. Selfishly focus on your stimulation if that will help you intervene in the anxiety cycle. Many couples eliminate the anxiety about birth control when the husband gets a vasectomy. You will be pleased how your intelligence and creativity enable you to resolve many stressors as you make effective interventions in the anxiety cycle.

5. Relaxation

Learning to relax is an essential part of dealing with anxiety. Everyone, at times in a lovemaking session, feels tense or anxious. Try taking in a deep breath through your nose and hold it a second or two, then slowly let it out through your mouth; repeat. Forget about creating sexual tension and just relax with your partner. Gently caress each other and enjoy being close.

Laugh and playfully tickle and tease each other. Allow the tension and anxiety to subside before focusing back on sexual arousal. Relaxation and an easy playfulness can be interspersed throughout your lovemaking, especially when anxiety occurs.

6. Playful Companionship

Become playful companions and take the time to build one-flesh intimacy. Emphasizing playful sensuality and making companionable connecting the goal of lovemaking will short-circuit anxiety—and many other pitfalls in marital relating. As you build your intimate partnership and begin to feel in love and become lovers, playful sex will thrive.

Chapter Twenty-One

Dealing with Infertility

One out of six couples has problems with infertility, according to recent estimates. The desire for children is so natural and yet becomes so painful when it is unfulfilled. Infertility takes a tremendous toll on marital companionship and love-making.

Infertility has an impact emotionally on both the individuals and the marriage. Despite efforts to minimize the influence, infertility and the attempts to overcome it will have a definite negative effect on a couple's sex life and their intimate companionship.

It is easy to take for granted that procreation will be a natural part of sex when you choose to begin your family. But that is not so for many marriages, and a season of turmoil and many difficult choices is entered. This chapter increases empathy, gives helpful suggestions and, most important, encourages couples to come through this crisis still in love and spiritually enriched.

Common Misconceptions About Infertility

It will be helpful to consider some of the misconceptions about infertility. You as a couple have probably struggled with many of them or heard them from a friend. People in the lives of the infertile couple don't mean to be so insensitive and hurtful, but they often are.

1. *It's just stress. Relax and hang in there; you'll get pregnant soon.* This is well-meant

advice, but infertility is not usually due to stress or emotional issues. In close to 90 percent of couples who seek medical help, there is a physical problem. It is also true that getting pregnant once does not ensure that you will get pregnant easily the next time. Fortunately, with improved techniques, medical help is effective, and many of the couples seeking treatment achieve successful outcomes.

2. *Perhaps it is not God's will that you have a child.* God has a will for each person's life, but infertility is a physical problem. It may have nothing to do with God's will around potential parenting. This is, like the disciples' question of "who sinned?" and our Lord's response of "no one," simply a chance for God to be glorified and His children to grow.

3. *It must be him. Nothing like this has ever happened in our family.* Actually, infertility problems are evenly divided in causation between the male and the female and aren't always hereditary. Because testing the sperm count is less intrusive, that is often the beginning point. It is disturbing that some couples will never know, even with infertility specialists, why they cannot conceive.

4. *Wait till you adopt a baby. I bet you get pregnant then.* Everyone has a story of this occurrence and is happy to share it. Studies have shown that only 5 percent of couples spontaneously overcome their infertility and conceive after adopting. This misconception has the harmful implicit suggestion that adoption is a cure for infertility rather than adoption being considered in its own right as a thoughtful decision and process.

5. *Fertility tests are terrible. I hope we survive.* Fertility testing can be painful and intrusive, though some husbands and wives find the process fascinating as they gain new knowledge and seek to overcome the problem. The pain and frustration often are caused not by the medical treatment but by miscarriages, continued disappointments, and fatigue.

6. *It's only a miscarriage.* Miscarriages are a part of the infertility process, but the loss is not diminished because the child is not brought to full term. Grieving must take place and the choice made about whether to continue with treatment.

7. *I have no control over the medical treatment process.* You are the consumer. You have the right to be informed about the treatment process and make choices about the costs: physically, emotionally, and financially. Educate yourself and never be afraid to ask questions or be a part of the decision making.

8. *Infertility may mean something is wrong with our sex life, but we will certainly have fun trying to conceive.* Sexual performance usually (unless it is vaginismus and an inability to have intercourse) has nothing to do with infertility. Unfortunately, sex on demand is not much fun, and infertility usually has a negative impact on making love—instead of providing opportunity for more fun. The stress may aggravate already existing marital and sexual problems.

9. *I must pursue this goal strongly. There is no price too great to pay to have a child of my own.* During the process, before you finally give up, you will have to take a recess from your efforts, now and again, to regroup. Neither of you will want to give up, but one, or perhaps both, of you will come to a place when enough is enough. You will have decreased motivation for the struggle, you will feel you have done all you can, and you will want to get life back to normal. There is a price in terms of health,

financial security, and your marriage that is too dear. Being a parent may start taking greater precedent than having a natural child of your own.

10. Maybe you should adopt and give a needy child a Christian home. It averages one to two years of waiting for an infant and approximately $11,000 to $25,000 in fees to an adoption agency. Those who are persistent still find it possible to adopt the healthy baby of their dreams, but it is not an easy road.

11. I will never get beyond the tragedy that I cannot have children. God will help you grieve and work through your anger and loss. Don't hold it in. Cry, and share your tears with the Lord and another person. Your toughest job may be taking your unborn children to a sacred place and leaving them there, forever, with Jesus. I am crying as I write these words because I know what a painful experience that will be. The grief and loss will still be triggered over and over, but there is healing and God fills the empty places with many special things.

Acknowledging the Problem

After waiting and worrying about birth control, a couple usually share a lot of fun anticipation and enjoy the extra sex in a haphazard way when the time is right to have a baby. You both are ready for parenting. You share your dreams about what your child will be like and how the three of you will create a family unit. You wonder if you should be more systematic in tracking the most fertile time, but you don't think you need to bother. You make love as often as you can about two weeks after menstruation, when ovulation is most likely occurring. It's a good time in your life.

There Might Be a Problem

You may not be sure exactly when it starts nagging at you that something may be wrong. You know nothing is happening, and it has been months that you have been trying to get pregnant. It isn't panic or severe anxiety, but you probably need to do something. This starts your journey into the emotional and intrusive world of infertility. Your lives will never be the same. At first, it isn't too bad, and there is still hope nothing major is wrong. This is a time of becoming more structured with a doctor's visit and charting temperatures and the beginning of intercourse on demand.

Not as much as later in the process, but the time of the wife's ovulation comes to take on a life-shaping significance. Her gynecologist does a basic pelvic exam. If no abnormalities are noticed, she is then given charts and the principles of taking basal temperatures. She starts charting her periods and around fourteen days before her next period begins, her temperature dips several tenths of a degree and then rises about four-tenths of a degree. Ovulation occurs right before the rise. It is recommended that you have intercourse right before and right after ovulation on alternate nights. Sperm lives up to forty-eight hours, and this will cover the fertile time. At other times of the month, you can be as spontaneous and carefree as you desire with making love—but at ovulation, planning is a necessity.

There Is a Problem

It will not take many months of charting and concentrating on sex in order to conceive, rather than make love, to begin taking a toll on frequency and enjoyment. As one woman at a support group meeting stated, "I'm tired of sex when I don't feel like it and ending up looking like a stupid question mark afterward." She was referring to the recommendation of keeping her legs in the air after intercourse so the ejaculate will be on the cervix for a few minutes, with more likelihood of sperm swimming into the uterus. It is easy to see how this could get old quickly and put a damper on sexual intimacy and connecting.

It is tough to cut through the denial, and you may wonder, "Why us?" As the months go by, you may be forced to acknowledge that there indeed is a problem. It is time for further tests to see if you can pinpoint what is wrong. Maybe there can be medical intervention that will resolve the problem.

The Biology of Conception

Do a quick review of the charts on male and female anatomy, which will help in understanding the journey through infertility. (Refer to figures 3.3 and 3.5 in chapter 3.)

Tests and Seeking Answers

This time of testing can feel very invasive, both physically and emotionally. It isn't just the tests. Emotionally, you want so much to have a child, and everywhere you turn you are reminded of your childlessness. You encounter babies in the malls; you walk by the nursery at church; your family asks you when you will be having children. All these circumstances make it even tougher on you—with a broad spectrum of emotions from sadness to anger to hurt to fear.

Sperm Count

Usually for the first medical test, the husband's sperm sample is evaluated for the amount and healthiness of his sperm. In a "normal" ejaculate there are 250 to 500 million sperm, with counts below 10 million considered poor.

Sometimes they have the husband give a sample on site, or he may be able to take it in. It is definitely not an ego-boosting or intimacy-enhancing process to walk in with jar in hand or to be required to give a specimen on demand. Infertility may come to seem like a maze in which you constantly bump into obstructions. Frustration and, sometimes, humiliation seem to be ever-present parts of the process.

The husband may be afraid before the results are known that he is sterile. Such fears are normal. Both spouses should talk through what that would mean. It may affect the husband's sense of masculinity. The wife can help him feel secure in his maleness.

You may decide that if the husband is sterile, you will begin adoption procedures. You may consider using a sperm donor.

Many Christian couples reject the use of artificial insemination by donor. Infertility is full of ethical issues that couples have to work through for themselves. Some Christian couples do use a donor. The husband may fear his reaction if his wife were carrying someone else's child, how he would emotionally respond. Some couples feel that the husband's sterility is God's closing the door on natural children for them. Both partners have to struggle before God and their consciences about when He says enough is enough, that He has another path laid out.

There are further tests and medical interventions for the couple whose problem is a low sperm count. There may be a problem with hormone levels or sperm motility, which will respond to intervention with drugs. Sometimes having surgery on a varicocele (dilated blood vessels similar to varicose veins) in the scrotum or unblocking the different ducts that carry the sperm is helpful. Semen can be processed to separate sperm from harmful antibodies, or the physician may collect a greater amount of healthy sperm, which are then placed in the wife through artificial insemination.

Hysterosalpingogram

The hysterosalpingogram and some of the other medical procedures are fascinating in their sophisticated biology, but the wife may find this exam very intrusive and painful. In this exam, radiopaque dye is injected slowly into the uterus. As the uterus fills up, there can be intense cramping, along with almost fainting. The dye spills over into the fallopian tubes and out the top of them if there is no obstruction. A fluoroscope and X rays are used to chart the flow of the dye. The test determines whether the tubes are clear.

Some women go through this test with no discomfort or reaction. With others, it can be among the most uncomfortable exams that they will experience. The husband can give his wife strong emotional and physical support. Infertility will force a couple to depend on each other. It is not comfortable being helpless and almost demeaned. At times you will wonder if the process is worth the toll it is taking on the body.

As the tests progress, you may be disappointed over and over again as nothing wrong is discovered and no answers are given. You feel like you are going down a path with no clear map in this foggy state of limbo, trying to reach a goal that is perhaps impossible. You keep seeking directions, and no one can help you, so you keep stumbling on. You want answers, and each test seems to bring you no closer to knowing what is wrong. It is important to formulate a careful game plan with your doctor and deal with the worst-case scenario and the subsequent steps to pursue. You may begin to wonder what exactly God is doing.

Your faith will be challenged throughout the infertility process. It is easy to read Scripture:

Have you not known?
Have you not heard?
The everlasting God, the LORD,
The Creator of the ends of the earth,
Neither faints nor is weary.
His understanding is unsearchable.
He gives power to the weak,
And to those who have no might He increases strength (Isa. 40:28–29 NKJV).

But it is very difficult to trust and rely on the Lord. You will be driven back to relying on His strength. Sometimes you must see God's provision in the caring demonstrated through Christian friends.

The Postcoital Test

It is traumatizing to a sex life when genitals and making love cease to be for pleasure and bonding—instead they are examined as a means of reaching the goal of pregnancy. This is certainly true of the postcoital exam. The couple are to have intercourse on the expected day of ovulation, no matter what the mood. Sexual arousal for both mates may take much longer than usual, with erections more difficult to stimulate. Some couples cannot comply with the sex on demand, and the test has to be rescheduled. After intercourse, the couple go to the doctor's office so the wife can be given a pelvic exam.

Some wives find this test especially embarrassing and intrusive as mucous is taken from the cervix. For others, this test is still a learning experience, trying to unlock the mystery of infertility. The mucous is examined because it has a certain consistency that changes with ovulation. A successful test shows the mucous to be more fluid with a sufficient quantity of sperm actively swimming in it. This exam can also check for sperm antibodies.

Sex may disappear except around the time of ovulation. You may have lost the emotional bonding and sexual excitement of making love. There is some release of sexual tension, but all in all sex has become engulfed in the process of becoming pregnant. The postcoital exam contributes to and symbolizes this unfortunate fact.

Laparoscopy

The thermometer remains a constant factor, with temperature taking and sex at ovulation. On the advice of your gynecologist, you may decide to have a laparoscopy done. A small incision is made near the navel after the abdominal cavity is inflated with carbon dioxide. The scope is inserted to allow the physician to observe internal organs and especially check for endometriosis. Endometriosis is a puzzling disease affecting women in their reproductive years. Endometrium is the tissue that lines the inside of the uterus and builds up and then is shed each month at a woman's menstrual cycle. In endometriosis, tissue like the endometrium develops in areas outside the uterus. It can adhere to the ovaries, fallopian tubes, and other areas of the pelvic cavity.

Endometriosis can be very painful and cause infertility. If it is present, a surgeon can remove the tissue and clear the ovaries and tubal area, though some of the scarring and other damage is irreversible.

Miscarriage

At some point, the wife may discover she is pregnant. She takes a home pregnancy test, then confirms the pregnancy with the gynecologist.

It is fun as both of you tell all your friends and family who have been praying for you. You wonder how a child will change your life-style, and you are so happy.

In your joy, the turmoil of the infertility process to that point is blurred. A baby is coming, and that makes up for everything. You are going to be parents! God has blessed you, and it is an accomplished fact. All is well with the world.

Working Through Grief

Then one day a couple weeks later, you think something might be wrong with the pregnancy but do not want to face it. Some bleeding and discomfort occur, but at this time there is strong denial. Deep down, you know what is happening but can't accept it. You know that with fertility problems there is a high risk of miscarriage, but finally your prayers seemed to be answered.

Eventually, though, you are physically faced with the fact that you have lost the baby. Both of you will be affected emotionally. No matter the stage of gestation, you have lost a baby and will need to grieve. Both of you will find friends, and in particular those who have been through infertility struggles, invaluable.

You have many feelings to work through, including anger at God that He has allowed your hope and happiness to be destroyed. You wonder exactly what He was doing. Express this anger to Him—knowing He can handle your feelings. Acknowledge the intense feelings of loss and the need to mourn the death of your child, along with all your dreams and expectations. Expect an intense roller coaster of feelings. Hang in there and work your way through these many feelings.

It may be especially rugged on the wife. The woman is the one who was carrying the baby and suffers even more intense loss with the miscarriage than the husband. He should try to be there for her in an extra-supportive way, to listen to her, and to hold her. Grieving is tough.

Dealing with Friends and Family

You told so many friends and family members. Now you have to repeat the story, feeling somehow embarrassed and hurt and at a loss for words. Some people come through with flying colors as they express sympathy and say they are there for you in any way that would be helpful. Others feel a need to try to fix things or give comforting advice: "You can try again"; or "Maybe God did not want you to be parents right now." Such advice does not help.

All who struggle with infertility have had to work through careless comments, advice, and very personal questions. Families can sometimes be more difficult than friends and acquaintances. You struggle with not isolating and try to be open to your church support group, family, and friends. You may want to withdraw and crawl into a corner to lick your wounds. Together, you can work at not doing this; experience the healing that comes with support and talking things through with others.

You may sense that people are uncomfortable and do not know what to say. Most people operate under many myths about infertility. It is not easy to keep open and avoid isolating. Sometimes you just have to shrug comments off, and other times you can seek to educate and express your feelings.

Sometimes infertility and even miscarriages are difficult for people to talk about because they involve sex. You can be open about many topics, but in the Christian church and society in general, sex is still not openly discussed. Most infertile couples encounter this problem of having a "socially unacceptable" issue, much like those who have a hysterectomy (female problems) or a varicocele fixed (male problems). Embarrassment prevents people from discussing sexual topics and supporting one another at times when it is needed the most. This is certainly true of infertility.

Miscarriage is difficult and intense to talk about. It is important to think ahead and plan some responses so you can comfortably manage the conversation. You may want to develop three levels of responses to personal tragedy. The first level of response is for those who are superficially curious and whose questions and comments sometimes come unexpectedly. "When are you going to start a family?" or "My sister had a miscarriage once." A level one response is polite but discourages further conversation until you wish to talk: "We're working on it," or "Thanks for your concern, but I don't feel like talking about it right now."

A level two response is more open and self-disclosing for friends and family who are interested but not wanting or able to be deeply involved: "I am really hurting right now and would appreciate your prayers," or "It's so confusing; if you have the time, I would be willing to sit down and share more about what is happening."

A level three response is for supportive friends and family you grieve with and count on for help. They want to know what is going on and will make sincere statements offering assistance. It is a more complete self-disclosure with tears and angry outbursts. You may sometimes have to make clearer what you want from them. You may have to say, "I need you just to sit and listen and hold my hand. You can't make it better, but thanks for being here."

It is helpful to think through how your family members choose to deal with problems and perhaps do some reeducating. They may be judgmental or quick to give advice, or maybe they are silent and never talk about anything personal. The silence may be worse than the quick response. It is worth making attempts to change these patterns and include them in level three responses. Because they are family does not mean you will always get the support that you wish from them. However, with encouragement and coaching, they may come through in ways that surprise you. Give them material to read, and keep them informed.

You may feel you are letting the family down, especially parents who desire grandchildren to enjoy. Sometimes when you are wrapped up in your own grief, you may miss how others grieve over your loss. Take the time to talk. Church and family can also be tough to handle as they unintentionally remind you of your childlessness.

Coping with Holidays and Constant Reminders

Holidays and traditional family times are tough, especially days like Mother's Day and Father's Day. It is like there is a national day in which everyone gets together and celebrates your loss. You may cry and not want to go to church. Thanksgiving and Christmas are even greater reminders of family togetherness.

You don't want to go through another Christmas without a child of your own. You dread family get-togethers and anything that forces you to deal once again with your childlessness. You hate going through busy shopping malls and seeing all the seemingly happy families. Holiday and vacation times are the pits.

Holidays are catalysts for all of us to have emotional turmoil. We are under more than usual stress but expect ourselves to be happy and contented from Thanksgiving through New Year's. At no other period of the year do we expect to go more than six weeks without a depressed or unhappy feeling. And those struggling with infertility have additional anxieties.

Use common sense as you cope with holidays. Plan special events that minimize the focus on infertility and fill difficult times. Create your own traditions, and enjoy each other as a couple. Allow yourself to feel a little depressed as you reach out for support. Celebrate your faith, and enjoy music. Practice strategic avoidance as you choose not to participate in activities you know will be especially painful.

Sadly, infertile couples may experience more than one miscarriage. In later pregnancies you are cautiously optimistic and do not tell everyone. But you cannot help having renewed hope and some anticipation. Could a baby truly be coming into your lives? Unfortunately, only weeks later the same cycle is repeated with another miscarriage. Perhaps the grief is not as intense, but a child is lost. Things get unreal after a while, and it becomes more difficult to deal with all the feelings.

Grieving on top of grieving takes place, with life a blur at times. You may grow fearful of getting pregnant and going through another loss all over again. Sex at this time may shut down completely. It isn't making love but risking pregnancy, which can result in another miscarriage and more pain. The prolonged effort takes a toll on all areas of life.

Dealing with Feelings

It is hard to keep talking to each other when you are sometimes hurting so much on your own that it is difficult being with anyone. The wife may have some feelings as a woman that she needs to talk over with another woman. She so desperately wants to miss a period and have a baby in her uterus.

You are even more grateful for people in your lives as support. The church body, and a close group of friends there, can really come through during this time. A couple who has been through the same experience can give empathy others cannot give. *You need interaction with caring people to get through the many feelings and constant turmoil.*

You will experience a range of feelings at various times on your journey through infertility. The feelings of grieving will be present with denial, anger, depression, and a desire to withdraw and lick your wounds. You may also feel guilt and wonder if God is punishing you because of past sins. Try to express these feelings and not let them build into deep resentment and depression. Friends and support groups can be empathetic sounding boards. Your intimate companionship will suffer under the onslaught of all these feelings, but work at maintaining communication. Mates have a special role in understanding and healing.

If you went on a deliberate quest for a great saboteur of a fun, playful, intimate, passionate sex life, you could not do better than infertility. Sexual arousal is based on your reflexive (autonomic) nervous system. Certain feelings short-circuit the natural arousal that normally occurs when spouses playfully enjoy each other's body, stimulate erogenous zones, and try to passionately connect. The main saboteurs of sexual enjoyment are anger, anxiety, depression, guilt, and grief. The couple struggling with infertility experiences most of them weekly if not daily.

The Final Round of Tests

Your gynecologist may complete the initial round of testing, then recommend a fertility specialist. This physician usually has added to training in obstetrics and gynecology a subspecialty in reproductive endocrinology (the hormonal system) and infertility. The national organization RESOLVE keeps a list and will make referrals in a given geographic area.

Be informed and well-educated consumers. Demand straight answers and quality care from the professionals you consult about infertility problems. If you are going through the journey of trying to conceive, please be assertive consumers. Read, go to RESOLVE meetings, talk with those who have been through the process, and ask questions. Here are five reasonable expectations in working through the infertility process and in dealing with your doctor(s):

1. Attend sessions as a couple, and both speak with the doctor. As a part of this process, make sure the management of both male (a urologist may need to be involved) and female aspects of infertility is coordinated.

2. Insist that questions be answered in language you can understand, and that each procedure be explained before it is done.

3. Develop a supportive relationship with your doctor, but retain the right to change doctors to get the type of care that you desire. Go with your hunches and find a doctor and staff with whom you are comfortable.

4. Know precisely what every procedure will cost financially, its probability of success, and a general idea of the toll in physical discomfort and danger to health.

5. Reserve the right to know when the price has become too high, physically, financially, and emotionally, and to stop without guilt or pressure to continue.

The whole process can become very expensive. Unfortunately, health insurance does not cover a lot of infertility testing and medical interventions. Many couples cannot afford in vitro fertilization, with its price tag of $5,000 or more per cycle and a success rate of 10 to 25 percent. Some couples endanger their future financial security and completely deplete their savings as they struggle to overcome infertility. Be wise stewards of your money, bodies, and companionship.

As with using a sperm donor, there are ethical issues involved with trying in vitro fertilization; many view the fertilized egg as life. In the in vitro procedure many eggs are fertilized, but only one is used. You may not want fertilized eggs to be discarded without any consideration. The infertility process continually forces you to make personal and ethical choices. You are being forced to make interventions in a natural process that has gone awry. You are also trying to contain the strain on your bodies and your relationship.

Artificial Insemination and Fertility Drugs

The endocrine system affects fertility and conception in many ways. God created a beautifully complex physical system to create life. The hormones and endocrine system help signal when the uterus should begin building up endometrial tissue in preparation for the fertilized egg. The ovaries are marvelously complicated; the hormones help eggs to be created and ovulated into the fallopian tubes on a monthly basis. Approximately half of female infertility is related to a problem with ovulation or the endocrine system.

The fertility specialist may examine for eggs in the wife's ovaries with a vaginal ultrasound. She may be given a fertility drug to help regulate ovulation. Unfortunately, a possible side effect is the development of cysts. In many of these procedures, there are often medical complications that need to be considered.

Your doctor may suggest artificial insemination. It is not exactly a procedure designed to nurture your sex life and create warm, exciting connecting. At the time of ovulation, the husband provides sperm. The physician inserts the sperm with a syringe at the mouth of the wife's cervix. This increases the chance for sperm swimming up into the uterus and to the fallopian tubes.

At this point, you may feel tremendous discouragement. Your life is still booby-trapped with reminders of your infertility and childlessness. Sometimes one of you will be depressed and the other will not know why. It might be the anniversary of the miscarriage or something that occurred during the day. You may begin feeling that you have done all you can. You still do not have any final answers. You may stop charting ovulation and going to the specialists regularly.

You may lash out at God and wonder, as more disappointments occur, what is going on. God is still loving and in charge and He often continues to demonstrate it through His caring people, but at times it's hard to see that. Like your sex life, your spiritual life will take some special attention during the infertility process.

Your Christian faith and your personal relationship with Christ give crucial meaning throughout your life. This never changes. In fact, the quality of your spiritual life deepens through suffering, but it is not an easy process. Infertility can result in bitterness or challenge you to growth. Lean on your supportive body of Christian friends and encouragers as you allow God to give guidance and hope.

Letting Go

After a third miscarriage, one couple learned that there might be an antibody causing the miscarriages. The unfortunate thing was that the way to prevent the antibody from operating was for the wife to take steroids during the entire course of her next pregnancy. There was no guarantee about what damage they would do to her body.

That was it for her; enough energy and effort had been expended. Her body had been invaded for the last time, and she was through subjecting herself to further procedures and drugs. It was time to finally accept that she would never have the joy of carrying a child to term and giving birth. There was much grieving, but she was slowly looking forward to adoption and parenting. The importance of her own pregnancy was diminishing, but the need to parent was increasing.

Her husband was still not sure if indeed they had gotten enough information and answers. He was not quite ready to give up. He still wanted a biological child and was angry with his wife for completely giving up. He wasn't willing to accept and let go of his desire for his own child. It took a major confrontation for it to finally sink in that she had indeed had all she could take! Even then his denial wasn't instantaneously dissolved. But it become increasingly clear that it was time to move on, and he became willing to check into adoption.

When you decide to stop infertility treatments, some severe grieving takes place and still goes on. This is a special kind of loss and grieving that not everyone can understand. Grieving over infertility is sometimes never worked through, but please do not let this happen to you. Recognize the complexity of infertility grieving and never having a natural child.

Part of the reason you may experience difficulty letting go is not knowing if you are truly infertile. It is also an indefinite loss. Miscarriages are more concrete and foster grief. It is more nebulous crying over never being a biological parent. Nebulous, but very real and traumatizing. You will appreciate the sensitivity and value of your support system, where your feelings are not denied. You may need to seek out couples who can understand this nebulous loss. At some point, both will be finally willing to say, "Enough is enough." The decision is right, and you will forever let go of having biological children.

It is not unusual for couples to experience great loss in frequency of sex and develop problems like temporary impotence. For some couples, a vacation and time spent making love revive the old passion. Others may need to do specific sex therapy to resolve issues that have developed or that the infertility has brought to the surface.

Adoption

Some couples, after going through the grueling process of infertility, decide to be child-free. They are too old, too spent, or too unable to adjust to not having their own biological child to pursue adoption. This can be a wise decision that a couple must pray through and decide between them and the Lord. For those who decide to adopt, they begin another long and complex process. It includes finding the right agency that they wish to list with. Many books list adoption resources. All agencies differ in their requirements of prospective parents and the way in which the adopted child is delivered to them. Certain state regulations must be complied with, also.

Endless forms must be filled out, and a home visit or two scheduled by the agency social worker. Fees vary anywhere from $11,000 to $25,000, and then couples have to wait one to two or more years. Couples feel like things are so out of their control during the infertility testing that they desire to be more in control of the adoption process. Unfortunately, that is not easily achieved.

One couple prayed every night and knew they would get a child. They named it and drew closer together as they prepared for the time they would be parents. They laughed and said that they were finding out that the seemingly trite advice they received from parents who had already adopted was true: "If you really want a child, you will get one"; "You will be able to resolve your grief over not having a natural child"; and "You'll love your adopted child as much as you would ever love a biological child."

They also found more misunderstanding and unhealthy attitudes about adoption than they expected: "Oh, she's adopted! You couldn't tell it isn't really your child." They now reveal the adoption strategically. Their experience in dealing with infertility has helped them make appropriate responses or choose not to answer questions at all.

Like many couples, you may be happy that one aspect of your relationship has returned to normal in the adoption process—your sex life. Intercourse once again is for connecting and is not regulated by ovulation. You are able to make love with all its God-intended excitement and intimate bonding. You are becoming one flesh and not simply trying to get pregnant. It is great!

The Final Steps

During the final waiting period for a child, you are still grieving, and pangs will get triggered as you see a family together. One father, who has adopted children who are four and six years old, stated that the scars of the infertility process never completely go away. He and his wife still have emotional reactions, but they have become less frequent and less painful.

One woman who recently adopted a child had to resolve three issues before she was ready to welcome the new child into her life. First, could she let go of fertility and accept that she would never have a biological child? She might never know why medically, but the issue needed to be resolved and forever finished for her. Second, could she take her unborn children (perhaps going to a place that is special and holy) and, with the necessary grieving, leave them forever in Jesus' hands? Third, was she able and ready to get excited about someone else's child?

Steps for Survival and Healing

1. Build and use freely a loving, nonjudgmental support network.
2. Express your feelings and carefully work through them.
3. Find someone, perhaps through the RESOLVE network, who has been through infertility and can be there for you. You will find a special camaraderie and kinship the moment you start sharing and will not feel so alone. Write RESOLVE National Office, 5 Water Street, Arlington, Massachusetts 02174-4814; or call (617) 643-2424.
4. Be an educated and assertive consumer as you wisely wend your way through the maze of infertility. Work with your physicians to formulate an overall game plan and the worst-case scenario so that you do not feel so helpless at each point of failure.
5. Realize your sex life will be affected. Try to keep as much privacy and loving tenderness as possible apart from ovulation. Take vacations and practice other parts of this book to keep variety and playfulness present.
6. Keep as balanced as possible, and resist letting infertility rule your whole life.
7. Choose to allow infertility to draw you together, not tear you apart. Communicate daily; continue loving and nurturing gestures; get away together as companions and ban infertility as a topic while away; make love as separate from infertility; enjoy times with other committed couples.
8. Keep close to the Lord. Be angry, cry, and allow Him to be there. He gently promises, "Come to me, all you who are weary and burdened, and I will give you rest" (Matt. 11:28 NIV).

Section Five

Resolving Problems

Chapter Twenty-Two

Male Malfunctioning

Three male malfunctions—retarded ejaculation (difficulty achieving an orgasm), premature ejaculation, and impotence—are indiscriminate. They strike out at most men with various levels of complication during the course of a marriage. Couples who are aware of this can anticipate and act positively to understand and resolve them.

One of my professors in sex therapy training stated that a man's penis may be one of the most honest parts of his anatomy. This is so often true. The guilty, hurt, or distracted man may be unable to focus his sexual attention and his penis is numbed to excitement—climaxes are difficult to achieve. The man who is angry with his wife may use premature ejaculation to passively sabotage her pleasure and get back at her. The husband who empathizes with his mate's discomfort with sex may become impotent to take her off the hook.

It helps to understand some of the causes of the male malfunctions as deeper changes are effected. In all of them, performance anxiety eventually plays a big role. The more they are reacted to, feared, and focused on, the more likely they are to occur. Both husband and wife have an important role in preventing this from happening. Sometimes rolling over and going to sleep without making a big deal of the malfunction are the most therapeutic responses. You can enjoy making love again later.

These malfunctions will not always go away once the cause has been diagnosed and understood. They have become a pattern that is maintained by the anxiety. The change strategies are included to intervene in this destructive cycle.

Retarded Ejaculation

Retarded ejaculation is less common than premature ejaculation and impotence. Statistics vary, and it depends on how retarded ejaculation is defined. If we define this phenomenon as a complete inability to achieve an ejaculation, it is indeed rare. If we expand the definition to being unable to achieve a climax through intercourse, it is less rare. A more accurate way to help us deal with this roadblock is to consider retarded ejaculation to be any time the husband cannot reach a climax as quickly as he desires. That is a common occurrence.

Understanding Retarded Ejaculation

Some of the common causes of retarded ejaculation vary, depending on the situation. With one widower, it was a combination of guilt and a new mate, which mentally and emotionally interfered with his ability to climax in his partner's vagina. Another man experienced stress and anxiety about a variety of mid-life experiences. His wife, with her own stressors, was not as active in the lovemaking process. All combined to lessen his sexual focus and arousal.

Other common reasons include letting sex lives become routine and a husband's finding his wife and lovemaking less arousing. As less excitement is incited while making love, going over the edge into a climax is less readily achieved. Some husbands focus too much on the wife's pleasure and consequently neglect their own buildup of sexual tension and pleasure. In a similar manner, a wife may find herself not as aroused when she more exclusively focuses on playing with and stimulating her husband. It is difficult to keep a balance in focusing on both helping your mate and attending to your own feelings.

The husband sometimes finds the vagina too loose or too lubricated to give sufficient friction. If that is so, the wife can practice Kegel exercises and tighten the muscles of her vaginal opening. She may wish to consult a gynecologist or a cosmetic surgeon to tighten the vagina if Kegel exercises don't improve friction. Proceed with caution. It might not be the vagina at all but a lack of sexual arousal and focused concentration. The ability to focus on growing sexual arousal is a crucial part of great sex.

Sometimes emotional scars, family repression, or other issues interfere with a man's ability to experience pleasure with intercourse. Often the husband can climax with manual stimulation but through intercourse only with difficulty. Perhaps he has been so indoctrinated about keeping himself pure and not getting girls pregnant that intercourse, even in marriage, seems wrong on an unconscious level. Maybe he viewed his mom as seductive, and as a boy, he shut down his sexual feelings; now he avoids active interaction with women. He may have experienced an abusive sexual relationship with a woman and be fearful of rejection or inadequacy.

A Change Program for Retarded Ejaculation

Emotional issues may emerge as you and your mate do the following behavioral work. Read the chapter on sexual communication and talk as you do these exercises.

You and your mate can be healing agents for each other. Process the emotions. Dispute the negative messages with positive affirmation statements. The husband may wish to repeat, "Intercourse is very exciting and I know I can climax," or "My penis is so sensitive to pleasure, and this is an exciting, bonding way to stimulate it."

Return to Playfulness

Take a shower together and play at soaping each other up, and enjoy the relaxing feelings of the shower spray beating down on you. Gently towel each other dry as you nurture and care for each other. Now get your favorite snacks and beverages and have a nude picnic in your bed. Don't worry about sex, but try to tell some jokes and laugh together. Gently and sensually caress each other's body as a part of this picnic. Playfully explore every inch of your mate's body, and come up with at least three new facts you did not know previously. Include a thorough and fun exploration of each other's genitals. Relax and be companions. Do not let this lead to making love or overt sexuality.

Practice Genital Sensate Focus

In the chapter on sensual massage, you learned the exercise of sensate focus—a sensual touching in which mates are active touchers or passive touchees. This is the same exercise, adapted to touching and enjoying the genital area. Both mates are nude. The environment is arranged by the active partner with temperature control, lighting, and any other mood setting desired. The exercise should not lead to intercourse or orgasm on that day. Block out thirty minutes, with each being the toucher and touchee for fifteen minutes. The purpose of this exercise is to take the focus off intercourse and orgasm. It will allow the couple to be sensual and let sexual arousal be incorporated into enjoyable loveplay. Mates will focus on personal pleasure and making love—not achieving a climax.

The active toucher. Touch the passive partner in ways that feel good to you. Unlike mutual lovemaking, you focus only on personal feelings and enjoyment of sensuality. There are no performance expectations but simply the goal of selfishly enjoying touching the passive partner in ways that give personal pleasure. Experiment with a variety of touches and strokes. Have the touchee lying on the back with genitals easily available. It is best to not have any communication at this point but to revel in individual sensations. If you are aware that touching a certain spot is causing discomfort, in love and respect move on to another part of the genital area.

The passive touchee. Lie passively and allow the active partner to touch, caress, and hold your genitals in ways that please the toucher. Often the touches that pleasure the active toucher also give stimulation and pleasure to the passive mate. You can increase self-awareness as you learn what areas and types of touching give you the greatest pleasure. You can ask for them and repeat them while making love at a different time. You are also learning about your lover—what kind of touching and caressing is sexually stimulating. Use the excellent data at future points in lovemaking as you arouse your mate.

This exercise is designed to decrease anxiety and increase warm playfulness and connecting. Don't let it lead into making love on the day you do it—let it be an end in itself and not a means to an end.

Focus on Building Pleasure and Tension

In these last two exercises, limit orgasms to intercourse with the penis in the vagina. This allows sexual tension to build and ejaculation within the vagina to be the goal.

The husband orchestrates making love to include the things that he finds very stimulating for him. Both partners focus on building his sexual pleasure and tension. This can include oral and manual stimulation of the penis. Allow the sexual tension to build for ten to twenty minutes before beginning intercourse. Tease and play as mates—enjoy each other. The husband should zero in on aspects of his mate and lovemaking that he finds arousing and sexy. Get away from negative thinking and routines. The goal of this exercise is building sexual arousal and focusing on pleasure, not having orgasms or worrying about what isn't happening.

The second part of this tension-building exercise is centered on intercourse. The husband again orchestrates and utilizes whatever position he finds most exciting to him—changing positions if he desires. He begins with slow thrusting and concentrates on the feelings of the penis. He may fantasize about past sexy scenes together and focus on building sexual tension in the penis and genital area. He should allow himself to receive pleasure and enjoy it, forgetting about the goal of orgasm and concentrating on the sensations of thrusting. If the husband desires, the wife may take her middle finger and forefinger and, reaching down, grasp the base of the penis as it comes in and out of the vagina. He should thrust more rapidly for a minute, slow down, then repeat this several times. Before stopping this exercise, he should thrust vigorously for a couple of minutes and enjoy the feelings.

Bridge Manual Arousal into an Orgasm with Intercourse

Begin with the husband once again orchestrating sexual arousal, and allow tension to build. This time manually or orally stimulate the penis to the point of ejaculation and immediately insert it in the vagina and continue stimulation with thrusting. He may have some mishaps as he perfects knowing the point of ejaculation. He should keep trying with succeeding sessions as needed. If he doesn't climax within a minute of intromission of the penis into the vagina, he should withdraw it and again stimulate the penis manually up to ejaculation and bridge over into active thrusting in the vagina.

Stop after trying five times. You are trying to decrease performance anxiety, not increase it. You may need repeated sessions to break down inhibitions and anxieties. It can be a fun time of bonding lovemaking as you practice until you are able to break through the retarded ejaculation. Have fun and enjoy focusing on your pleasure and arousal.

Premature Ejaculation

Wives feel cheated and both mates feel frustrated with premature ejaculation. Sometimes the husband is unpredictable and may last longer, only to relapse in the next lovemaking. Couples often settle for this unsatisfactory condition, even though this malfunction responds readily to treatment.

Understanding Premature Ejaculation

Premature ejaculation can be a learned behavior. When adolescent boys are first experimenting with sexual feelings and behaviors, it is often something they are afraid of being caught doing. If a boy is in the bedroom or bathroom masturbating and wondering when someone is going to knock on the door, leisurely taking time is not an objective. Sex can become nonrelational with a focus on attaining orgasms quickly. These habits can be carried into marriage and making love.

Premature ejaculation can also be an outcome of emotional tensions. A husband may be anxious or feel pressured, which can interfere with his control. If he is worried about climaxing too quickly, it becomes a self-fulfilling prophecy. A man can also use ejaculating prematurely to passively get back at his partner as he expresses his anger and aggression. He may unconsciously say to himself: "I don't like to be controlled; I'll get her and come so quickly she doesn't enjoy the experience."

Premature ejaculation may also occur from being too aroused and not knowing how to control the pace of lovemaking and the stimulation of the penis—stopping before the point of ejaculatory inevitability.

There are two stages to the male orgasm. The first stage includes contractions of the prostate, and the sphincter muscle closes off the bladder so the ejaculate goes out through the penis. The second stage is actual ejaculation. This includes muscle contractions along the urethra, seminal duct system, and penis, which expels the semen.

The first stage is only a few seconds, but with greater self-awareness, a man can anticipate it and feel it coming. At this point, interventions must be made and the arousal interrupted. The ejaculation stage is too late—with the completion of climax inevitable.

Once a man has passed over the point of ejaculatory inevitability, there is no returning; even a bucket of cold water won't stop it. An important part of controlling premature ejaculation, then, is recognizing the bodily signs when getting close to climaxing and backing off from active stimulation. The husband has to learn to stop and start and slow down as he regains control before passing the point of no return.

So how long must a husband last before he is not considered premature? Premature ejaculation can't really be defined in terms of time. It is better defined as the husband's not being able to control when he chooses to ejaculate. It is climaxing too quick to mutually enjoy the experience of intercourse. It can vary from couple to couple, but certainly anything over five to ten minutes should not be considered premature. An advantage of growing older is greater lasting power with an ability to thrust longer.

A Change Program for Premature Ejaculation

The following exercises are based on the stages of male orgasm and recognizing the point of inevitability. The Kegel exercises tighten the PC muscle in the genital area and around the prostate, helping control ejaculatory inevitability. Being able to accurately recognize the physiological signs that he is about to ejaculate allows a man to back off and keep from climaxing.

Use Kegel Exercises

The PC muscle in a man can be an invaluable aid for controlling arousal and helping to postpone ejaculation. It can be identified by starting to urinate and squeezing off the flow or, when standing, making the penis jump.

For one week, exercise the PC muscle by contracting it two times a day with ten repetitions per session. Contract the muscle while you count 1,001, 1,002, and then relax the muscle. Repeat this ten times and stop. Don't be macho and try to hold it tight longer or do thirty repetitions. You will grow sore and not accomplish more.

During the second week, repeat the two sessions per day with ten repetitions. Hold the count for 1,001, 1,002, 1,003, and then relax. This will help you identify the PC muscle and exercise it so it can more tightly grip the genital and prostate area. It will become a reflexive action that you can do easily and effectively.

Stop, Contract PC, Break, and Start

Practice these stop-and-start exercises for three months. It takes time to break old habits and learn new skills. There should be no intercourse or orgasm during these three months, except while practicing this program, or the skills can be jeopardized. It will be helpful to block out two to three thirty-minute sessions per week.

1. Start by manually stimulating the penis to the point of ejaculation and then stop and contract the PC muscle (tighten for the duration of 1,001, 1,002, 1,003 count). You may want to stop too soon rather than risk pushing beyond the point of ejaculatory inevitability. Become aware of your physiological arousal, and start training yourself when to stop. Allow a brief minute or so interlude as sexual tension decreases after the PC tightening—take a break from any active stimulation and be close. (A younger man will need to take a longer break than an older man to increase control.) Now repeat the process until you have practiced for fifteen to twenty minutes.

Here is a summary of this three-step technique for controlling ejaculation. Stop any movement and pair it with a quick contracting of the PC muscle and then take a break from any stimulation of the penis as arousal decreases: (1) stop, (2) tighten the PC muscle and (3) take a break from any penile stimulation for a minute or so.

You can practice this exercise alone, but it is important to approximate real life with the sexual stimulation of your wife present. It also helps to have your mate aware of the skills you are learning and participate with you. Your wife will profit from knowing that one extra pump or thrust may be too much. She is probably frustrated and needs to know that you cannot by willpower lengthen your staying power, but you can learn skills that will help. At the end of the session, allow your mate to bring you to an orgasm. Practice this exercise until you feel you are able to recognize your point of ejaculatory inevitability and can stop and decrease arousal. You should be able to comfortably stimulate the penis, with stopping and starting, for fifteen minutes without ejaculating.

2. The next step is called the quiet vagina. Begin with active loveplay manually, and if you approach ejaculation, stop, contract the PC muscle, and break to decrease arousal. After your mate and you are aroused sexually, enter her vagina but do not thrust. Just leave your penis in her quiet vagina. The wife is passive with no movements, she lies comfortably with a penis-in-vagina embrace. You will experience a special one-flesh closeness even though there isn't active stimulation. If this gets too exciting, withdraw the penis and use the stop-and-contract technique as needed.

After you are feeling less aroused sexually (a brief minute, or two if you are younger), remove the penis and begin again with loveplay. Repeat the quiet vagina five or more times over a twenty- to thirty-minute period. You are slowly teaching yourself that you can be in the vagina without climaxing. Practice this skill until you can comfortably have the penis contained in the quiet vagina without ejaculating and you are increasingly aware of your ability to keep from climaxing. Do not continue to orgasm with rapid thrusting at the end of these sessions. If you want release, do it manually.

3. After initial loveplay and arousal, enter the vagina with slow and shallow thrusts. The wife should remain more passive and allow you to enter about an inch and slowly move the penis in and out. If at any point in the thrusting you feel you are getting near to ejaculating, stop, contract, and go to the quiet vagina. If arousal is too high to remain in the vagina, withdraw completely as you stop and contract. Then go back to a quiet vagina until arousal decreases and you can begin the slow thrusting. Practice this until you feel able to control ejaculation during your thirty-minute lovemaking session. Again, don't ejaculate with thrusting but get relief manually as needed. You are learning new habits and working on orgasm control.

4. After loveplay and arousal, practice slow and deeper thrusting. The wife again remains passive. Don't be surprised to discover that she finds this stimulation very arousing and exciting to her. This is a very stimulating way to enjoy intercourse. Use the stop-and-contract technique whenever you approach ejaculation as you maintain control during your thirty-minute session. At first it may be necessary to completely withdraw the penis and stop all stimulation and then begin again with the quiet vagina. Don't berate yourself when you slip up and climax. Neither partner should make this a federal offense but laugh and know you will do better next time. You are learning together to maximize God's gift of sex. Even while building skills, lovemaking can be playful and intimate. Practice until you can accomplish this exercise comfortably and do not ejaculate during intercourse.

5. After loveplay, begin intercourse. This time practice varying slow with rapid thrusting. This is a crucial skill of the mature lover: intermittently varying rates and depth of thrusting. Intercourse thrusting might be charted like this: slow deep, rapid shallow, stop, rapid deep, stop, rapid deep, slow shallow, slow deeper, stop, rapid

shallow, and so on. As you approach an orgasm, the thrusting will become more vigorous and rapid. In this exercise, deliberately vary your rates of thrusting between rapid and slow. Whenever excitement builds toward ejaculation, stop immediately and practice your technique for decreasing sexual tension. Again as you progress, you may be able to use your stop-and-start technique without withdrawing. At the end of the session, choose when you want to ejaculate and do it.

Practice for a Lifetime

You have taken three months to practice new skills and to achieve your goals: being able to choose when you wish to ejaculate and enjoying prolonged intercourse. The stop-and-start technique with contracting the PC muscle is a skill you will need to incorporate into your lovemaking for the rest of your life. You will also be able to vary the rate of thrusting with intermittent stopping with the penis in the vagina and tightening the PC. You may discover that there will be periods in your lovemaking that you relapse and premature ejaculation comes back to haunt you. Take the time to go through the whole program again. You may be able to abbreviate it to a month this time. A great sex life takes some skills. Congratulations on learning some new ones.

Impotence

By the age of forty, around 90 percent of men have experienced one or more times of having difficulty getting or sustaining an erection. It still surprises most couples when it occurs, with an overreaction by both mates. This malfunction is prone to being made worse by anxiety and reactions.

Understanding Impotence

Erectile problems can be caused by physical or psychological problems, or a combination of both. The most common psychological difficulty is performance anxiety. Getting sexually aroused and getting an erection depend on the autonomic nervous system. A man doesn't will an erection—it happens as he is erotically aroused. These reflexive nerve responses are short-circuited by anxiety.

Various forms of stress can decrease your ability to focus on sexual feelings and become stimulated sufficiently. Environmental stressors can produce an inhibiting feeling such as *depression*. You lack energy and enthusiasm for life and can't cope well with everyday pressures. Depression is a common cause of sexual problems, and you will want to discuss with your doctor whether it might be a factor in your life. *Grief* is another emotion that can be a real sexual depressant and create less desire and an inability to become aroused. *Relationships* also have an important impact on your sex life. It may be the depression and grief your close relationships are creating with loss and hurt. It is a myth that men are never affected by their emotions—that they have instant erections and an ever-present libido. The penis is a very honest part of a man's anatomy. It reacts to hurt feelings, prolonged hostility, or stressed fatigue.

Other emotional and relational problems that many men face are anger, fear of rejection, rigid childhood sexual training, and guilt. *Anger* and other intense emotions efficiently sabotage great sex. Making love to someone you are fighting with and feeling hostile feelings toward is often not possible. If you do not want intimacy or are afraid of it, your penis may be very honest and not react with arousal. Perhaps you fear rejection or pick up on your wife's signals that she does not want to be close. This, too, can create erection problems. Perhaps you were raised in a rigid home in which sex was viewed as wrong or dangerous, and this *squelched sexuality* spills over into your marital sex life. *Guilt* can be an excellent sabotaging emotion. Guilt about being impotent can compound the problem: you feel you're not being there sexually for your wife. You want to nurture her but just do not feel like it physically or emotionally.

Trying to make love, regardless of your physical and mental states, can contribute to erection problems. Your wife may feel distanced and want to make love and experience some closeness. You may have had a particularly trying day at work and be exhausted. You hate to turn her down and you, too, desire to be close. But when you are unable to achieve an erection, the whole evening deteriorates further for you. You can learn better skills at making love and connecting without having to have intercourse and erections. This, as well as healthy assertiveness, can help take care of these situations.

Some physical problems can interfere with getting erections. The body mechanisms for achieving erection and sexual arousal are the endocrine system (hormones), the vascular system, and the nervous system. The hormones trigger desire, and the autonomic nervous system sends a signal causing the penis to engorge with blood and become erect. Diseases like diabetes, multiple sclerosis, and kidney problems can interfere with the nervous system and its functioning. Some surgeries like prostatectomy (removing the prostate) may destroy nerve paths. Radiation treatment can affect nerves and blood supply, creating leakage from the penis. The blood supply can also be disturbed by diabetes or arteriosclerosis.

An insufficient level of the hormone testosterone can create lack of desire and difficulty functioning. Hormone deficiency is easy to check out with a simple test by a physician and eliminate. It is actually quite rare, though many mates wish the problem could be solved so easily.

Drugs can also interfere with sexual functioning. They can depress or interrupt the nerve messages and affect the ability to get or retain an erection. The most common offender is alcohol. The more alcohol, the greater the negative effect on erectile functioning. Prescription medications, such as hypertensives for high blood pressure or antidepressants, can also have an effect. Consult with your physician. Different medications have differing effects on the body chemistry of individuals. It may be possible to change the medication to eliminate the side effects.

If impotence is physiological, consult a urologist. Sometimes, if there are partial erections, chemical injections will create a firmer erection. The chemical dilates the blood vessels, and it can be self-injected two or three times a week for lovemaking. It is important to keep under a physician's care; if the erection does not subside after four to six hours, seek medical help. There is also a vacuum pump that your physician can prescribe to pull blood into the penis with a ring to maintain the erection.

Newer surgical techniques sometimes help to increase the blood supply. Another common solution is a penile prosthesis. A physician can help in sorting through the advisability of a prosthesis as well as determining that the impotence is indeed physiological. Psychological counseling can help sort through both mates' feelings and sexual needs. Impotence does not prevent a man's having orgasms and ejaculation, and some couples adjust to the impossibility of having intercourse. They emphasize other aspects of making love and feel content and close. Others find a prosthesis revolutionizes their sex lives.

A Change Program for Psychological Impotence

An important part of dealing with impotence is heading it off before it becomes a chronic dilemma. Couples can wisely and lovingly handle some of the psychological issues and prevent an occurrence of impotence from evolving into a recurrent problem. Couples must remember to minimize the erectile difficulty and not overreact. The wife has an important role in taking incidents of impotence in stride and not panicking. Sometimes forgetting about sex until another time as you minimize the incident is the best medicine. Caress, play, and enjoy each other as you take the focus off intercourse! This is not a commentary on your skill or attractiveness as a lover. Learn to initiate and refuse around your lovemaking so you don't attempt sex when you are truly not in the mood.

If the ability to get or sustain an erection is an ongoing problem, the following program can eliminate performance anxiety and increase sexual arousal. Please don't panic, and do some self-talk as you enjoy each other inside and outside the bedroom. Engage in a lot of physical touching and close companionship.

As impotence gets into its vicious cycle with failure increasing anxiety and leading to more failure, making love can come to be dreaded. It is just another chance for pain and disappointment, and eventually, sex will be avoided entirely. Making love must be reclaimed as a sensual, relaxing, erotic experience. An essential part of dealing with impotence is redirecting your energy to pleasuring and getting rid of performance anxiety.

Sensual Touching

Do this sensual touching exercise without worrying about an erection. In fact, if the husband does get an erection, do not use it right now. Block out thirty minutes for this session, and relax with sensual feelings as each mate assumes the role of active toucher and passive touchee for fifteen minutes. Remember this exercise is to distract from performance and get each of you reinvolved in your sensual companionship. Do not engage in intercourse or other lovemaking on the day you do this exercise.

The active toucher. Touch the passive partner in ways that feel good to you. This touching is oriented toward individual learning and experiencing—not mutually attending to the partner. Focus only on personal feelings and enjoyment of sensuality.

There are no performance needs. The goal is selfishly enjoying touching the passive partner in ways that give personal pleasure. Experiment with a variety of touches and strokes. Start with the touchee lying on the stomach and begin at the top of the head and slowly work your way down to the feet. Have the passive partner roll over and work from the feet to the head. It is best to not have any communication at this point but to revel in individual sensations. Exclude any touching of the breasts or genitals. If you are aware of areas of the body that your partner does not like to have touched, in love and respect stay away from these areas.

The passive touchee. Lie passively and allow the active partner to touch you. Often the touches that pleasure the active toucher also give stimulation and pleasure to the passive mate. You can increase self-awareness as you learn what areas and types of touching give you the greatest pleasure. Focus on and enjoy your feelings. You can ask for them and repeat them while making love at a different time. You are also learning about your lover—what kind of touching and stroking is enjoyed. When you are the active partner, don't confine your touching by this information and begin to attend to your partner's needs. Do your active touching for yourself.

Repeat this exercise two or three times a week for two weeks as you take the focus off intercourse and erections. Enjoy your mate's body and your sexual responses.

Genital Pleasuring

Without fear and performance anxiety, the male and female genitals need to be reacquainted with each other. The husband needs to realize that it is normal for erections to come and go during lovemaking. Sexual arousal is an involuntary response to loveplay and enjoying the mate as lover. The wife has to deal with her fears and fatigue as she involves herself in making love to her husband's penis for her pleasure and not just to make him respond. Sensual touching helps. So can nondemanding genital pleasuring. It would be helpful to read chapter 11, which describes genital pleasuring.

1. Assume a comfortable sitting position, facing each other, with the wife's legs overlapped and the penis accessible to her vulva. Using the penis as a wand, the wife takes the flaccid penis and brushes it over her vulval area as both receive erotic stimulation. This exercise does not depend on an erection. Let the husband, as she lies back, also use the penis to touch the clitoral area, labia, and mouth of the vagina. Both relax and enjoy the sensual experience of the moment. Delight in the genital-to-genital sensations with no expectations. If the husband gets an erection, he should use it to stimulate the female external genital area. Don't engage in intercourse, but repeat this exercise at least twice a week for two weeks. The husband should refrain from orgasms during this time.

2. Assume a comfortable position with genitals to genitals, and begin enjoying each other. If the husband experiences an erection, he should use it to stimulate the clitoral area. As the wife becomes aroused, he should gently place the penis at the mouth of the vagina and penetrate half an inch as he manually continues to stimulate the penis. He is relaxing and becoming comfortable with enjoying and maintaining an erection in the vagina, almost like the exercises for premature ejaculation. Now he

should withdraw and reinsert the penis a little deeper; repeat this process as he enjoys the penis in the vagina without active thrusting. Do this two or three times a week for two weeks. Manually bring each other to an orgasm at the end of a session if desired.

3. Engage in loveplay, and as arousal builds, use a position of intercourse that feels great for both of you. Enjoy this process without demand as neither worries about erections, which will come and go. The goal is not orgasm but sensuously focusing on the experience of intercourse. Start with slow thrusts that are shallow and slowly penetrate deeper. Enjoy the feel. After at least ten minutes of slow, sensuous intercourse, begin varying the pace with more rapid thrusting. Enjoy this intermittent pattern of slow and rapid, shallow and deep. Come to an orgasm when you are ready.

For a month, alternate between the last two exercises. Every other time you will *not* engage in intercourse but enjoy genital pleasuring with manual orgasms as desired. Relax and be sensual; allow the desire and arousal to build. Keep your energy focused on sexual enjoyment as you allow your body and reflexive nervous system to do its erotic thing. God designed you to be a lover for your mate if you will get out of your own way.

If trouble recurs with performance anxiety and loss of erection, don't panic. Simply back up to sensual touching and start the process over. Enjoy again the pleasure of touching and being close together as you redirect your emotional energy to making love.

Male malfunctions are not catastrophes. They can be worked through. There are other skills that will be helpful as you and your mate work through these issues. Learn to communicate effectively and work on expressing emotions. These skills are invaluable for problem solving. Creatively enjoy variety and cultivate the ability to be sensual and create ambiance. Above all, build a loving companionship that is full of playfulness, honesty, and erotic tension.

Chapter Twenty-Three

Women and Painful Intercourse

Pain and discomfort can destroy a sex life. The medical term for pain during intercourse is *dyspareunia*. This condition occurs quite frequently and is not a problem that can be ignored. It is constantly brought to the forefront while making love, often affecting the rest of the marital companionship. Please never try to tolerate pain with lovemaking and intercourse. It needs to be medically explored and resolved through treatment or therapy. Like other sexual concerns, painful intercourse is complex and has many different causes.

Causes of Painful Intercourse

The following are six common causes of dyspareunia. Most wives will experience one or two of them over a lifetime of making love. Some of them can be self-diagnosed and treated, but others will require a doctor's visit or perhaps some therapy.

In exploring the causes of painful intercourse, you need to identify the onset of the pain. Has the pain always been there, or did it start after childbirth or a painful honeymoon experience? Did it surface after some surgery, or has sex always seemed wrong or intimidating? This information can help you sort through and begin to determine possible causes. It may be a psychological block that started with sexual abuse or a painful sexual experience. Possibly there is a fear of sex and intercourse resulting from a very restrictive sexual upbringing, and it has been present from the beginning of the relationship. Do you fear another pregnancy? It may be the result of some torn ligaments of the uterus or a painful surgical scar sustained during pregnancy or childbirth. Maybe there is an infection or perhaps a sexually transmitted disease of recent origin.

A second important factor to explore is when and where the pain occurs during your lovemaking. Describe the intensity of its discomfort. Does it occur as you experience arousal, or is it as the penis enters the vagina? Is it only with deeper thrusting or with rapid thrusting? Is it felt more in the vagina or in the abdominal area in general? Does the pain increase with orgasm, and is it still felt after coitus? This can help you understand if a tightening of the vagina or a lack of lubrication may be the culprit. If it is an infection, the pain may stay after intercourse, or if the pain is from a tear in the vaginal wall, it may occur only with thrusting in a particular area of the vagina. If the muscle spasms of orgasm create pain, it is more likely physiological in cause than psychological.

Many of these causes will have to be checked out with a physician, but it is helpful if you can play detective, too. You need to visit your gynecologist and rule out any physical problems before investigating possible psychological causes. Let's sort through these common causes as you build a better knowledge base of what may be happening to you.

1. Anatomical Factors

At the opening of the vagina is the hymen, a membrane that can close off part of the vaginal opening until it is stretched or torn. For the woman who has never experienced intercourse, occasionally there is a need for a hymenectomy. It is a simple office procedure in which your physician cuts the hymen if it is too strong to permit stretching or breaking. The hymen may have already been broken in the course of exercise, horseback riding, or other activity. In the weeks before attempting intercourse, the virgin bride-to-be can stretch the hymen and vaginal opening by inserting the thumb and pressing down toward the anus or inserting up to three fingers and gently pulling up on the vaginal opening. This is also an excellent exercise for becoming acquainted with the sensation of the vagina containing the penis and being stretched.

Sometimes there is a slight tearing of skin when the hymen is broken and brief pain ensues. Usually, the tear will quickly heal and not cause any enduring pain. The problem of experiencing any physical pain (e.g., hymen breaking with first intercourse) is that it can cause a fear of a recurrence of pain, which creates tension in the vagina. Subsequent pain may be more psychological in origin created by this tension than from any further physical stress.

In addition to the hymen, there are muscles and skin around the opening of the vagina. With some women, they remain tight, and intromission of the penis is uncomfortable. These muscles and skin can be stretched and should be able to accommodate a penis of any size. It may take patience, plenty of lubrication, and a prolonged stretching process, but it can be accomplished. This is helpful advice for the first time a women attempts intercourse. Gently go slow with artificial lubrication of the penis. Together place the penis at the mouth of the vagina and slowly try half an inch of penetration first, then slowly an inch, then two. Do all of this before any thrusting motion takes place. Thrusting should be shallow at first, then gradually deeper. Being as playfully comfortable and relaxed as possible with gentleness and patience is important in lessening the likelihood of pain.

Often a husband and wife jump to the conclusion that there is something wrong anatomically with the vagina and that it is too tight when it is normal. The wife's psychological tension is creating tightness and lack of lubrication—which creates pain. (We will discuss this in the next section.)

Another anatomical problem that can cause pain is a tipped or retroverted uterus. The ligaments that hold the uterus in place are weakened, which allows it to drop from its normal positioning. This pushes the cervix into the vaginal canal. In intercourse, the penis painfully hits the cervix rather than going into the fornix on the side of the cervix.

Couples may find it helps to decrease the depth of thrusting or place a pillow under the lower back or hips. Sometimes a shift in position (e.g., making sure the wife's legs are straighter) or lubrication can relieve the pain. Although a physician may identify what is causing the pain, the physician may not be able to alleviate the problem. Whether it is a retroverted uterus or some other physical anomaly, find treatment if possible and then work around it with shifts in position, lubrication, pillows, shallower thrusting, and other commonsense interventions that you can implement immediately.

After intercourse, some women report dull pain deeper inside the body in the lower back and abdominal area if they have not achieved a climax. With sexual arousal, the pelvic area becomes engorged with blood. An orgasm relieves this tension as muscles relax and blood leaves the area. This will happen naturally, with or without an orgasm, but for some wives, there can be a dull tension remaining that is uncomfortable. The obvious relief is taking steps together to help the wife achieve an orgasm.

2. Psychological Stress and Tension

So many factors can bring stress and tension to your lovemaking, such as personal fears that somehow you are inadequate as a lover or an uncomfortableness with new behaviors and situations. Many people are raised in environments where sex is never talked about or where it is at least implied that "bad girls" are sexual and "good girls" keep those impulses tightly controlled. More modest and shy personality styles can create inhibitions and tension. All of us have messages and expectations about sex from our past. For example, one woman's mother told her that sex would hurt but she would have to do it anyway. That certainly created some psychological stress during the first few times of intercourse.

Another cause of tension is being victimized in sexually abusive situations. Needless to say, if you have experienced sex in an abusive and traumatizing way, you will have to work through and heal those incidents and residual feelings. They could produce psychological stress and tension as you begin making love, even with someone you trust and love.

Whatever the reasons for the stress, a vicious cycle can get started in the lovemaking process. Psychological tension can cause the woman not to experience arousal as easily, which prevents the vagina from lubricating adequately. It can also produce, sometimes almost unconsciously, a tightening of the muscles in the genital area and the vagina. This tightening and lack of lubrication can cause pain on entry or chafing during the thrusting of intercourse. This pain sets off a chain reaction with further tightening of the vagina and less lubricating and more discomfort. Making love can become very uncomfortable and unfulfilling.

The vicious cycle can continue because the next time you make love, you fear the same thing will happen. Both husband and wife are on edge, which lessens arousal and in turn creates a tense and unlubricated vagina. The pain cycle keeps going, and sex becomes a frustrating experience for both partners. The most severe example of this is called vaginismus.

3. Vaginismus

Psychological stress can cause the muscles around the vagina to spasm and tighten so much that the penis cannot penetrate. Intercourse is impossible with the husband feeling his penis is pushing on a wall and there is no opening to the vagina. The woman has no conscious control over this tightening and cannot will it away. It is a reflexive reaction that husband and wife view as a tremendous hindrance but cannot control.

Vaginismus occurs for a variety of reasons. Sexual traumas—rape, molesting, a rough gynecological exam, or painful first intercourse—are common causes. A woman may have had a sexually inhibited upbringing, and sex is scary or seems wrong. Maybe there is a fear of pregnancy or a fear of painful intercourse after dyspareunia in past lovemaking sessions with her husband.

Couples sometimes hope the vaginismus will have a spontaneous cure as they become playful lovers. Unfortunately, this does not usually happen, and the vaginismus pushes them into seeking help. Often they want children and know the vaginismus will have to be overcome.

4. Vaginal Infections, Irritations, and Skin Tears

Remember the importance of identifying what kind of pain occurs and when it occurs. For example, acute stabs of pain or continuing irritations are usually physiological in origin. The remaining causes of dyspareunia explored in this section are physical in nature, not psychological.

The vagina has normal bacteria in it that can get out of balance and create yeast infections. Any infection affecting the external vulva or the vagina can create pain during intercourse and needs to be treated medically. Sexual activity and intercourse will probably be limited during the course of the treatment. Enjoy pleasuring in other ways. You may be especially prone to yeast infections and have to work with your physician on some preventive measures like medication and douching. Consult your doctor because sometimes douching can upset the bacterial balance in the vagina rather than help.

Sometimes there may be not a specific infection but an irritation of the vaginal opening or in the barrel itself. These skin irritations are common and painful. Again, you will want to think through when this began to occur and whether anything changed that might be creating the irritation. It may be an allergic reaction. Did you start using a new spermicidal jelly or foam? Were you tense or poorly lubricated? Did you experience some chafing? A couple of days to heal, a change of spermicide, and some liberal use of lubrication the next time you have intercourse may be all it takes to resolve the problem. It may also require specific medical attention and perhaps a visit to a dermatologist. Persist till you get the help you need.

If you are in menopause, maybe even prematurely in your late thirties or early forties, the vaginal walls could be thinning and creating irritation with intercourse. A physician can prescribe hormonal therapy that will help tremendously. Artificial lubrication for the thinning walls also enables you to enjoy intercourse and pleasure.

Pain in intercourse can be caused by a tear in the skin at the opening of the vagina or a cut in the skin within the barrel of the vagina. This kind of pain is different from an irritation. It is more acute and localized to the area of the tear. Women can often identify a particular place within the vagina that hurts or a more intense pain when the penis pushes into the opening and the skin tear is encountered. It may even be possible to put a finger on the cut or tear and locate the area of pain. If there is a localized pain, inform your physician of the exact place. These skin tears can often be treated with a topical ointment and quickly heal. Sometimes there may be a simple outpatient surgical procedure that will clear up the problem.

5. Endometriosis and Disorders or Diseases of the Pelvic Area

Endometriosis is a puzzling disease that affects women in their reproductive years. Endometrium is the tissue that lines the inside of the uterus and builds up and then is shed each month at a woman's menstrual cycle. In endometriosis, tissue similar to the endometrium develops in areas outside the uterus. It can adhere to the ovaries, fallopian tubes, and other areas of the pelvic cavity. It is generally not malignant or cancerous but can cause scar tissue and inflammation, and it can be very painful. The pain is often worse before and during the menstrual period. A common symptom of endometriosis is pain during and after any sexual activity.

This disease is so common and so devastating that an association has been formed to help women understand and cope with it. The address is International Headquarters, Endometriosis Association, 8585 North Seventy-Sixth Place, Milwaukee, Wisconsin 53223.

Endometriosis requires a physician's care. It can be treated in several ways. Sometimes hormones and medications can regulate it. It might require laparoscopic surgery in which a small incision is made and the endometrial tissue is removed surgically utilizing a laparoscope. In addition to endometriosis, other tumors can grow on the ovaries, the uterus, or other organs in the pelvic area near the vagina. They, too, can create pain during intercourse and may need to be surgically removed.

Any infection in the organs around the vagina can create discomfort and pain during sexual activity. A common offender is urethritis, which is sometimes called the honeymoon disease. It is an infection of the urethra and bladder and can be caused by physical trauma received during vigorous thrusting in intercourse. Infection in the anus and rectum, the bladder as well as urethra, and the uterus and any pelvic inflammatory disease can create pain during intercourse and must be treated medically.

Another fairly common cause of pain during intercourse is tears and damage to the ligaments that hold the sexual organs in place in the pelvic area. The ligaments of the uterus can get damaged during childbirth, or endometriosis can create scar tissue on them. The movements of intercourse then disturb the ligaments and create physical pain. This condition is treated medically, but shifting positions and going gently with adequate lubrication may also help.

6. Scars

The most common scars are those resulting from childbirth. In assisting natural birth, an episiotomy (surgically cutting the tissue at the mouth of the vagina toward the anus) is often needed. This takes time to heal and may need some minor surgery to correct if pain does not go away after six weeks. With childbirth by cesarean section or any other abdominal surgery, there may be scarring that creates some pain during intercourse. Sometimes when the hymen is torn, the tissue does not heal properly, and it creates a scar that can cause some pain as the penis comes into contact with it during intercourse. It may take a very thorough gynecological exam to discover the scar tissue.

Be patient and slow during intercourse immediately after childbirth or surgery. Without gentleness, you may create some actual physical pain that becomes the vicious cycle of psychological tension, fear of pain, and a tightening of the vagina in later sexual activity. In time the tissue often heals and there is no pain. However, a surgeon may have to remove scar tissue so that movement without pain can occur.

Treatment of Painful Intercourse

If pain during intercourse has been hampering your lovemaking, here are some solutions. The first and second solutions (medical and commonsense interventions) were developed somewhat in the previous section. The husband and especially the wife will need to deal with the psychological stress and tension about sex. Some of this you can do on your own, but it may take professional counseling, too. You must also work on breaking the vicious cycle of anticipating and fearing pain. A self-help plan will be presented as a fourth solution. It will help you as a couple to desensitize the fear out of sex and reprogram pleasure. Finally, you will consider a program that you can employ to overcome vaginismus.

Medical Interventions

Careful medical diagnosis and treatment of the many physiological causes of dyspareunia are necessary. Sometimes your internist or general practitioner can provide this care, but it may take the specialized attention of a dermatologist, surgeon, or gynecologist. (You should have regular Pap smears and breast exams anyway.) It is your body and your discomfort. Tell your physician details about the pain.

In selecting a physician, be a good consumer. The following are fair demands:

1. Being treated with respect, having a nurse present, demanding adequate time be taken, being properly gowned or draped, and refusing to put up with rudeness.

2. Having questions answered in language you can understand and each problem carefully explained. If there are any medications or procedures, they should be explained as to what is being treated, the prognosis, and any side effects.

3. Knowing precisely what every medical or surgical procedure will cost, its probability of success, and a general idea of the toll in physical discomfort and recuperation time.

4. Developing a supportive relationship with your doctor, asserting the right to be *persistent* in finding the cause of and treatment for the pain, and exercising your right to change doctors to get the type of care that you desire.

With dyspareunia, there will often need to be medical interventions, which are beyond your control. But you can control the type of care, and you can choose to actively be involved in the process. You can make a few medical interventions on your own. Some yeast infection medicines can be purchased with instructions over the counter at your pharmacy. If your spermicide is new and causing an allergic reaction, try changing to another brand. Most of the physical causes will need a physician's attention, however.

Commonsense Interventions

Purchase and keep on hand plenty of artificial lubrication. This usually is sold in the birth control section of pharmacies and can be jelly or more liquid in form. You can also use natural oils from coconut to olive oil, which may be appealing for smell and consistency. They are edible and don't interfere with oral stimulation of the genitals. Vegetable oils (corn or safflower) work fine if you have forgotten to purchase other artificial lubrication. The advantage of artificial lubricants is that they are often water soluble and easier for the vagina to be self-cleansing. Use lubricants generously when the vagina is irritated or there is tension present. It is amazing what a commonsense behavior like lubricating can do in preventing further pain and reversing the negative cycle.

Gentle and *slow* are crucial words in overcoming painful intercourse. Creating a safe and tender atmosphere is important in dealing with psychological tension and stress that may be present. Work on being playful and relaxing; set the pace that is most comfortable for the wife. Allow plenty of loveplay and arousal before attempting intercourse. Try using a position (wife-on-top) that lets her control penetration and depth. Take your time and enjoy the process. Be imaginative in creating ambiance, and unwind together.

Stop when there is pain! Make some shifts in position. Maybe cease from deep thrusting and go more shallow. Use your creativity, but don't ignore the discomfort as you try to make some immediate intervention. Prop a small pillow underneath the hips or lower back, use more lubrication, and maybe go back to loveplay as both relax again. With painful intercourse, it is better not to play through the pain and hope it will go away. That usually increases the problem. Do something about it. If no immediate intervention helps, stop making love or engage in other sexual activities until the problem can be checked out medically.

Use birth control wisely and increase precautions if the possibility of pregnancy is a source of sexual tension during intercourse. The husband may need to get a vasectomy. Discuss together how you might handle an unexpected pregnancy. Both partners may need to utilize greater care and take responsibility for birth control. Monitor the pills and hold each other accountable for never taking a chance.

Psychological Interventions

You will need to resolve your psychological tensions and stress as a part of overcoming painful intercourse. If you were raised in an environment where sex was never discussed or was considered wrong, undertake a personal educational program. Reading a book like this and doing the exercises with your mate will be very helpful. Communicating about sex and developing a comfortable language will greatly assist you in becoming more comfortable with sexuality. It will help to tune in to and talk through your fears and inhibitions. A loving, empathetic partner can be a marvelous sounding board, or you may find a same-sex friend who can lend a listening ear in a way your mate cannot. Get beyond embarrassment. No topic is too silly or taboo to discuss and resolve.

Mates who employ their creativity and band together to increase their enjoyment of sex don't always need professional intervention or a sex therapist. Increase your sensuality, and learn to play and tease together. Read aloud passages from this book as you desensitize yourself to being sexually explicit. Enjoy some of the exercises recommended in this book: take showers together, become comfortable with nudity as you have picnics in bed, plan sexual surprises, and get into sensual massage. Let making love permeate your relationship.

Survivors of sexually abusive situations will often need specific therapy to help them deal with unresolved feelings that impede sexual pleasure and create tension and pain with intercourse. Professional counseling may also be needed to deal with the guilt of a strict religious background or to resolve premarital experiences. Extramarital affairs can be crippling and may need a marriage counselor.

Never feel inferior if you cannot work out problems on your own. Wisdom and maturity allow us to reach out for the help we need. This is a very biblical principle. God created people with different gifts and the individual ability and intelligence to gain the skills to help us. Don't settle for remaining in psychological tension or physical pain.

Desensitizing

When you become sensitive to something, you know what it is like and come to expect it. A couple experiencing painful intercourse have become sensitized to pain and expect it. With the following exercises, you are going to take the fearful sensitivity and association with pain out of intercourse. You will become desensitized to pain and sensitized to pleasurable intercourse once again.

These exercises are needed, even though you may have resolved most of your psychological or physical causes of stress and pain, because the fear of pain and the tightening of the vagina continue involuntarily. You are sensitized to experiencing pain, and your body and mind react automatically when there is the threat of intercourse. These responses must be changed.

Block out at least thirty minutes for each of these steps. Realize that each step may need to be broken into a series of practice sessions. Repeat them twice or as many times as needed. Allow these three desensitization exercises to stretch out over two or three weeks. This process cannot be rushed. You may need to take a week or a month to hug nude, caress, and enjoy loveplay as you become desensitized and are then able to try these exercises. If you are experiencing vaginismus, skip ahead to the next section. You will be directed back to these exercises at the appropriate point.

1. Engage in loveplay that is fun and relaxing for ten to twenty minutes as you allow sexual arousal and emotional bonding to take place. Liberally apply lubrication to the head of the penis and the mouth of the vagina. Choose a position in which the woman can touch and guide the penis as she brushes the penis over the inner lips and lightly touches it to the mouth of the vagina without penetration. (This may be as

much desensitization as is possible in the first session; when you are ready, proceed further.) At the instigation of the wife, lightly apply pressure and let the head of the penis enter an inch and stop, gently leaving it there for several minutes. Remove and apply more lubrication. Now slowly penetrate two inches. Repeat this procedure at three and four inches, knowing it may take several sessions to reach this point, until the penis is fully contained in the vagina. Leave it there until the erection begins to ebb. If there is pain, stop and enjoy loveplay again for several minutes, then proceed with the exercise or wait till the next practice session. Do not start any thrusting with this experience. Manually stimulate each other to an orgasm after the full containment.

2. Repeat in this exercise the slow containment of the penis from the first step. Again, apply plenty of lubrication, and gently go slow. When the penis is fully contained, remove and apply more lubrication. Now start over with shallow penetration, and slowly thrust at a depth of an inch or so for ten or fifteen times. Remove and apply more lubrication, and thrust slowly at a depth of two inches. Remove and apply more lubrication if needed, and softly thrust with full penetration. Use as many practice sessions as you need to accomplish this step. If there is any pain, stop, engage in loveplay, and then go back to a more shallow depth. Do not attempt to ejaculate with intercourse; bring each other to a climax manually.

3. Enjoy some loveplay and apply lubrication as you begin with gentle penetration and slow thrusting in the outer two inches of the vagina ten to fifteen times. Remove and lubricate as you thrust halfway in ten to fifteen times—then fully penetrate and slowly thrust. Now try more rapid thrusting at the shallow depth. Remove, lubricate, and enjoy thrusting deeper but not so deep as to cause any pain. If there is pain, this time try to shift positions or thrust more shallowly or gently. If the husband is having trouble refraining from ejaculation, stop and allow his arousal to subside, then continue. Allow the husband to go through to an orgasm and manually bring the wife to orgasm if she has not climaxed.

You get the idea of desensitizing. You are gradually approaching intercourse with adequate lubrication and fun arousal. If there is pain, stop or shift as you make sure this experience is relaxed and painfree. There is no pressure, and you should take as many practice sessions as you need to comfortably accomplish all three steps. You will find in your practice sessions that reaching an objective (the head of the penis in the vagina) does not automatically ensure you can start at that point in your next session and proceed further. Sexual change is slow, and you may have to reach an objective several times before the desensitization is permanent.

Overcoming Vaginismus

The following program will help overcome vaginismus. The wife should do the first two exercises alone; the husband should be included for the last two exercises.

1. Take a warm bath, and adjust the bedroom temperature so it is comfortable to be nude. Lock the door to assure your privacy. Take a finger and lubricate it well and place it at the mouth of the vagina. Allow the fear to subside. (With each step, it is

good to take a few deep breaths and let them out slowly through your mouth as you expel the tension through the exhaled breath. Consciously allow your body to relax and repeat the breathing until the fear subsides.) Now gently insert the end of the finger, just slightly penetrating, and leave it there as you breathe and relax. Do not remove the finger for five minutes or more as you become used to an object being in the vagina. Now insert to the first knuckle and again leave the finger there as you relax. If the vaginal muscles start to spasm tight, stop and slowly breathe as you relax.

To get a greater feeling of control, practice deliberately tightening the PC muscle on your finger as in the Kegel exercises. Try two more stages of inserting the finger more deeply into the vagina, stopping each time to breathe, practice the Kegels, and become acclimated to an object being comfortably in the vagina. Repeat this exercise several times over the coming weeks until it becomes comfortable.

2. Take a bath and get comfortable. Always use plenty of lubrication. Start with one finger deeply penetrated; hold it there and relax with deep, slow breaths. Try wiggling the finger before pulling it out as you get used to motion and a different sensation. Now try inserting two fingers. Again, do it slowly and only to the first knuckle at first. Stop for five or more minutes and allow yourself to relax and become accustomed to the new feelings. Repeat the procedures with fingers penetrating more deeply and relax. Try moving the two fingers and allowing the vagina to feel comfortable with the motion. Do this gradually and repeat this session until two fingers are comfortable.

3. Now is the time to bring in your husband. He should go slow and listen to your instructions as he follows your desires. Do some sensate focus to relax and enjoy each other's body. Lubricate and start with one of his fingers (fingernails and cuticles clipped) and again hold for five minutes as you relax. Repeat the procedures with his finger instead of yours as you go deeper. Once that is comfortable, go to two fingers with motion until that is also comfortable within the vagina. If the muscles tighten, stop and enjoy some sensual massage as you relax—then begin again. It may take weeks or months to accomplish this step.

4. Now you are ready to begin with the penis and become desensitized to its feel. Do this by going through exercises one through three in the preceding section, "Desensitizing."

It may take two months to slowly work through the exercises, even after you have done preliminary months of therapy and sexual growth. It may take you longer, and that is okay. You may need to go back to caressing, hugging, and other sexual activity before continuing with the exercises.

Remember, never try to tolerate pain in lovemaking and intercourse. It needs to be medically explored and resolved through treatment or therapy. If you are already trapped in the vicious cycle of fear and tension, work out the psychological and physical parts of it first. Then slowly process through the desensitizing exercises. If you get stuck, seek out therapy. You are not alone, and pleasurable intercourse can be yours to enjoy. Don't give up!

Chapter Twenty-Four

Survivors of Sexual Abuse

Here is a frightening and tragic statistic. Recent surveys estimate that one out of three girls experiences a sexually traumatizing incident by the time she is seventeen—and boys are abused at almost the same rate. Confused couples are revictimized in their lovemaking over and over again by the unhealed wounds from the past. Mates are especially important in helping their partners reclaim a comfortable sexuality and enjoy, perhaps for the first time, the ability to relate intimately and truly make love.

Defining Sexual Abuse

Is sexual abuse only fondling of the genitals? Does it have to include penetration of the vagina or masturbation of the penis? No! Some of the worst cases of sexual abuse involve no physical touching at all. One young boy came home every day to find his mother in a see-through gown, and at night he would hear her with her lovers. He was deeply traumatized by the sexual confusion and abuse. One girl had the door taken off the bathroom and a window cut into the door of her bedroom. She had no privacy and was constantly observed by her stepfather while she dressed and bathed. Needless to say, the experience severely damaged her emotional and sexual development.

Sexual abuse is any behavior, attitude, or verbal response that hinders normal sexual development, bringing distortion and inhibition to personal sexuality and married lovemaking. It may be your grandfather leering at you and making suggestive remarks.

It can be Mom or Dad refusing to create an intimate relationship with the spouse and making you the little man or woman in the family. It can be an adult surreptitiously or overtly observing a child undressing or going to the bathroom. It can include the adult intentionally disrobing or exposing genitals. It can be an adult sleeping with a child and rubbing the genitals against the child or masturbating in the child's presence. The family that refuses to talk about sex and covertly makes it sinful or scary is guilty of a form of sexual distortion and abuse. This attitude definitely gets in the way of normal sexual development.

Having said all that, parents need not run scared or create unnecessary guilt. Some behaviors are not abusive, like washing children until they can wash themselves or cleaning the genital area when changing a diaper. Children need to be hugged and held with open demonstration of physical affection, especially when they become teenagers. There will naturally be some sexual tension and awkwardness as parents and children become aware of each other as sexual beings. This may occur before or at puberty. These feelings resolve themselves if appropriate boundaries are observed and privacy and private parts are respected. Sexually abusive situations have a different atmosphere. Sexuality is confusing, and boundaries and relationships are blurred. The adult is getting personal sexual gratification in inappropriate ways.

Effects of Sexual Abuse on the Survivor

In a healthy family, members have a right to privacy and to state assertively that they don't like behaviors that feel invasive or hurtful. Family members respect and validate one another's feelings and set consistent boundaries of what is appropriate and what is harmful. Without creating and understanding limits, people can hurt each other and demand too much or too little of each other.

In situations where sexual abuse occurs, the boundaries are unclear and confusing. A person is just developing a sense of self and its relationship with others in year one through the teen years. This is when the rules are set for defining the expectations and guidelines for sexuality and sexual relating as well as relationships in general.

These rules and sexual limits are distorted for the abuse victim. A child knows something is wrong but feels powerless, out of control, and helpless to stop the abusive behavior. This becomes a strong influence in the whole personality makeup. That person often dreads being out of control in adult life and rigidly tries to keep everything tidy and running smoothly. A double bind occurs in which an individual obsessively wants to be in control but does not have the skills to set the boundaries to truly be in control of life's events. This can result in constantly getting revictimized.

The personal and sexual relationships of abuse survivors are prone to confusion. They are not sure how relationships should function and how the boundaries should be set. They do not know how to express their needs and are not sure whether they deserve to have them met. They are often not very comfortable or adept with feelings. The victims were hurt and angry, but no one was there to validate those feelings. They begin to not trust themselves and their feelings.

Survivors are familiar with the feeling of shame. They often think that they should have been able to prevent or stop the abuse, that somehow they are responsible. It must be strongly emphasized that *a child is never responsible for sexual abuse*. One adult in looking back on the abuse wished he could have assertively said to his uncle, "Uncle John, you are not keeping proper sexual boundaries and are engaging in this activity purely for your own sexual gratification. I am not going to participate in these behaviors, I am going to report you to the proper authorities, and I strongly suggest you get some professional help." He laughed as he realized the impossibility of a nine-year-old child behaving so maturely. He still felt somehow to blame.

Masculinity and femininity, sex and sexuality, are profoundly affected by abusive experiences. Abuse victims are sexualized earlier than God intended and in a situation that was the farthest removed from the loving relational experience He designed. Sex becomes associated with fear, pain, and control. The positive feelings of love, joy, and pleasure are absent or distorted. As persons try to alter these experiences and enjoy making love in the present marital companionship, flashbacks are triggered. It is easy to get stuck in the past.

Mates as Partners in Healing

You and your mate indeed bring into marriage a whole backpack of garbage accrued in the years before you met each other. Because of the presence of evil and imperfection in this world, people hurt each other, and no one is exempt from these scars. That's the bad news. Now here's the good news. For every bad and hurtful relationship, there can be an opposite healing relationship full of love and truth. The fact is that wounds experienced in destructive relationships demand a positive healing relationship to regenerate wholeness.

How the Survivor Can Help the Partner

Both the partner and the marriage of the abuse survivor become victims of the survivor's abuse. This situation can create much confusion, feelings of rejection, and anger. When your mate is turned off by sex or avoids physical affection, it is difficult not to take that personally. The partner can know the cause and be sensitive to the abuse issues, but still there are personal needs and feelings. The partner may long for sex and desire to be close and not get pushed away.

It's easy to start doubting one's attractiveness and sexual appeal. Am I lovable? Is something wrong with my technique and ability as a lover? Sexual appeal and ability have little to do with what is going on, and both need to remind each other that the abuse is dampening sexuality. The male partner may experience difficulty with erections, and both partners may suffer a loss of sexual desire.

The excitement about making love is diminished when it seems full of confusion and, at times, painful flashbacks for the survivor. You, as partner, sometimes wonder if both might be better served by eliminating sex from the marriage. This idea, of course, causes shock waves of anxiety as you debate whether you could remain in a sexless marriage. Partners have these and many other feelings to work through. You, too, have to deal with grief as you wish that your mate had not been abused and that the marriage did not have to cope with these devastating aftershocks. You come to feel as helpless toward the abuse as the survivor did and have to work through to hope and healing.

Partners can become furious at the perpetrator. And sometimes it seems that the survivor gets all the attention and the healing takes precedence over all else. You know that there is a need for it, that until the sexual abuse is worked through, the lovemaking will never flourish. But it can seem very one-sided. You get lonely, too, and may have your own scars. You have feelings stirred up, and it is important that you get help and create a support network as well.

So how can the survivor help the partner?

1. Build and validate an understanding of the partner's position—feelings, needs, and reality. The partner probably has a very different reality and way of looking at life from the survivor's. Converse carefully as you practice active listening, and encourage your partner to deal with feelings in positive ways.

2. Keep affirming the commitment to the marriage and love for the partner. Even though sex may be difficult, maintain physical affection. Sensual caressing, with sex off limits, can be very affirming.

3. Remind the partner that difficulty with sex stems from the abuse and has nothing to do with the partner's attractiveness or ability as a lover. Reaffirm your commitment to working at the sexual part of the relationship and your determination that you, too, want your lovemaking to flourish. Remind your partner that you think you are married to a sexually attractive lover.

4. Recognize and appreciate the efforts of your partner in promoting healing. Express thanks for loving you with respect and patience. (There will be relapses and impatience, but affirm the helpful behaviors.)

5. Answer questions and try to be assertive in helping your partner understand what is comfortable and uncomfortable and what triggers flashbacks. Don't overreact to or take too personally your partner's frustration and anger and grieving.

How the Partner Can Help the Survivor

So much of the joy and freedom of life and relationships is destroyed as a result of sexual abuse. Survivors appreciate mates who will take the time to try to understand their reality in a loving and patient way—to get into the reality of the wounded child and perceive how tough it was. Your mate needs your empathy in comprehending what abuse is all about.

The survivor needs to be reassured that abuse will never have to be endured again. The survivor needs to be empowered to positively take charge of life and sexuality. The survivor has the right to say no and set sexual limits. Remember, the survivor did not have proper boundaries or the ability to take charge of life and express likes and dislikes in the abusive situation. Healing depends on the survivor's ability to learn these skills. You, as partner, can encourage and model healthy autonomy and safe boundaries.

You can assume a crucial role in empowering the survivor and breaking the vicious cycle of revictimization. You can help your mate to recognize potentially dangerous situations, assertively set limits, and confront as needed. Part of this will be affirming and increasing your mate's self-esteem. You can make clear that the survivor deserves good things. You can support the survivor in accepting God's verdict that everyone is created worthwhile and special. Compliment and build up the survivor's strengths and abilities.

Another way that you can empower the survivor is by helping the survivor place the blame and responsibility for the abuse on the perpetrator. You help your mate grow beyond disabling shame and guilt. Logically, the abuse will trouble you, and you will wish the survivor could have stopped the traumatizing behaviors sooner. Be careful not to imply that your mate could have done something about it, that somehow your mate chose to stay in the abusive situation. Your mate was a victim, who did not choose to be victimized. Your mate needs your support in distancing from the abuse and reclaiming the power to control life in a healthy way.

In a similar way, you need to work through any thoughts or feelings that the survivor is "damaged goods." Get beyond yourself. What happened to the survivor was not sex; it was violence and pain. Your mate needs your acceptance—not judgment or further victimization. You, as partner, did not ask for the abuse, and it creates many troubling side effects. Your mate did not ask for it, either. What has been done is cruel and vicious, and the survivor's personhood and sexuality need hope and healing.

Be gentle and empathetic. Don't place any sexual pressure. Let your mate know that your companionship is much more than the sexual part of it. Learn to touch and hold apart from sex, and make love with your clothes on. Your mate's life and sexuality are not irreparably damaged. It is a shame that both of you are having to pick up the pieces, but both will be closer and more committed for having walked the journey together. Jesus is using you "to heal the brokenhearted, to proclaim liberty to the captives" (Luke 4:18 NKJV). It is a role that only you, as partner, can accomplish.

Reclaiming Sexuality

There are many facets of working through sexual abuse. This section considers some of the significant issues, from finding a therapist to breaking the conspiracy of silence about the abuse to reclaiming sexuality. This journey will take time and patience, but there is hope. Many before you have worked their way through to peace, freedom, and healing.

The journey will be different for everyone. Many survivors have repressed their feelings for many years. Then perhaps in their late thirties, the feelings and flashbacks start to emerge, and life can become unmanageable. Sometimes the birth of a child or a child reaching the age of their own abuse triggers reactions and memories. Others find their marital sexuality seriously hampered, and they are nudged into working on the causes. This can bring to the surface sexual abuse that may or may not be already in the conscious mind. There may be repeated nightmares or flashbacks in certain situations.

Regardless of how the abuse surfaces or gets in the way, there comes a time when it is important to seek out healing. Please don't put it off. It is scary even to consider confronting the memories with their pain and terror. Unfortunately, the only way through is through. There is no shortcut to resolving sexual abuse; you must wade through the memories and resolve the pain and fears. Reading books is helpful, but working through the feelings and memories will require the assistance of a professional therapist.

Finding Professional Counseling

A professional therapist has been trained in psychological counseling and has special expertise in working with sexual abuse survivors. This counseling may come in several different forms. Working through the memories will probably take some individual work in a one-on-one office setting. Therapy groups help survivors work through their traumas together. A group can provide support and also be effective for bringing memories to the surface and promoting healing. Sometimes more concentrated therapeutic time is needed to work through intense grief and pain—especially if the emotions cause the person to have self-destructive thoughts. This may require a stay in a hospital that specializes in working with survivors.

Recent rape victims need specialized care. In larger cities there are crisis centers where you can get immediate help and be involved in support groups. As with sexual abuse, the effects will not just go away. The feelings can be repressed, but they will likely come back to haunt you and your marriage. You are not "damaged goods," and there is healing! If you cannot go to a crisis center, seek out therapy that can help you and your mate resolve the feelings of anger, helplessness, fear, shame, and pain.

One reason abuse survivors do not get help is that they are not sure where to go to find professional therapy. Use the yellow pages wisely. It may mean driving to a larger city to find a professional with the needed expertise, but more professionals are getting training in this area. Look under psychology and counseling centers or marriage and family therapists in the directory, then make some calls. Any therapist should be willing to give five minutes of time to answer questions.

In interviewing and selecting a therapist, consider these points:

1. Has the person had specialized training in working with sexual abuse survivors? Has the person been supervised by someone skilled in this area?
2. How many cases of sexual abuse has the person worked with, and is the therapist currently seeing any other abuse survivors?
3. Is the therapist familiar with helping a survivor work through repressed memories of abuse?

You may be able to find a therapist recommended by a professional counseling agency. (See appendix A.) A pastor or a friend may know of someone to recommend. That is better than starting cold, but the phone interview is still a good idea.

After you have started therapy, be aware of several issues. Every therapist has a different personality style, and you may get matched up with someone who does not fit well. Be a good consumer and find another therapist. Sometimes female survivors cannot get beyond the maleness of a therapist despite a gentle and sensitive style. They need to find a female counselor who can work more effectively with them.

Therapists who work with abuse survivors need to be able to set healthy boundaries. Obviously, if there are any sexual advances, find another therapist. Lack of boundaries will probably be more subtle, like keeping the role of therapist versus friend clear for you, or maybe even starting and ending counseling sessions on time. Talk to the therapist if any boundary issues come up and you feel uncomfortable. Never tolerate your therapist's implication that the abuse was your fault—find another therapist if this happens. Your therapist should be able to accept and appreciate that some of your symptoms (anger, avoidance) are coping habits that have helped you survive. They will have to be worked through and replaced slowly.

This will be one of the most important relationships of your life. Choose the person carefully and then commit to the process. It won't be easy; the pain and confusion usually get much worse before they get better. It is exciting to slowly see the pain leaving and yourself empowered to enjoy life in an assertive and whole way. The only way through is through.

Resolving Dissociation and Feelings

Dissociation is taking your sexual abuse and distancing yourself from it in your mind. This is an important mechanism you used to survive as a child. Abuse memories can be cataloged under the acrostic of BASK. It stands for Behaviors, Affect (feelings), Senses, and Knowledge. With dissociation, memories of the abuse are often taken apart and stored under each category. There may be behavioral memories (being pinned down, gagging), affective or feelings memories (feeling trapped, depressed, terrified), sensual memories (smelling a cologne, experiencing a certain look, hearing a sound, feeling chafed or sore), or stored knowledge (someone saying "just relax" like the abuser, remembering the time of year).

With some survivors, there is fairly accurate conscious knowledge of the abuse, even though they may never have talked about it with anyone. With most, there is dissociation, and the events have been stored away and are not remembered or are very fuzzy and minimized in the mind. This is not unusual because often the mind was turned off during the abuse and the event is stored in bits and pieces.

The goal in therapy is reassociating the memories and empowering the survivor to let go and move on. The behaviors and feelings and sensed data and knowledge of the event are all brought back together and experienced. It is a painful process to go back and acknowledge what happened and know that the abuse need never happen again. You are remembering so that you can let go of the pain and effects of abuse.

Forgiveness is not an instantaneous process unless you are God; He can instantly remove our sins "as far as the east is from the west" (Ps. 103:12 NKJV). With humans in relationships, we remember and hate and feel intense anger that certain deeds have been perpetrated on us and that our rights have been violated. Over time we slowly let go. Forgiveness is not condoning what the abuser has done or even choosing to ever see that person. It is a personal process that does not depend on the person who has hurt you. One woman who was kidnapped and raped was asked how she could forgive her rapist. She replied that he had gotten seven hours of her life and that was all he was getting. Forgiveness leaves the abuser to God's "day of vengeance" and frees your emotional energy for better uses than revenge, painful memories, and consuming hatred.

The Christian can appropriate God's love and power to do some of this inner healing. It is a *process* that lets Christ's healing presence into your pain. As you remember and reassociate the memories, you may want to work through them with a wise friend or counselor with healing prayer. One way to do this is to imagine walking back through your life and the traumatizing events with Jesus. Incident by incident you can pray and allow Him to put His healing touch on your hurts with compassionate understanding and restorative empowering.

Your Christian counselor can affirm this healing process by praying with you. After you have completed this inner process, it can be helpful to imagine Jesus gently holding you as one of His precious lambs, weeping with you that you have been wounded so badly, while His loving presence brings further comfort and grace to help you let go.

The primary feelings that you will have to understand and resolve are anger, pain, fear, and shame. The anger may have been repressed and never allowed to surface against the abuser or caretakers who failed to protect. There is special rage that occurs when you feel helpless and can do nothing about helping yourself. The hurt child was trapped and subjected to injury against his or her will without any recourse. You suffered both physical and emotional pain that you probably dissociated from. The pain has to be faced and lived through again, only this time you are remembering in order to let go and be healed.

The many fears must be confronted and understood better. The mind can then restructure the fears and make them manageable. It helps to go back and realize your reality as a little child. You can give that child reassurance that that was the past, and now there are more power and knowledge to prevent the same thing from ever happening again. There can also be mental reevaluation and restructuring of the shame. You can place responsibility squarely back on the perpetrator of the abuse. The timid, shame-ridden attitudes can be challenged and overcome. The abuser's brainwashing can be brought out in the open and shown for what it is.

Breaking the Conspiracy of Silence and Confronting the Abuser

Sharing your story with your spouse will be therapeutic. Remember, though, your spouse's reality will be quite different from yours. You may need some patience as you try to convey the feelings and reality of the wounded child. A professional therapist is helpful because of the ability to empathize and understand more easily. You will have to decide how you choose to break the silence and secrecy. Deciding whether to confront the abuser and other people connected to you during the abuse will be very difficult. They may be deceased, or you may have no continued contact, so the work will have to be done with you alone. Be sure to prepare before you choose to confront.

The danger is in being revictimized or having greatly disappointed expectations if the confrontation is not carefully thought through and planned. Think through why you want to confront and what the consequences of the confrontation will be for you. Are you willing to risk losing relationships and contact with family? Do you have a good support system? Can you take a negative reaction, denial, or no response without being victimized all over again?

The concern is to be strategic as you promote healing. If you don't confront people because you are full of shame or want to protect them, your reluctance needs further work in therapy. If there is legitimate fear of reprisal or no hope of anything but denial, don't confront and be revictimized. Perhaps you want no contact whatsoever, and you have dealt with your personal traumas and victimization in therapy. A confrontation may serve no purpose. Think through this step with a wise counselor and make strategic choices.

Healing and Reclaiming Sexuality

Wendy Maltz in her book *The Sexual Healing Journey* talks about the five false ideas most abuse survivors have in their attitudes about sex:

1. "Sex is uncontrollable." Sexual energy is wild and impulsive and cannot be controlled or contained. If it is unleashed, it probably can't be stopped and the desire is never satisfied. The perpetrator says he will stop but never does. Sex makes people irresponsible and divorced from everyday reality.

2. "Sex is hurtful." Sexual feelings and behaviors are emotionally and physically painful. Sex is full of betrayal and being used and can include hostility and rage. Penetration and rubbing cause torn skin and genital irritations.

3. "Sex is a commodity." Sexuality is an object or skill to use and is divorced from caring or relating. It is something to manipulate and bargain with as sex is exchanged for attention, love, and power. Sex is performance oriented and disconnected from emotion.

4. "Sex is secretive." Sexual behaviors are more exciting when sneaky or forbidden. Sex is shameful and should never be talked about with others. Sex is covert and furtive—never natural, open to discussion, and possessing a comfortable knowledge, with a healthy sense of privacy and mutuality.

5. "Sex has no moral boundaries." Sex has no right or wrong with limits but is whatever feels good to the other person. It is a game with winners and losers. There is no respect, trust, fairness, consequence, or virtue.

Challenge with words and actions that sex is a commodity and tied into earning love and commitment. Be assertive as you make sex natural and a conscious decision with the ability to say no whenever needed. Reaffirm your Christian beliefs that making love is a mutual experience and based on a loving, intimate companionship.

Male abuse survivors sometimes struggle with same-sex fantasies and an arousal by penises. That is a consequence of their abuse and not necessarily homosexuality. They can work through it with reconditioning and arousal centered on the mate. Male and female survivors sometimes find pain arousing sexually or have erotic dreams about the abuse. That, too, is a product of the abusive conditioning. They did not invite the abuse, and the reflexive arousal does not make them seductive, masochistic, or wanting sex with the abuser.

Prone to guilt and shame, the survivor may try to work things through without talking about them, thus sabotaging efforts to change attitudes and become comfortable with new behaviors. Don't keep secrets. Talk about these emotionally loaded topics with someone who is safe. Love and acceptance can be so healing. You may wish to unload some of this on a therapist and not just your mate, but it is important to get things out into the open without self-condemnation. Change attitudes that say it must be something you did or asked for.

With male and female survivors, a reconditioning process is a vital part of the journey. So much of sexual arousal, or pain, is built on conditioning. Sex in abuse is associated with the false beliefs of its being uncontrollable, hurtful, and secretive. Mates can begin a new set of conditioning as they pair sexual feelings and behaviors with fun, loving, respectful experiences. This slowly starts to make a real difference.

The pain, fear, and shame are often reflexive reactions and have to be continually challenged with healthy self-talk and healthy behaviors. Flashbacks occur unbidden and can be very disruptive. In the midst of lovemaking, you may panic in a certain position or sexual movement. Something your mate says or does may trigger old fears or pain.

Don't discount your feelings and reactions. Sort through your memories of the abuse, and try to find triggers from the past, even if you have to stop your lovemaking awhile. It will help your feelings seem more manageable. Take a deep breath and slowly let it out as you calm your automatic physiological response. You might say, "I am safe, and no one is trying to hurt me now." As you control your physical response, you will feel safer and more in control. Ground yourself in the present. Look around the room and notice, perhaps even touch, at least five things that are completely different from the abusive situation. Tune in to your adult self and remind yourself that you now have more power and control. Above all, choose a new response or behavior as you alter the old reality and continue healing, even in the middle of lovemaking.

Change to a different sexual behavior like engaging in intercourse rather than stimulating the clitoris. Find a way to alter the behavior a little and make it more acceptable as you try not to duplicate the past. Engage in a lot of pleasurable touching and holding before stimulation of the genitals. Sometimes you will have to face the trigger down and work through the feelings. Do something positive with your partner that can change your present reaction. All of this may take only a minute or two, but it puts you back in control.

It is not fair that anyone has to suffer sexual abuse. You are to be congratulated because you are a survivor. You indeed are on a healing journey, and God will bless your efforts. Stay courageous, and know that you can work through to the intimate lovemaking you so deeply desire.

Chapter Twenty-Five

Extramarital Affairs

An intimate marriage thrives on commitment, honesty, trust, comfortable companionship, and sex that is safe and connecting. Adultery strikes at the base of this special God-designed union—polluting and weakening it.

This chapter focuses on extramarital sexual affairs. It starts off with guidelines that can prevent you from falling into the trap of adultery. The second section explores the phases of an affair and the healing steps that are possible. The third section summarizes five commonsense but crucial ways to affair-proof your marriage.

Prevention: No Trespassing Allowed

In adultery everyone eventually suffers. Even if the affair is only an emotional adultery and never culminates in physical sex, if it is lived out in the mind and never acted upon, or if it is never discovered, the people involved and their marriages are damaged. They often live with a very poor excuse for what companionship is designed to be with a deep intimacy and powerful partnership. They also suffer spiritual deterioration with dishonesty and divided loyalty. They sacrifice the love and joy and peace that God promises His children who walk within His economy.

The following ten behaviors and attitudes are vital for keeping other people from trespassing into your intimate companionship. They can help you prevent adultery so that you never have to deal with its demoralizing consequences. How many of these fences do you have in place in your marriage right now?

1. Make a decision and commit to the fact that you will never have an extramarital affair. No circumstance or need or rationalization will ever make adultery right. You have determined, "Never!" and not "I don't think so." There is no waffling on that certainty. That door is shut and will never be opened. You have willfully determined this decision. Your "No Trespassing" sign is always up as you seek to protect and nurture your marriage.

2. Do not keep secrets or allow sexual feelings and fantasies to go unaddressed. Anytime you keep a secret, especially of a sexual nature, you invite trouble. Secrets need to be shared to prevent them from gathering energy and destructive possibilities. You are responsible for building an accountability network with which you can share secrets. Your mate is important, and anytime you avoid telling your spouse something, take note and examine what is going on. A trustworthy friend or colleague who shares your values is also invaluable. Infidelity is based on secrecy and dishonesty.

3. Keep all sexual fantasies that you willfully (intentionally) create focused on your partner. It may seem like trite advice, but your sexual thought life needs to be carefully disciplined. Sinful lust and acting out sexually are encouraged by obsessively making people sexual objects or continually fantasizing about a person or situation outside your marriage. Christ said that if we continually lust after someone, sin will usually result.

4. Set limits. Do not share intimate details of your marriage with a person of the opposite sex. Never complain about your partner or air your dirty laundry—even to a stranger on an airplane. Be careful how you provide a listening ear even in a church group. Revealing pain and frustration is a bonding behavior and makes you vulnerable to seek comforting. Mentioning your mate and children positively, refraining from long eye contact, avoiding intimate settings (riding alone in a car), including the whole group rather than seeking intense personal interactions—all help set limits with casual contacts. Affairs can start and flourish from a casual friendship.

5. Do not permit an intimate friendship with an opposite-sex person to grow without tight boundaries. Adultery often occurs among couples who have become good friends. Not only is the marriage damaged, but long-term friendships are lost forever. Some boundaries are including both mates in all activities, dealing with sexual attraction or ending the friendship, avoiding secret letters or phone calls, not playing therapist with bonding sessions over personal woes, controlling sexual talk and joking, and preserving modesty, especially on vacations. The most common and destructive affairs are built out of intimate friendships.

6. Do not spend unaccounted time together with opposite-sex colleagues, committee members, schoolmates, or exercise partners. Females and males enjoy interacting, and there will naturally be attraction—don't think you are invulnerable. That late night run or cup of coffee after the committee meeting, that study group meeting on Sunday afternoon or Saturday in the office, can be dangerous. One-on-one is intimate and increases temptation.

7. Be explicit with your mate about what is and is not appropriate behavior. One wife said that she knew her husband ate lunch with his secretary and they occasionally went shopping afterward, but she never thought they would go to a movie together.

Never let your marital rules on fidelity be unspoken. Discuss openly what you think is and is not appropriate behavior. One salesman never sees clients on the road after 7:00 P.M. A homemaker never allows her male neighbors in the house unless her husband is home. Don't assume you know how your mate thinks; discuss possible situations and talk to each other.

8. Pay attention to your guilty feelings. Guilt is a God-given specific feeling that a particular value has been violated and there is a need for recognition and change (the process of confession and repentance). A Christian trains the conscience so it is in accord with God's Word and values. If you are feeling guilty about something, especially if you are being tempted to keep it a secret, take notice and stop doing that behavior. When guilt flags a behavior or thought pattern as being inappropriate or dangerous, you should not engage in rationalizing. Examine what is happening and make changes.

9. Build an accountability network. You will not always recognize your rationalizations and errors in judgment. You need people in your life who know you well enough to indicate the times your attitudes and behaviors may be straying outside God's wisdom and economy. You can create structure in your life that keeps accountability and boundaries in place. For example, a pastor never counsels someone of the opposite sex without his secretary in the outer office, and he never chauffeurs women around town. God gives the wisdom for you to protect yourself from your sinful propensities with an accountability structure and network.

10. Never think that you are invulnerable. According to the Bible, pride can come before a fall, and resting in our strong character can lead us to quit growing and become very vulnerable. I pray so often, "Lord, please shine Your truth into my life and keep me from sin and stupidity." Being humble, constantly repairing your fences, maintaining close friendships with people of the same sex and couples who also value fidelity, never keeping secrets, disciplining your sexual thought life, and growing ever closer to Christ and His wisdom are invaluable if you don't want someone trespassing into your intimate companionship. Think through what might be the chink in your armor that Satan could exploit. What type of person and situation would be most seductive to you?

The old saying that "an ounce of prevention is worth a pound of cure" certainly applies to adultery. How many of these "No Trespassing" guidelines are you violating? How vulnerable are you? If you are ignoring some of these wise boundaries, please don't think that you are the one person in the world who can spit in the wind without its coming back to hit you in the face. Start making some changes today. Others of you are reading this chapter, unfortunately, after the fact, and you need to understand how to work your way through the affair and be able to heal your marriage.

Phases of an Affair

There are five common phases of an affair: (1) inception, (2) prediscovery, (3) discovery, (4) recovery, and (5) resolution. Many affairs go undiscovered and never get to the discovery and resolving stages. In some marriages, the undiscovered adultery and the problems that created it are resolved and the intimacy is restored. Unfortunately, that is usually not the case, and two things happen. First, the individual issues and flaws in the marriage are never dealt with, and often there is another affair or the partners settle for an unsatisfying relationship. Second, mistrust and dishonesty linger because the mate suspected the affair and a deeper intimacy never blossoms.

Confession and the discovery phase are vital for healing infidelity and its damage to honesty and the committed companionship. All marriages do not make it to a recovery phase. Although Christ permits divorce because of adultery, He does not mandate it. Most marriages in which both partners are committed to making the partnership work and go through the confession and repentance process can survive and become even more intimate.

1. The Inception Phase

How do affairs get started? Whose fault are they? Are the causes usually sexual in nature? Can they occur even in a reasonably good marriage?

Yes, affairs can happen in a fairly intimate and committed marriage. Affairs do not always signal that the one cheating has no love for the spouse. The reasons it happened may include a close friendship in which poor boundaries were set, sexual curiosity, reacquaintance with a former sweetheart, or a casual encounter.

No, adultery is often not centered on sex. Sex becomes a part of it, but it may have begun as a supportive friendship or an office flirtation that guaranteed ego strokes. For some, it is the thrill of the illicit and a sense of adventure. Often after the chase is over, the excitement and attraction are gone. Sexual curiosity and frustration initiate some extramarital liaisons, but sex is just one of many reasons affairs occur.

The offending spouse sometimes blames the mate or a deteriorating marriage for the affair. A poor companionship and a lack of lovemaking make a couple more vulnerable, but there is still a choice. If you leave the keys in your car and someone steals it, it is still the thief's fault. The adulterer chose to have the affair. Many deeper issues launch affairs: mid-life crisis, spiritual poverty, a poor sex life, unchecked sexual fantasy, family scars and adulterous parents, falling in love with someone else. These problems must be resolved, but the ultimate cause of infidelity is a series of poor choices. Adultery seldom begins by being blindsided.

2. The Prediscovery Phase

As the adulterous relationship comes into full bloom, there is a lot of guilt, excitement, stolen pleasures, much phone time, dishonesty and webs of deceit, and often not that much sex. The rendezvous take planning and deception, and there is more carelessness over time.

Some adultery involves a one-night stand, and there isn't a prediscovery phase. This is not to say that this type of affair is not destructive. It breaks the bonds of trust and faithfulness and love. Long-term infidelity takes an even greater toll on the marital relationship, and the cheated-on mate feels more deeply betrayed and blind for not discovering what was going on.

The one cheated on often knows something is not quite right but cannot put a finger on it. The one in the affair is often oblivious to the changes taking place: the different behavior patterns, the irritability or solicitousness toward the mate, and the increasing carelessness about the affair. The person does not see the deteriorating marriage and the distorted thinking going on: the partner is becoming less attractive, the tension is somehow the mate's fault, and the partner is no longer understanding.

Tremendous rationalizing and compartmentalizing occur in the mind of the unfaithful partner. One mate stated he didn't think he was that dishonest because he left his wedding ring on the whole time. A wife told her husband she had never taken all of her clothes off. The two worlds get more difficult to balance and keep separate. The dishonesty gets easier.

The prediscovery phase creates growing anger, frustration, and distance. Something is gravely wrong, but no one is talking about it, or denial reigns. Both mates are unsettled. Feelings oscillate from guilty excitement to self-loathing in the partner cheating and from confused hope to fearful desperation in the one cheated on.

Not every affair is discovered or confessed and worked through. An issue most people struggle with is the advisability of confessing undiscovered affairs, both past and present. Confession is vital in restoring honesty and rebuilding trust. It acknowledges that the adultery was destructive (sinful) and brings it to the light of day so the power of secrecy and guilt can be broken. Confession helps the guilty one feel accepted and forgiven despite the sinful actions. As James 5:16 encourages, "Confess your trespasses to one another, and pray for one another, that you may be healed" (NKJV). An ongoing or recent affair usually demands confession to one's mate as well as to God and His representative for healing to begin to take place.

Until this contrite spirit has been demonstrated and a recommitment to the marriage affirmed, it is impossible to create a true partnership again in which each has died to self and is unconditionally committed to the other's well-being. Trust takes time to rebuild, but with confession and reconciliation, the mates are back on the road to create a one-flesh union again.

The confession of past affairs is more difficult to determine. If the confession is just to share the guilt and the issues of the adultery have already been resolved, a better confessor may be your pastor or counselor. The past affair may have been suspected and is still creating mistrust. It may demand confession to clear the air. A good rule of thumb is to talk over the possible confession with a trusted advisor before proceeding.

3. The Discovery Phase

A profusion of feelings, issues, and reactions must be worked through during this time of discovery. How the affair was discovered doesn't seem to cushion the shock from the partner. It is devastating whether it is confessed or discovered via taped phone conversations, a private detective, or a growing collection of evidence and a

Extramarital Affairs 331

confrontation. It is all so tawdry and gut-wrenching and throws both mates into pain, guilt, betrayal, and deep loss. Choices have to be made, and a grieving process is entered.

Adultery is like a funeral and you need to view the body. Mates need a thorough, honest confession (viewing the body) to validate that a real loss has taken place. Then they can slowly grieve and reclaim the marriage. In Alcoholics Anonymous, recovering alcoholics go through twelve steps to promote healing. The fourth step is a very searching and fearless moral inventory in which they courageously write down all their past transgressions and then confess them to at least one person.

If affairs are a symptom of deeper issues, those problems must be dealt with as a part of the therapeutic process. For whatever reasons the affair occurs, a thorough confession helps clear the air and create a better understanding of the problems needing resolution. The confession also helps the betrayed mate feel that secrecy is being broken and the partnership restored.

After this confession, encourage process questions and not detail questions. The couple need to view the body, but eventually, it can become ineffective if they keep digging it up and do an endless autopsy with detail questions. Process questions deal with what was missing from the person's life and the relationship that caused the affair. How did the love for someone else grow? What needs to change? How could one help the other trust more? Detail questions—when, where, how many times, what positions—create vivid nightmares and are counterproductive as the imagination runs wild.

A betrayed mate feels the need for this interrogation. The one who has committed adultery will grow weary, but it is important for the cheated-on spouse

- to break through the shock and denial and ventilate feelings as the grieving process is worked through.
- to prevent with enough questions and knowledge another affair from happening.
- to completely reclaim the mate by destroying all secrets and having everything in the relationship mutually shared knowledge.
- to exact some penance and perhaps some vengeance as the partner squirms and atones for the feelings of pain and being duped that the one cheated on feels.

After the denial stage of grieving is broken through, intense anger will surface. The interrogation is a part of this, but it is also feeling duped and wondering how foolish the individual must seem to others. Trust and fidelity, very special and important qualities, have been lost and violated. Healing is a tortuous process for both mates.

4. The Recovery Phase

In the recovery phase, the interrogation can continue. New outbursts of feelings and questions are occasionally triggered, and the adulterer is awakened in the middle of the night or receives a barrage over the phone while at work. A wrong number, a new sexual technique, twenty extra minutes getting home at night, and the angry attacking begins all over again. The one cheated on needs to remember to keep the questions more process and not detail in nature. Sometimes the cheater needs to make a simple answer to a detail question to lay an issue to rest. The cheater wonders if it will ever stop and trust will ever be rebuilt. This is part of the penance and price paid to restore intimacy and heal the damage done.

An adulterer has stolen intimacy and commitment from the partner. Restitution in kind seems appropriate, not only to heal what has been damaged but also to help that person grow through penitence and make some real changes. Time, money, and energy should be invested in rebuilding the marital intimacy that has been so damaged by the adultery.

In recovery, the one involved in the affair is ready to move on long before the wounded partner is able. Both can grow weary in the processes of grieving, rebuilding intimacy, and forgiving. The initial choice of forgiveness on both partners' part may be done quickly, but the process of forgiving and letting go and rebuilding respect and trust takes time. Forgiving is not condoning what has been done or instantly forgetting. Partners don't forgive and immediately forget—they slowly let go as trust is earned.

New bubbles of resentment and hurt will pop to the surface as recovery goes on, and forgiveness will have to be an ongoing process. The recovery stage can be very different for various couples. Certain factors complicate the restoration process and demand more work for healing to take place:

- The length and intensity of the affair, especially feelings of love and friendship, relapses or making contact with the person again
- The state of the marital intimacy before, during, and after the affair—the depth of dishonesty, broken commitment, and disrespect and the breakdown of one-flesh bonding
- The level of individual scars and immaturity and the amount of environmental pressures (finances, children, illness, work) that are present in addition to the stress of the affair

Even with all of these complex factors, God's healing grace abounds. If both partners are committed to restoring the marriage, they almost always succeed. The trauma often creates a deeper and more realistic intimacy with better boundaries in place. Greater maturity grows out of the crisis they have weathered.

Not everyone in the recovery phase chooses to stay married, however. The adultery may have tapped a deep core fear within the soul of the one who was betrayed. Trust may be irreparably shattered as the couple try to pick up the pieces but cannot. Sometimes the affair has pointed out deep flaws in their relationship, which they don't think they have the energy or respectful desire to repair. A tragic fact is that adultery can result in divorce.

After evaluating the marriage, the one in the affair may decide to get a divorce and marry the person involved in the affair. It is easy to be deceived into compounding the mistake. Affairs are very idealistic and are not the best perspective from which to choose a life partner.

If you have fallen in love with someone else but decide to honor your marital commitment, be aware of how difficult it can be to break that other bond. There is no good way to end it other than to stop it cold turkey. You will be vulnerable. Get in place an accountability network to support you in resisting temptation.

See your spouse as an apple and your former lover as an orange. Focus on apples. One husband put an index card in his wallet and reviewed it daily for a while. On one side were all the wonderful qualities of his wife. On the other side were the flaws in the adulterous relationship and what he stood to lose.

Some couples experience a second honeymoon as a part of the recovery phase. This response is understandable and can help to heal wounds. The one involved in the affair is relieved to be beyond the secrecy and guilt and is rediscovering some of the reasons for the original attraction to the partner. The one cheated on, after dealing with anger and betrayal, is excited not to have lost a mate. After their marriage had such a close call, both have their adrenaline flowing and deeply appreciate that the disaster was averted. Sex has been forced out into the open with romantic activity and libido running high. The problem with the honeymoon is that it can sweep issues under the rug, which can later come back to haunt the marriage. Individual and relational problems are not uncovered and resolved.

5. The Resolution Phase

The couple working on recovery slowly reestablish the equilibrium and deepen the intimacy of the partnership. Now comes a crucial time in the marriage—the final resolution phase of an affair as the healing process merges back into the humdrum of routine existence. The angry questioning is largely gone, and the grief and causes of the adultery have been worked through. The marriage now continues to grow stronger from the base of recovery and all the changes that have been made—or it settles back into the same routines and is prone to future affairs, sometimes with mates changing roles.

Changing personal and relational patterns in a permanent manner is not easy. The emotional and spiritual growth will come slowly as you continually resist sliding back into old patterns. The scars of the affair may still haunt you occasionally. Do not try to avoid the flashbacks, but talk through them. Keep strengthening and protecting your intimate companionship.

Relapse Prevention and Affair-Proofing

You have already considered ten different behaviors and attitudes that can keep other people from trespassing into your sacred partnership. The ten behaviors that set solid fences in place to keep out trespassers are vital. Here are five other protective and growth-producing suggestions that you need to have in place as you affair-proof your marriage and prevent relapse:

1. Flag some behaviors that can warn that the partnership is losing some of its intimacy and you are becoming vulnerable. Set in place some warning signals that you as mates will notice and act upon to make changes. Here are various behaviors that other couples have found helpful to flag:

- Making love infrequently and falling short of their sexual goals
- Avoiding conflict and gunnysacking anger
- Neglecting spirituality: no prayer, poor church attendance, and so on
- Keeping any secrets or tiptoeing around some issue
- Canceling date nights and spending little time alone together

2. Love and affirm the beauty of your mate and marriage. Resist the "greener grass" syndrome. If you focus on your mate's flaws and stay dissatisfied with your partnership—rather than make needed changes or affirm strengths—you adulterate your one-flesh union and invite trespassing. Focus your energy and attentions on your garden instead of noticing every beautiful plant and the green grass outside your fence.

3. Learn the biblical and relational skills of confrontation, repentance, confession, grieving and expressing feelings, forgiveness, and making amends. These are vital processes when sin has damaged your partnership.

4. Get your act together—personally and maritally! Remember that problems often precipitate affairs. Do whatever you need to do: learn communication skills, deal with addiction or anger or some other personal problems, overcome your fear of conflict, get some therapy, take action—or the problems may manifest themselves through adultery.

5. Build an intimate marriage and learn to truly make love to your mate. Mates who are creating the one-flesh partnership that God designed and are falling more deeply in love are much less vulnerable to temptation. They are more aware of the damage infidelity would do to the beautiful, trusting companionship that they have worked so hard to build and nurture. This is also true of a fulfilling sex life. Affairs are often not sexual in nature, but making love frequently and passionately is a great prevention of adultery. Don't have sex, but truly learn to make love to your partner and "know" your partner inside and out. Be tender, excited, nurturing, communicative, and loving. The "No Trespass" signs seem to be obvious to all looking in on a truly intimate marriage.

Chapter Twenty-Six

Sexual
Short Circuits

God gives each person and every marriage the beautiful gift of sexuality. Making love can create pleasure, drain off negative emotions, and help bond two individuals into one flesh. This chapter explores four saboteurs of sexuality that are commonly encountered. It is not for the idly curious but for you who have had to live with these terrible secrets with their sexual distortion and painful confusion.

For you, sex is often not joyful but filled with guilt, pain, and self-loathing after you have acted out. You are not alone, and there is hope for restoring a warm, intimate sex life with your mate. The steps will not be easy, and the journey to healing will be time-consuming and necessitate giving up your will to God's will.

An important part of healing is breaking the conspiracy of silence for these secrets. Part of their power is that they probably have never been brought out to the light of day and been carefully sorted through. I am sure you have tried to make changes and have vowed repeatedly that you will never engage in these behaviors again—only to relapse months or weeks later. You never seem to get to the root of the problem and achieve a depth of understanding so that you can make the deeper changes that are needed.

This chapter is also for the mates who have cried through years of deep frustration, suffering through a sex life that has never grown into intimacy. Making love has become confusing, hurtful, or perhaps nonexistent. One wife shared about her husband's sexual quest: "He is like a bucket with no bottom. Nothing sexual ever satisfies him or brings us closer together." Thank God, there are hope and healing for your relationship if your mate is willing to admit the problem and seek to make permanent changes.

You may be in the category of those who wonder if changes are indeed needed. You see it as your mate's problem for being rigid and narrow sexually. If your mate would cooperate, together you could minimize the effects of the problem and incorporate it into your sex life somehow. I hope that this chapter will point out the futility of doing this, and that you will grasp God's sexual economy and realize how you have been sabotaging what He desires your lovemaking to be.

Pornography

Pornography makes persons into sexual objects and robs them of the three dimensions of being a real person: body, soul, and spirit. Oh, it includes the dimension of a body, but that is simply an imaginary sexual image in a secret, one-dimensional world the user creates. There is a fear of truly going beneath surface sexuality and connecting with a real person, of allowing sex to have depth with strong connection to an intimate partnership. Pornographic sex becomes an unfulfilling, nonintimate activity in a distortion of God's intended pleasure.

I am not trying to debate whether you should look at a piece of art of a nude or watch a romantic scene in a movie that is sexually explicit. I am getting to the essence of pornography, and that is making a human being, created in God's image, into a depersonalized object for one's selfish sexual gratification.

Pornography divorces sex from relationship. It stems from being afraid of going beneath the surface and experiencing true intimacy. It distorts and shuns love, tenderness, and playful companionship. Sex becomes a commodity or an emotional buzz, a drug to create a high or numb the pain. This is far from God's design for a one-flesh sexual union.

Pornography is more an attitude than an action. It is objectifying another person to the detriment of the marriage and the mate. In the chapter on sexual fantasy, partners were encouraged to make the enhancement of their lovemaking and the sexiness of their mates their primary sexual focus. Looking at sexually explicit pictures and creating fantasies that exclude the mate and the relationship can degenerate into pornography.

We are able to create pornography everywhere, not just with sexually explicit movies or magazines. We can look at our mates and use them in a one-dimensional way that is pornographic—if we don't hook up our emotions and relationship. The environment can become a place to enjoy our mates and sexuality, or a place to lust destructively and become pornographic. Sexual desire is not wrong, but the way we indulge it can be. James 1:14–15 so aptly states, "Each one is tempted when he is drawn away by his own desires and enticed. Then, when desire has conceived, it gives birth to sin" (NKJV). Men and women other than our mates will be sexy to us, but a person should never be reduced to the common denominator of sex, as personhood and the soul are lost. This is pornography and ultimately destructive of God's design for intimate sexual relating and fun.

Sex Addiction

Sex is a very powerful force, and pornography often gets hooked up with sexual compulsions. Lovemaking truly gets short-circuited in the world of sex addiction. The mate loses importance, and the person is more guided by the need to alter the mood than playfully, passionately unite with the mate. The sex addict forfeits creativity, greater passion, and a lifetime of making love and enjoying sex in an infinite variety of ways and feelings with the mate. Sex addiction is a miserable and sexually sterile existence.

Defining Sex Addiction

Sex addiction, like pornography, uses people and sex to alter the mood in a one-dimensional, unfulfilling fashion. An individual can act out in many ways. The husband sneaks to his stash of magazines and masturbates while viewing them. The youth pastor cruises to find a place to exhibit his genitals. The wife frequents the downtown hotels for quick, casual sex. The husband wants his wife to look at sexually explicit movies and constantly try different and more sexually stimulating activities but is never satisfied. The deacon is arrested for shoplifting lingerie, or the newlywed calls phone sex lines, running up an eight-hundred-dollar bill. The person frequents prostitutes while maintaining a pious facade and teaching Sunday school. The husband sneaks out at night to look in windows, waiting hours for one brief glimpse of someone undressing. The mate engages in affair after affair and is constantly on the alert for sexual involvement. The husband visits the strip bars twice a week.

When the addiction is discovered, the partner often wonders why the addict doesn't use willpower and make better choices if the marriage is really valued. The addict must not really love the partner, or the addiction would have stopped. The partner is confused about why the addict keeps sinning and hurting the relationship without appropriating God's help. This is an addiction, and many factors have contributed to making the addict fall into sexually compulsive behaviors. It is not a simple matter of willpower, sin, repentance, and instant change. Deep-seated issues and long-term habits must be painfully worked through. It is a process, like so many other facets of becoming Christlike, as the person grows and renews the mind and heart.

Understanding the Addict

Here are seven factors that can contribute to someone's being prone to falling into sex addiction. These factors also contribute to the addict's staying stuck in the addictive behaviors. These are not excuses for addictive behaviors. Showing causes or contributing factors for addiction helps the partner and the addict understand that the addiction is greater than willpower. The addict is powerless without help. No one engages in dangerous affairs, drives hours to go to adult movies, shamefully hides pornography, or peeps in windows because it is fun and fulfilling. There is a compulsion fueled by many underlying problems. It is a time-consuming and costly addiction that needs increasing amounts of sexual activity to alter the mood.

1. Sexual abuse, early sexualization, and dysfunctional family. The sex addict often was exposed to pornography or explicit sex early in life. Dad may have had pornography, or parents may have engaged openly in extramarital affairs. There may have been physical as well as psychological sexual abuse, and the addict repeats the victimization, only now being the perpetrator. In victimization, sex is associated with power and intrusion into another's life in a one-dimensional fashion for personal sexual gratification. The addict repeats this intrusive sexuality. The family itself may have been rigid and very private, with an inability to demonstrate intimacy and playfulness. The child in growing up may have been starved for affirmation. In high school or late adolescence the destructive sexual patterns were further solidified with sexual acting out—continuing into the present.

2. Insecurity, lack of self-esteem, and loss of purpose. The addict often feels worthless and insecure. This feeling may be especially focused in the area of interpersonal relationships and interaction with the opposite sex but can extend into work and all areas of life. The person lacks self-assurance and the ability to confidently direct life. This of course is aggravated by the addiction and the shame and confusion that it produces. The person feels out of control and has strong fears about the future—what to expect from the marriage and what to be sure of spiritually. In the midst of fear and a poor self-image, it is difficult to love the Lord, feel in relationship with Him, and allow His truth to bring peace. It is almost impossible for addicts to love themselves and bring meaning to the injunction, "Love your neighbor as yourself."

3. Impostor phenomenon and dual lives with despair. The impostor phenomenon says that if others truly knew me, they would not accept and love me. The addict tries to compartmentalize and balance two separate lives: the secret world of sexually compulsive behaviors that can consume literally hours of time and demand a web of lies to conceal and the public world of marriage and family and job that would probably be forfeited if everything came out into the open. The person feels guilt and deep despair because often the addiction violates important values and beliefs. The Christian especially knows the acts go against God's truth, and the person often loves (as deeply as possible) the mate and family. Nevertheless, the person can't stop the addiction or admit the need to alter the mood. Addiction can produce real moral bankruptcy as the lies and sinful behaviors erode character and take so much time and energy to maintain—with a hopelessness permeating the core of life.

4. Isolated and socially shallow and lonely. The addict often is socially isolated with no real close friends. There may be comrades in the addiction as they try to hold off loneliness for each other, but the relationships are far from healthy. Because of dishonesty and lack of trust and intimacy, relationships and even the marriage stay casual and shallow. It is not surprising that the inability to relate goes hand-in-hand with the casual sexual objectifying and fear of intimacy. Sometimes addicts wish that sex would drown out the pain and create instant intimacy, but that is not God's design for sex. Authentic lovemaking is deeply relational. Genuine connecting with others could bring so much healing, but it is impossible while walls and defenses stay rigidly in place. It can be very lonely behind those walls.

5. Constant and intense guilt, shame, and pain. Shame both causes and is created by the addiction. It can be a vicious cycle. The addict feels intense shame and feelings of being unacceptable, and then acts out sexually to change and soothe these feelings. More intense feelings of shame and guilt occur, which can lead to more acting out. There are deep psychic pain and feelings of being unfulfilled, but the sexual fix does not relieve them except for a short time. Instead, it exacerbates the shame and pain. Some of this pain can be traced back to childhood and the confused and conditional love demonstrated in the family while growing up. The child needed acceptance, affirmation of worth, and a format to love and be loved. The child needed clear boundaries to guide life. In a shame-based dysfunctional family, none of that happened.

6. *Stress and living on the edge with fear and adrenaline.* An important part of acting out sexually is the risk that adds excitement and diverts attention from the current stressors and pain. The addict may be more likely to act out when there is a lot of stress. The behaviors need to have illicitness and an emotional charge of fear to create the desired effect. Cruising and anticipating exposing oneself, sneaking into a motel and watching videos all day, calling an escort service—all have a certain illicitness and excitement, or they would not have appeal for the addict. The addict has a need to be outrageous and live on the edge. Often, peaceful feels abnormal and can be very uncomfortable at first. The addict needs the fear and adrenaline rush of excitement.

7. *Obsession and objectification of sex with no fulfillment.* Sex becomes the drug of the addict. It is used to relieve stress, to celebrate a significant accomplishment, or to overcome boredom. It is not connected with intimacy, playfulness, relationship, satisfaction, or mutual enjoyment. Sex becomes objectifying and using others and results in tremendous guilt and dissatisfaction. The addict loses perspective and comes to feel that sex is the most important need in life. Sex has lost its true meaning of uniting the one-flesh companionship, and it is used for many other nonsexual and destructive purposes.

Recovering from Addiction

Here are several aspects of recovery that you cannot neglect if you wish to get beyond your addiction.

A Support Network

This network will need to include your mate, but your partner cannot be your therapist and group support, too. Part of healing will be working through your family issues, stress management, lack of intimacy, and shame. You will need the help of an individual who can counsel you and offer guidance as you sort through problems and make changes. A group of fellow addicts who are also working to recover can help you slice through the denial and support you through the grieving that will occur as you move beyond your addiction. You will need accountability and help, or the changes will not be deep and permanent.

Sobriety

It may seem obvious, but the addict must stop the sexual self-destructive behaviors. This may require a time of complete sexual abstinence or at least completely limiting sex to mutual activity with your mate—no masturbation. You must resist, with the help of your support network, engaging in any of the shameful but exciting activities. You will experience withdrawal and grief, and there will be relapses. Relapse does not mean you are back to ground zero; make new resolutions and continue to grow and change.

Addicts often talk about being in the zone, that place of compulsion when they know they are going to act out. They are on their way to the bookstore or out cruising. It is best to choose sobriety before you get into the zone. Call a friend or therapist or mate, and let the person help restore sanity before you get fully into the zone. Remember you will be prone to denial and some very slick thinking. One addict related that he was at the stoplight in front of the adult bookstore. At that point he was so in the zone it was like the car had a mind of its own and went right into the parking lot. When asked what he was doing near the bookstore, which is miles from his home, he stated that he was taking a shortcut home and happened upon the bookstore. Rationalizations and distorted thinking will come like second nature as your mind and personality rebel in withdrawal pains. Lean on your network as you maintain sobriety.

Relentless Honesty

In your secrets and dishonesty lies the power that perpetuates your addiction. You must become rigorously honest with yourself and others. You lied so much as you lived in your two worlds that truthfulness will not come naturally at first. Scriptures stress the importance of honesty. Read this message from Ephesians: "Having lost all sensitivity, they have given themselves over to sensuality so as to indulge in every kind of impurity, with a continual lust for more....Therefore each of you must put off falsehood and speak truthfully to his neighbor (4:19, 25 NIV). Honesty will help break the chains of continual lusting and give meaning back to your life and marriage.

Part of healing is a thorough confession in which you get honest with yourself and at least one other person, probably your therapist or pastor rather than your mate. Your mate will need honesty and confession, but you need others in your accountability network, also. Confession helps break the impostor phenomenon as someone knows all about you and still accepts and unconditionally loves you. Again, being honest will not come naturally, but it is irreplaceable for recovery.

Intimate Relating

Part of the pain and shame is generated by the desire to be close to people but a fear of what might happen. Addiction is the opposite of intimate companionship: trusting, caring, playfulness, positive sense of self, warmth, lightheartedness, comfort, and open communication. You will need to provide opportunities that stretch you into relating on a deeper, more intimate level with your mate and other friends. Groups are great places to practice new relational skills and especially find a same-sex friend.

You will not feel very comfortable with allowing yourself to be close to others, and getting close will produce real anxiety at first. Hang in there, and you will come to enjoy intimacy very much. The marriage companionship will require special work as you learn to communicate. Get some counseling, go to a marriage enrichment seminar together, read some good books on intimacy, and take vacations in which you play together. You will need to help your mate work through personal feelings, too. Your mate will need to sort and grieve through the losses and hurt sustained with your addiction.

Sexual Recovery

Sexual recovery has many dimensions to it. You are building an intimate marriage perhaps for the first time and including sex as a part of relating—not objectifying. This will mean building solid communication skills and learning to nurture your mate and yourself as Scripture exhorts. Reread chapters 1 and 2. A part of sexual recovery will be learning God's economy for great sexual relating. You will have to build the character traits of a mature and expert lover. Growing spiritually and allowing God into sex and the bedroom are also important. It will be a totally different experience as you bring God and His guidelines into your sex life rather than try to hide and hope He is ignoring your secret world.

Overcoming and recovering from addiction involve a process. This is also true of the Christian life in general as you allow God to continually shine new truth into your life helping you change areas of immaturity. No one ever gets it all together, but you can become more Christlike with honesty, love, and intimacy permeating your life in wonderful ways and revolutionizing your lovemaking.

Cross-Dressing

Cross-dressing is wearing the clothes of the opposite sex. The male dressing in female clothes is more common than people suspect. Consider these reasons it occurs and suggestions for dealing with this problem.

Understanding Cross-Dressing

Sometimes cross-dressing is done by homosexuals who wish either to make a dramatic statement or to take the role of the opposite sex. It is easy to assume that if your spouse is cross-dressing, there must be innate homosexual tendencies. That is probably not true. The cross-dressing dealt with in this section is usually done by heterosexual men.

Another type of cross-dressing occurs with gender confusion and what we call *transsexualism*. Transsexualism is a very complex problem that is still being understood within Christian theology. This is often more of a congenital condition and has nothing to do with homosexuality. It is a person who wants to be heterosexual and yet feels trapped in the body of the wrong sex. Sometimes the only way the person feels a sense of wholeness is by surgically changing the body. Before we condemn, we must have compassion. Transsexualism is not dealt with in Scripture, and it is a torturous journey for those in this condition. Transsexualism is not discussed in this section.

Why do heterosexual men who love their wives get caught up in cross-dressing? Here are several explanations:

Feminine apparel paired with erotic arousal. A fetish is something a person has paired with erotically arousing activity and sexual excitement until it can elicit erotic arousal. Female clothes can easily become a fetish. The feel of lingerie or a slinky dress or high-heeled shoes can be paired with sexually exciting feelings so that just putting the item on or caressing it can give a sexual rush. The sexual rush it creates can become an important cause of cross-dressing.

Sex addiction. Something illicit or different, like erotically charged feminine apparel, can trigger a real high for the addict. Having that satiny feel of women's lingerie on the skin can create an all-day high at first. It is paired so closely with female genitals that the addict allows the lingerie to trigger flights of sexual fantasy. The addict may break into houses and collect lingerie because of its close association with female sexuality.

Feminine apparel paired with female companionship. One man would put on pantyhose and masturbate while stroking the hose. Like some sex addicts, he had poor social skills, and this put him in touch with female sexuality so that he could be both male and female. When sex becomes an isolated and nonrelational activity, the person may need some token of femininity that becomes erotically charged. It may be lingerie, shoes, or dresses, as intimate companionship is completely short-circuited and sex becomes self-centered. The man is trying to be himself and also represent an imaginary female companion.

Enjoying illicitness or escaping. All of us want to be unique and different at times. Dressing in women's clothes can meet that need, as a man feels he is doing something others don't. If every man wore dresses, the way women often wear more masculine clothes as a fashion statement, it wouldn't have the same charge and would cease to be illicit. In our culture, though, cross-dressing in women's clothes can still meet some men's need to be different and special. Cross-dressing can also represent a desire to escape. Wearing a dress and makeup can create a different life. Usually, cross-dressers want their own stash of feminine clothes that become special to them as they create a secret fantasy world.

Tuning in to femininity. Some men say that when they have on female clothes, they more easily tune in to the gentle and soft side of themselves. The cross-dressing becomes a ritual that allows them to be different or more aware of a female side. This may go back to childhood deficits and a poor identification with both the same-sex and the opposite-sex parent. There may be some gender and role confusion. Each of us has a more masculine (aggressive, analytical) and feminine (soft, nurturing) side, and we should be in touch with both. Men shouldn't need to cross-dress to accomplish this as they rest comfortably in their masculinity but avoid any stereotypes.

Changing Cross-Dressing Behaviors

Probably each of you who is struggling with this problem has at one time or another thrown away all of your stash of female clothes and vowed never to engage in that behavior again. That didn't change the inner attitudes and correct the bad habits you had in place, so you started back again with the same shame and guilt. You may be wondering if perhaps your mate could incorporate it into your loveplay. As I study intimate sexuality and the roles within the marital companionship, I believe that cross-dressing is an immaturity that would be better abandoned and replaced with other behaviors. It can hurt respect and distort gender roles and detract from the ability to enjoy your mate and for your mate to enjoy you. Please engage in dialogue with your mate as you sort through the problem and bring the secrets out into the open. That in itself will be healing.

These four suggestions may help. Like any addictive habit, it will change only if you accept your powerlessness and humbly ask God to help as you mobilize a support network and grow up certain areas of your life.

1. In breaking any habit, you have to practice abstinence and truly want to change the behavior. You may not see any great harm and think your mate should adjust to it. You may need to give it up as a gift to her, but it will help your own sexual adjustment. Fight through the denial and rationalizations as you honestly look at the behavior and sort through it openly and carefully. Talk especially with your mate but also with another person you respect as you truthfully try to understand the whole phenomenon. How did it start, and what will be the most difficult hurdle in stopping the behavior?

2. Determine what needs cross-dressing fulfills within your life. It is never wise to leave a vacuum, or it often gets filled up with the old behavior. Think of other ways that you can meet those needs. At first they won't be as fulfilling, but they can come to take the place over time. Maybe tune in to femininity and become comfortable with your wife as a lover in a more open and easy way. Pair new erotic behaviors and fantasies that are centered on your lovemaking as you extinguish the old erotic charges of the cross-dressing. Create an escape by making your home or study a safe haven without the dressing. Employ sexual variety in many different ways. Be different by changing your hairstyle, joining a repertoire group and hanging out in cafes, or finding an unusual hobby like skydiving. Try to understand and meet the need—don't just quit.

3. Deepen your support network and include people in addition to your mate who can hold you accountable. Get into a counseling relationship that can hold your feet to the fire and support you as you make changes. Don't keep secrets. Increase the depth and richness of your intimacy network, and especially work on your marital companionship. Some of cross-dressing is similar to other sexual compulsions, and you will fit the profile of the sex addict. (See the suggestions for breaking sex addiction.) Build self-esteem and overcome your imposter phenomenon as you confess your inner thoughts and gain acceptance as a person. Grieve through the loss of the behavior as you lean on your support network. Honesty and intimacy are great healers.

4. Read this book and others on sexuality as you work through any insecurity and immaturity. Grow to be a very competent lover with all the character traits and relational skills. This can help you grow beyond the cross-dressing. Learn to revel in your lovemaking, and appropriate the excitement and closeness that God intended for your one-flesh union. It won't be an easy journey—changing habits never is. The rewards are great as you grow beyond the double life and marital tension and experience a new wholeness sexually.

Homosexuality

There are many theories about why the short circuit of homosexuality affects certain people. Some have seemed to struggle for a lifetime, and others can point to some trauma or confusion that helped them fall into this behavior that causes such internal conflict. Usually, a whole constellation of factors converged to create the struggle: a breakdown in the family, lack of intimate bonding with a detached father, a sensitive and often passive personality style, emotional and sexual traumas, early sexualization, some masculine or feminine role confusion, and a breakdown in meeting affection needs, especially with the same sex and feelings of rejection.

Understanding the Complexity of Homosexuality

We are called to compassion and not a fear or revulsion of homosexual behavior. The danger in taking a strong stance on any moral issue is that the persons do not feel we can empathetically listen and help them deal with the problem—they are unwilling to tell us the story of their tortuous journey for fear of rejection or pat advice. That does not have to be so. Christ carefully distinguished between sinner and sin, between the person and the actions. He associated with sinners and yet never compromised His values, loving and accepting the sinners into change. We as a church will have to do much better at lovingly working with those who are entrapped in homosexual behavior and need our acceptance (of the person) and help.

For you whose marriages have been distorted and damaged by homosexuality, there are no easy answers and no way to adequately understand the pain and suffering you have been through. The spouse has often already traumatically worked through to a place of compassion and acceptance about the presence of homosexuality. Most spouses are not homophobic with fear of and disgust for the homosexual. They just wish that there were some way to make changes and rid the marriage of the saboteur.

Part of understanding and making changes is carefully exploring and understanding the evolution of the homosexual behavior and the personal issues behind the confusion and habit. There will have to be a careful consideration of the family background, especially the relationship with the same-sex parent. So often there are anger, feelings of rejection, and other unfinished business.

In many people's lives and especially in the homosexual's, confusion can occur as the person tries to meet nonsexual needs sexually. A special trap is the thinking that sexual behavior is the most and only truly intimate expression of affection. It is easy to have an important friendship and sexualize it without considering that the friendship will be forever changed. In a society of instant gratification, it is easy to hope that instant sex will create instant intimacy—or to hope that sex will meet deeper needs for closeness and connection with the same sex in ways that were never fulfilled by the same-sex parent.

Rejection is a significant aspect to deal with in understanding the origins of homosexual behavior. It can be perceived rejection by the same-sex parent or actual acts of rejection experienced by the person in growing up. The anger and issues with parents must be resolved. Tied in with rejection are some of the same struggles of the addict with deep feelings of worthlessness and uneasy acceptance of masculinity or femininity. The tendency can be to isolate while desperately desiring to be close.

As with the addict, there was often early sexualization or abusive, confusing situations in sexual development. There may have been sexual repression or a lack of information and comfortable, appropriate values. This confusion may have been further compounded in dating relationships—or a lack of such relationships.

Recovering from Homosexual Confusion

Homosexual feelings and behaviors are so complex that hurting mates often ask, "Is there hope for change with such a deep-rooted problem?" Absolutely! There are possibilities for real changes. But it will take a strong four-pronged plan of attack: (1) sobriety from the behavior, (2) personal changes, (3) a renewed enjoyment of intimate companionship, both maritally and interpersonally, and (4) a reliance on and relationship with God.

1. Sobriety

If spouses want to get beyond the effects of homosexuality, the individual struggling with these desires will need to believe it is wrong and truly want to change the behavior. If this is impossible, I think Christ's allowance for divorce because of sexual immorality applies, and the mate is better off moving on than staying with the offending partner and risking further abuse. If the partner with homosexual confusion wants to change, a program of sobriety will have to be inaugurated, which applies to thoughts as well as actual behaviors. Active sexual fantasy should involve only your mate and heterosexuality. The goal is not to make you heterosexual but whole and able to make love with your mate.

Staying sober will probably be impossible without a support network. Build a strong friendship with a same-sex mentor who can set healthy boundaries on the friendship and model appropriate behaviors. Have an accountability group to help you work through the problems of making changes. Your mate, pastor, therapist, and other Christian friends can also encourage your staying sober from homosexual acting out.

2. Personal Growth

An essential part of maintaining sobriety is growing into wholeness and healing the damaged areas of your life. You will need a counselor who can guide you through this process, someone who can help you explore your family background and find healing. Your mate, your sponsor, and other friends can also be helpful in encouraging, confronting, and overcoming blind spots in your self-awareness. You will have to be ruthlessly honest and courageous as you grow personally in all areas, especially in the spiritual and relational aspects of your life.

Sort through the sexual distortions and bad habits and attitudes. Set goals and structure a growth program in which you dispute ineffective attitudes ("sex is the primary way to experience intimacy," or "I am flawed and unable to create close friendships") and create new behaviors. You will have to pair new behaviors with erotic excitement and allow them to gain momentum in producing arousal. You will have to choose to let the opposite sex and especially your mate be the focus of your sexual arousal and permit the homosexual preferences to slowly fade. It will take time and repeated conditioning before you have extinguished the old arousal patterns and established new ones with your mate. This is perhaps the most difficult part of this journey. Don't become discouraged.

3. Renewed Intimacy

Love and deeply intimate relationships will be the most effective agents of healing in your life. Your mate, your sponsor, your group, your growing network of friends, and your therapist will demonstrate affection and acceptance, which will help heal the wounds of the past. God's plan for healing the hurts of past negative relationships is to go through a healthy relationship and this time have your needs for intimacy and affirmation truly met. We could call this reparenting or refriending. Your mate and friends can help you redo negative experiences in the parenting or friendship process, and real healing can result.

Build intimate relationships with those people the Lord has placed in your life to love and accept you. Lean on them in overcoming temptations, and draw strength from them when the problems seem insurmountable. Work and play at sorting through your sexual distortions, and allow your mate to become your lover in a bonding and exciting manner. You will be able to make changes that you never thought possible. You must also build deeply intimate, nonsexual same-sex friendships. It is often helpful to have a therapist of the same sex.

4. Relationship with God

Only as you admit your powerlessness and trust Him to provide growth and healing can you work through needed changes. Daily draw closer to Christ and appropriate His power. Give yourself up to His love and truth as you learn to trust and be intimate. He can set you free.

Appendix A

How to Find Helpful Resources

Proverbs tells us that "without counsel, plans go awry, but in the multitude of counselors they are established" (15:22 NKJV). Many resources and much wise counsel are available to help you with your marriage and the sexual part of that relationship. But before we discuss some of them and especially talk about choosing a therapist, you need to consider some general principles. We do not always wisely use and manage our counselors, or advisors.

Wisely Managing Your Advisors

You know the guilt and frustration generated when you know you should be doing something but never get to it. Working on your marriage and sex life can be like that.

Prioritize and Tackle the Important

As you have read this book, you have become aware of different areas of your marriage and lovemaking that you would like to make changes in. Sit down as mates, and each of you make a list of your top five improvements and prioritize the order in which you think they should be tackled. Now select the top two from both lists and start with them. You will have a more manageable task, and you will be more motivated to work on the changes you think most important.

Be a Smart Consumer

Wise consumers seek out the products that will most effectively meet their needs. The second section of this appendix lists several resources available to you as a couple. You have already chosen your two improvements you wish to tackle. Now choose the way or resource that will best help you make the changes that you desire. As a wise consumer and steward of your time and energy, check out and choose an effective resource. Ask your friends, consult with people who have used the resource, try to preview it, and do whatever you can to ensure it is what you need. If you start and it doesn't meet the need, pick another one and be persistent until you get satisfaction.

Get Psyched

You will have to believe you need to make changes before you will ever follow through. You will also have to believe the changes are profitable and worthwhile. Think of the two areas you desire to make changes in, and list at least three good reasons why it is critical to work on them right now. What is in it for you? Why will it be beneficial to follow through? Visualize the payoffs, and listen to others who have made similar changes. Get yourself psyched. Without some motivation you will never follow through.

Structure a Growth Routine

Part of effectively making changes is getting a routine in place. If you are constantly doing busy work and trying to mobilize your change network, you will grow weary in well doing. Do the time-consuming preparation work. If you need baby-sitters to go to counseling, line them up for four months. If you are going to do some self-help exercises, set a time each week and keep it. If you want to attend a workshop, plan months in advance so you can schedule around interference. Buy that book and keep it beside your bed with a pen to highlight ideas you want your mate to read, also. Anything that is planned and can become a habit and routine is more likely to be accomplished.

Sabotage Your Saboteurs

How are you going to sabotage your routine or plan for change? Sit down and think through with your partner how you two usually sabotage the things you want to do. What are they? Emergencies with the kids? Lack of energy and time? Poor planning? Not choosing a good resource? Work demands? Now how are you going to overcome these typical saboteurs? Get a backup baby-sitter. Do the self-help on the weekend at a slower pace. Plan your job around your change program. How can you ensure that you will sabotage your saboteurs?

Resources for Change

Even after you know you need to make changes, it is a little intimidating to wisely choose the right resource. I've listed possible advisors that could provide wise counsel and be change agents. Counseling is last not because it is the least important but because I want to develop it the most.

Bibliotherapy

Biblios is the Greek word for "book," and *bibliotherapy* refers to reading books to find help. Reading some good books on intimacy and marriage, especially from a Christian viewpoint, will be helpful. Go to a bookstore and browse as you read jacket covers and skim a few pages. Reading is an excellent way to gain new insights and make changes. If you are a poor or unmotivated reader, have your mate read the book and underline selected chapters or sections as the highlights. Do the same with this book as you glean the help you need.

Don't neglect the Bible. Though it is not a marriage or sex manual, it details God's economy for life and spiritual growth and marriage. Remember that a great sex life is based on being a mature person. Be sure to read the Bible and some other books that will encourage your inner spiritual life to mature and become more Christlike.

Self-Help Growth Program

This book is designed with many exercises that you as a couple can work through and grow on your own. You will need to structure a routine and not be haphazard about it. Think through some areas you want to tackle first. You may want to read through part of chapter 6 on goal setting and choose personal and marital goals for yourself in lovemaking. Be active as you engage in your growth program. Anything that you write, discuss, or practice in some way is more likely to initiate changes and more deeply affect your intimate companionship. Mobilize your willpower as a partnership, encourage each other, and structure your growth program.

The Church

The church may seem an odd resource for change to you. Churches are marvelous places to find friends, gain practical insights, and learn more about God's guidelines for being a mature lover and an intimate companion. If you neglect growing spiritually and appropriating the help of the Holy Spirit, you have disregarded the foundation of a one-flesh partnership and a deeper intimacy. You will find that the church is like so many of the other resources; you get back what you are willing to put into it. If you participate in Sunday school, worship, and Bible studies, the church will have more of an opportunity of being a change agent. Churches are also excellent places to find the next two resources.

Workshops and Seminars

Many churches, counseling centers, and educational institutions offer seminars and workshops on various relationship-building topics. It may be a communication workshop, assertiveness training, or a seminar on making love. These powerful tools for teaching won't change long-term habits or completely alter your marriage or sex life. They will give hope and inspiration, specific skills and suggestions for implementing change, and get you as a couple started in understanding and talking about the changes that you need in your marriage. You will feel encouraged and not as alone. It may necessitate a sacrifice of time and money, but a workshop or seminar on a specific needed topic may be a resource to implement important changes.

Groups

It may be a self-help group, a Bible study for couples, or a therapy group for you as an individual or a couple. I am not referring to a large nonparticipative Bible study or Sunday school, which doesn't present the same dynamics as a small group. Small groups give people the opportunity to learn and to practice insights as they interact together. Many counseling centers and therapists offer group therapy directed to various concerns: sexual abuse survivors, men's growth issues, or relationship building. Other general therapy groups may be designed to allow members to work through areas of personal growth. Groups provide gentle interaction and confrontation. Open up and share and take away from the group the richness you can receive as an active participant.

Even when several couples get together regularly for fun and fellowship, group dynamics take place with encouragement, communication skills, humor, tension release, and some confrontation. Get together with other loving couples who are committed to making their marital partnership work to reaffirm mutual commitment to marriage and model the best for one another.

Counseling

Many Christians have a real stigma about going for counseling. Unfortunately, some pastors and other Christian leaders have not understood counseling from a Christian perspective and they have perpetuated this fear. They regard most of counseling as suspect, promoting values not in accord with scriptural teaching. They have also taught that counseling is unnecessary if a Christian conforms to the Bible and lives a Spirit-filled life. This mistaken belief has denied many Christian individuals and couples the help they desperately needed.

Romans 12:4–8 tells us God gave the church many differing gifts so we could help each other grow and become Christlike. There is not a specific gift of counseling, but people who do counseling are placed in the body to help believers and often have selected spiritual gifts for a special empowering.

How then can you be a good consumer and hook up with someone who has the gifts and skills to help you heal and make needed changes? Here are five suggestions:

1. Understand the complexity of the counseling field and become a good consumer. Many educational and career paths lead to someone's decision to be a marital or sex therapist or counselor. You may see a clergyperson (M.Div., Th.M., D.Min., Ph.D.), a psychiatric nurse (M.N.), a social worker (M.S.W.), a psychotherapist (M.A., M.Ed., Ed.D., Ph.D.), a psychologist (Ph.D., Psy.D., Ed.D.), a psychiatrist (M.D.), or a medical doctor, such as a family practitioner, urologist, or gynecologist. Each person may have special training and supervision in the given field of marital therapy or working with sexual problems.

How important is it to find a Christian therapist? God does not limit His truth and knowledge to Christians. You will benefit more from a qualified nonbeliever who does not feel the need to change your belief system than from a nonqualified Christian who does not understand marital or sex therapy. However, if you are working on areas of Christian values, like working through an affair or overcoming homosexual desires, you will benefit more from someone who shares the same belief system.

What if you've just moved to an area and don't know how to find a good counselor? Start by trying to find a referral from your pastor, a friend, or your physician. You will still need to check out the therapist and not operate on blind faith. Try national Christian organizations that you might hear about on Christian radio or from Christian psychiatric hospitals. They often try to maintain a national referral network. Two secular professional organizations provide supervision, training, and certification for sex therapists; you can contact them for a list of their members: the American Board of Sexology (1929 Eighteenth Street NW, Suite 1166, Washington, D.C. 20009; 202-462-2122) and the American Association of Sex Educators, Counselors, and Therapists (435 North Michigan Avenue, Suite 1717, Chicago, Illinois 60611-4067; 312-644-0828). Then check out referrals as to style of counseling and belief system.

You may have to use the yellow pages and look under psychologists, marriage and family therapists, or mental health. A national organization—the American Association of Marriage and Family Therapists (AAMFT)—has set requirements of education and supervision before allowing clinical membership as a marriage and family counselor. AAMFT often advertises in the phone book, too. Larger cities have counseling centers that advertise and list specialties for the consumer's benefit. Be a good consumer and get on the phone and let your fingers do the walking. Before interviewing a therapist, you can often find out from a receptionist the fee structure and the therapist's educational and professional qualifications and areas of specialization.

2. Interview the potential therapist and feel free to shop around until you find the right fit. You are entering into an intimate relationship, and you should feel comfortable with the person. You need someone in your corner as you make changes. All therapists should give you five to ten minutes of time for an initial telephone interview. If someone is curt or threatened by questions, choose someone else. Ask questions that are important to you: "What is your approach to therapy?"; "Will you interact with me and be directive?"; "Are you Christian in your religious beliefs, and how are they incorporated in therapy?"; "Are you under any kind of supervision and accountability presently?" (all counselors should be in some kind of supervision and should continually be learning and working on their own growth); "What kind of training and experience do you have in working with my specific problem?"; "How many problems like this have you worked with in the past year?"; "Are you the right person to help me make the changes I need, or do I need to be referred to someone else?"

If you feel comfortable after this initial contact, make an appointment. Plan to have several sessions in which you work on issues, and mutually make certain this person can help you. Being a good consumer does not mean staying with someone you don't think is the right fit or bailing out of a relationship because you are running scared as you are asked to face tough issues or feel uncomfortable trusting anyone. Counseling is a real relationship, and you and your therapist will have to work through confrontation and disappointments. You as involved client will have to discuss when you don't understand some point or question the wisdom of a given homework assignment. Don't sit on things, say when you think the change is not going quickly enough or you are feeling frustrated with the process.

3. Realize that your problems have been a long time in the making and significant changes won't occur quickly. The benefit of therapy is that you can speed up your change and growth process. It will still take months (six to eighteen) and much investment in time and money. Some of the issues you need to work on sexually or maritally may never be resolved without therapy. Other problems will probably, with time, be worked through. But why take two to three years to do this? Counseling will provide the discipline and the structured environment to effect changes. A therapist can also encourage and be there for you as a safety net.

4. Build a complete support network and ways to prevent relapse once the counseling stops. A crucial aspect of therapy is not only encouraging changes but also putting in place the attitudes, skills, and support network to prevent relapse. Therapy and sexual goals should be individually tailored to meet the needs of your unique one-flesh relationship. Do whatever you need to do to ensure that you will nurture your love life and prevent backsliding: structure in vacations, create a good baby-sitting network, put your sexual feelings on the front burner, and honor God's injunction to enjoy the rich gifts He has given you.

5. The more you invest, the more you will reap a rich sexual harvest of satisfying changes and mutual happiness. The emphasis is not on investing money, though there is a need to invest financially in your sex life; the emphasis is on investing time and energy. The Bible is accurate that we reap what we sow. If you are willing to appropriate resources for enriching your lovemaking and to follow through with making necessary changes and learning new skills, you will be blessed with an intimate and exciting love life.

The journey of becoming one flesh sexually is exciting and fulfilling but requires an investment. Talk, do some exercises, and never settle for mediocrity.

Appendix B

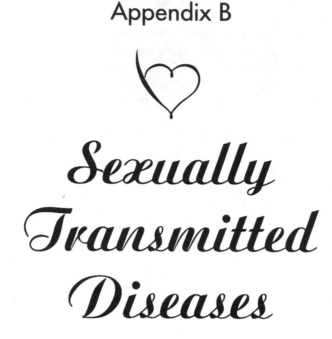

Sexually Transmitted Diseases

Wₑ will first consider several of the most common sexually transmitted diseases (STDs). We will then explore some questions and fears that need confronting. (For further information, the Centers for Disease Control has an STD hotline: 1-800-227-8922.)

Common Sexually Transmitted Diseases

One couple contracted herpes (simplex II, a virus that in simplex I is a cold sore) after being married six months. Neither suspected the other was involved in an affair, but great doubts and some distancing occurred. They learned from their physician that someone can be a carrier without having actual outbreaks of the disease and therefore not even know it is present. One of them had apparently acquired the disease in a previous sexual relationship and gave it to the partner after marriage. This is true of most STDs in a small percentage of people; a person can be a carrier and spread the infection without having active symptoms.

Bacteria and viruses of STDs can be spread without sexual contact, but it is a very unlikely possibility. Catching a sexually transmitted disease from shaking hands or sitting on a toilet seat is statistically very remote, though a common excuse of mates who have contracted an STD. A standard comment is that the only way you catch an STD from a toilet seat is if someone else is sitting on it.

Don't avoid getting these diseases diagnosed and treated because you feel guilty or embarrassed. They won't go away, and ignoring them can have serious health consequences. With bacterial infections like gonorrhea, both mates will have to undergo treatment to ensure the bacteria are killed and aren't passed back and forth. There is no recourse but an honest disclosure to your (future) mate about any STD that you might have.

Gonorrhea

Gonorrhea is the most common kind of STD, and it is a bacterial infection. With men, the symptoms are a yellowish discharge and burning with urination because the urethra gets infected. Many women have gonorrhea without noticeable symptoms or very mild symptoms at first and so go untreated. The symptoms when they are noticed are vaginal discharge, painful urination, irritation of external genitals, and abnormal menstrual bleeding. Untreated gonorrhea can cause pelvic inflammatory disease (PID), which is the most common cause of infertility. PID can cause scarring that blocks the fallopian tubes. The symptoms of PID are nausea, fever, lower abdominal pain, and perhaps pain with intercourse. Penicillin and other antibiotics can cure gonorrhea.

Genital Herpes

This STD is caused by a herpes virus that is in the same family as chicken pox and cold sores. Genital herpes can be spread by herpes simplex I and II. The infection is usually contracted through intercourse or direct genital contact or oral sex with a partner who has an outbreak of the disease. Important to note is that cold sores (simplex I) can create herpes breakouts on the genitals with oral to genital contact. Some mates falsely accuse their partners of an affair when they have transmitted the simplex I. In rarer cases, genital herpes can be transmitted by a carrier without any symptomatic breakout of the skin. The symptoms of genital herpes are small painful blisters on the pubic area, penis, vaginal opening, cervix, or rectum. The first episode of herpes is usually the most severe with fever, headaches, and painful irritation at the site of the blisters and subsequent sores when the blisters burst. With some people there is never a second breakout, but others incur more blisters, often stress- or illness-induced.

Presently, there is no cure for genital herpes. The drug acyclovir (Zovirax) helps some people lessen the painfulness of the symptoms and shorten the healing time of the blisters, especially in the first occurrences. If taken on a long-term basis, it can reduce the rate and duration of recurrences. With some, there is only an initial breakout; others break out frequently under stress. Women need to be conscious of two health hazards, which their physicians can monitor. There is risk to the fetus at birth if there is a breakout; a cesarean section may be required. Added caution must be taken to watch out for cancer of the cervix and vulva.

It is very difficult to keep from infecting a mate, but refraining from intercourse during active recurrences and at least two days after an episode has healed will help. During this time, using separate washcloths and not having contact with the sores are essential. Use of a condom can prevent spreading infection, though sometimes all the area is not contained within the condom or other genital contact occurs before the condom is put on.

Genital Warts

Genital warts are transmitted by the human papilloma virus (HPV). These warts appear on the genitals and with women in the cervical area. They can be removed with liquid nitrogen or laser treatment in an office procedure. Care must be taken to watch out for cervical and genital cancer.

Chlamydial Infections

These infections are caused by *Chlamydia trachomatis*. It may be the most common bacterial STD, though it has not gotten much attention until recently. In men, chlamydia bacteria can cause infection in the urethra and the epididymis. The damage is much more severe in women because the bacteria attack the reproductive tract and can cause pelvic inflammatory disease (PID) and infections of the endometrium and complications during pregnancy. Often there is an initial lack of symptoms until the infection has progressed, but some antibodies testing diagnoses the disease earlier. Penicillin will not treat the chlamydial bacteria. Fortunately, various other antibiotics are effective.

Pubic Lice

Sometimes called crabs, these parasites attach themselves to pubic hair and can cause intense itching. They can be killed with a special medicated shampoo or cream but not by simple washing.

AIDS

Acquired immune deficiency syndrome has become a horror that affects all our lives. It is caused by the human immunodeficiency virus (HIV).

Many people are very frightened and worry that AIDS can be contracted with casual contact. HIV is transmitted through sexual contact and the exchange of bodily fluids. HIV is present in saliva but in much lower concentration than in blood or sexual secretions.

Completely safe sex is possible only if there is no exchange of bodily fluids, though use of a latex condom lessens the risk. After infection, the HIV antibodies can be detected within two to three months usually. Immediately going for an AIDS test is not effective. Testing positive for HIV does not mean having AIDS. Many people remain a carrier of the virus for three to five years without developing AIDS or AIDS-related symptoms. There is no cure presently for AIDS, and everyone who is HIV positive will eventually contract AIDS. There is not enough research to definitely say how long this will take.

Coping with Sexually Transmitted Diseases

Too often we as a Christian community are not on the vanguard of bringing hope and help to wounded souls who need our loving ministry. We sit in judgment rather than reach out. Each of us must become involved and learn more about AIDS. Persons living with AIDS need our understanding and tender care, and we can do this without endangering our health. We will have friends and relatives who need our hugs and support.

Because there is no cure for herpes, many individuals see it as a badge of shame. They fear a Christian dating partner will immediately reject them if it is known. The persons suffer intense emotional pain and worry as they wear a capital *H*. Any sin is able to be forgiven. We are much more than our sinful mistakes. Like any skeleton in the closet, it should not be revealed immediately in a dating situation. However, as trust and commitment build, it must be disclosed and worked through with your partner. If the person cannot deal with this aspect of you, that is a commentary on the person's values and needs—not your worth and ability to be loved.

Herpes or other STDs need not destroy a potentially intimate marriage and a great sex life. Consult a physician, and get appropriate medical help immediately. It will take work to ensure that the wounds and emotional issues are healed and will not come back to haunt the companionship and lovemaking. You may be able to talk it through together, or you may need a wise counselor to assist you in this process. Persevere. God can help bring a gracious healing. Together you can help each other find wholeness and unconditional love and acceptance within your intimate partnership.

Bibliography

Sexual Enrichment

Dillow, Joseph C. *Solomon on Sex*. Nashville: Thomas Nelson, 1977.

LaHaye, Tim and Beverly. *The Act of Marriage: The Beauty of Sexual Love*. Grand Rapids: Zondervan, 1976.

Penner, Clifford and Joyce. *The Gift of Sex: A Christian Guide to Sexual Fulfillment*. Waco: Word, 1981.

Marriage and Intimacy Enhancement

Diehm, William J. *Staying in Love: What Wives and Husbands Can Do to Keep Their Love Alive*. Minneapolis: Augsburg, 1986.

Harley, Willard F. *His Needs, Her Needs*. Tarrytown, N.Y.: Revell, 1986.

Leman, Kevin. *Sex Begins in the Kitchen: Renewing Emotional and Physical Intimacy in Marriage*. Ventura, Calif.: Regal Books, 1981.

Rosenau, Douglas. *Slaying the Marriage Dragons: Protecting Your Marriage from the Enemies of Intimacy*. Wheaton, Ill.: Victor Books, 1991.

Smalley, Gary, and John Trent. *The Two Sides of Love: What Strengthens Affection, Closeness and Commitment?* Colorado Springs: Focus on the Family Press, 1990.

Wright, H. Norman. *Communication: Key to Your Marriage*. Ventura, Calif.: Regal Books, 1974.

Sexual Affairs

Carter, Les. *The Prodigal Spouse: How to Survive Infidelity*. Nashville: Thomas Nelson, 1990.

Dobson, James C. *Love Must Be Tough*. Dallas: Word, 1983.

Joy, Donald M. *Rebonding: Preventing and Restoring Damaged Relationships*. Dallas: Word, 1986.

Specific Sexual Issues

Penner, Clifford and Joyce. *Restoring the Pleasure: Complete Step-by-Step Programs to Help Couples Overcome the Most Common Sexual Barriers*. Dallas: Word, 1993.

Sais, Michael R. *Counseling the Homosexual*. Minneapolis: Bethany House, 1988.

Sexual Abuse and Recovery

Morrison, Jan. *A Safe Place: Beyond Sexual Abuse*. Wheaton, Ill.: Harold Shaw, 1990.

Scripture Index

Index

Note: Bold page numbers indicate pages with illustrations.

arousal, 50–51, **49, 51**
condoms, 66, **66**
genitals, 42–45, **43, 44**
as lover, 190–99
orgasm, 52–54, 177, **49, 55**
becoming orgasmic, 241–54
perspective of sex, 173–78
sex drive, 180–81
Fertility drugs, 289
Finances, handling, 8
Foreplay. *See* Loveplay
Freud, 54

G spot, 186
Gender. *See also* Female; Male
characteristics, 16
differences and similarities, 15–16,
47–48, 53, 88–89, 272–73
Genital herpes, 355–56
Genital warts, 356
Genitals
female, 42–45, **43, 44**
male, 39–42, **40, 41**
Goals, sexual, 79–81
Godly sorrow, 32
Gonorrhea, 355
Grafenberg, Ernst, 186
Grafenberg, the, 186
Grief, 204, 256, 285–88
Guilt, 32–33, 238–39, 259

Hayakawa, S. I., 106
Health, 78
Heraclitus, 21
Herpes, 354–56
HIV (Human immunodeficiency virus),
66, 356–57
Homosexuality, 257, 345–47
Honesty, 29–30
Honeymoon disease, 217, 311
Honeymoons, 7–8
Hormones, 35, 216–18
HPV (human papilloma virus), 356
Human immunodeficiency virus (HIV),
66, 356–57
Human papilloma virus (HPV), 356

Hygiene, 72–73
Hymen, 43, 307, 311
Hysterosalpingogram, 283

Illness (as disability), 211–12, 256, 302
Impotence, 301–305
Individuating, 6
Infertility, 256
and adoption, 291–92
and miscarriage, 285–88
misconceptions about, 279–81
testing for, 282–85, 288–90
Infidelity. *See* Adultery
Injuries (as disability), 210–11
Intercourse, 159–62, **160**. *See also* Sexual
activity; Lovemaking
and aging, 167–68, 170, 219
painful, 306–16
positions of
crosswise, 166–67, **166**
for disabilities, 163, 169, 170, 171
face-to-face, 169–70, **170**
husband-on-top, 165–66
missionary, 165
during pregnancy, 166, 167, 171
with props, 170–72, **171**
rear-entry, 167–68, **167**
side-by-side, 164–65, **164**
standing, 168–69, **169**
wife-on-top, 163–64, **163**
Intimacy, 1, 137–38, 260
Intimate Behaviour, 139
Intrauterine device (IUD), 67–68, **68**
In vitro fertilization, 289
IUD (intrauterine device), 67–68, **68**

Jung, Carl, 15

Kegel, Dr. Arnold, 193
Kegel exercises, 193–94, 299
Kissing, 183–84
Kubler-Ross, Elisabeth, 204
K-Y Jelly, 69

Labia, 42, **43, 44**
stimulation of, 44–45

Pair bonding, 138–45
Pairing, sexual, 45–46, 251, **46**
Parasympathetic nervous system (PNS),
  35–36
Passages of Marriage, 222
Pavlov, Ivan, 46
PC (Pubococcygeal muscle), 161,
  193–94, 299
Pelvic inflammatory disease (PID),
  355, 356
Penis, 39, **40, 41**
  size-of myth, 180
  stimulation of, 42, 153–58, 197
Perineum, 42, 45
Personality differences, 71
Petroleum jelly. *See* Lubricants
Peyronie's disease, 218
Philia, 2–3
Physical fitness, 78
PID (Pelvic inflammatory disease),
  355, 356
Plateau phase, 51–52, **49**
Playfulness, 25–26
Pleasuring, genital, 23, 150–53
  with making love, 154–58
  oral, 157–58
  positions for, 153–54
PNS (Parasympathetic nervous system),
  35–36
Pornography, 337
Positions of intercourse. *See* Intercourse,
  positions of
Postcoital test, 284
Pregnancy, 60–62
  intercourse positions during, 166,
    167, 171
Premarin, 217
Progesterone, 218
Progestin, 63
Props, 83–84, 170–72
Prostate, 41, 218, **41**
Prosthesis, penile, 211, 303
Provera, 218
Pubic lice, 356
Pubic mound, 42
Pubococcygeal muscle (PC), 161,
  193–94, 299

Quickies, 199

Recuperative time, 53, 215
Reflexes, sexual, 35–36
Refractory period, 53, 215
Relationship. *See* Companionship, marital
Religious prohibitions, 257, 263
Renshaw, Dr. Domeena, 32
Resentment, 259
Resolution phase, 54–56, 109, **49**
RESOLVE, 288, 292
Resources for change, 348–53
Retirement, 221
Rhythm method, 62–63
Romance, 30–31, 177–78

Scars, 311
Scrotum, 39–40, 42, **41**
Seductiveness, 195–96
Self-esteem, 26–28
Self-image, sexual, 258–59
  and disabilities, 201
  during pregnancy, 61
Self-pleasuring, 151–53, 242–49
Selfishness, 18–19
Semen, 53
Seminal vesicles, 41, **41**
Sensate focus, 37–38, 114–16, 296–97
Sensuality, 81–83
Sex addiction, 338–42
Sex drive
  female, 180–81
  male, 188
Sex life, fulfilling, 1, 14–24
  principles for, 2–11
  saboteurs of, 255–67
Sexiness, 258–59
Sexual abuse, 261, 309, 317, 323–26
  counseling for, 322–23
  definition of, 317–18
  effects of, 318–19
  mates of survivors, 319–21
Sexual activity. *See also* Intercourse;
    Lovemaking
  frequency of, 10, 31–32, 71–72, 77–81
  initiating and refusing, 110–11
  phases of, 48–56, **48, 49, 55**

About the Author

Douglas Rosenau received a Th.M. degree in theology from Dallas Theological Seminary and did further graduate work at Northern Illinois University, earning an M.S.Ed. and Ed.D. in counseling with specialties in marriage and family therapy and sex therapy. He received sex therapy training at Loyola University Medical School. He is licensed as a psychologist and a marriage and family therapist with a private counseling practice in Atlanta, Georgia, and he leads therapy groups, workshops, and seminars. He is a clinical member of the American Association of Marriage and Family Therapists and the author of the book *Slaying the Marriage Dragons*. He is committed to the integration of Christian values with relationships and sexuality.